THE AGE
OF
ANXIETY

Contents

PART SEVEN

Legacy

Must a government of necessity be too strong for the liberties of its people, or too weak to maintain its own existence?
—Abraham Lincoln

We should be eternally vigilant against attempts to check the expressions of opinion that we loathe and believe to be fraught with death.
—Oliver Wendell Holmes

Preface to the Paperback Edition

Dramatic developments have intensified America's anxieties—and added new ones—since publication of this book. Taken together they reinforce its major theme: how fear of national insecurity can be exploited for demagogic purposes, just as it was in the Cold War era of Joseph R. McCarthy. Then, fear of Communism created opportunities for a demagogue like McCarthy to play on public insecurities through false accusations in order to gain political power. Now, fear of terrorism has been exploited to gain, and retain, power.

Since 9/11, America has experienced new examples of McCarthyistic tactics: smearing opponents; impugning the patriotism of critics; attacking the media, Congress, and Judiciary to produce acquiescence; "leaking" classified information selectively to demonize dissenters; destroying the careers of public servants; besmirching the reputation of military officers; manipulating public opinion through false charges;

launching illegal covert surveillance operations; employing lie-detector tests in McCarthy era–type witch hunts to intimidate government whistle-blowers; abusing civil liberties; relying on pervasive governmental secrecy to cover up mistakes. All these are now part of the contemporary record forged against a background of fears of terrorism. That record also documents a pattern of deceit emanating from the Office of the President. Unlike the McCarthy era, when the Republican president, Dwight D. Eisenhower, loathed and opposed McCarthy and his campaign of defamation, this time it is the Republican president, George W. Bush, who has set the tone for many abuses that have occurred. As Bush has said, "I'm the decider, and I decide what's best."

Key among new developments is Hurricane Katrina, America's worst, and worst-managed, natural disaster. When placed alongside scenes of daily disasters in Iraq and of the outbreak of war between Israel and terrorist organizations in Lebanon and Palestine, the government's failure to provide effective emergency relief for Katrina victims—and then its concealment of its failures by refusing to cooperate with lawful investigators—dealt a devastating blow to Bush's pledges to make America more secure from dangers abroad and at home. Bush's misplaced praise for the hapless director who bungled the Katrina response—"Brownie, you're doing a heckuva job"—also didn't reassure the public about the competence of Bush's administration or the security of the people.

As for Iraq, the U.S. invasion of March 2003 now takes its place among the great strategic blunders in American history. Instead of enhancing America's sense of security, the Iraqi misadventure spawns greater insecurity and renews feelings of anxiety about the nation's direction and leadership.

A reminder of McCarthyistic character assassination occurred in November 2005 when Pennsylvania's veteran congressman, John Murtha, a conservative Democrat and the
most respected congressional supporter of the American military, denounced the administration's Iraq policies and called
for a phased withdrawal of American forces. Murtha, who
had been decorated for heroism as a Marine in Vietnam, was
branded a "cut-and-run coward" by a right-wing member
of Congress. The White House and the Republican Party
launched a coordinated fear-and-smear campaign against
Murtha in which he was accused of advocating "surrender
to the terrorists" and of "sending mixed signals to our troops
and the enemy." Vice President Cheney suggested that such
calls for withdrawal from Iraq were examples of Democrats
peddling "'cynical and pernicious falsehoods' to gain political advantage while U.S. soldiers die in Iraq." Conservative
bloggers were even more vitriolic. They filled the electronic
ether with slogans right out of Joe McCarthy's playbook. "The
Democratic Party is the party of TREASON!" one such
blogger proclaimed. Two intensely controversial events—an
abortive ports security deal with Dubai and the embittered
controversy over border security and illegal immigration—
have since surfaced to demonstrate anew how fears of national insecurity can be exploited.

Cumulatively, these and other events have already had a
great impact on the nation. They have shattered the public
standing of the president, splintered the conservative coalition that has ruled Washington for more than a decade, and
set the stage for two of the most significant elections in recent
U.S. history. The first is the midterm elections of 2006, which
will determine control of Congress and set the nation's political

priorities for the remainder of George W. Bush's term. Important as that election is, it is only a prelude to an even more crucial one—the presidential battle in 2008.

In my afterword to this paperback edition, I will assess these and other major developments since this work was first published. What follows is my original narrative, as written, chronicling how the parallels between the Cold War era that created McCarthyism and the present "war on terror" stand, as I wrote then, "as a warning of what can happen when fears and anxieties combine to create hysteria in public and political life."

—H. J.
April 2006

To the Reader

America's preemptive war against Iraq, representing a radical new policy of unilateral "regime change," grew out of the attacks on September 11, 2001, that shattered the nation's sense of invulnerability, initiated a global war on terrorism, and spawned a wave of apprehension and fear. These events made it seem that Americans had entered an unprecedented era of stress and danger—an Age of Anxiety unlike anything experienced before. This is not so. The Age of Anxiety I chronicle here dates to the beginning of the Cold War more than half a century ago.

The reader should know that I wrote the prologue to this book as American forces were invading Iraq in March 2003. I have not since amended my suggestions of the consequences that could flow from that military operation resulting from grievous U.S. misrepresentations and miscalculations. Now, two years later, the calamitous effects of this war, the post-9/11 abuses of civil rights and liberties at home, and the revelations of systematic torture of Iraqi prisoners abroad, seem likely to affect the standing of the United States in the world and the lives of Americans for years, if not decades, to come.

All this forms the backdrop for the story I tell. Part narrative, part political and social commentary, and part personal memoir, this book retells the reign of terror in the 1950s called McCarthyism and examines the way it shaped the context in which we fight today's war on terror. McCarthyism stands as a warning of what can happen when fears and anxieties combine to create hysteria in public and political life.

Political repression and threats to liberty neither began nor ended with Joseph McCarthy at mid-twentieth century. They are woven throughout American history. What is happening today holds disturbing similarities to past events, as I will show. Examining McCarthyism and terrorism in light of one another is imperative as Americans face a new Age of Anxiety and the ever more difficult task of balancing the needs of national security with those of personal freedom.

H. J.

THE AGE
OF
ANXIETY

Prologue

A New Kind of War

In the third month of the third year of the new millennium, after a period of unparalleled prosperity, after emerging from the long Cold War as the world's only superpower, after achieving unsurpassed economic, technological, and military might, the United States of America suddenly found itself waging what its president described as a "new kind of war."

Abroad, the nation's armed forces were racing along the fertile plain between the Tigris and Euphrates rivers where Greek and Roman legions once marched to occupy the ancient Middle Eastern "cradle of civilization," known then as Mesopotamia. America was engaged in a brief but brutal war that promised to affect the country's global standing and perhaps even its character, though the full consequences would not be known until long after combat ended. At home, the United States confronted the threat of more deadly terrorist attacks of the kind that had traumatized the nation a year and a half earlier on September 11, 2001.

Americans, the most optimistic of people, now faced unnerving official terror warnings—Yellow, Orange, and the ultimate, doomsday Red. Their television screens broadcast alerts. Their newspapers published emergency preparedness articles full of alarming instructions on how to protect themselves from biological, chemical, or radiological attacks. Their government authorities, already vastly expanding the surveillance and interrogation of citizens suspected of being security risks, advised them to be on the lookout for terrorists. "Spy tips" posted on billboards along freeways, bridges, and tunnel entrances advised citizens to call a special number to report "suspicious activity." Their school-aged children practiced huddling inside designated "safe" rooms. Their politicians and some members of their press exchanged accusations about who was the most patriotic, who was a "good" or "bad" American, who was guilty of giving "aid and comfort" to the enemy. And their newest federal agency, a behemoth called the U.S. Department of Homeland Security, whose 180,000 employees were hastily gathered together from twenty-two different federal agencies, produced full-page national ads that set off more ripples of fear.

Under a somber photograph of this agency's troubled-looking director, a headline proclaimed:

You've Probably Wondered, "Is There Anything We Can Do to Protect Ourselves from the Threat of Terrorism?"

While advising citizens that "there is no reason to feel helpless in the face of terrorist threats against the United States," the official message was far from encouraging. "All of us should be able to survive comfortably on our own for at least a period of three days," the ad announced. "That's the amount of time you may need to remain in your home until the danger from a biological, chemical or radiological attack has passed." Listed below were the steps each citizen should take: from making "an emergency supply kit" and "a family communications plan" to "being informed."

Citizens rushed to carry out their government's instructions to "be prepared." They stocked their homes with emergency supplies of food and water, duct tape and plastic sheeting, flashlights and battery-powered radios, first-aid kits, toiletry items, protective chemical suits and additional layers of clothing, gas masks, and maps of escape routes "in case you're advised to evacuate"—all the while attempting to adjust to new government-imposed restrictions on their travel and movement.

Americans were urged to visit the government's new website, http://www.ready.gov, for more details. Some of the advice found there unintentionally provided material for a *Saturday Night Live* parody: Graphics instructed people not to run if they were on fire and to hide behind a door in case of nuclear attack.

Such bureaucratic foolishness offered mordant relief, but it did not allay the new state of foreboding. Nor was there anything humorous about convergence of war abroad and terror at home. Coming as they did amid around-the-clock televised "breaking news," in which routine events were depicted as being as unique and troubling as the approach of Armageddon, these threats made it seem that Americans had entered a time of the gravest peril. This impression ignored the years immediately following World War II, when hopes for a more peaceful world were dashed by the emergence of the Cold War and with it, the prospect of nuclear incineration.

Nothing in human experience matched the fears that then enveloped the United States: fear of a cold war turning hot; fear of a Soviet Union that had detonated an atomic bomb, ending the United States' monopoly on nuclear weapons; fear of traitors within who were stealing the fruits of victory from the United States. Civil defense shelters blossomed in American cities. In cellars and backyards, home bomb shelters were constructed and stocked with essentials. In schools, children crouched under classroom desks, supposedly learning how to safeguard themselves against nuclear attack.

So pervasive was this fear that millions of Americans began to believe that civilization, life itself, was teetering on the edge of extinction. Out of this devil's brew of fear, suspicion, and paranoia—and cynical political opportunism—came McCarthyism.

In today's America, no less than in the time of McCarthyism, fear again contributes to a climate in which abuses of power, infringement of liberties, and pervasive secrecy thrive. It brings to mind the acts of hubris that my old mentor, J. William Fulbright, called "the arrogance of power," quoting the Shakespearean lines: "It is excellent to have a giant's power, but tyrannous to use it like a giant."

Years will pass before we understand all the ramifications of the chain of events beginning with 9/11 that led the United States into its "new kind of war," though some of the effects already seem clear. That the consequences will be profound there is no doubt, but many questions remain: In the end, will the United States be regarded as a liberator or conqueror, its people peace-givers or imperialists, not only by an Islamic world already seething with rage and resentment against the U.S. but also by nations that for decades have been America's staunchest allies? Will the U.S. have won the war but lost the peace, become safer or less secure from new acts of terrorism? Will the task of fighting faceless global terrorists so expand the powers of the new security state that fundamental American freedoms are threatened—or lost? While these and other questions cannot yet be answered, looking to the past offers lessons for understanding the present.

PART ONE

McCarthyism

Chapter

ONE

The List

I have here in my hand.

Thursday afternoon was overcast, the temperature hovering just above freezing, when the black-haired, heavyset man carrying a bulging, battered tan briefcase boarded a Capital Airlines plane for the two hundred-seventeen-mile flight from Washington's National Airport to Wheeling, West Virginia. "Good afternoon, Senator McCarthy," he heard the stewardess say after he took his seat. He looked startled, then pleased, not realizing the stewardess had been waiting to greet him after noticing a senator's name on her passenger list. "Why, good afternoon," he replied, flashing a broad smile. "I'm glad somebody recognizes me."

There was no false modesty in his remark. On February 9, 1950, Joe McCarthy was neither a household name nor a recognizable public face. In four years as a freshman senator, a position he held by virtue of the 1946 Republican sweep of both houses of Congress, his record was so undistinguished that in a recent poll Washington correspondents had voted him America's worst senator.

As he boarded the plane, McCarthy's career was in shambles. In his home state of Wisconsin, critics were calling him the "Pepsi-Cola kid" because of reports that he had taken $10,000 from a manufacturer of prefabricated housing and obtained an unsecured loan of $20,000 from a lobbyist for Pepsi-Cola. Then it was disclosed that he recklessly lost the money speculating on soybean futures.

A year prior, McCarthy, a lawyer, had come close to being disbarred by the Wisconsin State Board of Ethics Examiners; he had run for the U.S. Senate while holding a state judicial office, a practice deemed both unethical and illegal. The board found that he had acted "in violation of the constitution and laws of Wisconsin," but dismissed a petition to discipline him by concluding that his infraction was "one in a class by itself which was not likely to be repeated."

McCarthy's reply was contemptuous. Paraphrasing the board's ruling, he mocked, "Joe was a naughty boy, but we don't think he'll do it again."

He was also in trouble in Washington.

In a clubbish Senate that relied on hoary tradition and deferential collegiality, on rigid seniority and elaborate courtesy, his repeated violations of Senate rules and customs had lost him the respect of influential colleagues in both parties and denied him a place among the players who would shape the legislative future. Already he had alienated both Republican and Democratic colleagues by lashing out during floor debates with false accusations against them. Once, in the spring of 1947, he so enraged two fellow Republicans, Ralph E. Flanders of Vermont and Charles W. Tobey of New Hampshire, that both arose in protest and, claiming personal privilege, accused McCarthy of having falsified their positions. This came after McCarthy told the Senate that both Flanders and Tobey had just informed him that they intended to introduce a "fictitious amendment" designed to "deceive the housewife" on a bill to extend wartime sugar controls for a year. So furious was Tobey that, red-faced and shouting, he accused McCarthy of lying and attempting to confuse the Senate.

As McCarthy was acutely aware, for these reasons and others his prospects for reelection in 1952 were imperiled. He had been consulting, in fact, his advisors about finding a cause to bolster his public standing and reverse his political slide. All this was about to change when his plane took off that February afternoon for West Virginia.

The way west is the most enduring of American legends, and in its time Wheeling, West Virginia, played a central role in that saga.

There, where the last battle of the Revolutionary War was fought at Fort Henry, a flood of pioneers and adventurers found their overland gateway west through Wheeling's gorges to claim free land beyond the Alleghenies in the Ohio River Valley. By the time Joe McCarthy's flight landed that February afternoon, Wheeling, once West Virginia's capital and leading city, had become a cultural and economic backwater. Its population had sunk to fifty-nine thousand from its peak of seventy thousand, and the exodus was accelerating. Wheeling was hardly the place for an obscure freshman senator to make his mark in history, especially at a political boilerplate event like the annual Lincoln Day speech to the Republican Women's Club of Ohio County—in a state that had voted Democratic in the last five presidential elections, including Harry S. Truman's two years earlier.

———

As unlikely as the backdrop was, when Joe McCarthy flew into Wheeling, West Virginia, the stage for McCarthyism had already been set.

Each morning that week, citizens of Wheeling had awakened to find the pages of their newspaper filled with frightening reports of treachery, spies, Communists, terrible new nuclear weapons, and a Cold War turning hot. Everything pointed toward a war of incalculable destruction. There seemed no end to alarming news flashes. Typical was the eight-column banner headline spread across the *Wheeling Intelligencer*'s front page, two days before McCarthy left for Wheeling:

FBI Hunts Fuchs' Aides in Atom Theft

The headline decks told the story, reported out of Washington:

Hoover Relates
Spy Activities
To Congressmen

British Scientist
Faces Trial Friday
For Betraying U.S.

Klaus Emil Fuchs, a British subject of German extraction who as a physicist had worked for three years in the United States on the ultrasecret atomic bomb project, had been arrested in London. Fuchs, "weedy, with a large head and narrow, rickety body," as the writer Rebecca West described him, was charged with transmitting to Soviet agents in the U.S. "all he knew" about America's A-bomb development. As the record revealed, Fuchs knew a lot.

Days after these shocking revelations, a federal jury found Alger Hiss, a top diplomatic aide to Franklin Roosevelt at the Yalta Conference, guilty of perjury in a highly-publicized espionage trial. An ex-Communist named Whittaker Chambers had accused Hiss in House Un-American Activities Committee testimony of being a Soviet agent who passed him secret government documents. After Hiss's conviction, Secretary of State Dean Acheson drew protests for telling reporters, "I do not intend to turn my back on Alger Hiss." Then Acheson made matters worse by invoking the words of a forgiving Jesus in the Sermon on the Mount in connection with the case of a convicted traitor.

Coming on the heels of Fuchs's arrest, and Hiss's conviction, President Truman's announcement that the United States had begun work on the hydrogen bomb only intensified national anxiety. The hydrogen bomb was the deadliest weapon yet known to humankind. Albert Einstein, the father of the nuclear age, appeared on national television warning that "radioactive poisoning of the atmosphere and, hence, annihilation of any life on earth has been brought within the range of possibilities." Einstein's conclusion: "General annihilation beckons." In this context, one of the staunchest Republican anticommunists, Homer Capehart of Indiana, cried out on the

Senate floor: "How much more are we going to take? Fuchs and Acheson and Hiss and hydrogen bombs threatening outside and New Dealism eating away the vitals of the nation. In the name of heaven, is this the best the nation can do?"

If this was not enough material for Joe McCarthy to exploit in West Virginia, another front-page story ran just before he arrived:

GOP Bares New Platform for 1950

Party Charges Truman With Promotion of Socialism in America

"The Republican Party opened its 1950 campaign tonight with a new platform charging the Truman administration with promoting socialism in America and allowing 'Communists and fellow travelers' to infiltrate the government," the wire service lead from Washington read.

There it was. All that was lacking was someone like McCarthy to light a bonfire and elevate campaign rhetoric into a movement that would ruin lives, discredit the United States, and affect the country for years to come.

In Wheeling, McCarthy strolled across the platform in the ballroom of the McClure Hotel, waved a sheaf of papers, and told the Republican women: "While I cannot take the time to name all of the men in the State Deparment who have been named as members of the Communist Party and members of a spy ring, I have here in my hand a list of 205 that were known to the Secretary of State as being members of the Communist Party and who, nevertheless, are still working and shaping the policy of the State Department."

Most of McCarthy's speech was a turgid pastiche of the GOP's standard attack rhetoric of the time. He shamelessly lifted paragraphs without attribution from other political addresses, congressional hearings, and newspaper articles such as a recent *Chicago Tribune* series about Communists in government, which the paper had said was proof that Franklin Roosevelt was sympathetic to Communist aims and "thus a willing partner in a conspiracy directed against his own country." McCarthy had stuffed the old speeches and reports from which he was lifting material into his briefcase before setting out on his way west into history.

In a blatant appropriation, McCarthy repeated as his own ideas large portions of a speech Richard Nixon had delivered about the Hiss case days earlier in the House of Representatives.

Nixon in Congress	**McCarthy in Wheeling**
The great lesson which should be learned from the Hiss case is that we are not just dealing with espionage agents who get 30 pieces of silver to obtain the blueprint of a new weapon . . . but this is a far more sinister type of activity, because it permits the enemy to guide and shape our policy.	One thing to remember in discussing the Communists is that we are not dealing with spies who get 30 pieces of silver to steal the blueprint of a new weapon. We are dealing with a far more sinister type of activity because it permits the enemy to guide and shape our policy.

McCarthy's speech was original in only one sense—the boldness with which he twisted facts, or invented them, to make grave and unsubstantiated accusations against the highest leaders of the United States at a moment of intense national fear. Without the one explosive paragraph containing his "I have here in my hand a list" accusation, the speech would not have been memorable in any way; but that brief paragraph was enough to change the course of history. And even McCarthy's famous "list" was a fraud. There was no list. What he held in his hand that night was a four-year-old letter from a former Secretary of State, James Byrnes.* It contained no names, no list, no mention of traitors working within the State Department, nothing about "spy rings," not *any* reference to Communist Party membership.

———

The only reporter covering McCarthy's speech that night was the *Intelligencer's* Frank Desmond, who along with two Republican officials met McCarthy at the airport and rode with him into the city. McCarthy gave Desmond a copy of his text to follow, and Desmond was in the audience as McCarthy spoke; he then returned to his paper's offices to write his story.

Some intriguing what ifs arise: What if Desmond had asked to see McCarthy's famous "list"? What if he had asked

---

*The 1946 letter was in response to Democratic Congressman Adolph Sabath of Illinois asking Byrnes to respond to Sabath's Cold War concerns about the loyalty of federal employees. Byrnes replied that of 3,000 government employees transferred to the State Department from other agencies at the end of World War II, a loyalty screening board had recommended against employing 284; of those, 79 had been separated from government service, leaving 205 employed by the State Department on July 26, 1946. This supposed McCarthy "list" was given him by Willard Edwards of the *Chicago Tribune* before he left for Wheeling. Though McCarthy implied he was disclosing this "list" for the first time as proof of his conspiracy charges, Sabath had promptly inserted the letter in the *Congressional Record* four years before.

McCarthy for proof of his allegations? Would Desmond then have reported McCarthy's charges without qualifying them?

Desmond asked McCarthy neither of these questions. His front-page story the next morning was written as if he were unaware of the significance of McCarthy's charges, but nevertheless assumed everyone knew they were true. The story reads like a report on a local Kiwanis meeting.

> Joseph McCarthy, junior U.S. Senator from Wisconsin, was given a rousing ovation last night when, as guest of the Ohio County Republican Women's Club, he declared bluntly that the fate of the world rests with the clash between the atheism of Moscow and the Christian spirit throughout other parts of the world.

> More than 275 representative Republican men and women were on hand to attend the colorful Lincoln Day dinner of the valley women which was held in the Colonnade room of the McClure hotel.

> Disdaining any oratorical fireworks, McCarthy's talk was of an intimate, homey nature, punctuated at times with humor.

> But on the serious side, he launched many barbs at the present setup of the State Department, at President Truman's reluctance to press investigation of "traitors from within" and other pertinent matters.

> He said that recent incidents which brought traitors to the limelight is the result of an "emotional hangover" and a temporary moral lapse which follows every war. However, he added:

> "The morals of our people have not been destroyed. They still exist and this cloak of numbness and apathy needs only a spark to rekindle them."

> Referring directly to the State Department, he declared:

Finally, in the eighth paragraph, just before the story jumped off page one to continue on an inside page, came the soon-to-be famous words:

> "While I cannot take the time to name all of the men in the State Department who have been named as members of the Communist Party and members of a spy ring, I have here in my hand a list of 205 that were known to the Secretary of State as being members of the Communist Party . . ."

Wheeling readers had to turn to page six to find the McCarthy quote continuing, "and who, nevertheless, are still working and shaping the policy of the State Department."

The rest of the article was filled with bromides, right down to a final McCarthy quote: "Today, we are engaged in a final, all-out battle between Communistic atheism and Christianity. The modern champions of Communism have selected this as the time, and, ladies and gentlemen, the chips are down—they are truly down."

That was it. But this article contained the spark that started a conflagration.

———

After Desmond turned in his story that night, the paper's managing editor, Norman L. Yost, a part-time "stringer" for the Associated Press, called the AP's night editor, Charles R. Lewis, in the wire service's Charleston, West Virginia, bureau. Yost dictated a paragraph or two from Desmond's story, then hung up.

An AP reporter in Washington, Bem Price, later reconstructed how McCarthy's allegations reached America via the

AP. "As Lewis began writing the brief story," Price reported, "he came to a figure he questioned—205 Communists in the State Department? He called Yost back and asked him to verify it." Yost told him to hold on. He would have his reporter recheck with McCarthy. In a moment, Yost came back on the line. The figure was accurate. Shortly after two A.M. the 110-word story clattered over the teletypes.

———

When Joe McCarthy headed to the airport the next morning, Friday, February 10, on the next leg of his journey west, he was accompanied by Francis J. Love, a former West Virginia Republican congressman who had been one of McCarthy's hosts in Wheeling. Love showed McCarthy coverage of his speech in that morning's *Intelligencer*, and McCarthy savored it. However inadequate Desmond's story, the paper had trumpeted the *real* news.

Across the top of page one was a banner headline:

McCarthy Charges Reds Hold U.S. Jobs

This was McCarthy's first clue that he had found his issue. His new course was set.

Aside from the one sensational paragraph in his speech, McCarthy's political sales pitch was no different from those of a score of other, much better known, Republicans. They, too, had been dispatched across the country by the Republican National Committee to hammer home the GOP's new campaign platform accusing Democrats of being "soft on Communism" and allowing "Communists and fellow travelers to infiltrate the government." They all were on the road giving Lincoln Day speeches inveighing against Communism, Red infiltration and subversion, treason sanctioned by the highest councils of government, spies and betrayal, and rampant immorality and un-Americanism.

Joe McCarthy stood so low in the Republican hierarchy that GOP leaders had not picked him as one of their speakers. Desperate for a chance to bolster his political profile, he had had to phone the Republican National Committee to volunteer. Even then, the party assigned him dismal, out-of-the-way appearances in Wheeling, Salt Lake City, Reno, Las Vegas, and Huron, South Dakota, with airport stops along the way. Yet now, as he boarded a Wheeling flight out of West Virginia, McCarthy was poised to catapult himself into a position of power above all others then exploiting the anticommunist issue. His life had changed, and so, shortly, would the country's.

——————

In William Manchester's narrative history of America from 1932 to 1972, *The Glory and the Dream,* Manchester describes how McCarthy, leaving Wheeling, "realized that he had stumbled upon a brilliant demagogic technique." As Manchester put it, for McCarthy this meant that because "others deplored treachery, McCarthy would speak of *traitors.*"

To Manchester's assessment, I would add: Not only would McCarthy speak of traitors. *He knew who they were. He knew where they were. He had a list. He had their names.* And the President of the United States and the Secretary of State knew who they were, too—or, at the very least, could find out. They could expose, remove, and prosecute these traitors, *if they wished,* assuming they were not traitors themselves.

McCarthy was aided by powerful factors that at that moment combined to make Americans feel threatened by fearsome forces at home and abroad.

Americans had confronted the deeply disturbing knowledge that spies and traitors did exist, and had been operating as the nation faced the possibility of nuclear war. And now, when they looked to the world beyond their borders, daily events made global conditions appear more dangerous. Berlin remained a tinderbox. The 1948 American-led airlift to break the Russian blockade had saved Berliners from starvation, but it had not eliminated the threat of war between the two existing superpowers. Mao Zedong's Red armies had driven Chiang Kai-shek's Nationalist forces from the Chinese mainland to the island of Taiwan in the East China Sea. Days before Hiss's conviction, Mao had seized American consular property in Shanghai and Beijing, presaging the imminent withdrawal of American personnel from the Chinese mainland and, more ominously, the signing of a defense pact between the two great Communist powers of Russia and China. The Korean War, and nearly forty thousand U.S. battle deaths and another hundred thousand combat casualties, was four months away.

Another factor powerfully made McCarthy's charges of traitors operating at the highest levels of the government seem credible: that anyone in a position of high public office—and McCarthy was not only a United States senator but also a Marine veteran of World War II—would deliberately level such falsehoods against leaders of the country. It was simply unbelievable that such a person would stoop so low. Besides, a senator was in a position to know things ordinary citizens could not. *There must be something there,* people thought.

McCarthy built on this belief. In the next hours of February 10, he did not let an opportunity go by without adding fuel to his bonfire. He generated the kind of national press attention he craved. And it was then that he demonstrated his genius for dominating headlines by countering questions about his facts by denying what he was reported to have said, by changing the figures he used and his characterization of them, and by making dramatic new charges and countercharges. In Wheeling, and for the next five years, Joe McCarthy proved himself a master manipulator of the press, someone who understood how to use journalistic deadlines to keep advancing a story by making more and more sensational charges. The charges kept him in the headlines. The rebuttals, if any, remained in the background.

When McCarthy landed in Denver later that morning, on the way to another speech in Salt Lake City, reporters were waiting for him. By then the State Department had issued a denial of his charges. "What about it, senator?" the reporters shouted as they gathered around McCarthy's plane on the tarmac of Stapleton Airport. McCarthy was unfazed. Now he gave the reporters a different account. He said he had in his possession "a complete list of 207 'bad risks' still working in the State Department."

This time the reporters asked to see his list with its names of, if not Communists, then "bad risks." In a moment of such high farce that it is hardly believable now, McCarthy began rummaging through his bulging briefcase, then said he had left the list in his baggage on the plane. *The Denver Post*, in one of the few humorous moments in the entire McCarthy saga, ran a front page photo of McCarthy "pawing" the contents of his briefcase while standing beside his plane. The photo caption read: "Left Commie List in Other Bag."

Before departing Denver, McCarthy told the reporters that if Dean Acheson called him when he reached Salt Lake City, he would read the list to Acheson over the phone. Then McCarthy was off again.

In Salt Lake City, he cited a different number of Communists in the State Department—fifty-seven. (He soon changed the number to eighty-one.) He also raised the political stakes, and the news coverage, by making a direct challenge to Acheson during a radio interview that afternoon.

A transcript of the interview between McCarthy and local reporter Dan Valentine illustrates McCarthy's technique of dodging and weaving, then delivering sneak punches:

> McCarthy: Last night I discussed the "Communists in the State Department." I stated that I had the names of 57 card-carrying members of the Communist Party. I noticed today that the State Department has denied that. They say they don't know of a single one in the State Department. Now I want to tell the Secretary of State this, if he wants to call me tonight at the Utah Hotel I will be glad to give him the names of those card-carrying Communists. I might say this, however, Dan, the day that Alger Hiss was exposed the President signed an order to the effect that no one in the State Department could give any information as to the disloyalty of the Communistic activity of any State Department employee. Then later they went a step further. They said, in addition to that, no one in the Department can give any information as to the employment of any man in the State Department. Now, obviously, before we will give him the information, give him the names of the Communists whom we, names he should certainly have himself (if I have them, he should have them) I want this: an indication of his good faith. The best way to indicate that is to say that at least as far as these 57 are concerned, when you give their names

then all indication of their Communistic activities, as to their disloyalty, will be available to any proper congressional investigating committee. Have I made myself clear, Dan?

He had delivered a bombfog. It enveloped the reporter, who, in his confusion, bought the version McCarthy intended:

Valentine: In other words, senator, if Secretary of State Dean Acheson would call you at the Hotel Utah tonight in Salt Lake City—

McCarthy [interrupting]: That's right.

Valentine [continuing]: you could give him 57 names of actual card-carrying Communists in the State Department of the United States—actual card-carrying Communists.

McCarthy: Not only can, Dan, but I will on condition—

Valentine [interrupting]: I don't blame you for that.

McCarthy [continuing]: that they lift this veil of secrecy and allow the congressional committee to know about the Communistic activities and disloyalty in the Department.

Though McCarthy first said he would read Acheson the names and then withdrew the offer, his charge about "card-carrying Communists" went across the country via the wire services. It produced headlines such as one in the *Washington Evening Star*, then the capital's wealthiest, oldest, and most careful paper: "McCarthy Charges 57 in State Department Hold Red Party Cards."

McCarthy had employed the tactics he used from then on: to always put the onus on others; to never answer challenges to his own credibility; to repeatedly make new charges; to move from city to city outside of New York and Washington; to count on headlines to keep him ahead of his critics. Now it was the Secretary of State who was on the defensive. McCarthy's public challenge sent the message that Acheson must either act according to McCarthy's dictates, or be seen as covering up or guiltily refusing to cooperate with a reasonable request.

Then McCarthy was off again, this time to Reno—and this time his target became the president.

———

Reno was a watershed for Joe McCarthy. When he arrived Saturday morning, February 11, he found that Deputy Undersecretary of State John E. Peurifoy had sent him a telegram refuting his accusations point by point and demanding that he provide any information he had about Communists in the department. Rather than backtracking or answering directly, McCarthy went on the attack. In consultation with his staff in Washington, he began drafting a telegram to President Harry S. Truman in the White House.

The night before in Salt Lake City, McCarthy had introduced a fellow Republican senator, George Malone of Nevada. This night, in Reno, Malone was to introduce him at a Lincoln Day dinner. Knowing this and knowing of McCarthy's schedule, reporters Edward A. Olsen of the Associated Press and Frank McCullough of the *Reno Gazette* set out that morning to interview McCarthy about his charges. They found him in Senator Malone's office in the Sierra Pacific Power Company building. McCarthy's behavior was even more bizarre than it had been in Denver.

"We opened the door and walked in," Olsen of the AP later recalled. "McCarthy was talking on the phone, to his

Washington headquarters or his staff. The gist of his questioning was, 'How's it going? Are we making an impact? Are we getting some publicity out of it?'"

While McCarthy talked on the phone, he continually tapped his front teeth with his fountain pen. Occasionally, he hit the phone mouthpiece. Why was he doing that? the reporters asked after he hung up. "I'm breaking up the wiretap," McCarthy answered dramatically.

"We tried to interview him about his allegations of Communists in the State Department," Olsen said, "and asked him if he could name some names for us. Well, he did. He named three or four eminent people . . . I asked him would he name these names in his speech that night, because I didn't want to run them as an interview unless he was really on the record about it. His reply to that was, 'Young man, I know more about libel than you do. I'm a lawyer.' So I didn't run his interview at all, and [Olsen's superiors in] New York agreed."

———

In the archives of the Truman Presidential Library in Independence, Missouri, is the original Western Union telegram that Joe McCarthy sent from Reno, Nevada, to "The President, the White House" on February 11, 1950. It is stamped as having arrived in the White House that night at 7:31 P.M. Eastern Standard Time (5:31 P.M. in Reno). So typical of McCarthy's way of attack is this document that it deserves to be quoted at length.

IN A LINCOLN DAY SPEECH AT WHEELING THURSDAY
NIGHT I STATED THAT THE STATE DEPARTMENT HARBORS
A NEST OF COMMUNISTS AND COMMUNIST SYMPATHIZERS
WHO ARE HELPING TO SHAPE OUR POLICY. I FURTHER

STATED THAT I HAVE IN MY POSSESSION THE NAMES OF 57 COMMUNISTS WHO ARE IN THE STATE DEPARTMENT AT PRESENT. A STATE DEPARTMENT SPOKESMAN FLATLY DENIED THIS AND CLAIMED THERE IS NOT A SINGLE COMMUNIST IN THE DEPARTMENT. YOU CAN CONVINCE YOURSELF OF THE FALSITY OF THE STATE DEPARTMENT CLAIM VERY EASILY. YOU WILL RECALL THAT YOU PERSONALLY APPOINTED A BOARD TO SCREEN STATE DEPARTMENT EMPLOYEES FOR THE PURPOSE OF WEEDING OUT FELLOW TRAVELERS. YOUR BOARD DID A PAINS-TAKING [sic] JOB, AND NAMED HUNDREDS WHICH IT LISTED AS "DANGEROUS TO THE SECURITY OF THE NATION," BECAUSE OF COMMUNISTIC CONNECTIONS.

WHILE THE RECORDS ARE NOT AVAILABLE TO ME, I KNOW ABSOLUTELY THAT OF ONE GROUP OF APPROXIMATELY 300 CERTIFIED TO THE SECRETARY FOR DISCHARGE, HE ACTUALLY DISCHARGED ONLY APPROXIMATELY 80. I UNDERSTAND THAT THIS WAS DONE AFTER LENGTHY CONVERSATION WITH ALGER HISS. I WOULD SUGGEST THEREFORE, MR. PRESIDENT, THAT YOU SIMPLY PICK UP YOUR PHONE AND ASK MR. ACHESON HOW MANY OF THOSE WHOM YOUR BOARD HAS LABELED AS DANGEROUS HE FAILED TO DISCHARGE. THE DAY THE HOUSE UN-AMERICAN ACTIVITIES COMMITTEE EXPOSED ALGER HISS AS AN IMPORTANT LINK IN AN INTER-NATIONAL COMMUNIST SPY RING, YOU SIGNED AN ORDER FORBIDDING THE STATE DEPARTMENTS [sic] GIVING TO THE CONGRESS ANY INFORMATION IN REGARD TO THE DISLOYALTY OR THE COMMUNISTIC CONNECTIONS OF ANYONE IN THAT DEPARTMENT, [sic] DISPITE [sic] THIS STATE DEPARTMENT BLACKOUT, WE HAVE BEEN ABLE TO COMPILE A LIST OF 57 COMMUNISTS IN THE STATE DEPARTMENT. THIS LIST IS

AVAILABLE TO YOU, BUT YOU CAN GET A MUCH LONGER
LIST BY ORDERING SECRETARY ACHESON TO GIVE YOU A
LIST OF THOSE WHOM YOUR OWN BOARD LISTED AS BEING
DISLOYAL, AND WHO ARE STILL WORKING IN THE STATE
DEPARTMENT.

McCarthy demanded, as "the minimum which can be expected of you in this case," that Truman order Acheson to
give the president and the proper congressional committee
"the names and a complete report on all of those who were
placed in the Department by Alger Hiss, and all of those still
working in the State Department who were listed by your
boaard [*sic*] as bad security risks because of the Communistic
connections."

In closing, McCarthy went much further. In effect, he accused not only Acheson, but also the President of the United
States, of treason:

> FAILURE ON YOUR PART WILL LABEL THE DEMOCRATIC
> PARTY OF BEING THE BED-FELLOW OF INTER-NATIONAL
> COMMUNISM. CERTAINLY THIS LABEL IS NOT DESERVED BY
> THE HUNDREDS OF THOUSANDS OF LOYAL AMERICAN
> DEMOCRATS THROUGHOUT THE NATION, AND BY THE SIZ-
> ABLE NUMBER OF ABLE LOYAL DEMOCRATICS [*sic*] IN BOTH
> THE SENATE AND THE HOUSE.
> JOE MC CARTHY U.S.S. WIS.

At a presidential news conference five days later, Truman
told reporters that there was "not a word of truth" in Mc-
Carthy's charges of Communists in the State Department.
Truman, a peppery little man with a hair-trigger temper,
never let himself get into a charge-and-countercharge debate

with McCarthy, and in his memoirs he makes no mention of McCarthy's telegram.

His real feelings, however, leap out in another document found in a McCarthy file in the Truman Archives.

Marked "Draft," and written in Truman's own unmistakable voice, it reads:

> My dear Senator:
>
> I read your telegram of February eleventh from Reno, Nevada with a great deal of interest and this is the first time in my experience, and I was ten years in the Senate, that I ever heard of a Senator trying to discredit his own Government before the world. You know that isn't done by honest public officials. Your telegram is not only not true and an insolent approach to a situation that should have been worked out between man and man but it shows conclusively that you are not even fit to have a hand in the operation of the Government of the United States.
>
> I am very sure that the people of Wisconsin are extremely sorry that they are represented by a person who has as little sense of responsibility as you have.

As far as can be determined, this draft letter, signed "sincerely yours" and under that the initials "HST," was never sent.

———

One morning in March, only weeks after the Wheeling speech, readers of the *Washington Post* opened their papers to find an editorial page cartoon by Herblock. It showed Republican leaders pushing a reluctant GOP elephant toward a shaky tower fashioned of ten bespattered tar buckets, complete with tar brushes. At the very top, Herblock labeled the largest oozing bucket: *McCarthyism.*

Chapter TWO

Tail Gunner Joe

America needs a tail gunner.

In still the best-written, most trenchant portrait of McCarthy, Richard Rovere addressed the central enigma about him:

"When I was gathering materials for my book *Senator Joe McCarthy,*" Rovere wrote in his uncompleted memoir *Final Reports,* which was published posthumously in 1978, "I found that a good many reporters had spent a considerable time in and around Grand Chute, Wisconsin, McCarthy's birthplace and early home . . . I think I can sum up their findings in a sentence. The fifth of nine children born to a poor farm family—Irish in background, Roman Catholic by religion—McCarthy was a physically unattractive boy and something of a bully, but nevertheless a reasonably bright, ambitious, and industrious one. Nothing in that sentence helps explain the emergence of Joe McCarthy, the most formidable and gifted demagogue of the century."

Much as I admired Rovere, I could not accept his judgment about the unfathomable mystery of Joe McCarthy. So decades later, in the summer of 2003, I found myself retracing the territory Rovere and many others before and after him had explored. Though I thought I knew the basics of McCarthy's life story and had engrossed myself in the literature about him, the picture that emerged was darker, more complex, and more disturbing. Not that what was revealed about the life and character of Joe McCarthy came as a great surprise. That he was a rogue, both charming and brutal; a primitive; a reckless prevaricator; a daring risk taker; a compulsive gambler at poker, dice, horses, casino tables, and stock markets; a cheat at games; an astonishingly bold bluffer; a man with little respect for truth and incapable of admitting he was wrong, are facts essentially well known. But I came to see McCarthy as infinitely more formidable than I had suspected.

Joe McCarthy possessed something like a photographic memory—his mind was like a "sponge," or a "blotter," his college classmates said—that enabled him to spew forth answers "lightning quick" in cram sessions and on exams. From the beginning of his career, he demonstrated a kind of instinctive political genius that owed nothing to campaign consultants or image makers. He was not interested in ideas, except in appropriating the thoughts or opinions of others if they helped him exploit an issue like Communism. His law degree and native intelligence notwithstanding, he was ill educated, had no sense of history, and was incurious and carelessly ill-informed about the great public questions—again, like Communism—that he addressed with such assurance. He did not read books, with one fascinating exception: Hitler's *Mein Kampf.*

Two men, both of whom became judges, separately—and very differently—recalled to McCarthy scholars McCarthy's early admiration for *Mein Kampf.* Once, in the late 1930s when McCarthy was a young judge in Appleton, Wisconsin, he shocked a fellow lawyer, Gustavus Keller, by bringing out Hitler's book in his judicial chambers and citing it as "the source of his political strategy." Urban P. Van Susteren,* who also became a judge, was McCarthy's closest friend from boyhood until his death, and told how McCarthy "never read books" with the exception of *Mein Kampf,* adding: "And he only read half of it, and it was *my* [copy]."

As for McCarthy's interest in *Mein Kampf,* Van Susteren cautioned biographers not to make too much of it. "Lots of people read *Mein Kampf* in Appleton," he said. "Hitler had support here. But Joe, I think, was more taken by the tactics, by the means and not the end. He had no use for Hitler or anything the Nazis did. But when he looked at *Mein Kampf,* it was like one politician comparing notes with another. Joe was fascinated by the strategy, that's all."

Rovere was not alone in being unable to resolve McCarthy's behavioral contradictions. Those who knew him well saw him either as "tricky, very tricky" and "slippery," or as "intensely human" and the most warmhearted of friends with a gift for inspiring loyalty. He was "basically insecure, highly emotional, even romantic," or tough and utterly unsentimental. He was a lovable rake whose exaggerations, however outrageous, were merely examples of his "Irish blarney," or of his having a "genius of the half lie."

Scholars who spent years trying to understand McCarthy

---

*His daughter, Greta Van Susteren, is a noted cable TV commentator and talk show host, for Fox News.

came away no less perplexed. In 1976, biographer Thomas Reeves wrote to Van Susteren to confess that having studied fourteen manuscript collections, constructed extensive files, and interviewed fifty people who knew McCarthy well, he was unable to solve a number of problems that threatened the reliability of his book. In some accounts of McCarthy's formative years, Reeves said, he had been described as "the family's shy, ugly, inferiority-ridden little boy, constantly hiding in his mother's apron, being assured by her that some day he would amount to something"—this inferiority complex supposedly stemming from McCarthy's relationship with his stern, almost cruel, father. Since McCarthy family members had refused to cooperate with Reeves, he had appealed to McCarthy's friends for help.

Equally puzzling, however, were the sharply contradictory descriptions of McCarthy given by Van Susteren and Thomas Korb, McCarthy's close friend, law-school classmate, professional associate, and "best man." The key to understanding Joe McCarthy, Korb had told Reeves, "is an understanding of his deep sense of personal insecurity." Quoting from interview notes, Reeves said Korb told him: "Joe was *not* a 100% extrovert. That was all a show. He was extroverted in compensating for his acute sense of inferiority." Korb also saw McCarthy as a "sentimental slob" who "exhibited great emotionalism" and privately "often broke into tears." After five years as a senator, McCarthy "would still get tears in his eyes at the sight of the Capitol." Korb added: "Joe never really accepted the fact that he was a senator. The position was too awesome. He would say on various occasions, 'pretty good for a guy that wasn't educated,' and the like. Joe always really felt himself . . . inferior."

Van Susteren's reaction to Korb's assessment was dismissive. It was "bullshit." McCarthy was not a slobbering, sentimental man; Van Susteren had never seen McCarthy cry, not even at the deaths of his mother and father; he was a tough, realistic man. Insecure? The opposite was true. Joe McCarthy's "major fault was that he was in awe of no one; he thought almost everyone inferior to himself."

In the end, the enigma of McCarthy's character and personality remains. There can be no question, though, that Joe McCarthy was a blunt force with a lust for power and a willingness to do anything to prevail.

———

Outside of Appleton, in Outagamie County, a hundred twenty miles north of Milwaukee in Grand Chute Township, the two-lane McCarthy Road still runs straight as a string past fields of corn unmarked by suburban sprawl and cookie-cutter developments. When I visited there in 2003, nothing seemed to have changed from decades past. At the very end of the road, on the left, stands the old McCarthy homestead. There, in the 1850s, Stephen Patrick McCarthy of Tipperary County, Ireland, cleared land; built a log cabin; planted crops; raised corn, barley, cabbage, oats, and hay; bought dairy cattle; and in the second year of the Civil War married another immigrant who lived on a farm directly across McCarthy Road: Margaret Stoffel from Bavaria, one of numerous German, Dutch, and Irish settlers who made their way west to Wisconsin. Timothy, the third of Stephen and Margaret's ten children, married another woman of Irish descent, Bridget Canall, and fathered nine more McCarthy children, the fifth of whom they named Joseph Raymond. By the time of my visit, the farm's old barn was gone, but there remained the road named for Joe's ancestors and the homestead, now modernized and occupied by a furniture repairman. Standing in the driveway, a few hundred feet from the rural free delivery mailbox, the present owner pointed out sites along the skyline—here, there—where other McCarthy offspring had made their farms, and where some descendants still did. No clues to unraveling any McCarthy mystery existed there.

Nor, at first, did Appleton seem of much help.

No historical markers informed strangers that here was where the saga of Appleton's most famous—or infamous—native son began. This had not always been so. Not long before, visitors to Appleton would have found a large bronze bust of McCarthy prominently positioned inside the Outagamie County Courthouse lobby. Local officials and dignitaries from Washington placed it there with appropriate ceremony two years after his death. But over the forty-two years that the bust dominated the lobby, this tangible tribute to Joe McCarthy became an object of increasing controversy. Finally, after a decade-long campaign by county supervisors to have the bust removed from the courthouse, it was donated in 2002 to a temporary museum exhibit in Appleton. When the exhibit closed in 2004, it was removed and placed in storage. All physical reminders of McCarthy in Appleton were gone. Hardly any residents had personal memories of him and the legacy he left; the rest probably didn't care whether or not he was celebrated in bronze.

Such was not the case when he died. At the time of McCarthy's funeral, which was attended by twenty-one United States senators, all of Appleton's public offices, schools, and businesses were closed in his honor. Thirty thousand local mourners filed by the open casket. Later, they waited patiently outside St. Mary's Catholic Church to follow the hearse carrying the flag-draped coffin to burial ceremonies at the parish cemetery. By 2003, no signs told visitors how to find the gravesite.

St. Mary's Catholic Cemetery, a mile southwest of the church, lay on a bluff nestled against the Fox River, a small oasis of calm. A narrow asphalt driveway ran off West Prospect Avenue and led toward a small chapel, curling past immaculately tended lawns and graves along the way. Some graves bore small American flags; most were decorated with flowers. Strolling across the grounds on a sunlit summer day with a fresh breeze and cloudless skies, I saw carved on the tombstones names that mutely testify to the Irish and German roots of those who rest here: *McGrath* and *Konz, McMahon* and *Treiber, McLaughlin* and *Sturm, MacDonald* and *Bierstalken.* Only one name broke the ethnic pattern—and produced a personal surprise: *Bonner.* It is my middle name, of English, and I think before that, of French derivation, but of what possible distant family connection, if any, I know not.

I had to search among the tombstones to find McCarthy's grave. Finally, there it was: gray marble, larger but in no way dominating the rest, it stood alone, backed up to the very edge of the bluffs, the Fox River below, surrounded by a magnificent stand of trees and bushes. The words carved into the marble read simply:

Joseph R. McCarthy
UNITED STATES SENATOR
November 14, 1908   May 2, 1957

On top, embedded in the headstone, was the Marine Corps emblem with eagle, globe, and anchor, and a scroll bearing the Latin words *Semper Fidelis,* "always faithful." Barely visible a few feet in front were two small stone markers lying flat in the grass. They designated the graves of McCarthy's mother, Bridget, and father, Timothy.

On this summer day, there were no other visitors to the cemetery. Standing steeped in silence before his tombstone, I thought how ironic, yet fitting, it was that a life that produced such raging controversies and claimed so many victims should end in so tranquil a setting. Suddenly, out of nowhere, a summer storm threatened. Dark clouds passed swiftly over the cemetery grounds. A stiff wind rose from the river, whipping the trees along the bluff and bending toward the ground the tall pines directly over McCarthy's grave. Then, as quickly as it had arrived, the turbulence passed. Sunlight and calm returned. I don't offer this act of nature as a sign or clue as to the forces that shaped McCarthy, the man, and propelled him on his reckless journey from Appleton; but for me, at least, it symbolized the stormy nature of that life and those times.

As for the essence of Joe McCarthy, I continued my search. Appleton was quiet, its pace slow, its streets largely deserted: a midwestern town slumbering in the summer sun. The Outagamie Historical Society, site of the Outagamie County Museum's McCarthy exhibit, was an old, buff-colored stone mansion fronting East College Avenue. Also housed there was a permanent display devoted to another local celebrity, the fabled trickster and escape artist Harry Houdini. For now, the museum's focus was on McCarthy.

I confess that out of eastern snobbishness or plain ignorance, I was prepared for an exhibit that praised, if not glorified, the local boy, ignoring, or glossing over, his failings. I could not have been more wrong. Captured on the walls and in the glass display cases of three rooms were the essentials of

Joe McCarthy's life and career accompanied by candid and often harshly critical assessments. He got no hometown breaks.

Greeting visitors to the second-floor exhibit was a group of large photos showing McCarthy from 1930 to 1954. Above them, in bold black letters, was the name of the exhibit:

Joseph McCarthy: A Modern Tragedy

and underneath, its theme:

> Joseph McCarthy lived a modern tragedy. He became Wisconsin's junior senator as the United States entered a Cold War with the Soviet Union. With increasing conviction in his anti-Communist crusade, McCarthy recklessly attacked some of the country's leading public officials. His ambition and independence became character flaws which led to a disastrous ending—his censure by Senate colleagues in 1954.

Photos on surrounding walls showed a younger McCarthy: in overalls, with his family, standing before the old homestead; with classmates outside his one-room rural school; with fellow Marquette University students, striking a swaggering pose in front of college buildings.

Studying these images, it was apparent that one of Rovere's findings was demonstrably wrong. Joe McCarthy was clearly not "a physically unattractive boy." Eventually standing just over five feet eleven inches and weighing a compact one hundred sixty pounds, he was a handsome youth and young man: dark haired, clear eyed, looking alert and sharp, and, at least in pictures taken in these early years, always smiling. Even in the old black-and-white pictures, he appeared to exude charm. Yet in later photos, especially those taken during the final "McCarthyism" years, something else emerged. He became heavier, fleshier, darker. He scowled instead of smiled, stared with a fixed, almost deadened gaze instead of displaying the sparkling blue-eyed countenance previously captured by the camera.

As for other Rovere findings, that McCarthy was "something of a bully" and also a "reasonably ambitious and industrious" person, the exhibit offered no evidence on the first, but it clearly existed. From his days in Wisconsin through those in Washington, numerous people testified to a peculiar strain in McCarthy's character. One moment he could be most charming, backslapping, generous, friendly ("entertaining and fun," as someone remembered); then, suddenly, he would turn on you viciously. Van Susteren observed this kind of behavior. "You could watch Joe's eyes light up as he figured out almost immediately how to screw an opponent," he told Reeves. To Van Susteren, McCarthy's combative tactics resembled those of the Irish Republican Army: "cut their balls off."

As for the second of his findings, Rovere much underestimated McCarthy's ambition and industriousness.

From the beginning, McCarthy was possessed of enormous raw energy; it was the trait most often mentioned by those who knew him best. "Joe worked like the devil," a neighboring farmer of the McCarthys said of young Joe.

> I remember one day when he was helpin' Tim load hay into the barn. We was usin' a team of horses and a rope and pulley to hoist the hay up. Joe's job was leadin' the horses. He had to lead them across the yard and through a ditch and clear to the road. The ditch was near fulla water, but Joe plowed right into it, up to his knees, leadin' them horses. Never even slowed down. One of his boots came off in the mud and I remember he didn't go pick up that boot till all the hay was in. Joe was always like that—a hard worker.

McCarthy was driven from his earliest days by a fierce ambition to rise above his roots. He wanted to be somebody. Gustavus Keller remembered McCarthy telling him years before becoming a national figure that he would "be the first Catholic president of the United States." McCarthy was always looking up to the next rung on the ladder. He always believed he would win. Until nearly the very end, he always did.

McCarthy's "good side" was faithfully represented. The museum exhibit showed how he rose so far so fast from hardscrabble beginnings: how he quit school at the age of fourteen to run a chicken farm, which failed; how later he managed a local Cashway grocery store and again struck people as intensely ambitious ("I never saw anybody so steamed up," an acquaintance recalled. "He just couldn't ever relax; he worked at everything he did. He was pushing all the time."); how, in 1929, he moved northwest to Manawa after the grocery chain relocated its Appleton store; how the same year, at the age of twenty, he left the store to enter Manawa's Little Wolf High School; how the principal allowed him to complete course work at his own pace, with the result that he finished grades nine through twelve in one academic year and graduated from high school at the age of twenty-one; how the principal admiringly wrote McCarthy's father that his son had completed his schooling in one year "by will power, unusual ability, and concentrated work!!!"; how McCarthy then moved to Milwaukee to enter Marquette University and began literally working around the clock to put himself through school, laboring as a gas station attendant, "janitor, salesman, short-order cook, and construction worker," even selling flypaper door-to-door, all for as little as thirty cents an hour.

His admittance to Marquette exposed McCarthy's willingness to break the rules: he lied to get in. McCarthy had not spent four years at an accredited high school, as required by Marquette of entering freshmen, but when he (or his teacher?) filled out Marquette's entrance forms, he answered the question, "Did you attend four years of high school?" by writing "Yes."

He often worked for ten to twelve hour stretches at night while maintaining a full college class load in the afternoons. He also found time to join the university's debate and boxing teams, both of which provided experience that became useful in his political career.

He was a "punishing puncher . . . he could hurt you," one of his classmates and fellow boxers later recalled. He was a slugger, a brawler. And he was fearless when fighting bigger, heavier, or more skilled opponents. He never gave up, even when, as in one fight, he and his opponent were left "lying in the dirt, covered with blood." His capacity for absorbing, even courting, punishment and pain was extraordinary, and apparently part of his makeup. A high school classmate recalled how McCarthy, who couldn't swim, repeatedly jumped off a high diving board with an inner tube around his waist, each time bruising himself terribly and ending the day's outing literally black and blue.

Nor was he above fighting dirty; for years, he would recount the advice an "Indian Charlie" had given him on how to fight: "start kicking . . . as fast as possible below the belt until the other person is rendered helpless."*

---

*Virtually every McCarthy biographer recalls his "Indian Charlie" story, but I can't determine where it comes from and when he first began telling it. In his memoir about the Army-McCarthy hearings, Army counsel John G. Adams cites McCarthy boasting during a secret hearing to fellow senators about the lessons: "He had learned from an an 'old Indian friend' named 'Indian Charlie' that 'when anyone approached him in a not completely friendly fashion, [to] start kicking that person in the balls and continue to kick him until there was nothing but air where the balls used to be.'"

When McCarthy took up debate he was not a talented speaker. In fact, he had to overcome a problem that had been apparent in high school: he stuttered. His high school principal, proud of his determined older student, thought he was giving McCarthy an honor by inviting him to address a student assembly. Instead, the experience was a nightmare for the nervous, tongue-tied McCarthy. Yet, typically, after that speech McCarthy diligently worked to improve his public speaking technique and his stage confidence. At Marquette, he joined the oldest forensic society on campus. Though he always lacked eloquence, as a politician he employed a debater's rhetorical style to keep opponents on the defensive as he aggressively made assertions to win points and carry the day.

Despite the museum exhibitors' earnest attempt to be even-handed in their assessments, however, the negatives in McCarthy's life far outweighed the positives.

Beneath each presentation of an episode in McCarthy's life, visitors were asked, in bold black letters:

What Do You Think?

This approach continued when the subject turned to Communism. One assessment, in fact, coincidentally expressed the theme of this book. After noting that "many Americans in the 1950s saw Communists as a danger to national security" and that "in fighting that danger, they weighed the effectiveness of McCarthy's anticommunist tactics and their impact on civil liberties," the commentary added:

"Debate about national security and citizen rights continues today in a new form. The terrorist attacks on the Pentagon and New York's World Trade Center towers started a new wave of anxiety."

As for McCarthy's success in fighting Communism, the exhibit's judgment is negative: "McCarthy named a few federal employees with Communist associations" and "identified one espionage agent"—a United Nations employee in 1950—but "McCarthy made little distinction between a Communist, a former Communist, or a Communist spy."

When the exhibit assessed his professional career, the negatives became more pronounced.

The museum's look at Joe McCarthy's life revealed a pattern of engaging in practices that, at best, skirted the edges of legality and, at worst, descended to outright deception and fraud. In an early example, McCarthy was shown, at the age of thirty-one in 1939, campaigning for the position of Tenth District judge against a long-time incumbent, Judge Edgar V. Werner. McCarthy won, and became the youngest man ever elected circuit court judge in Wisconsin. Beneath a picture of him as a new sitting judge, however, a caption noted: "The Wisconsin Supreme Court criticized Judge McCarthy for destroying a court record in 1941. McCarthy had removed one page from a court transcript to hide his comment that a trial in the Quaker Dairy case was a 'waste of the court's time.'" Much later, he was criticized for turning his court into a "divorce mill" by granting "quick" divorces, sometimes as political favors, and using the fees to help pay for his campaign expenses. He was also constantly facing investigations—by the Internal Revenue Service, by the state tax agency—into his financial dealings and his failure to pay taxes, as well as his staving off demands for repayment of substantial loans he had received from local banks. Until much later, most of these incidents were not known to the public; some never received public airing.

The exhibit referred briefly to something even more telling: how McCarthy won his judgeship. He engaged in dirty tricks.

Though he knew better, McCarthy issued a campaign letter misstating Werner's age (then sixty-six) by seven years and suggesting that if reelected Werner would be eighty when his term expired. In a campaign ad that ran just before the election, under a bold headline that asked WHAT ABOUT THIS AGE QUESTION?, McCarthy implied that his opponent was approaching senility. McCarthy also courted, and won, a large Menominee Indian vote in the district. Later, he boasted to friends that he would introduce himself to tribal leaders, then have them introduce him to other members of the tribe, "as the young man running against 'that feeble fellow' who is now judge." In fact, Judge Werner was in good physical and mental health.

In another campaign ad, McCarthy lumped together everything Werner had earned while in public office, a grand total of between $170,000 and $200,000—an enormous sum in the Depression era—leaving the impression that the judge had grown wealthy by dipping from the public trough. During a thirty-five-year career in public service—including twenty years on the bench, another six years as district attorney, and six more as city attorney—Werner's average annual earnings of between six and seven thousand dollars were in keeping with salaries for lawyers of that time and place. Yet Werner lost. For the rest of his life, he remained embittered by McCarthy's tactics.

Judge Edgar V. Werner became Joe McCarthy's first victim.

Years later, when McCarthy was at the peak of his power in Washington, Judge Werner's son said of McCarthy: "He not only drove my father to his grave but turned longstanding family friends against our whole family. He didn't just add years to my dad's age; he accused him of all sorts of evil. It was amazing how one man could wreck the reputation of a man loved and honored in this community."

Nor was this the first example of McCarthy's willingness to push the limits of fair play, as an incident that took place during his law school days at Marquette showed. "Joe and I were opposing candidates for Class President," recalled Charles P. Curran years later when he was practicing law in Mauston, Wisconsin. "I suggested to Joe that we vote for each other and he agreed."

When the ballots were counted, McCarthy and Curran were tied. "The Dean called us both into the office and inquired as to whether we would like to cut cards, draw straws or flip a coin in order to determine the winner," Curran remembered. "I told him that either of such methods would be satisfactory to me but Joe said, 'No, I would like to have another election.'" In the second election, after a two-week campaign, McCarthy was declared the winner by two votes. "Subsequently," Curran said, "in a friendly inquiry, I inquired of Joe which votes he had switched on me in order to be successful." McCarthy told Curran "that he had worked so hard trying to convince his classmates that he was the best candidate" that he decided to vote for himself.

McCarthy joined the Marines in 1942 at the age of thirty-three while still holding his judicial seat, and then served in the South Pacific. To his credit, he did not have to serve; his judicial position deferred him from the draft. But according to the testimony of his friends, he was motivated at least in part by the need for a military credential to further his political career.

Van Susteren remembered how McCarthy "shocked" a local reporter by confiding in 1942 that he planned to run for the U.S. Senate, a decision McCarthy had apparently made at least a year earlier. Typically, McCarthy knew nothing about the Marine Corps' traditions or its history of courageous action, but after hearing Van Susteren explain them, McCarthy decided the Marines were for him.

McCarthy never told the truth about *how* he entered the service, and continued to lie about it for the rest of his public career. He claimed then—and later in his campaign literature and congressional biographical entries—that he had "enlisted as a buck private in the Marine Corps" and was "sent to an officers' training school," where he earned a second lieutenant's commission. The local paper wrote of McCarthy's enlistment as a "buck private" with no promise of a commission or any special favors as an action that "breathes the spirit that founded America, developed its rugged slopes, harnessed its ceaseless energies and is not only willing but anxious to protect it."

In fact, McCarthy arranged to enter the service as a commissioned officer; he wrote a letter on court stationery requesting that he receive an officer's commission. He was sworn in as a first lieutenant. Nor did he resign his judgeship, enabling him to campaign for the Senate two years later as "a Judge and a Soldier." He rose to captain before he chose to end his military duty on December 11, 1944, to return to the bench in Wisconsin. This was months after he lost, while still in the service, the 1944 United States Senate Republican primary in Wisconsin against the veteran Senator Alexander Wiley. McCarthy apparently never expected to win, but counted on his candidacy to gain favorable publicity for later attempts—which it did. Upon entering the race, he was hailed by the *Green Bay Press Gazette* as a model of a vanguard of patriotic citizen-soldiers, "honest acting men who are heralds of a new and more decent day in American politics."

About this first McCarthy attempt to gain national office, museum visitors were informed dryly: "McCarthy's 1944 campaign for U.S. Senate came under criticism. He broke an election law when he diverted money into his campaign through family and friends. McCarthy left the Marines in December, 1944, to begin preparations for the 1946 Senate race."

How McCarthy financed that first attempt at national electoral office in 1944 revealed another thread that ran throughout his career—what one scholar called his "obsessive preoccupation with money." His private financial affairs, Michael O'Brien writes, were "compounded of mysterious borrowings, unexplained bad debts, speculations in the bonds of bankrupt railroads, and other wildcatting operations." His most successful known speculative venture came during the World War II period, when an investment of some seven thousand dollars in defaulted railroad stocks—where and how he got the money to invest remains unclear—returned a profit of $43,353.92 in 1943. With part of this money, he financed his campaign against Senator Wiley. "He could not do so openly," O'Brien writes, "because a state statute limited to $5,000 the amount a candidate could contribute to his own campaign. He did it covertly, therefore, by funneling $17,600 through his relatives. Campaign records listed contributions of $10,600 from his brother Howard, $3,000 from his brother-in-law Roman Kornely, and $4,000 from his father Timothy. None of the three could have afforded to make such contributions without assistance."

Exactly when McCarthy had decided to become a Republican was a mystery. He had been an active Democrat—treasurer of his Democratic Party county organization and chairman of the Young Democrats of the Seventh Congressional District—as well as a fundraiser for FDR's 1936 landslide reelection. His first political race, for district attorney in that same year of 1936, was as a Democrat; he campaigned as "a militant New Dealer," dispensing Works Progress Administration patronage to constituents. He attacked local Republicans for offering no alternative to New Deal programs and for allying themselves with the more reactionary elements in their party. He assailed the GOP presidential nominee, Alf Landon of Kansas, a progressive, for his "hare-brained, illogical and senseless" policies. In a two-day period at the close of the campaign, he made fourteen speeches for FDR and the Democrats, employing the same sarcastic style and flagrant language he later displayed to the country. Of Landon's campaign, he said it offered nothing to the people. Of Landon's appeal for voter support, he said contemptuously: "Of all the brainless, halfbaked, cockeyed pleas which have ever been made to a voting public, that absolutely tops them all in asininity." As for FDR, whose New Deal policies he would later demonize, he had nothing but praise for a president "every drop of whose blood and every faculty of whose mind and body is devoted to that great noble, unselfish task . . . of serving all the American people."

This early campaign taught McCarthy useful lessons. One, as Michael O'Brien wrote, was that a "hard-hitting, personal assault that hurt an incumbent opponent suit[ed] his style best." Another lesson McCarthy learned was that the press could be exploited, that it would "print his charges verbatim and make no attempt to evaluate them." Still another lesson went to the core of his political philosophy. During the campaign McCarthy had asked the most prominent Democrat in his county to read a speech he had prepared. After reading it, the Democrat, Grover Meisner, asked whether McCarthy believed what he had written. "Hell, no," McCarthy said. "I don't believe in all that. But if you want to get anywhere in politics, you've got to feed the public what they want to hear and not what you believe."

His early foray into politics showed that neither McCarthy's changing his political ideology from liberalism to conservatism, nor his later switching parties to become a Republican reflected his beliefs. He simply saw the Republican Party as offering a greater opportunity for success in Wisconsin.

How, and why, McCarthy chose to leave the Marines was also revealing. During the 1944 primary campaign, he had requested, and received, a thirty-day leave to return to Wisconsin. When he returned to the Pacific after losing the primary, he requested another leave, claiming that he was neglecting his judicial duties in Wisconsin. After the leave request was denied, McCarthy in July 1944 was reassigned to duty on several California military bases, then resigned his commission and was officially discharged in December. The Marine Corps had given McCarthy the option of resigning after the Corps rejected his request for another leave to attend to "pressing duties at home"—his plan to run for reelection to his judgeship in 1945.

At this point, the bloodiest fighting in the Pacific War lay ahead at Iwo Jima, Okinawa, and the Philippines, with the final planned assault on Japan long in the future. But Joe McCarthy was back home in Wisconsin, still holding his judicial seat while actively laying the grounds for his next U.S. Senate campaign two years away in 1946.

Joe McCarthy was not a coward or unpatriotic. He did experience danger and served his country honorably when he did not have to serve. At the same time, he used his service as a means of advancing himself politically, and misled the public about his military record. The Appleton exhibit devoted much space to his military career, and to the false claims McCarthy made about it.

Among the exhibit's many photos taken during McCarthy's service were those showing him posing in the tail gunner's seat of a Marine dive bomber and standing beside a plane in a tail gunner's uniform—photos McCarthy used extensively in his political campaign.* On the wall, visitors read:

---

*Not that he was the first politician to exploit his service record. Within days of the attack on Pearl Harbor, Lyndon B. Johnson entered the Navy and became the first congressman to go into uniform. Like McCarthy, he was not obliged to; he could have remained in Congress. Again like McCarthy, he did not resign his official seat. Through political influence and his position on the Naval Affairs Committee, Johnson gained an instant commission as a lieutenant commander—a rank career officers would have spent years to achieve. When he wearied of his first assignment in a San Francisco military office, he made a personal trip to the White House to obtain a more interesting job overseas: going to Australia to serve with General Douglas MacArthur and prepare a report for President Roosevelt. He flew on one reconnaissance mission over New Guinea; the plane was fired on, hit, and forced to return to Australia to make an emergency landing. For merely being a passenger on that flight, Johnson was awarded the nation's third highest decoration for valor—the Silver Star. MacArthur, one of the most political generals in American history, personally presented the medal to Johnson, who was widely known as a favored FDR protégé. After serving seven months, LBJ resumed his congressional seat; as president, he almost always wore a Silver Star ribbon in his lapel. Another future president, Richard Nixon, who also served with the Navy in the Pacific, embellished *his* record. In his first political campaign after the war, Nixon boasted that he knew what it was like to be in the mud when the guns were blazing. In fact, he never saw combat; he was a supply officer removed from combat operations. In the 2004 presidential election, Democratic nominee John Kerry made his naval service—and decorations for heroism—a centerpiece of his campaign.

McCarthy ran for the U.S. Senate as a Wisconsin Republican in 1944, while in the Marines. He portrayed himself as an airplane rear gunner, calling himself "Tail Gunner Joe." While McCarthy worked for most of the war at a desk as an intelligence officer [*whose duty was to brief pilots before flights and question them on their return about enemy activity*] he did volunteer for 11 flight missions as a photographer and tail gunner.

There was more, however, to the true story of "Tail Gunner Joe," as McCarthy styled himself in his campaign material, which proclaimed "America Needs a Tail Gunner." While on active duty, McCarthy carefully burnished the legend of Tail Gunner Joe and saw to it that local papers in Wisconsin were supplied with accounts of the fighting judge's exploits, however false. McCarthy kept increasing the number of tail gunner missions he supposedly flew. In his 1944 Senate campaign, he claimed fourteen missions. Two years later in his victorious second Senate campaign, he claimed seventeen. In 1951, he claimed to have made thirty-two missions.

More wall postings:

"McCarthy strafed Jap ground positions with 4,700 rounds of ammunition."
—Appleton *Post-Crescent,* January 20, 1944.

Directly beneath:

"This is worth 50,000 votes to me."
—Captain McCarthy discusses Appleton
Post-Crescent news coverage, 1944.

Years later, a Marine pilot who served with McCarthy wrote an angry letter to the editor of the *Madison Capital*

Times urging the editor to have reporters check McCarthy's official service jacket in Washington, which would "expose the guy for the fraud he is."

The historian David M. Oshinsky would one day tell the story of what happened in 1943, on Henderson Field, Guadalcanal, where McCarthy's squadron was based.

> Sometimes, to ease the boredom, the pilots would try to break every flight record on the books—most missions in a day, most ammunition expended, and the like. According to one Marine, "Everyone at the base who could possibly do so went along on the ride on some of these missions—it was hot, dusty, and dull on the ground, and a ride in an SBD was cool and a break in the monotony. It was also quite safe—there weren't any Jap planes or anti-aircraft gunners around." Apparently Joe wanted to break the record for most ammo used on a single mission. So he was strapped into a tail-gunner's seat, sent aloft, and allowed to blast away at the coconut trees. As a matter of routine, the public relations officer gave him the record and wrote up a release for the Wisconsin papers. A few weeks later McCarthy came into the fellow's hut waving a stack of clippings. "This is worth 50,000 votes to me," he said with a smile. The two men then had a drink to celebrate the creation of "Tail-Gunner Joe."

Nearby in the museum exhibit, a glass case held medals McCarthy had been awarded, along with pictures showing them being pinned on him while he was a senator. Again, the exhibit captions told the true story.

Beneath a photo of a solemn McCarthy being presented on December 29, 1952, with two major commendations—the

Distinguished Flying Cross and the Air Medal—the caption read: "McCarthy received these medals at the height of his political career. He applied for them in 1951, saying he flew in 32 squadron missions. Military leaders, some sympathetic to the senator, accepted his number and awarded him a Distinguished Flying Cross. Wartime log entries list 11 missions under McCarthy's name. Usually, soldiers who completed 25 missions received the prestigious Distinguished Flying Cross medal."

McCarthy's deceit was breathtaking. As a U.S. Senator, McCarthy supplied the Air Force with documents supporting the award of these high honors. Among the documents was a letter praising his combat record, which supposedly had been signed by McCarthy's commanding officer, Major Glenn A. Todd, and then countersigned by Admiral Chester Nimitz after the letter was forwarded up the military chain. Later investigation showed that Major Todd neither wrote nor signed the letter. McCarthy, in his capacity as the unit intelligence officer, apparently wrote the letter himself, forged Todd's name to it, and then dispatched it through channels whereby it would be routinely endorsed by Nimitz. The exhibit did not address this fraud. It did, however, encourage the viewing public to react to what they had seen. About McCarthy's war record, it asked:

Do you think
McCarthy's exaggeration
of his military career
as a tail gunner was a
necessary political tactic
to win office?
You be the Judge

Visitors learned that when McCarthy resigned from the Marines on December 11, 1944, "He publicly attributed his departure to a 'war wound.'" The exhibit commentary then added: "McCarthy had broken a bone in his foot during a hazing ceremony on board a ship in 1943."

For the rest of his life, McCarthy milked the false war wound story, even at times affecting a limp when campaigning before constituents in Wisconsin, telling numerous people that he carried "ten pounds of shrapnel" in his leg, and referring to a "crash landing" in the Pacific. "I had a leg badly smashed up, burned, and broken," he told a reporter in Wisconsin in 1952. "I got a citation from Nimitz based on that." The truth lay elsewhere. McCarthy was injured on June 22, 1943, aboard the USS *Chandeleur*, a seatender, during a traditional "shell-back" hazing in which initiates ran a gauntlet of paddle-wielding sailors when the vessel crossed the equator. "I was within 15 feet of Joe when the accident occurred," John F. Mitchell later wrote Reeves. "He was wearing a fifty pound leaded diving boot. After [McCarthy was] wet down with a hose of salt water, a sailor touched his bottom with an electrically charged fork. His twisting reaction snapped his fifth metatarsal" in his foot.

Many years later, when the *Milwaukee Journal* exposed the false war wound story, McCarthy accused both the reporter and the paper of being "pro-Communist."

At the end of the Appleton exhibit, two bulletin boards displayed a blizzard of small white cards containing handwritten responses to the museum's request for visitors to express their feelings about McCarthy and McCarthyism.

From "Helen": *McCarthy was correct. The Communists had penetrated our entire government and were working against our country. The truth can be found in papers now available from USSR since the fall of Communism. Vernona* [sic] *papers.*

From "F.J., 2003": *Joe was a hero. He fought for freedom.*

From "Lexi," who wrote in a childish scrawl and at the bottom of her card drew a crude picture of an American flag flying from a pole: *I think he was cool.*

From an unnamed member of the viewing public: *We need a hundred Joes today to save our country. Many of these comments are un-American.*

But here was one from a Tess Muszyowski: *He was a dork and should have known what he did was wrong.*

These reactions were testaments to passions that radiated from the Cold War period to our own, legacies bequeathed by Tail Gunner Joe after he left Appleton to unleash suspicions that haunt America still.

Chapter
THREE

Progressivism to McCarthyism

Like having the Ringling Brothers Circus come to town.

For decades, Wisconsin earned a reputation as the nation's most liberal state. It was the "Ideal Commonwealth," in Lincoln Steffens's term, and the state that Theodore Roosevelt said "has literally become a laboratory for wise experimental legislation." It was also the birthplace of Lincoln's Republican Party, which espoused the radical position of freeing the slaves and providing "free soil and free speech." Even more, Wisconsin embodied the heart of the Progressive movement that transformed American life for much of the twentieth century and played a major role in New Deal reforms.

After McCarthy, American liberalism no longer would look to Wisconsin for inspiration; henceforth, as Karl E. Meyer observed, Wisconsin would be regarded as the cradle of McCarthyism, "a creed as loathsome to the orthodox liberal as Progressivism was odious to orthodox conservatism."

———

The shift from Progressivism to McCarthyism was set in motion when McCarthy defeated an icon of American liberalism and ended one of the nation's most remarkable political dynasties. The icon was Senator Robert M. La Follette, Jr., known popularly as Young Bob to distinguish him from his late father, Fighting Bob (or Old Bob) La Follette, the founder of the dynasty. Until 1946, when McCarthy defeated Young Bob, a La Follette had been elected as either Wisconsin's governor or as one of its United States Senators for forty-six years in unbroken succession.*

Not only had Fighting Bob first popularized the word "Progressivism"; as William Allen White, a principal player in and chronicler of those times, wrote of La Follette's influence on national reforms: "No other living American has impressed himself so deeply upon the life and thought and institutions of America."

This was no idle praise. Through Fighting Bob's tireless efforts on behalf of "the people" (farmers, workers, teachers) versus "the interests" (political bosses, corporate titans),

———

*Another son, Phil, was a popular three-time Progressive governor of Wisconsin from 1931–33 and 1935–39. The mother, Belle, was a full partner with her husband and sons. She was an early suffragette and supporter of liberal causes, including desegregation and disarmament. When she married Old Bob, she asked the minister to delete the words "to obey" from her wedding vows. In addition, she was the first woman to graduate from the University of Wisconsin Law School.

Wisconsin led the way in instituting reforms such as the direct primary, workmen's compensation, stringent regulation of railroads and public utilities through the establishment of independent regulatory bodies, equal and fair taxation of corporate property, and management of public resources in the public interest. At Progressivism's philosophical heart was La Follette's belief in using the powers of the government to achieve social and economic justice. His theme, sounded for years in countless speeches, was: "Who shall rule—wealth or man?"

La Follette was an extraordinary figure, passionate, eloquent, incorruptible. With his shock of thick white hair, piercing eyes, and strong jaw, Fighting Bob was the very model of a political crusader. On the stump, touring county fairs, standing on a farmer's wagon, he would speak for hours, rip his collar from his throat, faint, and swear he would die on the field for the people. He was feared. And hated. As one Wisconsin businessman told Lincoln Steffens: "If we don't stop him he will go out and agitate all over the United States."

La Follette took the lead in opposing the United States' entry into World War I. War, in his view, was "an outgrowth of commercial and imperial rivalry." Instead, he urged that America's resources be put to work achieving domestic reforms: "more wages; more education; more money to fight infectious diseases."

These controversial positions created what Karl Meyer described as "an almost unprecedented wave of persecution against La Follette and his followers." Many observers believed that La Follette's career was doomed. But in 1922, in his third successful Senate campaign, La Follette received in both the Wisconsin primary and the general election the largest majority ever given a Senate candidate. The six million votes out of thirty million cast that he received two years later as the presidential nominee of the Progressive Party he founded still represents the largest percentage won by a third party candidate in America. A year later, when La Follette's hold on the people of Wisconsin had never been greater, he suffered a heart attack. As he lay mortally ill, gasping for breath in a death scene Dickens would have savored, his family gathered at the foot of the bed waiting in anguish until his last breath had expired. Then, one by one, they filed silently to the head of the bed, leaned over, and kissed the old warrior on the forehead. Fighting Bob's death that June day should have signaled the end to the La Follette story. It did not. For another twenty-one years the dynasty continued under the leadership of Young Bob La Follette, who took his father's Senate seat. Remarkably, the achievements of Old Bob were eclipsed by the record of Young Bob in the Senate.

Few, if any, men in the Senate were more respected or admired than Young Bob La Follette—and respected across the ideological political spectrum by both liberals and conservatives. "If Franklin had not been a Roosevelt," said one White House insider at that time, "I am quite certain he would have liked to be a La Follette." Young Bob put his stamp on legislation from social security to labor reforms and unemployment relief that affected the life of the nation for decades. As biographer Patrick J. Maney observed in 2003, it is hard to imagine a senator standing up in twenty-first century America and proclaiming, as La Follette did repeatedly, "that the rich have too much money and the poor too little; that the federal government should use the tax system to redistribute the wealth; . . . that a national referendum should be conducted before the United States could enter a war; or that everyone's income tax return should be open to public inspection."

This was the man—and the legacy—that Joe McCarthy confronted.

———

By 1946, much of the New Deal's domestic reform agenda, which owed so much to the La Follettes, had been enacted, and a strong backlash was underway against New Deal liberalism and what its enemies called its big government, big spending, big taxing, socialistic ways. It had been a bad sign for La Follette and the Wisconsin Progressive tradition when, two years earlier, FDR failed to carry Wisconsin for the first time. The election returns signaled other problems for Progressives. Over the years, the success of the New Deal had drawn many liberals away from the Progressive Party to FDR's Democrats. Labor had defected to the Democrats, farmers to the Republicans. The Progressive Party was moribund.

As La Follette assessed the political scene of 1946, he was fifty-one years old, had served in the Senate for twenty-one years, and was still by far the most formidable Wisconsin political figure. He decided his best strategy for remaining in the Senate was to run as a Republican in the primary. Immediately, he became the overwhelming favorite. La Follette's return to the Republican Party—the party he and his brother had bolted during the Depression—was exactly what the regular Wisconsin GOP leaders, long bitterly opposed to La Follette's Progressive policies, feared most. They began scrambling to back the strongest candidate they could find to run against him in the state primary.

Their first choice was not the small town judge and Marine veteran from Appleton, Joe McCarthy. The leader of Wisconsin's regular Republicans at that time was Thomas C. Coleman, a "smooth, suave, impeccably dressed" conservative Madison businessman with a lifelong loathing of the La Follettes and their Progressive followers. "Boss" Coleman, as he was known, vowed to put an end to the La Follette dynasty in 1946. He was not impressed by McCarthy's prospects, and told him so a year before the primary. He was "disinclined" to support McCarthy or offer him the party's considerable financial help. McCarthy was said to have replied: "Tom, you're a nice guy and I like you. But I got news for you. When that convention is over next year, Joe McCarthy will be the Republican-endorsed candidate for U.S. Senator."

Boss Coleman was not the first politician to underrate or misjudge McCarthy. In the year since his return from the Pacific, while the war was entering its climactic stage, McCarthy had been planning his 1946 campaign.

The available McCarthy correspondence from this period is revealing. Writing in March 1945 to Urban Van Susteren, then an Army captain on active duty, McCarthy said: "I have been doing a great deal of speaking—fence building for 1946. The work in Circuit Court is at a minimum, which gives me a lot of time to beat the bushes throughout the state." A month later, on April 23, in another letter to Van Susteren, he appended this postscript: "Have been doing a tremendous amount of speaking lately, and frankly am getting damn good."

The McCarthy-Van Susteren correspondence is revealing in another sense. Nothing in McCarthy's letters gives any hint of the great events that were then transpiring. In all of McCarthy's available correspondence from the mid-thirties to the final point of World War II, there is not a single reflection on any of the historic tides—from Nazism to Communism to iso-lationism to New Dealism to the death of FDR—that were reshaping the world. Instead, the letters contain references to personal political calculation along with near-constant ac-counts of his financial speculations, investments, stock tips, and deals—tips and advice he offers privately to such a friend as Van Susteren.

When Van Susteren returned from the service to become McCarthy's 1946 campaign manager, he found McCarthy had already worked out his political strategy. He knew La Follette was hated by regular Republicans; he knew the Progressive Party was breaking up; he knew many Progressives had de-fected to the Democratic Party; and he knew La Follette had shifted to the GOP as his best prospect of retaining his seat. As McCarthy outlined his strategy, he would first get the state Re-publican convention to endorse him—something new for that body, which traditionally did not make endorsements—on the grounds that action was necessary because the GOP was being "raided by outsiders." McCarthy wrote each delegate asking for their support, warning them that the Republican Party was being taken over by Progressives. He won the endorsement. Next he had to win the party establishment's backing.

Van Susteren met with Boss Coleman to plead for his sup-port. McCarthy had a system for winning, he told Coleman, describing how McCarthy had won his judgeship campaign in 1939. The Boss smiled slightly. There is no such thing as a "system for winning," he said dismissively. No, Van Susteren insisted, Joe did have a system, and it worked. (He also had a system for beating the roulette wheel.)

In his campaign against Judge Werner, as biographer Reeves recalls his "system," McCarthy spent three months, six or seven days a week, traveling over icy roads, "shaking hands, swapping farm stories, complimenting wives on their cooking, patting children on the head; he even milked a few cows."

After leaving a farm, McCarthy dictated details of his visit into a recording machine, making sure he wasn't seen by the farming family. The recording tape cylinders were given to his secretary who used the information to write postcards to each family, including personalized remembrances of the Mc-Carthy visit. She then signed each card—which featured on its opposite side a photo of McCarthy, in suit and tie, "wearing his glasses and appearing earnest and responsible"—with McCarthy's name.

McCarthy used the same technique in all the towns he visited, "darting in and out of stores, barbershops, and restaurants introducing himself." He sat in on card games, pretending not to know certain ones, then happily bought drinks all around for opponents and spectators. Later, he fed the name of *every* person he met into his recording device; they all received personalized postcards seemingly signed by Joe. Mc-Carthy examined each postcard before his secretary mailed it. He insisted each card be written neatly and that each one contain a slightly different message. When he returned to the town or farmhouse, he called people by their names, greeting them as old, dear friends. It was, one local recalled of a Mc-Carthy visit, "like having the Ringling Brothers Circus come to town."

Using local phone books and directories, he and his secretary compiled a list of every household. They, too, received postcards with a pitch for McCarthy's candidacy and a signature, always by hand, as if McCarthy himself had penned it.

In his 1946 Senate primary campaign, McCarthy employed the same tactics—except he expanded his reach to cover the entire state. Every Wisconsin household received booklets and brochures. Seven hundred fifty thousand post-cards personally were signed (by McCarthy's friends and workers) as if from Joe.

Boss Coleman, after seeing McCarthy attract growing Republican support, reversed himself. He funneled thirty thousand dollars from the Republican volunteer committee to the McCarthy committee to pay for McCarthy's postcards and booklets. Other sums, largely unaccounted for, came from personal and business donors; some were in the form of personal loans, reportedly large, to McCarthy—and may not ever have been repaid.

Joe McCarthy was a superb campaigner. As David M. Oshinsky records McCarthy's manic race across Wisconsin, "He cut a 250-mile swath across the state in fifteen hours, personally fixing three flat tires, junking his automobile, hiring a cab and then two private planes to make a final late-night appearance near Lake Superior." By primary day he had traveled thirty-three thousand miles across Wisconsin, literally wearing out two automobiles in the process.

Criticism of him during the campaign—that he hadn't paid state or federal income taxes when overseas in 1943; or that he was running despite Article VII, Section 10 of the Wisconsin Constitution prohibiting state circuit and supreme court judges from running for any other office "during the term for which they are respectively elected"—never took hold with the public. It was "the year of the veteran"; one didn't dare challenge their wartime credentials. Or their veracity. Nor did the press examine such subjects.

It was the Joe McCarthys who had won the war for America, the Joe McCarthys who had come home to lead America toward a better future, the Joe McCarthys who formed the legion of American politicians whose lives, and careers, were shaped by World War II. Beginning with the political commanders of that war, Roosevelt and Truman, the next eight American presidents had all worn a uniform during World War II: Eisenhower, Kennedy, Johnson, Nixon, Ford, Carter, Reagan, the first Bush. The war proved to be McCarthy's greatest asset and credential. He adopted the cloak of a statesman. In his judicial office in Appleton's Outagamie County Courthouse, he installed a wall plaque that became a feature in articles written about the young judge seeking a Senate seat. The plaque read: *A politician thinks of the next election; a statesman of the next generation.*

He ran on his military record. He ran against the New Deal. He ran against La Follette.

The Joe McCarthy who offered himself to the voters in this first post-war election of 1946 was the humble war hero and small town judge, supposedly wounded in the service of his country, who possessed the perfect Horatio Alger résumé: the poor boy who had made it on his own. He campaigned by exaggerating his military record. Typical of his approach was a newspaper campaign ad:

JOE McCARTHY was a TAIL GUNNER in World War II. He wants to SERVE America in the SENATE. Yes, folks, CONGRESS NEEDS A TAIL GUNNER.

Wisconsin was flooded with campaign literature containing photos of McCarthy in his tail gunner Marine uniform. Some showed him with bandoleers of ammunition draped across his chest; in others he posed behind a gun in the tail of a combat aircraft.

He labeled La Follette a "New Deal Senator," and always referred to him as "the gentleman from Virginia," implying La Follette was far removed from his Wisconsin roots, an out-of-touch liberal living in luxury on a Virginia estate.

During his years in Congress, La Follette *had* become a more distant figure in Wisconsin, spending less time in the state and more in Washington on the work of the Senate. Mc-Carthy's insinuations about his "Virginia estate," however, were false. Years later, Roger T. Johnson set that record straight in his *Robert M. La Follette, Jr. and the Decline of the Progressive Party in Wisconsin*. La Follette, he wrote, "had once owned a small and run-down house in Virginia, a house in which he had never lived and which he had sold years before 1946; he owned and lived in a modest house in the District of Columbia."

Nonetheless, much as during his campaign against Judge Werner, McCarthy kept hammering on the theme of his opponent's having profited from his years in public service:

"Mr. La Follette, the gentleman from Virginia, and his group are staking their political futures on the hope that all of the honest labor vote, all of the honest labor leaders, can be wrapped up and delivered to them by the few selfish, self-proclaimed, misnamed labor leaders for whom the New Dealers and La Follette have been taking orders . . . If, however, the gentleman from Virginia is right, if the great masses of votes can be packaged and delivered, then the group that is now in power shall finish the job which they have begun. They shall do what no enemy from without has ever been able to do with this country. They shall destroy this nation from within."

Another McCarthy charge struck hard at La Follette's "man of the people" image. La Follette, continually worried about his financial affairs, had bought interest in a Milwaukee radio station, WEMP, in 1942. Within three years he realized a return of fifty thousand dollars. McCarthy implied that La Follette was guilty of not only hypocrisy but also a conflict of interest, pointing out that the Federal Communications Commission had approved the radio station license and that La Follette had voted for FCC appropriations. Every member of Congress had voted for the appropriations, but McCarthy implied that La Follette's vote made him guilty of fraud. In statewide ads, McCarthy left the impression that La Follette was corrupt: "How Did La Follette Get That Money?"

While McCarthy was on the attack, so was Boss Coleman. In a letter to the party faithful, Coleman accused La Follette of being the man "who is more responsible for the confusion in this nation today than any other single person in the Senate . . . Go back through the New Deal administration of government and you will find La Follette trotting along with it on practically every evil that it promoted."

Then, twisting the knife, Coleman contrasted La Follette's lack of military service (he was forty-six in 1941 when the war began) with McCarthy's war hero claims, implying that La Follette was a slacker, if not a coward: "Did this Progressive senator who returns to the state only intermittently from his estate in Virginia, chiefly for campaign purposes, make any sacrifice at all?"

McCarthy also inaugurated what became his most familiar political tactic: accusing an opponent of giving aid and comfort to the Communists.

In one radio speech, McCarthy charged that La Follette's isolationist background, like that of his father's, was "playing into the hands of the Communists" because of La Follette's "failure to do anything to promote industrial peace." He also charged that La Follette's congressional votes "have paved the way for what the Communists have since done in Poland and the rest of Eastern Europe."

This was three and a half years before the Wheeling speech.

Of all the ironies in La Follette's defeat, surely the greatest was that he "expressed more concern about that threat of Communism," as one scholar put it, than did Joe McCarthy. La Follette's militantly anticommunist position cost him critical support among the group that he had long and ardently championed, organized labor—specifically among the leadership of Wisconsin's most liberal union wing, the CIO.

At the Progressive Party convention in 1944, La Follette spoke out strongly against what he saw as the post-war dangers to world peace posed by the Soviet Union's expansionist policies. A year later, in May 1945, in a three-hour speech in the Senate, he delivered a more extensive attack on Soviet Communism's global ambitions. After his Senate speech, the state CIO unleashed a barrage of criticism deploring La Follette's "denunciation of our great Soviet ally." Writing in the *Wisconsin CIO News,* one outraged CIO leader said that La Follette "actually charges that the Soviets are trying to force their system upon other countries."

In a conspiratorial twist to the plot, it has been charged— apparently with some accuracy—that the leadership of the state's CIO was then in fact controlled by Communists. Years later, Wisconsin's state CIO president, Herman Steffens, said Communists and "fellow travelers" had been removed from organizational control at the union's statewide convention in December 1946, a month after McCarthy became a new senator. "The Communists definitely were responsible for the election of McCarthy," he claimed. "We did all we could to offset Communists in the state and Milwaukee councils but were outnumbered."

That Joe McCarthy owed his election to Communist support was a myth given wide circulation in Jack Anderson and Ronald May's 1952 book, *McCarthy: The Man, the Senator, the Ism.* Describing actions of the Communist-controlled state CIO during that campaign, the authors wrote: "So they cranked out reams of hate-La Follette literature and rallied workers behind McCarthy. When Joe was asked by reporters about this, he said: 'Communists have the same right to vote as anybody else, don't they?'"

While Communists did oppose La Follette in 1946, their support was not decisive, either against him or for McCarthy. In reality, La Follette was caught in the crossfire between the Left and Right. To the Republican Right, he was, as McCarthy and Boss Coleman kept arguing, a despised New Deal liberal. To the Left, he had turned against his liberal past and defected to the Republicans. La Follette, the erstwhile New Dealer, was now arguing that the federal government should balance its budget and that Communists had too much influence in American society. Not only that, he was an isolationist supported by "Mr. Republican," Robert A. Taft himself.

The appeal of a young, aggressive supposed war hero such as McCarthy, the pull of a new generation of young warriors coming to power, and the fact that McCarthy was outspending La Follette nearly twenty to one, would all seem to have been enough to defeat Young Bob. Not so.

More than anything, Bob La Follette was the agent of his own defeat. He refrained from active campaigning, remained for the most part in Washington working on Senate business, and refused to answer attacks on him by dignifying them with a public response. As he told Wisconsin voters in a radio speech opening his reelection campaign—and delivered from Washington—he was "running on my record" and staking his prospects "on my twenty years of service to the people of Wisconsin and my fight for the liberal principles which the Progressive movement has pioneered." To the voters of Wisconsin, he simply said: "All the evidence is there for you to read, discuss, debate, and decide."

Despite the factors arrayed against him, La Follette remained the overwhelming favorite to the end. As James Reston reported for the *New York Times* the day before the election: "Senator Robert M. La Follette is expected to prove tomorrow in the Wisconsin primary election that a man can bolt the Republican party and get away with it."

Delivering the last radio address of his brief campaign on election eve in Madison, La Follette finally displayed a defiance—and a fire—he had not exhibited during his lackluster reelection effort. "I am proud of the enemies I have made," he said. "I am proud that the little group that sits in Communist headquarters in Milwaukee and the tight little corporation that sits in Coleman headquarters here in Madison . . . have chosen me to be the target of their venomous attacks, their fraudulent propaganda, and their neurotic editorials."

At last, a touch of Fighting Bob. But it came too late.

Turnout the next day was extremely light, with only a third of eligible voters going to the polls—often a negative for a reelection candidate, whose supporters tend not to be as motivated as an opponent's. Still, La Follette took the early lead and the race was neck-and-neck to the end. When the final votes were tabulated, McCarthy had received forty-one percent of the ballots, La Follette forty percent. The actual count was McCarthy: 207,935, La Follette: 202,557. McCarthy had won by a mere 5,378 votes.

The *Milwaukee Journal* described McCarthy's victory as "one of the most startling stories in the history of Wisconsin, an upset that not only stunned the state but bewildered political observers all over the nation." The next day, commenting on the demise of the La Follette dynasty and the role the family had played in twentieth century American history, the *New York Times* said: "In our day only the Roosevelt family, in both its branches, has overshadowed it." And of Young Bob, it added: "Perhaps he, too, recognizes it as the end of an era."

He did. Years later, he told *Time* magazine: "I didn't go back to talk to the voters. My father did just what Joe McCarthy did [to win], and I guess I made a mistake."

———

In the general election three months later, Joe McCarthy overwhelmed his Democratic opponent, Howard J. McMurray, a former New Deal congressman and political science professor at the University of Wisconsin, to become the state's newest United States senator and the Senate's youngest member. The election's outcome was never in doubt. McCarthy garnered 630,430 votes to McMurray's 378,772 for a winning margin of 251,658.

The campaign was memorable not for McCarthy's victory, but for the tactics he employed to win. In the final weeks he increasingly attacked his opponent's patriotism, loyalty, and falsely attributed to him a predisposition for Communism. He accused McMurray of being, among other things, "a little megaphone" used by the "Communist-controlled PAC." As election day neared, to quote Reeves's account, "Red-baiting became one of the McCarthy campaign's most distinctive features."

During a statewide radio broadcast, McCarthy promised to "make every effort toward removing the vast number of Communists from the public payroll." In another broadcast, he charged: "We have been victimized by a seditious serpent, which has wrapped us in its cunning constrictions until we stand in a perilous position. The snake is Communism."

McCarthy called Communist infiltration "a vital issue in America" and in his home state. Then, in words that foreshadowed the coming era of McCarthyism, he said that while "all Democrats are not Communists . . . enough Democrats are voting the Communist way to make their presence in Congress a serious threat to the very foundation of our nation."

Once again, the press was a critical factor in McCarthy's successful campaign. As Reeves concluded, "Pro-McCarthy newspapers were almost reckless in their denunciations of McMurray." To McCarthy's hometown *Appleton Post-Crescent*, McMurray was "a noisy, unbearably egoistic gentleman upon whom the American editor of the Moscow *Pravda* slobbered." To the *Green Bay Press-Gazette*, McMurray was "in favor of the enemies of our country." Reeves's research found that many of the newspapers "printed Joe's charges against the loyalty of his Democratic opponent but would not run McMurray's rebuttals." He cited the *Wisconsin State Journal*, which during the campaign printed only two stories on McMurray longer than five inches while publishing several forty-inch-long stories on McCarthy. This became a familiar pattern in years to come.

———

The most crucial factor in the 1946 election was fear of Communism. Having failed for years to break the Democratic hold on Washington by equating New Deal liberalism with socialism, the Republicans exploited instead the specter of Communism. It worked. When the GOP captured both

Houses of Congress for the first time in a generation, Mc-Carthy simply rode the crest that had carried his party to victory.

The Republican national political message was hardly subtle. Four months before Americans went to the polls, Republican National Committee Chairman Carroll Reese said the election would offer a stark choice between "Communism and Republicanism." This was so, he added, because "the policy-making force of the Democratic Party [is] now committed to the Soviet Union." The day before the election, House Republican Leader Joseph Martin declared: "The people will vote tomorrow between chaos, confusion, bankruptcy, state socialism or Communism, and the preservation of the American way of life." Striking the theme McCarthy would sound four years later in Wheeling, he promised: "Congress will ferret out all those who [seek] to destroy the American way of life." In California, Richard Nixon, running for his first term in Congress, distributed campaign literature that said: "A vote for Nixon is a vote against the Communist-dominated PAC [Political Action Committee of labor's CIO] with its gigantic slush fund." On the eve of the election, Nixon's campaign headquarters accused his opponent, Jerry Voorhis, of voting "the Moscow-PAC-Henry Wallace line."

For Democrats, these attacks resulted in disaster.

At the peak of the New Deal, after the FDR landslide of 1936, the Democratic lock on Congress was overwhelming. Democrats held three hundred thirty-four House seats to Republicans' eighty-eight. The ideological tilt toward liberals was even greater: seven members of the Progressive Party were also elected to the House, along with three Farmer-Labor candidates. The toll was worse for Senate Republicans, who were left with a mere sixteen of the ninety-six Senate seats. Democrats held seventy-six seats, the Farmer-Labor Party held two, and the Progressive and Independent parties each held one. Democratic senators were so many that twelve of their freshmen had to take their seats on the traditionally Republican side of the aisle. By 1944, Democrats still held two hundred forty-two House seats, or sixty-four more than the Republicans, and fifty-six Senate seats, or eighteen more than the GOP.

But the 1946 election for the 80th Congress produced the largest midterm GOP Senate gain since 1894, with Republicans picking up thirteen seats. In the House, they captured fifty-five seats from the Democrats. (One Farmer-Labor congressman was elected.) In control of Congress for the first time since the 1920s, Republicans set their sights on winning back the White House in 1948 by continuing to play on fears of Communism.

Chapter
FOUR

The Remarkable Upstart

What makes you think you're important?

After arriving by train at Union Station on a cold rainy day, December 1, 1946, and settling into his downtown hotel, McCarthy phoned the White House and asked to see President Truman. Never mind that he had not been sworn in as a senator, that hardly anyone in the capital knew him, or that the new session of the now Republican-controlled 80th Congress would not begin for more than a month. As he explained on the phone to a presidential aide, he wanted to share with the president some ideas he had about the coal strike then paralyzing the nation. His request for an appointment was politely refused. Perhaps he might see President Truman after the new Congress convened.

Unabashed, McCarthy immediately called a press conference for the next day. A roomful of reporters and photographers showed up. It was a slow news period, and they couldn't remember when a senator-elect had summoned reporters on his second day in town. Besides, they wanted to get a look at this most junior senator who had pulled off the great upset of Young Bob La Follette.

Their questions were revealing, as were McCarthy's responses.

"Mr. McCarthy, what makes you think you're important enough to call a press conference?" one of the reporters asked.

"Now, let's get down to business," McCarthy replied. "About this coal strike. I've got a solution. The Army should draft the striking miners. That would solve the problem."

"What about John L. Lewis?" someone called out, referring to the coal miners' formidable union president.

"Draft him, too."

"And what if they refused?"

"Then they would be court-martialed for insubordination and you know what that means."

"You mean you would line up men like John L. Lewis and have them shot?"

"Lewis should be directed to order his miners to mine coal. If he does not do that, he should be court-martialed. We should go straight down the line . . . All this talk about you can't put four hundred thousand miners in jail is a lot of stuff. They won't go to jail. They will mine coal first."

As provocative and unconstitutional as his proposal was, it didn't rock the nation—but it did win him desired headlines from the *New York Times,* the *Washington Post,* and other news organizations. McCarthy had effectively called attention to himself.

McCarthy's youth also set him apart. At thirty-eight, he was ten years younger than the average incumbent and more than twenty-five years junior to the average Senate committee chairman. He had no need to pretend to be younger than he was. But he did, claiming to be a year younger in his official biographical sketch for the *Congressional Directory*. La Follette, upon succeeding his father in 1925 at the age of thirty, had been the youngest elected senator since Henry Clay. As McCarthy had already shown, their behavior would be very different.

McCarthy was pleased with the press notice he received. As a sign of his appreciation, he sent several wheels of Wisconsin cheese to the bar at the National Press Club, along with a message to the national reporters: "When you want me, don't hesitate to call me, night or day."

McCarthy continued to court the press, going out of his way to make friends with reporters. He established a particularly close relationship with photographers, often going to the race track or sharing investment tips with them. He invited female correspondents to a fried chicken dinner at the Georgetown home of a Republican official, and, donning a ruffled apron, cooked the meal himself after letting them know he had been a short-order cook while working his way through Marquette. He grilled the steaks at a cookout he hosted for eighteen newsmen.

McCarthy's efforts paid off. *Life* magazine published a pictorial about the first day in office of the Senate's young giant-killer. *U.S. News* hailed him for his "hustling, whirlwind" style. *The Saturday Evening Post* commissioned a laudatory article with a title he surely loved: "The Senate's Remarkable Upstart."

In public appearances, McCarthy continued to burnish his Tail Gunner Joe image by spinning a maudlin yarn that he would repeat for years. In his telling, it was a scene "painfully clear before my eyes at this instant": all the pilots and gunners "of our dive and torpedo bombing squadrons" had gathered in a tent for a briefing before launching "one of our first and roughest bombing attacks." After the briefing, McCarthy recalled, "my skipper" turned to a chaplain, saying: "Chaplain, we know that some of us shall die today. Might you have some words to say?" Then McCarthy would say dramatically:

> As the chaplain rose, no other sound could be heard. That chaplain's body today lies on the floor of a vast moon-swept, wind-tossed Pacific, but his words I know are burned deep into the hearts and minds of each of those young pilots and gunners who still live, and this is what he said:
>
> "If each of you young men shall remember two fundamental truths, two truths taught by all religious groups since the beginning of time, if you will remember first, that there is a God who is eternal, and second, that each of you has a soul which is immortal, then regardless of whether you die within the next few hours or live another fifty or sixty years, you shall serve yourself, your country, and your God to the last full measure."

That, McCarthy would say in his peroration, "is the American concept of life, a concept so foreign to the Communistic concept, a concept preserved over the years by the expenditure of blood and flesh and steel. That concept of life we must preserve. That concept of life we shall preserve."

Melodramatic and hyperbolic, to be sure—and made up out of whole cloth. Veterans who served with McCarthy could recall no such briefing and no such speech by a chaplain.*

As a way of indicating his own model for statesmanship, McCarthy posted on the wall of his Senate office a copy of Lincoln's famous remark: *If the end brings me out all right, what is said against me won't amount to anything. If the end brings me out wrong, ten angels swearing I was right would make no difference.*

Among the wealthy hosts and hostesses who comprised the self-appointed, and self-important, elite of Washington's incestuous "cave dweller" society, the new young bachelor war hero was much in demand. Joe McCarthy was on the town and, on the evidence, having a helluva time, squiring young women, going to parties and receptions, giving interviews, doing radio shows, and making connections that proved valuable in years to come. It was a whirl.

The sheer power of McCarthy's personality was a major factor in his rapid rise among Washington's political players. People liked him. Even many colleagues who strongly disagreed

---

*I find it startling how much the rhetorical style of this apocryphal tale so resembles one that Ronald Reagan repeatedly told later, always with choking voice and often shedding of tears: how a U.S. bomber pilot, returning from a mission over Germany with his plane badly shot up, orders his crew to bail out, then just before jumping himself, hears his tail gunner informing him over his earphones that his ball turret has been so damaged by enemy fire that he's trapped and can't evacuate. The pilot then tells him, "Never mind, son, we'll ride this one down together." The plane crashes. Reagan's story ends when he dramatically says: "Medal of Honor, posthumously awarded." No Medal of Honor was ever awarded during World War II for any such action resembling Reagan's fable.

with his views found him genial, a good companion. He exuded a kind of rugged charm and was thought by some of the
female staffers to be physically most attractive. Years later
Christine McCreary, who worked then on the staff of Senator
Stuart Symington, still vividly remembered literally running
into McCarthy stepping from a Senate elevator. "He looked at
me, and I looked into the most piercing blue eyes you ever
saw," she said of that first encounter. "Beautiful eyes." She
laughed, and repeated: "He had the most piercing blue eyes
you ever saw. He was a nice looking guy."

Absent access to McCarthy's office logs, appointment books,
private correspondence, and financial records, all of which remain sealed nearly half a century after his death, it cannot be
determined just when—or how—he developed what became
an extremely close (and private) relationship with J. Edgar
Hoover and other important figures of the right-wing anticommunist network such as the Hearst columnists Westbrook
Pegler and George Sokolsky.

In these formative Washington days, Joe McCarthy was
struggling to establish himself as a national force. While he
had employed the Communist smear in his 1946 campaigns
against La Follette and McMurray, and sometimes wielded it
now in Washington, it still was not his *only* political weapon.
After Wheeling, it was.

Chapter
FIVE

The Way to Wheeling

Mr. McCarthy has lost his temper.

A fter the highly publicized launching of his Washington
career, the "remarkable upstart" sank into the back ranks
of the Senate, largely ignored and, among colleagues of both
parties, largely discredited. He was already in peril of losing
reelection.

McCarthy's response to his political problems was to go on
the attack. His answer to *Madison Capital Times* articles that
criticized his practice of holding "quickie divorces" for his
campaign contributors and exposed his tangled financial affairs, including his failure to pay taxes, was to accuse the paper
of being part of a Communist conspiracy to destroy him. Early
in November 1949, all daily and weekly newspapers in Wisconsin, as well as radio stations, received an eleven-page, three-
thousand-word McCarthy statement, mailed at government

expense. "Has the Communist Party with the cooperation of the Capital Times Corp. won a major victory in Wisconsin?" his statement began. McCarthy then cited J. Edgar Hoover's belief that the Communist Party sought to place its members in important positions in America's newspapers, and especially those published in college towns such as Madison, "so that the young people who will take over control of the nation someday will be getting daily doses of the Communist Party-line propaganda under the mistaken impression that they are absorbing 'liberal' and 'progressive' ideas from an American newspaper."

That the *Madison Capital Times,* an ardent supporter of the La Follettes, had for years campaigned vigorously *against* Communism did not deter McCarthy. He falsely smeared the paper's city editor as "an active and leading member of the Communist Party." He compared the paper to the Communist *Daily Worker,* called for patriotic citizens to boycott it, and asked rhetorically, "Is the Capital Times Corp. the Red mouthpiece for the Communist Party in Wisconsin?" He answered his question by saying: "The simplest and most infallible way to answer this question is to examine the method of handling news by the Capital Times Corp. to see whether it follows the Communist party-line . . . for as someone has said, if a fowl looks like a duck, walks like a duck and quacks like a duck, then we can safely assume that [it] is a duck."

McCarthy shielded himself from libel laws by employing his government printing frank. Then, in a speech at a Shriners Club luncheon in Madison, he struck what seemed a bold stance—daring the *Capital Times*'s editor to sue him for libel—but cautiously adding words that protected him from libel suits: "I'm not going to tell you that [the editor and city editor] or anyone else is a Communist." Notwithstanding the disclaimer, he implored his audience to boycott the paper, saying: "When you expose a paper as Communistic, then I believe businessmen should never send in a check for advertising. When any man pays a nickel for a newspaper he is contributing to the Communistic cause."

McCarthy's battle with the Madison paper continued for the rest of his career. In particular, the paper's investigations of his financial affairs and the heavy debts he had accumulated in loans from Wisconsin banks to cover his stock market speculations and gambling losses spurred others to examine his private business dealings. In 1947, a Pepsi-Cola lobbyist had bailed him out by arranging for an unsecured twenty-thousand-dollar loan to cover McCarthy's mounting stock losses. McCarthy's efforts on behalf of real estate interests and housing industry lobbyists sparked even more controversy.

From his earliest days in the Senate, McCarthy accepted large fees to speak before real estate and housing conventions. His behavior at the Association of Building Standards convention in Columbus, Ohio, left an indelible impression on the businessman, Robert Byers, Sr., who had invited McCarthy to speak. McCarthy had been in Columbus less than an hour before he began borrowing money to shoot craps in his hotel room. As Byers recalled the scene:

It was a disgusting sight to see this great public servant down on his hands and knees, reeking of whisky, and shouting, "Come on babies, Papa needs a new pair of shoes." He did stop long enough between rolls to look over the gals his aides brought to him: on some, he turned thumbs down, but if one suited his fancy, he'd say, "That's the baby, I'll take care of her just as soon as I break you guys." The baby in question sat patiently on the bed, awaiting her chances for a ten-dollar bill. I overheard McCarthy tell one aide to keep a couple of others around just in case. If these statements are denied, one or more of the gals who were there are eager to testify as to what they saw.

None of this was a transgression of the more lax ethical standards applied to politicians then, and it was a side of McCarthy the public never fully saw. McCarthy's close connection to the housing industry, however, attracted public notice, especially his dealings with the Lustron Corporation. Lustron, then negotiating a multimillion-dollar loan from the federal government, was a manufacturer of prefabricated housing in great demand in the post-World War II housing boom fueled by millions of veterans returning home.

Early in 1949, McCarthy called a press conference to announce that Lustron had purchased an article he wrote on the housing shortage. McCarthy told reporters that his author's fee was "embarrassingly small. Besides, I have to split it with ten people who helped me." Much later it came out that Lustron had agreed to pay him $10,000 for his article—a large sum in that period. By contract, Lustron would market the article by publishing 10,000 copies in pamphlet form, sell them for thirty-five cents each, and pay McCarthy a dime on top of his $10,000 fee for every one sold.

As Oshinsky writes, McCarthy was then vice chairman of the Joint Committee on Housing and a member of the banking subcommittee reviewing loans from the Federal Housing Authority to Lustron. The next year, Lustron declared bankruptcy, thus "squandering $37 million in government credits." Later investigation, as Oshinsky said, "turned up another interesting fact: McCarthy had not written the article. The real work—the research, writing, and editing—was done by employees of Lustron and the Federal Housing Authority. Nor, for that matter, had McCarthy split the fee with 'ten people' who helped him. A check of his tax returns showed the full $10,000 listed as earned income."

McCarthy had already promised the money to the Appleton State Bank, which was sending dunning letters demanding that he pay back interest for notes on his debts to the bank. Though McCarthy pledged in writing to the bank president to "assign the book royalties to the bank" and to "assure you that any monies received . . . will be immediately applied in full measure to improve the picture," he instead used the money to buy two thousand shares of stock in Seaboard Airlines Railroad—an investment that ultimately returned tens of thousands of dollars of profits.

The Lustron deal never received the kind of detailed public airing it deserved. However, a single event did give the public, the press, and politicians—or should have given them, had they been paying attention—the most unvarnished view of what Joe McCarthy was like. This was McCarthy's involvement in the so-called Malmédy massacre affair.

———

Richard Rovere had just begun to write his incisive "Letter from Washington" articles for the *New Yorker* when he first encountered Joe McCarthy in action at a congressional hearing. As Rovere recalled the scene years later in his posthumous memoir, *Final Reports:*

> One pleasant day in May of 1949, I found myself at a noisy hearing of charges of alleged American mistreatment of a

number of German SS men—members of an outfit known
as the Blowtorch Battalion—who had some years earlier
been accused of massacring Belgian civilians and American troops at a crossroads village named Malmédy. The
noise came mostly from an obscure young senator from
Wisconsin, Joseph McCarthy, who was disrupting the proceedings and accusing the investigators of whitewashing
some Americans who, he said, had conducted their own
atrocities. The investigation was a sham, a fraud, and an
outrage, he shouted, and he stormed out of the hearing
room, saying that he was going to take the case to the public. Curious as to what he was making such a fuss about, I
walked out behind him and asked him what kind of case
he thought he had to take to the people. He invited me to
his office and I spent a dizzying hour or two watching him
shuffle papers and rattle off names and numbers that told
me nothing except that I was in the presence of a con artist
of considerable talent. A few months later, that talent was
everywhere on display and remained so for a run of four
[five] years.

Why McCarthy decided to take part in the congressional
hearings into the Malmédy massacre—or to take on the role
he played—remains a mystery. The defense of SS Nazi mur-
derers was hardly a cause for an American politician to embrace, especially when memories of World War II were still
vivid. The massacre was a fact. Eighty-three American soldiers, after being surrounded and surrendering during the
Battle of the Bulge, were herded into a field and executed by
Germans firing eight machine guns into their disorganized
ranks. Their corpses were found strewn across the snow-
covered fields.

After Germany surrendered, war crimes investigators learned of other Malmédy massacres, resulting in the deaths of another five hundred soldiers and civilians in the area. Seventy-four SS men were charged with the crimes and sent to Dachau for trial. In 1946, in unanimous verdicts, all but one were found guilty. Forty-three were sentenced to death.

Two years later, a pacifist group initiated charges that American troops had committed atrocities, including torture, against the Germans in order to extract false confessions from them. The American secretary of the Army created a special commission, headed by a Texas supreme court justice, to investigate these allegations. It was against this complicated and emotional background that, in the words of biographer Arthur Herman, McCarthy "somehow convinced himself that the Army was engaged in an elaborate coverup of judicial wrongdoing and browbeat the Senate into holding public hearings" led by a subcommittee of the Senate Armed Services Committee. Nothing emerged in these hearings, or subsequent examinations, that disproved the original charges against the Nazis or proved there had been an American coverup of U.S. atrocities against German prisoners of war.

Joe McCarthy was still in search of an issue to further his political career, and politics certainly motivated his decision to involve himself in the Malmédy investigation hearings. Alexander Wiley, Wisconsin's senior Republican, warned the subcommittee chairman, fellow Republican Raymond E. Baldwin of Connecticut, to "watch out for this fellow McCarthy." When Baldwin asked Wiley why he thought McCarthy was so interested in Malmédy, Wiley replied: "Ray, there are an awful lot of Germans in Milwaukee."

McCarthy was already interested in an issue of obvious appeal to Wisconsin's large German-American population: the repatriation of German prisoners of war. By 1948, an estimated six hundred forty thousand Germans were still held captive in the Soviet Union, despite Soviet pledges to repatriate them promptly. McCarthy introduced an amendment to the European Recovery Act, or Marshall Plan, requiring the return home within a year of all such POWs as a precondition of U.S. assistance to Europe. By further appealing to the Wisconsin German-American community as a defender of fair treatment for German prisoners of war, including those arrested for crimes at Malmédy, McCarthy could hope to reverse his political fall.

Other McCarthy scholars, including Robert Griffith, have raised the question of whether McCarthy was influenced by his close political and financial ties to Walter Harnischfeger, a wealthy Milwaukee industrialist known to be ardently pro-German, if not pro-Hitler. Harnischfeger had lobbied for a negotiated peace with Germany during World War II and denounced the Nuremberg trials as "worse than anything Hitler ever did." His firm, a global leader in the mining and construction industries producing cranes, diesel engines, and excavating equipment, had been cited for refusing to employ Jews or blacks. His nephew, Oshinsky writes, "had strutted around the University of Wisconsin, telling of his family's great admiration for Hitler and proudly exhibiting a copy of *Mein Kampf* that the Fuëhrer had autographed for him."

This motive for McCarthy's push for the hearings remains speculation, to which I'd add another bit of speculation: McCarthy's great desire to attract attention to himself by dominating press coverage, which he captured in the Malmédy episode.

Headlines: "McCarthy Scores Brutality," "McCarthy Charges Whitewash," "McCarthy Challenges Testimony." But whatever McCarthy's motives, the Malmédy episode is perhaps the one case in which he has had virtually no defenders. Writing from a staunch conservative perspective and as an otherwise strong defender of McCarthy, biographer Herman concludes: "By every objective standard, he made a fool of himself. It was a strange and self-defeating performance." The transcripts of McCarthy's performance during the long congressional hearings give the impression of a seriously disturbed person.

McCarthy treated virtually everyone he confronted with contempt—bullying, rudely interrupting, making false charges, and questioning the integrity of both witnesses and his fellow senators. Even more worrying were his darkly conspiratorial insinuations about coverup plots by American officials and his claims to have uncovered secret information containing "charges of a very serious nature that go beyond the Malmédy case," charges that "can do irreparable damage to the Army . . . and make it difficult for our State Department to operate."

His choice of language was flagrant in the extreme. To McCarthy, the attitude of the secretary of the Army, then testifying in defense of his troops' actions, was "fantastic." A statement by the judge advocate general was "the most phenomenal I ever heard." American military judges were "morons," the military courts in Germany were run by "brainless" and "imbecilic" American judges. McCarthy's personal disparagement of those who said something he didn't like was vicious and intimidating. Responding to legal testimony with which he disagreed, McCarthy said that anyone who acted like the witness in his court would have been "immediately disbarred." As an afterthought, he added that he would "perhaps first commit him to an institution for observation."

McCarthy's relationship with his fellow senators was contentious, but in this instance McCarthy more than met his match in the hearings' chairman, Raymond Baldwin of Connecticut. Throughout, Baldwin conducted the proceedings with dignity and dispassion. He maintained his poise despite repeated badgering from McCarthy. His quiet but firm demeanor and his carefully worded responses left McCarthy visibly enraged and frustrated. "The Chairman regrets that the junior senator from Wisconsin, Mr. McCarthy, has lost his temper and with it the sound impartial judgment which should be expressed in this matter," Baldwin said at one point. At another, he told McCarthy: "The committee does not intend to be swayed by any emotional threats or charges." And at still another moment, after being repeatedly interrupted by McCarthy, Baldwin said: "Let me say to my distinguished friend that I am not going to let him incorporate misstatements of facts in this case, because sometimes, in his exuberance, he is a little reckless in statements which do not normally appear in the testimony."

In the hearings' climactic denouement, witnessed by Richard Rovere, McCarthy launched an all-out assault on Baldwin. Speaking in the menacing monotone that soon become familiar to the American people, McCarthy directly addressed Baldwin: "I might say I think the chairman is inherently so fair and honest that the day is going to come when he is going to bitterly regret this deliberate and very clever attempt to whitewash. I think it is a shameful farce, Mr. Chairman, and inexcusable. Goodbye, sir."

With that, he picked up his papers and stormed theatrically from the hearing room.

In a speech before the full Senate two months later, on July 26, 1949, McCarthy accused the mild-mannered Connecticut Republican of whitewashing the Malmédy hearings in order to protect a law partner from a conflict of interest charge. He declared Baldwin "criminally responsible" for a miscarriage of justice.

This egregious violation of the Senate rules against personal attacks on fellow members was too much for senators of either party. In a stinging rebuke to McCarthy, the Senate Armed Services Committee passed a bipartisan resolution expressing full confidence in Senator Baldwin and his handling of the Malmédy hearings.

The resolution's language was extraordinary both for the severity of its denunciation of McCarthy and for its unqualified support of Baldwin: "We, his colleagues on this committee, take this unusual step in issuing this statement because of the most unusual, unfair, and utterly undeserved comments" McCarthy had made about Baldwin. Even more striking were the names of the senators who signed it: Among Democrats, such towering figures as Richard Russell of Georgia, Lyndon Johnson of Texas, Harry Byrd of Virginia, Millard Tydings of Maryland. Among Republicans, stalwarts such as Leverett Saltonstall of Massachusetts, William Knowland of California, and Styles Bridges of New Hampshire.

These men represented the very heart of the Senate establishment. They were among its most powerful and influential leaders. With this almost unprecedented public blow to Joe McCarthy, many who thought they knew the workings of Washington best believed Malmédy signaled the end of the political career of the "remarkable upstart" from Wisconsin. Instead, it marked the end of Baldwin's Senate career. In December 1949, he resigned from the Senate to accept an appointment by the governor of Connecticut to that state's supreme court, where he served with distinction. His distasteful battles with McCarthy, Baldwin later told reporters, were the last straw in his decision to leave politics. He would not be the last distinguished public servant to leave elective office in disgust at McCarthy's tactics.

PART TWO

The Past
as Prologue

Chapter
SIX

In the Beginning

Reign of Terror.

McCarthyism was not a new phenomenon in America, but a recurrent manifestation of a basic element of the American condition and character that keeps reappearing during times of national stress and crisis. Three previous periods had produced the same kinds of abuses that stained the nation during the McCarthy era. The first occurred in the earliest days of the Republic, when the French Revolution sparked ideological conflict in the new democracy. The second came during the upheaval of World War I that resulted in the Russian Revolution, the rise of international Communism, and fears that radicalism threatened the United States. The third was spawned by the despair of the Great Depression and the conservative reaction to the liberal New Deal reforms of Franklin D. Roosevelt.

The McCarthy era cannot be understood without examining

the similar fears and anxieties at work in these previous periods. To begin at the beginning:

THE ALIEN AND SEDITION ACTS

America's first "reign of terror" began eleven years after the Constitution of the United States was adopted "to form a more perfect Union, establish Justice, insure domestic Tranquility . . . and secure the Blessings of Liberty to ourselves and our Posterity." In the face of this idealized hope for the new democracy, Congress in successive weeks passed four notorious measures that became known collectively as the Alien and Sedition Acts.

These acts, pushed through Congress in late spring and early summer of 1798 by the Federalist Party that came to power with America's second president, John Adams, were enacted against the backdrop of the French Revolution. Democratic clubs, backed by the Federalists' bitter Jeffersonian rivals, had sprung up across the country. Meeting in these clubs, working-class citizens discussed not only the principles of the French Revolution but also their application to domestic political concerns. This was anathema to the Federalists. They denounced the clubs as "demonical societies" and "nurseries of sedition."

The Jeffersonians and their allies in the Democratic clubs became locked in a fierce battle with the Federalists. Anyone believed to harbor pro-French ideas was smeared as a "subversive" and accused of being "disloyal" or tainted by "The French Stamp."

Out of this atmosphere came the Alien and Sedition Acts.

The first act severely tightened the immigration laws that admitted "aliens" who planned to become U.S. citizens. The act was aimed at the rising numbers of Irish immigrants, who the Federalists feared were too closely allied with the Jeffersonians. Amid accusations that the Irish were plotting to overthrow the government, the Federalists sought to have them summarily deported.

The second act gave the president extraordinary powers to deport aliens he believed to be "dangerous." Its sweeping grant of presidential legal authority began with the remarkable words: "It shall be lawful for the President of the United States at any time during the continuance of this act, to *order* all such *aliens* [italics in original] as he shall judge dangerous to the peace and safety of the United States, or shall have reasonable grounds to suspect are concerned in any treasonable or secret machinations against the government thereof, to depart out of the territory of the United States."

The third act, the Alien Enemies Act, held that in the event of war, invasion, or "predatory incursion," whether "declared or threatened" against the United States, alien males aged fourteen and older "shall be liable to be apprehended, restrained, secured, and removed, as alien enemies." The act specified no crimes that might have been committed; the president was empowered to have the person arrested merely because he was an alien suspected of "disloyalty" or "subversion." Elements of this act reappeared in the twenty-first century with the passage of the Patriot and the Homeland Security acts, which granted new powers to detain and remove those suspected of being terrorists or of associating with terrorists. Creating secret military tribunals to try "enemy combatants" without benefit of counsel was another reaction to fears in the new Age of Anxiety.

Fourth came the Sedition Act, which contained provisions that obliterated constitutional protections guaranteed every citizen under the Bill of Rights. This act made it unlawful:

if any person shall write, print, utter or publish . . . or shall knowingly assist [in] . . . any false, scandalous and malicious writing or writings against the government of the United States, or either House of the Congress of the United States, or the said President, or to bring them, or either of them, into contempt or disrepute; or to excite against them, or either or any of them, the hatred of the good people of the United States, or to stir up sedition within the United States, or to excite any unlawful combinations therein, for opposing or resisting any law of the United States, or any act of the President of the United States done in pursuance of any such law.

Jail terms and fines could be imposed on anyone conspiring "to oppose any measure or measures of the government of the United States." So much for freedom of speech, or the right to dissent peacefully against the policies of the government and its elected officials.

No sooner had these acts passed than a wave of terror swept the young Republic.

Carey McWilliams captures that dark page in American history best in his 1950 *Witch Hunt: The Revival of Heresy.*

Mobs broke into the headquarters of the Democratic Clubs. Artisans employed in the manufacture of war materials were driven from their jobs with charges of being "pro-French" and "disloyal." Newspapers screamed that any person who doubted the wisdom of either the Alien or Sedition Act deserved to be listed as disloyal, and the Right Reverend Bishop White of Philadelphia announced that those who opposed either measure "resisteth the ordinance of God." . . . Editors were arrested and convicted under the Sedition Act; Congressmen were threatened with arrest for the offense of writing letters to their constituents; and lawyers who defended those charged with sedition were denounced from the bench for "propagating dangerous principles."

This repression lasted for three years, from 1798 until 1801, until power changed in Washington with Adams's defeat by Jefferson.

THE GREAT RED SCARE

Nothing like the Alien and Sedition repression reoccurred in the United States until the aftermath of World War I. Then, during what came to be known as the Great Red Scare, it was worse.

The Red Scare resembled the McCarthy era and our own Age of Anxiety. Citizens were suspected of plotting to overthrow the government, and accusations of disloyalty and subversion were hurled. Loyalty oaths were imposed. People were perscuted through guilt-by-association tactics. An attorney general of the United States bent, or broke, the law to seize "dangerous" people and keep them imprisoned without allowing them to see or talk with attorneys or family members. And it was during the Red Scare that a militant superpatriotism emerged in America. This ethos sought to impose conformity of thought and expression, dividing citizens into two camps: loyal ones, who practiced Americanism; or disloyal ones, who exhibited un-Americanism.

These were the results of waves of fear set off across the United States by tidal changes then sweeping the globe. In 1917, a year before the end of World War I, the Russian Revolution had toppled the czars and brought to power Lenin and Trotsky. Communists pledged to create, through violent insurrection if necessary, a new order throughout the world—including the United States. "Communism does not propose to 'capture' the bourgeoisie parliamentary state, but to conquer and destroy it," the manifesto of the Communist Party of the United States proclaimed upon its founding in 1919. "It is necessary that the proletariat organize its own state *for the coercion and suppression of the bourgeoisie* [emphasis in the original]."

Then, as later, the number of Communists and anarchists in the United States was grossly exaggerated. Best estimates put the U.S. membership of the Communist Labor Party during this period at ten to thirty thousand, and the membership of the Communist Party at thirty to sixty thousand. As for the Socialist Party, which had established a long and venerable history in the United States, membership was an estimated thirty-nine thousand. Communists could muster at most one-tenth of one percent of the adult American population. All three parties together—Communists, Communist Labor, and Socialists—represented no more than two-tenths of a percent of the workforce. Moreover, party membership didn't mean that a majority of these minuscule numbers advocated achieving their goals through illegal actions. Still, fears sparked by the menace of radicalism trumped a logical assessment of the threat Americans faced. Just as in the post-9/11 Age of Anxiety, the Great Red Scare was initiated by murderous acts that triggered a national reaction of fear and anger.

It began in April 1919, while President Woodrow Wilson was in Paris negotiating peace accords.

———

In Seattle, Mayor Ole Hanson found in his mail "an infernal machine big enough to blow out the entire side of the

County-City Building." The mayor had been traveling the country warning of the new Red threat to America.

The next afternoon, an African-American maid named Ethel Williams opened a package addressed to U.S. Senator Thomas R. Hardwick at his home in Atlanta. Her hands were blown off when a bomb inside the package exploded. Hardwick, as chairman of the Senate's immigration committee, had proposed restrictive immigration legislation intended to keep out Bolsheviks and suppress Bolshevism.

Early the next morning, a New York City postal clerk riding the subway home to Harlem was reading about the attempted bombing of Senator Hardwick when something about the newspaper's description of the package containing the bomb reminded him of packages he had recently placed on a shelf because of insufficient postage. Immediately returning to the post office, he found sixteen small parcels wrapped in brown paper. They were addressed to the Attorney General of the United States, the Postmaster General, the Secretary of Labor, the Commissioner of Immigration, a Supreme Court justice, a federal judge in Chicago, and a number of prominent capitalists including J.P. Morgan and John D. Rockefeller.

The clerk alerted police, who carefully removed the packages to a nearby firehouse and there found each to contain a bomb. Succeeding investigation discovered at least thirty-six such packages had been shipped through the U.S. mails. No suspect was ever found.

On May 1—a day Soviet leaders had adopted as a holiday summoning workers to "arise and cast off your chains"— traditional May Day events held to celebrate "the struggle of the working class" turned violent. In Cleveland, an Army lieutenant enraged by the sight of a Communist (or Socialist) Red Flag carried at the front of a peaceful Socialist parade proceeding through a public street demanded that the flag be struck. He then led a group of soldiers and sailors who charged into the parade, attacking the marchers. Police responded by also moving against the marchers, igniting riots throughout the city. One man was killed, scores were injured, and the Socialist headquarters building in Cleveland was demolished.

In New York City, another mob of soldiers and sailors stormed into a reception honoring the opening of the office of the *New York Call,* a Socialist newspaper. When celebrants refused to tear down "Bolshevist" posters, the servicemen waded into the crowd of hundreds of men, women, and children, smashing the office, destroying the party literature set out on tables, driving the crowd into the street, and clubbing many so severely that they were hospitalized.

The public's desire for security prompted other anti-Bolshevik riots and even more extraordinary actions. An Indiana jury deliberated only two minutes before acquitting a man for shooting and killing an alien because he had shouted, "To hell with the United States." In Chicago, on May 6, a sailor shot a man merely for failing to rise during the playing of "The Star Spangled Banner." The next morning, readers of the *Washington Post* awoke to find a wire dispatch describing the incident under the headline:

Chicagoans Cheer Tar Who Shot Man

Sailor Wounds Pageant Spectator Disrespectful to Flag

Disrespect for the American flag and a show of resentment toward the thousands who participated in a victory loan pageant here tonight may cost George Goddard his life. He was shot down by a sailor of the United States navy when he did not stand and remove his hat while the band was playing the "Star Spangled Banner." . . . When he fell at the report of the sailor's gun the crowd burst into cheers and hand-clapping.

An America reeling from reports of terrorist mail-bombers was shocked even more when, on June 2, a series of bombs detonated within an hour in eight cities, including the nation's capital.

Attorney General A. Mitchell Palmer, in office barely two months, had just left the first-floor library in his house, turned off the lights, and started to go upstairs to bed when he heard a loud bang, as if from something hitting his front door, followed by an immense explosion. The man who had been carrying the bomb up Palmer's front steps had not set the fuse correctly and was blown up; pieces of his limbs were found outside the house. Across the street, a startled neighbor raced to his front door and stepped outside to see what had happened. Assistant Secretary of the Navy Franklin D. Roosevelt found blood and bits of flesh on his doorstep.

The public reacted to these events with spontaneous attacks on Bolsheviks, Socialists, and aliens. These were only a prelude to the most notorious offenses of the period: the so-called Palmer Raids.

Alexander Mitchell Palmer, always identified publicly as A. Mitchell Palmer, is remembered by historians as perhaps the worst U.S. attorney general, rivaled for that distinction

only by Harding's Harry Dougherty and Nixon's John Mitchell.*
Palmer remains the only one whose name will be forever
linked to repression.

During World War I, Congress passed three pieces of
legislation—whose names will be instantly familiar from an
earlier period—that gave Palmer statutory power for his repression: the Sedition Act of 1917 and the Espionage and
Alien Acts of 1918. The worst was the Espionage Act, which
strengthened provisions in the Sedition Act. As characterized
in Henry Steele Commager's *Documents of American History*, this act "made the Sedition Act of 1798 look very mild
indeed. Under Attorney-General Palmer the Espionage Act
was drastically enforced, and freedom of speech and of the
press temporarily disappeared."

The Espionage Act called for fines of up to ten thousand
dollars and twenty years in jail for all offenders, "whosoever,
when the United States is at war, shall willfully utter, print,
write, or publish any disloyal, profane, scurrilous, or abusive
language about the form of government of the United States,
or the Constitution of the United States, or the military or
naval forces of the United States, or the flag . . . or the uniform of the Army or Navy of the United States, or any language intended to bring the form of government . . . or the
Constitution . . . or the military or naval forces . . . or the flag
of the United States into contempt." At one point in its drafting, the legislation called for the death penalty, if recommended by a jury verdict. Had it been enacted, this provision

---

*It's too early to render historic judgment on Attorney General John
Ashcroft during the George W. Bush years, but his record has been one of
the most troubling in decades.

would have subjected Vietnam era protesters to execution for burning their draft cards.

In another relic exhumed from the Alien and Sedition period, Congress gave the government sweeping powers to deport aliens. The Alien Act of 1918 made it legal to deport any alien who opposed organized government (the anarchist belief), who advocated overthrow of the government by force, or who was a member of any organization teaching these views. Armed with these broad legal powers, the attorney general set in motion the policies for which he is remembered.

He did not act alone. On August 1, 1919, two months after the bomb attack on his home, Palmer hired a twenty-four-year-old former law clerk to head the new unit he was creating within the Justice Department—the General Intelligence Division, later renamed the Anti-Radical Division. Palmer's pick to lead this unit was John Edgar Hoover, a pug-faced man whose demeanor matched his zealous personality.

From that moment, through the administrations of ten American presidents from Wilson to Nixon, Hoover was the nation's most formidable and feared fighter against "subversives" and "subversion." He became one of the most powerful figures in American history.

The history of McCarthyism cannot be told without understanding the critical role Hoover played. He is best remembered as the man who headed the Federal Bureau of Investigation from its creation on May 10, 1924. But Hoover's part in forming and leading the anticommunist crusade began with his invaluable service to Palmer during the summer of 1919; it continued for more than half a century until Hoover's death on May 2, 1972.

———

J. Edgar Hoover (like A. Mitchell Palmer, he never used his full name) began compiling dossiers on those suspected of supporting the radical ideas of anarchism, socialism, and Communism. He proved to be as determined a worker as he was a committed ideologue.

By the fall of 1919, his files on suspected radicals numbered one hundred fifty thousand. Within two more years, the number of people in his dossiers had risen to four hundred fifty thousand. Out of those, Hoover created files on sixty thousand persons he considered "key agitators." Assisted by a growing number of agents assigned him by Palmer, Hoover cross-indexed his file system to identify each suspect's place of residence and political affiliation. From there, he expanded his investigatory reach into a network of public and private groups that extended across the nation. Local police Red Squads, private security firms such as Pinkertons, and patriotic organizations like the American Legion all assisted Hoover in gathering intelligence, often through anonymous informers. Over the decades, during boom or bust, peace or war, this network grew as the Hoover-led hunt for subversives continued. The FBI became his private army.

Palmer used the press to get across his message: America faced an imminent radical revolution. He distributed leaflets that pictured fearsome-looking Bolsheviks with bristling beards and asked Americans whether they wanted these kinds of men to rule over them. In speeches before business and farm owners, he said the Reds would take away everything they had—from their homes and businesses to their personal property and bank accounts. Politicians added fuel to the fire by repeating incendiary remarks such as: "My motto for the Reds is S.O.S.—ship or shoot."

Meanwhile, a series of deadly race riots made it seem as though the nation were coming apart. The riots began in Washington on a hot Saturday night in July. A screaming white mob surged through the downtown area, past the White House and Treasury and down Pennsylvania Avenue, attacking any black in sight. Thousands ran wild. Blood literally flowed in the streets. Even with the addition of four hundred United States cavalry, infantry, and Marines, Washington's police force of seven hundred was unable to stem the mob's fury. It took the dispatch of two thousand more federal troops, plus a driving rain, to establish an uneasy end to the violence days after it had begun. Within a week, however, racial animosities spread to Chicago, resulting in riots that lasted thirteen days and left thirty-eight dead and a thousand families—most of them black—homeless. In the next two months, other race riots followed in East St. Louis, Illinois; Knoxville, Tennessee; Omaha, Nebraska; and Elaine, Arkansas.

Only weeks after the last of the riots was suppressed, another ripple of fear swept the country. This time the focus was on Boston, where eleven hundred seventeen of the city's fifteen hundred forty-four policemen went on strike, leaving the city virtually defenseless; mobs quickly smashed windows and looted stores. The Boston police strike faded into history, but the fear of lawless insurrection lingered.

Against this background, Palmer and Hoover plotted a series of raids on suspected radicals that began in the fall of 1919 and continued through the following May. The purpose, as Palmer explained later, was "to tear out the radical seeds that have entangled American ideas in their poisonous theories."

———

Without warning, and often without warrants, hundreds of Palmer's agents and local police forces carried out raids in a twelve-city sweep in November 1919. Four thousand people were arrested, and many of them were badly beaten. They were crowded into temporary holding pens lacking adequate toilet facilities, medical care, and even, in some cases, food and water. Their possessions were destroyed, as were the offices in which they had worked. All were held for days or weeks without bail and without access to counsel or to the judicial process. Many were held incommunicado; family and friends didn't know where they were. Most were never told what, if any, charges were being made against them.

In Detroit, more than a hundred men were herded into a bull pen measuring twenty-four by thirty feet, and "kept there for a week under conditions which the mayor of the city called intolerable." In Hartford, visitors who came to see any of the hundred being held were themselves arrested and jailed. Authorities regarded such visits "as *prima facie* evidence of affiliation with the Communist Party." In Boston, five hundred shackled prisoners were led through the streets on their way to the Deer Island Prison. In New York, three hundred whooping policemen mobilized by Hoover raced into buildings to round up hundreds of "radicals." In a notorious incident, an Italian immigrant named Gaspare Cannone, who spoke limited English, was arrested (again, without warrant or charges) by Justice Department agents in New York. When he refused to give evidence against others, he was beaten and kicked. After being held in secret for seventy-two hours, Cannone was turned over to U.S. Bureau of Immigration officials on Ellis Island, the place symbolizing America's call to the world to "give us your tired, your poor, your huddled masses yearning to breathe free." Cannone refused to sign a document acknowledging that he was an anarchist; nonetheless, his signature was forged to it.

The next month Palmer's agents rounded up two hundred forty-nine radicals and American Communist leaders, including the feminist activist and self-professed anarchist Emma Goldman, and deported them to Russia, via Finland, on the ship *Buford.* Americans jokingly called the ship "The Soviet Ark." Standing on the dock when the *Buford* departed at five o'clock on the morning of December 19, 1919, was J. Edgar Hoover. These deportees were removed from American shores though they had not been proven guilty of any crime.

On New Year's Day 1920, after careful planning by Hoover, the Palmer forces mobilized to launch a dragnet sweep throughout thirty-three cities. The specific targets on the next day's raids were Communist, Communist Labor, and Socialist leaders and organizations. Again operating without warning or warrants, the raiders smashed party offices and union headquarters. As many as ten thousand people* were arrested, jailed, and held under the same miserable conditions as experienced by those seized in November. Of these detainees, seven hundred more eventually were deported.

The Palmer raids, despite their appalling abuses of civil liberties, drew wide support. Following Congress's lead, and encouraged by Palmer's call for stronger legislation throughout the country, many states enacted their own sedition laws.

---

*Total numbers cited for arrests in these raids are in conflict. Some sources say 6,000, others 10,000.

Some fourteen hundred people were arrested under these state laws.

————

The combination of public hysteria and political zeal produced a climate that inhibited political discussion and the teaching of ideas. When the New York State Legislature introduced a measure to expel five Socialist representatives after citing them for being members "of a disloyal organization composed exclusively of perpetual traitors," and yet offered no proof of that charge, a Republican representative, Teddy Roosevelt, Theodore's son, arose to defend them. Roosevelt, who later distinguished himself in battle and died as a U.S. general in the D-day invasion, was immediately rebuked by the Speaker of the House. The legislature expelled the Socialists after an overwhelming majority voted in favor of the motion, leading the *New York Times* to comment: "It was an American vote altogether, a patriotic and conservative vote. An immense majority of the American people approve and sanction the Assembly's action."

Public school teachers, college professors, writers, and intellectuals also became targets. The New York Council on Education found membership in the Socialist Party "incompatible with the obligations of the teaching profession." On those grounds, a number of Socialists were removed from their teaching posts.

Concern over the loyalty of teachers prompted New York's State Legislature in 1921 to pass the Lusk laws, which required a loyalty oath for all teachers. Under this legislation the New York secretary of state was given power to deny a place on the ballot to any "disloyal" political party. The head of the state's education department was also empowered to deny accreditation to any Socialist school. These laws led to the harassment of educators and a flood of investigations for "disloyalty." The mere threat of being investigated was intimidating enough to instill conformity. Use of what the distinguished American historian Howard K. Beale called "the censorious eye" was more effective than force or coercion because "dismissals would have raised protests whereas terrorization gained its end without unpleasant publicity."*

By the early months of 1920, the fear of revolution began to subside and leaders of the bar and bench started speaking out against Palmer's abuses. Among the first to decry the repression was a pillar of the Republican conservative establishment, Charles Evans Hughes—former governor of New York, GOP presidential nominee (against Wilson in 1916), U.S. Secretary of State, and Chief Justice of the United States. Then, on May 12, a panel of judicial leaders, including Felix Frankfurter and Roscoe Pound, published a widely publicized report that documented dozens of instances of due process violations. Their report concluded: "There is no danger of revolution so great as that created by deliberate violations of the simple rules of American law and American decency." Other judges ruled that many deportations had

---

*I'm delighted to tip my hat to my old major professor from graduate school. When I was his graduate history assistant, Mr. Beale was the foremost scholar on the life and times of Theodore Roosevelt. Either I forgot, or didn't know, about his splendid defense of academic freedom much earlier.

been illegal. Palmer was forced to resign. America turned to other matters. The Great Red Scare was over; its pattern of abuses was not.

THE DEPRESSION YEARS

How many Americans flirted with Communism, or became Communists, during the hopelessness and anger of the Great Depression cannot be accurately determined. While the total number of Communists and "fellow travelers" was highly exaggerated, Americans were in a mood to demand changes in the social and economic order. In the Midwest, farmers bearing shotguns and pitchforks opposed sheriffs who came with foreclosure notices to seize their homes and land. Jobless veterans marching on Washington battled U.S. Army forces called out to suppress them. Influential writers looked favorably on Russia and the supposedly popular revolution then underway. "I have seen the future and it works," the writer and progressive muckraker Lincoln Steffens proclaimed after returning from a trip to the Soviet Union. At the least, significant numbers of Americans were attracted by the promise of a revolution to shift the balance of power, to put simplistically, from owners to workers.

As John Earl Haynes and Harvey Klehr note in *Venona: Decoding Soviet Espionage in America,* Soviet agents found easy targets for recruitment or assistance among "the bright young idealists who had flocked to Washington in the heady days of the early New Deal." Based on decryptions of secret cables between Soviet spies then operating in the U.S. and their Moscow superiors—the results of an ultrasecret U.S. code-breaking effort known as the Venona Project, which was only made public in 1995—the authors conclude that several hundred of that early New Deal cohort joined the Communist Party. They were assigned "to secret party cells." Of these recruits, "many willingly turned government information over to the party in hopes of assisting Communist political goals," and of this group, "a few score went further. When they found themselves in positions with access to secret government information helpful to the USSR, they did not hesitate to give it to Soviet intelligence officers."

By 1934, in reaction partly to President Roosevelt and the New Deal, and partly to the perceived Communist threat, the Hearst press had launched a national campaign against "radicals" in schools and colleges. The same year, a campaign to make the Pledge of Allegiance a requirement in school began. This was all part of a drive for "patriotic conformity." Within five years, fourteen states had adopted laws requiring teachers to take loyalty oaths.

———

The term "un-American" was employed often during the Red Scare, and perhaps even during the Alien and Sedition period; but it was the creation of the congressional House Un-American Activities Committee that made the word such a lightning rod of both opprobrium and approval.

From its birth in 1938 until its demise nearly forty years later, HUAC, as it came to be known, was a rallying point for anticommunists and a symbol of the worst governmental abuses for liberals. To its critics it was the committee that spent the most money, called the most witnesses, published the most pages, visited more places, ruined more lives, and was responsible for the least legislation of any committee in the United States Congress. To its supporters, it was the forum where Communist treason was exposed.

The 1938 congressional resolution creating HUAC authorized the committee to investigate the extent, the character, and the objects of "un-American propaganda within the United States." Its second mandate was to investigate "the diffusion within the United States of subversive and un-American propaganda that is instigated from foreign countries or from a domestic origin and attacks the principle of the form of government as guaranteed by our Constitution."

HUAC's charter gave the committee seven months to investigate and submit its final report by New Year's Day 1939. When the deadline neared, HUAC's flamboyant chairman—a six-foot-three-inch, gum-chewing, cigar-smoking Texan named Martin Dies—pleaded with his congressional associates to extend it by another year. There was more un-Americanism and subversion in America than he had realized, Dies told them. The committee's life was extended, and extended again. Decades passed before HUAC left the American scene.

It was the mission of HUAC, as pronounced by its chairman and members, not to draft legislation, but to expose subversive Americans by subjecting them to rigorous publicity—publicity generated by the government at public expense. And this exposure was free from the constraints of libel laws; because HUAC operated under grant of congressional immunity, it could not be held legally responsible for defaming people called before it.

Dies and his staff, many recruited from Hoover's FBI, demonstrated a gift for creating headlines through sensational charges. The chairman's name-calling and shouted epithets against witnesses became staples of HUAC hearings. Witnesses were: "un-American," "atheistic," "immoral," "irreligious," "radical," "communistic," "unpatriotic," "disloyal." They were: "fellow travelers," "subversives," "agents of Moscow." They were: "Communists," members of a "Communist front," or in thrall to other "foreign-controlled" organizations.

McCarthy not only adopted as his own the themes and rationale upon which HUAC operated, but also repeatedly employed the same epithets during his anticommunist investigations.

Above all else, it was the duty of HUAC and good Americans to restore "Christian influence" in America and to oppose the teachings of Karl Marx as diametrically opposed to those of Jesus Christ, for "Marx represents the lowest form of materialism," while "Christ symbolizes the highest and noblest conceptions of the spiritual." It was this "irreconcilable conflict between the teachings of Christ and Marx" upon which "the future of Western civilization is staked." As we've seen, McCarthy used nearly the exact words in his Wheeling speech, and continued to employ them in his subsequent public addresses and hearings.

In Dies's view, another idea "the good American" rejected was "absolute social and racial equality." Those who disagreed were subversive. This theme—and it also became an ugly conspiratorial refrain during the McCarthy years—was a constant in HUAC hearings. Take, for example, Dies's questioning of one witness early in the committee's history during a hearing August 12, 1938:

> The Chairman: Before you testify, Miss Saunders, let me
> say we are not interested, as a committee, in the racial
> question, except only insofar as it forms a vital part of

Communistic teachings, practices, and doctrines. Later
on it will be developed that Communists are working
among the Negroes in certain sections of the country,
and their appeal is racial equality.

Miss Saunders: That is right.

The Chairman: Only as we link that in with Communist
practices, doctrines, and methods—only to that extent
we are concerned with your testimony.

The Dies committee became infamous for two other vir-
ulent strains in addition to such racism: unabashed anti-
Semitism, and a pathological hatred of a New Deal it believed
infested with liberals, radicals, Communists, and traitors. To
Dies, and later McCarthy, "liberals" were the same as radicals
and Communists. Liberals were un-American. And this was
years before HUAC conducted the hearings on Communism
in the movie industry that resulted in the blacklisting of the
Hollywood Ten, or the hearings that unmasked Alger Hiss. It
was also years before McCarthy struck identical notes to play
upon Cold War fears that nurtured, and made possible,
McCarthyism.

Chapter SEVEN

Cold Warriors

It legitimized Red-baiting.

At one o'clock in the afternoon of Wednesday, March 12, 1947, Harry S. Truman stood at a marble rostrum, faced the assembled members of Congress, and against the backdrop of a huge American flag began delivering one of the most fateful presidential addresses of the twentieth century.

In words broadcast live via radio to an anxious national audience, Truman addressed what he called an "extremely critical situation" that required immediate congressional action. His speech amounted to a declaration of war, one that did not require congressional authorization, but one that would commit the United States to doing battle for nearly half a century. Though the term Cold War is now solidly anchored in history, it is a misnomer. America actually fought a decades-long "hot war." Before it ended, nearly a hundred thousand American lives were lost in the conflicts of Korea and Vietnam. Millions more lives were lost in covert and overt military operations worldwide. The nation expended eleven trillion dollars to wage the war, plus a vast amount of its military, scientific, and technological resources.

Ostensibly, Truman was asking Congress for an emergency appropriation of four hundred million dollars to aid Greece and Turkey, free nations then being threatened by a Communist takeover from within and without. But as the president made clear to the joint session of Congress and to his national audience, he was asking for a commitment of infinitely more. He was putting "the world on notice that it would be our policy to support the cause of freedom wherever it was threatened." The threat was Communism. Whatever the risks, no matter the costs in blood and money, however long it took, the United States would oppose Communism.

The Truman Doctrine, as this speech became known, had an immediate effect on American lives and long-term consequences for the world. Not until George W. Bush announced a U.S. policy of "regime change" and "preventive war" more than fifty years later would there be as significant a foreign policy shift as the Cold War formulation of Truman.*

How great an impact the Truman Doctrine had on average American families then I didn't fully appreciate until many years later after both my parents had died. Then I found a letter my father had written to my mother the day

---

*Bush's second inaugural address on Jan. 20, 2005, strongly echoed Truman's sweeping assertion that it was the policy of the U.S. to "support the cause of freedom wherever it was threatened."

after Truman's address. My father had been a war correspondent in the Pacific, covering among other actions the invasions of Iwo Jima and Okinawa and the surrender ceremonies on the decks of the U.S.S. *Missouri* in Tokyo Bay before returning home to report the post-war scene from New York. Obviously, his still-fresh memories of World War II were much on his mind when he wrote my mother, then visiting relatives in Charleston, South Carolina, describing the anxiety he and others felt after listening to Truman.

"Lots of concern here, and elsewhere, over Truman's speech to Congress on the Greek crisis," his letter to my mother began.

> I am confused, don't know what to believe, and I guess there are millions of other Americans like me. Truman certainly didn't mince words. He said, in the bluntest language a president can use, that we were serving notice on the world that we would oppose the spread of Communism, economically and militarily, anywhere in the world. It amounted, for the present, to an economic declaration of war on Russia. There seems to be strong support for the president's position, even among the Republicans, but with grave misgivings as to where this new, aggressive policy may lead. To another war? There are many who think so— and very soon. I wish I knew what to believe.

Then he wrote, in a personal reference that transported me back to that long-ago time when I was in high school at the dawning of the Cold War:

> Our Haynes, who is far from dumb, as you know, put his finger on the trouble spot at breakfast this morning when

he said: "This means that we'll have to have a standing army all over the world. I do not want to go to the Middle East. I can see no future in that for me." He's right, of course. Haynes will soon be 16, just ripe for another war, if there is one. You can't help but think of things like that, can you? Well, I guess the only thing we can do is to sit on this keg of dynamite and hope for the best—that it won't explode!*

I believe my father was expressing the thoughts of countless others who suddenly saw their hopes for a post-war peace dashed by the prospects of a new, potentially more terrible, global war.

There are two ways to look at the Truman Doctrine and the role it played in subsequent developments, including McCarthyism. The first involves Truman's mind-set about the Communist threat to the United States as he saw it at that moment.

Exactly a year earlier, on March 5, 1946, before the term *Cold War* had entered the language, Winston Churchill forever defined the fearsome new era by declaring that the Soviet Union had erected an "iron curtain" dividing the Communist world from the democratic Western one. The text of Churchill's famous speech at Westminster College in Fulton, Missouri, reveals that even such an ardent anticommunist

---

*Lest I appear to puff myself up with this passage citing my alleged youthful wisdom, my father quickly put me in my place when he also wrote my mother in the same letter: "Our careless Haynes has just had to have a new lens for his glasses. This makes about the umpteenth time he has broken them, doesn't it? I wish he weren't such a blunderbuss."

leader as Churchill played down the *internal* Communist threat to British and American interests. *"Except in the British Commonwealth and in the United States where Communism is in its infancy* [italics added]," he said, "the Communist Parties or fifth columns constitute a growing challenge and peril." This undercut the anticommunist crusaders' central thrust of the peril America faced from *domestic* Communist subversion.

In the year following Churchill's address, Truman and his key aides, notably George Marshall, Dean Acheson, and George Kennan, watched with growing alarm as more and more nations fell under the external Soviet advance. They concluded that the United States had to take a stand—what Truman described as "America's answer to the surge of expansion of Communist tyranny."

Truman, in his memoirs, first articulated what later became known as the "domino theory,"* saying the loss of Greece to Communism had wider implications than the stability of the eastern Mediterranean. Unless the Communists

---

*Eisenhower later coined that phrase when asked at a 1954 press conference about the strategic importance of Indochina (Vietnam) to the free world, citing what he termed "the falling domino principle": "You have a row of dominoes set up, you knock over the first one, and what will happen to the last one is a certainty that it will go over very quickly." The loss of Indochina would be followed by Burma, Thailand, the Malay Peninsula, and Indonesia "until you are now talking about millions and millions of people." The dominoes would continue to fall until Australia and New Zealand were threatened and the defensive island chains of Japan, Formosa, and the Philippines were forced to turn toward the South—to the Communist East. Often forgotten is that this Cold War formulation was first articulated by Truman seven years earlier.

were checked, Truman believed, nation after nation would become part of an expansionist Soviet totalitarian empire. The United States and the Western democracies would be imperiled.

In fact, America was not in danger of being defeated by the Soviet Union. It was the Soviet Union that was declining, and to such an extent that its eventual disintegration could be foreseen decades before its final fall. What's more, the U.S. security services were well aware of the Soviet Union's deteriorating condition. The American public was not, and much of the nation's political leadership either did not seek such knowledge or for political reasons chose to ignore it.* So fierce was the bureaucratic infighting among the security services, notably between the FBI and the CIA, that as Derek Leebaert concluded in his study *The Fifty-Year Wound,* neither Truman nor Acheson "knew that U.S. counter-intelligence was reading Soviet spy traffic. The CIA would not

---

*In an important, but sadly little-noted volume, *Secrecy* (Yale: 1998), the late Senator Daniel Patrick Moynihan concluded that the Soviet Union was on the point of economic, social, and political collapse since at least the mid-1970s, thus making unnecessary the cost and dangers of the continuing Cold War U.S. military buildup. Moynihan further concluded that knowledge of the true state of Soviet affairs was well known within the U.S. intelligence community for years before that, but its "culture of secrecy" kept even presidents of the United States uninformed about these facts. He also believed that "the most baleful consequence of the Cold War—the fissure in American culture that developed during the Mc-Carthy period and the fathomless debts accumulated during the arms buildup of the Reagan years—could have been avoided had it not been for the secrecy that concealed from the American people what the government knew and what it did not know."

be alerted to Venona's astounding revelations until 1952. FBI Director J. Edgar Hoover kept the information in his personal vault." The same kind of bureaucratic unwillingness to share vital information was a prime factor in the intelligence failures of the 9/11 terror attacks.

In any case, there is no reason to doubt the sincerity of Truman, Marshall, and Acheson's conviction that the United States faced a *foreign* Communist threat. At the same time, there can be no question that the administration greatly exaggerated for political reasons the *domestic* threat posed by Communism. They were spurred by fears that the Republicans' success in labeling Truman and the Democrats "soft on Communism" in 1946 not only led to the Democrats' loss of Congress but imperiled Truman's 1948 presidential election prospects as well.

Clark Clifford, the president's top political strategist, boasted in 1947 that the administration's new hard-line stance had "adroitly stolen" the anticommunist issue from the Republicans. It hadn't. If anything, it intensified Republican allegations that the Democrats coddled Communists at home and abroad.

Clifford wasn't referring only to the Truman Doctrine. Nine days after his address, the president issued Executive Order 9835, instituting a sweeping federal "loyalty-security" program that perhaps more than anything else initiated America's second—and greater—Red Scare.

Hastily conceived, vaguely defined, rife with abuse, and reflecting the anticommunist agenda of J. Edgar Hoover, who handpicked the commission chairman who established its rules and guidelines, the loyalty-security program was created essentially to forestall domestic political attacks on the

124 / COLD WARRIORS

administration. It encouraged employers in the federal service to screen their employees for their political beliefs and remove "potentially disloyal" people. In the same copycat style in which states and municipalities passed loyalty and anti-sedition laws during the World War I Red Scare, similar purges were instituted by local governments. Such screening then spread throughout the American work force. Before the scare ran its course, one in every five Americans, as a condition of employment, had to complete a loyalty statement or otherwise be granted some kind of security clearance.

The Truman loyalty program aimed not merely at ferreting out employees considered disloyal because of their affiliations, past actions, or suspected acts of treason or espionage. In targeting "potentially disloyal" persons, it sought to remove those who, because of attitudes or ideas "they entertain today or subscribed to yesterday, might in the future undertake action contrary to the best interests of the United States." As such, the program abused fundamental tenets of Anglo-American jurisprudence and, as one scholar later concluded, violated a basic principle of law: "that one cannot be punished for merely *considering* the commission of a crime, or for *thinking* in such a way that a body determines that one might undertake action contrary to the law [italics added]."

Excerpts from transcripts made during various loyalty board hearings reveal how "potentially disloyal" Americans often were unable to learn the source of the accusations against them—and even discovered that the loyalty board members *themselves* did not possess that knowledge. In one board hearing, the following exchange took place:

Board Member: Did you ever act as an organizer for the Communist Party or attempt to recruit others?

Employee: No.

Board Member: [It] has been corroborated, checked and verified—

Employee's lawyer, interrupting: By whom?

Board Member: I can't tell you. . . . We don't even know who the accuser is.

Witnesses who believed in racial equality, socialized medicine, labor unions, equalization of economic opportunities, or a larger governmental role in the economy were believed to harbor left wing or liberal views. It was assumed that these were Communist views. Therefore, anyone holding such beliefs *could* in the future become a Communist agent. By that thinking, whether or not they were disloyal, their jobs should be terminated.

From the transcripts, isolated fragments:

Question: There is a suspicion in the record that you are in sympathy with the underprivileged. Is this true?

* * *

Question: Did you see—X—soliciting funds for strikers?

* * *

Question: Have you ever had Negroes in your home?

* * *

Question: In your recollection, do you recall ever discussing any topic which might be sympathetic to Communist doctrine?

Answer: Yes.

Question: Would you care to state what it was and who it was made to?

Answer: I have been sick for years, and so I have discussed
what they call nationalized medicine.

In addition to such absurdity, another theme winds
through the hearings. It's the familiar one of prejudice against
immigrants—the "aliens" among us, citizens or not, who by
their mere foreign backgrounds, looks, or accents were suspected of holding un-American, and thus dangerous, views.

Question: Was your father native born?
Answer: Yes.
Question: How about his father?
Answer: Yes.
Question: Your mother, was she native born?
Answer: Yes.
Question: How about her parents?
Answer: Yes.

The loyalty-security program was soon augmented by the
so-called attorney general's list. The list of ninety-three organizations deemed a threat to the nation's security was made
public that November—compiled by the attorney general
under Truman's authorization—and forwarded to the new
loyalty boards. Members of the groups were to be screened
for evidence of "Communist sympathies or affiliations." The
outcome was often dismissal of the employees from their jobs.

From the beginning, the list was out of date. Many of the
groups named, such as the pro-Nazi German-American Bund
or the North American Committee to Aid Spanish Democracy, were already defunct or were in the process of disband-
ing. Nonetheless, in the way of bureaucracy, the list grew.

Within three years it had expanded to encompass one hundred ninety-seven organizations. And the number increased in the Eisenhower years.

Injustices were rampant. Authorities allowed anonymous informants to remain hidden, abridging the fundamental right of a citizen to confront his accuser. People found themselves fired, as one scholar put it, for being on the "wrong" mailing lists, owning the "wrong" books, having "politically suspect" relatives and friends. If an employee chose to contest charges, the review process was cumbersome, personally humiliating—and expensive. The government refused to provide free counsel for suspects. Not surprisingly, thousands—one estimate puts it as high as twelve thousand—of those involved in loyalty-security proceedings chose to resign rather than fight to clear their names or be reinstated.

It was in this context that in 1947 the House Un-American Activities Committee conducted its loyalty investigations into Hollywood. These resulted in the blacklisting, browbeating of witnesses, and ruin of reputations that forever discredited such congressional inquisitions. They also formed a model for the even more destructive McCarthy witch hunts to come.

Two factors greatly added to the Hollywood inquiries' impact on the public. First was the advent of television, which became a powerful vehicle for reaching unprecedented numbers of citizens and for advancing political careers through manipulation of evidence and airing of charges of disloyalty. Second was the Truman administration's new loyalty-security policies, which made more credible anticommunist crusaders' claims that America faced a grave threat from enemies within.

In the decades since, as scholars have examined and attempted to explain the origins of both the Cold War and McCarthyism, a consensus has emerged holding Truman and his administration responsible for contributing to the repressive political climate that culminated in the McCarthy era. "The Truman Administration legitimized Red-baiting at home by the institution of a federal loyalty-security program," historian Robert Griffith writes, "which applied sweeping standards to all government employees, not just those in sensitive positions, and by the promulgation of the attorney general's list, which, based on the concept of guilt by association, rapidly became the most widely used litmus test for 'subversive tendencies.'" On January 15, 1948, two months after making public his list, Attorney General Tom Clark told the Cathedral Club of Brooklyn: "Those who do not believe in the ideology of the United States shall not be allowed to stay in the United States." Later, Truman appointed Clark to the U.S. Supreme Court.

A more conspiratorial view of Truman's loyalty-security program emerged among so-called New Left historians during the divisive Vietnam War era. David Caute's *The Great Fear: The Anti-Communist Purge Under Truman and Eisenhower* perhaps best expresses their revisionist conclusion about the negative effects of Truman's anticommunist policies: "It was the liberals, rather than the reactionary Right or the heirs of Teddy Roosevelt's Rough Riders, who set the United States on the disastrously interventionist and egotistical course that culminated in the horror of the Vietnam War."

Certainly liberals cannot escape judgment for contributing to the climate that finally produced McCarthyism. By naïvely dismissing threats to U.S. security from Communist penetration of sensitive government agencies as entirely figments of a conspiratorial right-wing mentality, many liberals provided ammunition for the zealous anticommunists.*

Not *all* liberals were blind to the terrors imposed by Stalin's bloody regime, however. By the time McCarthyism arose, many liberals were already distancing themselves from youthful, and now dangerous, left-wing views and so-called front organizations. They saw clearly that Communism represented a very real threat to the Western democracies; that fear of Communism *was* warranted; that the Cold War stemmed in large measure from the Soviet Union's ambition to impose its will globally through overt force of arms, internal subversion, or a combination of both. At the same time, recognition of Cold War realities posed an anguishing dilemma for American liberals. As the historian Irving Howe writes of what he calls "ideas in conflict," "Wherever Stalinism conquered, freedom vanished . . . The Socialist intellectuals either went underground or abandoned socialism. The more thoughtful worked out a system of opposing both

---

*The political fissure that developed among liberals who warned about the reality of the Communist threat and those who dismissed it was perhaps best expressed by Arthur M. Schlesinger, Jr., in a *New York Times Magazine* article Nov. 2, 1947, when he wrote about the growing debate over loyalty: "Those who believe that the agitation over purging liberals—that this is a repetition of A. Mitchell Palmer and the Red Raids—are themselves mistaking a part for the whole. Times have changed a lot since A. Mitchell Palmer. In 1919 the U.S.S.R. was a torn and struggling nation with its back to the wall. Today, Soviet totalitarianism is massive, well-organized and on the march. Its spies and agents are ubiquitous. We face here not just a figment of the reactionary imagination but a proved problem for the security of free nations."

Communism and McCarthyism. The sudden upsurge of Mc-
Carthyism was to prove a crucial test for the intellectuals."

The revisionist view placing responsibility for McCarthyism on the liberals within the Truman administration ignores,
as political scientist Nelson Polsby says, two critical factors: the
role of the Soviet Union in creating anxieties during Mc-
Carthy's heyday, and the bitterly partisan Republican Party
politics of the time. It also ignores the fact that it was the administration's increasingly influential conservatives who helped
fashion the policies that contained the seeds of McCarthyism.

———

In the summer of 1950, the *American Scholar* published a disturbing survey gauging the impact of the Truman loyalty program on career federal service employees.

> The atmosphere in government is one of fear—fear of
> ideas and of irresponsible and unknown informers. Gov-
> ernment employees are afraid to attend meetings of polit-
> ically minded groups; they are afraid to read "liberal"
> publications; they screen their friends carefully for "left-
> wing" ideas. Government employees are in very real dan-
> ger of dying intellectually and politically. Everyone knows
> of someone who has been accused of disloyalty—and it
> amounts to an accusation of treason—on ridiculous
> charges. Nobody wants to go through a "loyalty" investiga-
> tion. The inclination and inevitable result are simply to re-
> strict one's own freedoms. All Americans suffer thereby.

———

By the time Truman left office in 1953, enormous damage had
been done. Derek Leebaert provides the following statistics:

"By 1953, the FBI had made some 26,000 field investigations under Truman's original sweeping executive order on 'loyalty.' That was in addition to 2 million 'name checks' of federal employees overall, resulting in about 2,700 dismissals within three years. It had 109,119 informants [one of whom was listed in FBI files as "Ronald Reagan, Warner Brothers Studio, Hollywood," who was assigned identifying number T-10] at more than 10,745 'vital facilities,' such as defense plants, research centers, dams, and telephone exchanges."

This was in addition, Leebaert notes, to the FBI's carrying out 23,800 "black-bag jobs" (breaking and entering), most of them without legal warrants, on homes and offices of suspects; accumulating painstakingly kept archives "on seemingly everyone except the officers of the Daughters of the American Revolution"; and launching vendettas against anyone who dared criticize the bureau publicly. This included, he writes, "A year's long investigative vendetta . . . waged over the 'hostility' of Senator Albert Gore, Sr., for daring to criticize Hoover, and the gathering of more than six hundred heavily censored pages on composer Leonard Bernstein, dating from the 1940s and beyond, "replete with insight [obtained] from his household garbage."

In California alone, reflecting states' copycat committees investigating un-American activities, "twenty thousand people were spied on before the records were sealed in 1971."

———

There was, as the historian Stephen Ambrose has written, an Alice in Wonderland-like quality to the charges McCarthy and his adherents later leveled against Truman, Acheson, Marshall, and other administration leaders.

It was, after all, Truman who dropped the first atomic bomb initiating the nuclear age and then oversaw the development of the hydrogen bomb, missiles, and families of lesser atomic weapons; Truman who approved the containment policies that shaped the Cold War and led the United States into its role of the world's policeman; Truman who negotiated peace treaties with enemies Germany and Japan that led to German rearmament and the exclusion of Russians from Japanese soil; Truman who forged U.S. alliances with fifty nations, enabling American military forces to be stationed in one hundred seventeen countries and to establish bases that hemmed in Russian and Chinese Communist forces everywhere; Truman who instantly committed U.S. armed forces to the Korean War; and Truman who created the Central Intelligence Agency, the Marshall Plan, and NATO.

By the time Truman left office, as the historian Walter Millis later observed, the country possessed "an enormously expanded military establishment, beyond anything we had ever contemplated in times of peace. . . . It evoked a huge and apparently permanent armament industry, now wholly dependent . . . on government contracts. The Department of Defense had become without question the biggest industrial management operation in the world; the great private operations, like General Motors, DuPont, the leading airplane manufacturers had assumed positions of monopoly power."

Despite its record and its domestic loyalty program, the Truman administration found itself increasingly on the defensive against charges of not doing more to confront Communism. In reaction, Truman's Cold War acts escalated at home and abroad. Stephen Ambrose describes the consequences well: "Chickens had come home to roost. From the time Truman had 'scared [the] hell out of the American people' in

March of 1947 to the explosion of the Russian bomb and the loss of China, Democratic officials in the State Department had been stressing the world-wide threat of Communism along with the danger of internal subversion in foreign governments. McCarthy and his adherents followed the same path, only they went further with it."

PART THREE

Dealing With a Demagogue

Chapter

EIGHT

The Press

*Many of the most celebrated excesses of "McCarthyism"
had occurred before he entered the scene, but most of
those earlier Red-baiters have been forgotten. What was it
about McCarthy that enabled him to dominate the
headlines, incense the Democrats, to make McCarthyism a
dictionary word, and to stamp the years 1946 through
1954 "the McCarthy decade?" All the answers to this
question concern McCarthy's relations with the press.*

—**Edwin R. Bayley,** *Joe McCarthy and the Press*

Without the massive publicity McCarthy generated, or his
extraordinary skill at manipulating the news media, Mc-
Carthy never would have imprinted himself so powerfully upon
the consciousness of the country. Nor, without the assistance of
the press, would his name have been transformed so quickly
into a common noun in the dictionary: **Mc·Car·thy·ism
1.** *public accusation of disloyalty to one's country, esp. through*

pro-Communist activity, in many instances unsupported by proof or based on slight, doubtful, or irrelevant evidence. **2.** *unfairness in investigative technique.*

The press's failure to hold McCarthy accountable was especially critical in the month after his Wheeling speech. First and lasting impressions about Joe McCarthy and his charges of traitors operating from the highest levels of the U.S. government were planted in the public mind. "If the press, through superbly accurate and interpretive reporting, keen news judgments, and brilliant headlines, had been able to show up McCarthy for the fraud that he was, this is when it would have had to be done," Bayley wrote of the days immediately following Wheeling. This was the time when "McCarthy's tactics should have been perceived and analyzed, when he was out in the open, without staff, feeling his way, developing the techniques that he employed later with more skill as he 'used' the press."

To the lasting discredit of the press, this did not happen.

Still, though the press helped create and perpetuate McCarthyism, it cannot be blamed for all the damage done the nation. Indeed, in the months and years to come as McCarthyism grew more powerful, spreading fear and doubt throughout American society, many reporters, columnists, and commentators tried admirably to hold him accountable for his falsehoods.* If anything, the responsibility politi-

---

*Standing out in that journalistic honor roll is the work of Mary McGrory, Murray Kempton, Richard Rovere, Marquis Childs, I.F. Stone, the Alsop brothers, Walter Lippmann, Edward R. Murrow, Drew Pearson, Martin Agronsky, Alan Barth, Murray Marder, Herblock, and the collective work of the *Washington Post*, the *New York Times*, the *New York Herald-Tribune*, the *New York Post* (in its liberal phase), the *St. Louis Post-Dispatch*, the *Milwaukee Journal*, the *Madison Capital Times*, the *New Yorker*, the *Nation*, and the *New Republic*.

cians bear for McCarthy's abuses is greater than that of the press. The politicians possessed the power to check McCarthy. They knew his true character. They knew his basic charges were false and his tactics disreputable. Their failures, coupled with those of the press, made possible the phenomenon of mass demagoguery that became known as McCarthyism.

Among the Red-baiters of his era, only McCarthy attacked the press itself, repeatedly singling out the news media as a central part of the Communist conspiracy. More so than any other example from the American experience—Nixon's press-bashing in the 1940s and 1950s, Agnew's attack on the "nattering nabobs of negativism" in the 1960s, or right-wing talk radio and attack TV commentators relentlessly targeting the press in the 1990s up to the present—McCarthy set in motion the ideological forces that demonized the press, sowing doubt about the media's credibility and even its patriotism. McCarthy's message—that the American press was infested with biased liberals and, of course, Communists and Socialists—has been a source of national political divisiveness and public distrust ever since.

Paradoxically, McCarthy enjoyed excellent personal relations with members of the press. He not only courted reporters and photographers but seemed genuinely to enjoy their company. They reciprocated. They socialized with and in many ways protected him. McCarthy and his friends in the press did each other favors. It seems private profit was also involved for some, particularly some of the photographers with whom McCarthy became close.

"Joe loved to play the horses," George Tames of the *New York Times,* one of the greatest of Washington photographers, recalled years after McCarthy's death. "Every time he wanted to make a bet, he would tell one of the boys what horse he wanted, and they would call it in. They would go to the race track quite often together."

This kind of closeness was relatively innocent, even if it contained an inherent conflict of interest for press and politician; not so innocent, however, was an incident Tames remembered involving McCarthy and a land deal in nearby suburban Virginia.

"One of my photographer friends came to me and said, 'Look, we've got a scheme. We can make a lot of money. We need ten photographers to come up with two thousand dollars each,'" Tames said.

His friend explained how the scheme would work. "South of Alexandria is a piece of swampland that's for sale for half a million dollars," he told Tames. "With twenty thousand dollars we can get an option to buy that land. Then we can go to the federal government and get a loan to build an apartment there. Not only that, we can get a loan of five million dollars [at an interest rate of only 2 percent], and it's only going to cost four and a half million to build it. Instead of giving the money back to the federal government, we divide the money."

"You can't do that," Tames replied.

They could, the friend said, "because we're going to get ten photographers and Joe McCarthy is going to be our silent partner. He's going to be in on it, as one-eleventh of the ownership. He's going to make all the arrangements to push it through."

Tames remained dubious. "I just couldn't believe it could be done," he recalled. "My mind just didn't work that way." But he said it *was* done. "Joe was going to see it done. And the beauty of it was, like I say, that not only did you build it and own it, but you divided half a million dollars and you had all this money. A lot of people became multimillionaires doing it." As for Tames, it turned out to be "another lost opportunity": he turned down that investment offer.

Tames also recalled an incident involving McCarthy's drinking. "He would preside over a hearing and he would excuse himself and go to the men's room, which was next to the elevator" near a hearing room on the fourth floor of the Russell Senate Office Building, Tames recalled, "and he'd have a flask of booze up [hidden] on top of the stall."

One day, with McCarthy absent and no hearing in progress, Tames entered that restroom. "I was by there and looked up and damn if his flask wasn't there . . . so I went up and got it. I have it . . . as one of my memorabilia [of my journalistic career]."

This kind of McCarthy behavior was never reported. It was all part of the game, an insider game in which press and politician forged a cozy, mutually beneficial relationship. Rules of the game, unwritten but observed, held that a reporter protected his sources; let himself be used in order to gain greater access and, thereby, exclusive stories; did not reveal politicians' personal misbehavior (drunkenness or sexual affairs), which might attract public notice; and clung to a specious journalistic standard of objectivity. By this standard, a public official's charge of egregious misconduct, corruption, or even treason was always reported as a lead news item, then somewhere in the same story duly (but never truly) balanced by denials from the subject of the charge. The accuracy of the charge often went unexamined. Even if it *was* analyzed or the charge put in perspective, dramatic headlines dominated the story and the news, creating for the public indelible impressions of conspiracy and wrongdoing. The headlines recounting the original charge made the front page; the follow-ups, if any, invariably did not.

Two episodes from those rancorous days after Wheeling are revealing.

The first took place when two reporters tracked McCarthy down in Reno before another Lincoln Day speech, only to see him tapping his teeth while on the phone, ostensibly to "break up the wiretap" Communists had placed on the line.

McCarthy had promised the press that he would name at least four "known Communists" in the State Department when he spoke that night. As the reporters watched McCarthy talking on the phone to his Washington office, they heard him say, "That's great, great," and, "Give me some more names," all the while furiously taking notes. Looking at McCarthy's pad, they saw he had written down one name as "Howard Shipley." This turned out to be one of the names he cited—incorrectly—in his speech that night. The person's name was actually Harlow Shapley.

Two things were apparent to the reporters who witnessed this scene. First, McCarthy had no idea who the people were whose names he was jotting down to include in his speech only a few hours later. Second, the only research he had done on the four people he promised to name as traitors was to call his staff and ask for names.

The reporters, Edward A. Olsen of the Associated Press and Frank McCulloch of the *Reno Gazette,* were confounded by what they observed. They were also distrustful of McCarthy's claim that he would "name names," which he warned could be cited in their stories only "at your own risk" of libel. To protect themselves, they hired a stenographer to take down McCarthy's exact words while he spoke.

The speech was classic McCarthyism, employing not only guilt by association, but also guilt by inference. McCarthy gave the appearance of naming traitors without actually doing so by naming four people but refusing to label them anything more than security risks. As McCulloch reported the next day in the *Gazette*, McCarthy made the inflammatory charge that spies had "been planted in the State Department to shape the policy of our government and rob this nation of its potency." But McCulloch also wrote that when a reporter asked McCarthy after his speech whether he meant to identify further the four people he had just cited as traitors, McCarthy answered: "I did not [call them traitors], and you will notice I did not call them Communists, either."

Olsen of the AP never had a harder time writing a story about a speech in his life, he later said. "The man just talked circles," he said. "Everything was by inference, allusion, never a concrete statement of fact. Most of it didn't make sense. I tried to get into my lead that he had named names but he didn't call them anything. AP New York didn't know what to do with it, and they asked me to file the whole text [of McCarthy's speech], which I did. But they couldn't do any better with it."

The second episode that struck the reporters as odd took place in the Mapes Hotel bar, where McCarthy and the two frustrated journalists continued their talk after the speech. "By three or four o'clock in the morning, we were stony drunk, McCarthy worst of all," Olsen recalled. "He and McCulloch and I were hollering back and forth about what a phony he was, and what phonies we were. At the end he was screaming at us that one of us had stolen his list of Communists. He'd lost it, and he knew he'd made a fool of himself." McCulloch commented sardonically: "He lost his list between his eighth and ninth bourbons." Earlier, McCulloch's managing editor told him that he had seen McCarthy that afternoon in a bar called the Sky Room, drinking with "an old Marine Corps buddy" who lived in Reno.

None of this was reported—not that McCarthy got the names of his alleged Communists over the phone, not that he didn't know who the accused were or how to spell their names, not that he had been drinking before his speech and later was involved in an angry drunken exchange in a Reno bar.

As Ed Bayley later said, "Reporters covered politics then as if it were a stage play; only what happened in public counted."

These journalistic practices did not end with the McCarthy era. Too many journalists still rely too heavily on official sources. They still fail to hold sources accountable; still accept too passively the secrecy that increasingly pervades government; still allow themselves to be used by becoming the recipients of anonymous high-level "leaks" intended to advance the position of the leakers and to discredit—or destroy—the reputations of critics who possess damaging information.*

---

*A disgraceful example occurred in 2003 when anonymous top Bush administration officials "leaked" the name of a CIA undercover operative, Valerie Plame, to a prominent Washington columnist, Robert Novak. The agent's husband, Joseph Wilson, a former ambassador, had investigated and disproved the President's public claim that Iraq was secretly seeking to obtain nuclear bomb-making material from the African nation of Niger, thus undercutting the president's case for launching war against Iraq. The leak occurred even though it was illegal to disclose an undercover agent's name, and the columnist ran the agent's name in print.

Some things have changed, of course. In our present tabloid news culture, with its ceaseless preoccupation with trivial scandal and the search for sensational—or deplorable—details about the private lives of public figures, Joe McCarthy's excessive drinking and public drunkenness would never go unreported. Nor would certain of his other less attractive character traits. But now the journalistic standard for effective coverage of issues of public interest has been so lowered, if not obliterated, that the very reliance on scandal coverage too often becomes lead news. This makes it difficult for the public to gain insight into the complicated, far more significant issues of the day. In this, the lessons of McCarthyism still apply.

––––––

Despite reporters' failure to provide a fuller accounting of McCarthy's behavior and deceitful practices during his Reno stopover, his public performance was enough to produce some critical stories. The headlines from the *Milwaukee Journal* read, "McCarthy List Down to Four; 'Not Reds or Traitors'"; the *St. Louis Post-Dispatch* said, "McCarthy Names Four in Red Charges and Then Hedges; Senator Lists Them as 'Specific Cases of People with Communist Connections.'" In an editorial entitled, "McCarthy Does Some Backtracking," the *Post-Dispatch* pointed out that not only was McCarthy using different numbers every day in his claims about the known Communists in the State Department; he was also deflating his charges as he traveled. The rival *St. Louis Globe-Democrat* commented that, in addition to there being no Communists or traitors on McCarthy's "Red list," three of the four people he named in Reno were not even employed by the State Department.

These headlines and editorials were notable exceptions. More typical of the coverage McCarthy received was the Huron, South Dakota, *Plainsman's* account of his appearance at another Lincoln Day event. The page one story, printed under a two-column picture of McCarthy, read, in words echoing Wheeling's coverage: "A grim picture of a United States that is in a 'showdown fight with Communism' while its foreign policy is shaped by 'traitorous actions' in the State Department was painted by a fighting Irishman and ex-Marine."

Such coverage generated strong grassroots support for McCarthy. He had barely left Huron when a South Dakota state senator introduced a concurrent resolution in the legislature demanding that Congress and the president check on "the loyalties of the men employed in the State Department from Dean Acheson on down." The resolution passed both houses of the legislature four days after it was introduced— with no debate.

———

On the last leg of his swing through the American hinterland before he returned to Washington, McCarthy flew from South Dakota to Wisconsin. In Milwaukee, he phoned a *Milwaukee Journal* editorial writer named Paul Ringler and suggested they meet for lunch. McCarthy knew that Ringler had already written two critical editorials about his charges and wanted to repair any political damage done by the paper with the largest circulation in the state.

"Joe tried to maintain good relations with *Journal* people until the end," Ringler recalled. "Partly I suppose this was good political sense, but even more it was a total failure to understand why we were opposing and criticizing him. He was so totally amoral that he believed we should understand that this was all political gamesmanship—that no matter what he said, it shouldn't make any difference between friends."

Ringler accepted McCarthy's luncheon invitation as an opportunity to find out what information McCarthy really had about traitors in high places. Because he wanted to protect himself by having witnesses present when he and McCarthy met, he asked two *Journal* reporters who later became noted Washington correspondents, Robert H. Fleming and John Hoving, to accompany him.

They met McCarthy on a Saturday afternoon at Moy Toy, a small Chinese restaurant popular with *Journal* people. "What a session that was!" Ringler remembered. "The three of us used everything but the third degree in trying to get some hard evidence. He was at his evasive best. We cajoled, we pleaded, we insulted. Finally, I said, 'Joe, I don't believe you've got a goddamn thing to prove the things you've been saying. It's all a lot of political hogwash.'"

McCarthy flushed, pounded the table, and shouted: "Listen, you bastards. I'm not going to tell you anything. I just want you to know I've got a pailfull of shit and I'm going to use it where it does me the most good."

This conversation went unreported, as did a critical part of a session with reporters that took place immediately after McCarthy returned to Washington.

On his first day back in the capital, McCarthy, now a national figure, found his outer office filled with journalists waiting amid the din of ringing phones. Two correspondents representing smaller Wisconsin papers elbowed their way through the crowd and into McCarthy's inner office, where he had agreed to give them an interview.

"We'd like the names," one of them told McCarthy. "The two hundred five Communists."

"Look, you guys," McCarthy said, "That was just a political speech to a bunch of Republicans. Don't take it seriously."

"Don't you have any names?"

"Oh, one was a college professor," McCarthy said.

"Where?"

"A professor of astronomy," McCarthy answered. "Another was a professor of anthropology, a woman. But it was just a political talk."

In accounts filed for their publications, the journalists didn't report McCarthy's breezy dismissal of the Wheeling address as "just a political speech to a bunch of Republicans." Instead, they focused on the national controversy McCarthy was stirring. Hours later, McCarthy prepared to take his case before the United States Senate, where he promised—he announced grandly to the press before going to the Capitol—to give his fellow senators "detailed information" about Communists in the State Department.

Chapter

NINE

The Politicians

*Let me have him for three days . . . and he'll never
show his face in the Senate again.*

—Democratic Senator Millard Tydings on Joe McCarthy

The enormity of the lies Joe McCarthy set forth on the
night of February 20, 1950, was staggering. Nothing like
the audacity of his attack, the boldness of his bluff, and the
shamelessness of his falsehoods had ever happened before.
Nothing like it has happened since. When it was all over,
shortly before midnight, McCarthy had demonstrated how
unprepared his colleagues were to deal with him, and how
difficult it was going to be for the political system to check
such a consummate demagogue.

A few minutes after five o'clock, McCarthy, clutching his bulging tan briefcase, strode across the Senate floor to the podium and began to address his colleagues. He was going to lay out before them, he said, "a subject which concerns me more than any other subject I have ever discussed before this body." That was "the extent to which Communists have infiltrated into the State Department and are shaping its policy."

He had pierced the "iron curtain" of State Department secrecy, he claimed, with the help of anonymous patriotic informants—"some good, loyal Americans in the State Department" whose identities he would forever protect. Through these informants he had obtained damning new information about the espionage and treason threatening America, documented by the photostatic files of classified investigatory dossiers crammed into his briefcase. Or so he maintained, speaking solemnly and with deliberate sincerity. "I know that the State Department is very eager to know how I have secured this information," he said. "I know that the jobs of the men who helped me secure it would be worth nothing if [their] names were given."

He was explicit about the contents of his briefcase: "The files which I have here show the source of the information," he said. "I contacted one of the federal intelligence agencies, one of the investigative units. I asked them if they would care to go over what I have to say before I say it, and red-pencil anything which they thought might in any way divulge the source of information, that would in any way inform the Communist spy ring of the information they have."

He quickly backtracked on a promise to let the Senate "see them," saying it would be improper to make the files public until a Senate committee studied them in executive session, lest "one man [be labeled] a Communist when he is not a Communist." He also reneged on a promise made that night to permit fellow senators to examine the files later in the privacy of his Senate office.

It was all a fraud. There was no such "State Department list." McCarthy had not obtained new secret State Department files from patriotic anonymous sources. Instead, the papers he pulled from his briefcase and read to the Senate were from old State Department loyalty investigative files compiled three years earlier by a House Appropriations Committee investigator and friend of McCarthy's named Robert E. Lee.

———

The Lee list was neither new nor entirely accurate; since 1947 it had been widely circulated throughout congressional and executive department offices—though apparently not so much in the Senate, as it was a House document. Originally, it contained one hundred eight dossiers on past and present State Department employees and many job applicants. McCarthy pared down the Lee list, saying he possessed eighty-one dossiers on "loyalty risks." He would now reveal details about them. Long before McCarthy recited this old material before the Senate, every person on the list had been fully investigated by the FBI. By the time he spoke, only about forty persons were still State Department employees. Nor did the Lee list ever claim that the "derogatory information" included about the individuals investigated meant they all were Communists, traitors, or spies. The Lee list never named its subjects; instead, it identified them by numbers, beginning with a dossier labeled Case No. 1. To obscure the source of his material, McCarthy randomly changed the numbers on the Lee

152 / THE POLITICIANS

list. For instance, his Case No. 1 was actually Case No. 51 on the Lee list. His No. 9 was Lee's 99. His 12, Lee's 107. While McCarthy pretended he didn't name these disloyal government employees because of a desire to protect them from false accusations, his real reason was dishonorable. Though he told the Senate that he had the names of all eighty-one suspects, not until a month later would he obtain a key to the Lee list that matched the names of those investigated with the numbers on their case reports. Until then, he had no names to name. He didn't know who they were, or even if they still held government jobs. The fraud McCarthy was perpetuating was immense.

In addition to changing the numbers, he altered the language in each case report, twisting the findings of the original investigation, exaggerating testimony, adding new and fallacious material of his own, and throughout, as Robert Griffith noted, wringing from it "the most sinister and sensational implications." He eliminated modifying or exculpatory facts and conclusions, and omitted all qualifiers. Where the Lee list described one person as "inclined toward Communism," to McCarthy "he was a Communist." Someone identified as a "liberal" on the Lee list, became to McCarthy someone "Communistically inclined." An "active fellow traveler" became "an active Communist." McCarthy transformed an unsuccessful job applicant into someone who had been given "a top-secret job clearance." The "considerable derogatory information" on one Lee list individual became to McCarthy "conclusive evidence of . . . Communist activity."

McCarthy's characterization of the Lee list suspects had been, biographer Reeves writes, "one of the most fantastic and supremely dishonest performances ever witnessed on

THE AGE OF ANXIETY / 153

Capitol Hill. Even William F. Buckley, Jr., and L. Brent Bozell later said that Joe deserved Senate censure for lying about the source of his information." But case by case, his citations from the Lee list that night in the Senate seemed to document treasonous behavior at the heart of the American government.

> The Lee list: This employee is with the Office of Informa-
> tion and Educational Exchange in New York City. His
> application is very sketchy. There has been no investi-
> gation. C-8 [an anonymous informant] is a reference.
> Though he is 43 years of age, his file reflects no history
> prior to June 1941.
>
> McCarthy: This individual is 43 years of age. He is with the
> Office of Information and Education. According to the
> file, he is a known Communist. I might say that when I
> refer to someone being a known Communist, I am not
> evaluating the information myself. I am merely giving
> what is in the file. This individual also found his way
> into the Voice of America broadcast. Apparently the
> easiest way to get in is to be a Communist.

> The Lee list: A report of December 31, 1946, reflects that
> witnesses describe her as being: "liberal," "pink," "no
> more of a security risk than many others if kept under
> proper supervision." She has been quoted as saying,
> "Everyone in Russia has equal rights" and that in this
> country minority rights are persecuted.
>
> McCarthy: A security report dated December 31, 1946, de-
> scribes her as being "pink" and as advocating that we
> substitute conditions in Russia for those in the United
> States.

> The Lee list: The informant also advised that a brother of
> the subject was a member of, and active in, the Jack-
> son Heights, Long Island, Branch of the Communist
> Party in 1944. Further information was obtained that
> the subject himself has been a member of the Commu-
> nist Party.

> McCarthy: His brother, who either was or is in the State
> Department, was a member of the Jackson Heights
> Branch of the Communist Party. . . . The file indicates
> that this man is not only very active as a Communist,
> but is a very dangerous Communist.

McCarthy also excluded any material that expressly
cleared an individual. In his Case No. 1, McCarthy didn't
mention that a full field loyalty investigation found "nothing
derogatory" about the person examined. His Case No. 6 omitted this finding from the Lee list: "On January 7, 1947, a memorandum summarizing the investigation stated that nothing
was developed tending to affect adversely the subject's loyalty." His Case No. 46 correctly noted that a State Department report of March 22, 1947, raised questions about an
individual's loyalty. But McCarthy did *not* tell the Senate that
the Department's security officer, in a memorandum of June
18, 1947, concluded: "It is not believed by this office that the
information at hand raises a reasonable doubt as to [subject's]
loyalty to the United States and, accordingly, security clearance is recommended."

McCarthy did not merely raise the alarming specter of
traitors in high places. He also smeared these "loyalty risks"
by claiming the files contained anonymous allegations about
their immorality, their homosexuality, their disbelief in a "Supreme Being." One file, he said, disclosed "unusual mental

aberrations of certain individuals in the Department." He quoted—anonymously—"one of our top intelligence men in Washington as saying, 'You will find that practically every active Communist is twisted mentally or physically in some way.'" From then on, McCarthy branded Communists and traitors as either being, or associating with, "queers" and secret homosexuals. His explicit homophobic attacks became part of his blanket characterization of un-Americanism, just as did his linking "godless" or "atheistic" Communism with liberals. These themes won him support among cultural conservatives in Middle America and the Deep South.

––––––––

In the months and years to come, there would be many moments when the political system would attempt, and fail, to counter Joe McCarthy. But if there was one moment when the system could—and should—have stopped him, it was this night. Yet McCarthy emerged from this moment before his Senate colleagues stronger than ever.

His success wasn't for a lack of critical reaction to him. From the beginning, three Democrats—Majority Leader Scott Lucas of Illinois, Brian McMahon of Connecticut, and Herbert Lehman of New York—confronted McCarthy. They demanded that McCarthy name the "card-carrying Communists" he had talked about on the road. They demanded he provide dates, facts, documentation. They demanded that he clear up the many discrepancies in accounts of what he had said in Wheeling and his other Lincoln Day appearances. Had he mentioned two hundred five, fifty-seven, two hundred seven, or eighty-one Communists? Which was it? Did he actually have complete State Department files? If so, he should make them available now.

The exchanges became heated and ugly. Lucas interrupted McCarthy sixty-one times, McMahon thirty-four times, Lehman thirteen times. To every interruption, every challenge, McCarthy responded in character. He fought back, made more false accusations. He pulled a mass of papers from his briefcase and spread the pages out on two tables. As he parried interruptions and challenges, he pawed through his papers to retrieve and read from yet another case that supposedly proved pervasive disloyalty. His language, as usual, was evasive and confusing. At one point Lehman, who had succeeded Franklin Roosevelt as governor of New York and played a prominent role in the New Deal before being elected to the Senate, demanded that McCarthy tell his story in clear language. McCarthy replied contemptuously: "I am afraid if it is not clear to the senator now, I shall never be able to make it clear to him, no matter how much further explanation I make."

Standing behind his lectern piled with documents, McCarthy said any senator who wanted to examine his evidence was free to do so. Only one senator, Herbert Lehman, tried to take up McCarthy. Stewart Alsop, the columnist, watching that scene from the press gallery above, captured a moment that demonstrated the degree to which McCarthy had intimidated the Senate. "With his funny waddling walk and his heart full of courage," Alsop wrote, "Herbert Lehman came over to McCarthy's desk and stood in front of it, his hand held out for the documents." He stood there alone, waiting. Then, as Alsop reported what happened next:

> The two men stared at each other, and McCarthy giggled his strange, rather terrifying little giggle. Lehman looked

around the crowded Senate, obviously appealing for support. Not a man rose. "Go back to your seat, old man," McCarthy growled at Lehman. The words do not appear in the *Congressional Record,* but they were clearly audible in the press gallery. Once more, Lehman looked all around the chamber, appealing for support. He was met with silence and lowered eyes. Slowly, he turned and walked [back to his seat]. The silence of the Senate that evening was a measure of the fear which McCarthy inspired in almost all politicians. . . . Old Senator Lehman's back, waddling off in retreat, seemed to symbolize the final defeat of decency.

As the bitterness of the exchange increased that night, so did the partisan divisions. Now Republican ultraconservatives—Ferguson of Michigan, Mundt of South Dakota, Capehart of Indiana, Wherry of Nebraska, Brewster of Maine—rallied behind McCarthy. They answered the Democrats for McCarthy, rescued him when he faltered, prompted him with softball questions, jeeringly reminded Democrats that many in their party had stood behind the traitor Alger Hiss, who had been convicted just a month before.

Republican moderates, including distinguished figures such as Henry Cabot Lodge and Robert A. Taft, personally had little respect for McCarthy. But they kept their silence. Everyone understood that Communists in government would be a major issue in the midterm elections that fall. McCarthy, respectable or not, could be the key to Republican victory. Taft, for one, was looking beyond the 1950 elections: he was already planning to run for president in 1952. Taft was later quoted as calling McCarthy's behavior that night "a perfectly reckless performance" and McCarthy's charges "nonsense."

Nonetheless, he began backing McCarthy publicly and encouraged him to "keep talking." He was quoted as privately advising McCarthy: "If one case doesn't work out . . . proceed with another."

Not a single Democrat present seems to have been aware that McCarthy was reading from the old Lee list that night. As David Oshinsky writes, the Democrats were "curiously unprepared" and "their lack of preparation made an effective counterattack almost impossible." Not so the Republicans. At least one Republican senator, Ferguson, clearly followed McCarthy's presentation with a copy of the Lee list before him. At one point, referring to the cases McCarthy cited, Ferguson even asked McCarthy, "I wondered why the senator took them out of order. Is there any reason why he did not take them in order, beginning with number one and going down through them?" McCarthy brushed the question aside, then returned to more accounts of dangerous loyalty risks. Ferguson did not pursue his question.

When a weary Senate adjourned late that night, a profound political turn had occurred, though not everyone recognized it then. Joe McCarthy had directly confronted his critics, in both press and politics, and far from backing away from his charges, had escalated them. By evening's end, Democrats realized that Joe McCarthy would not easily be vanquished. Nor would he go away. They would have to deal with him more aggressively and definitively.

———

Once more, McCarthy won the battle of the headlines. He was portrayed as having taken his evidence directly to the Senate, and held his ground in the face of politically motivated heckling and interruptions. Determining the accuracy of his charges that night was near impossible for the press, but in at least some news accounts McCarthy was credited with having provided key senators with new and authentic documents. The Associated Press, for instance, reported to its worldwide subscribers that McCarthy had shown senators "photographs of records."

The next evening, after huddling in a private day-long session, Democratic leaders reached an agreement: they would call for an official Senate investigation into McCarthy's charges. The Democrats remained clueless. They believed that McCarthy's falsehoods were so transparent and outrageous that they would emerge victorious from any encounter with him. They still controlled the Senate and believed the public would back them when they challenged McCarthy. They thought McCarthy, whom they considered the Republican Party's weakest as well as most controversial senator, could even be an asset for them. Exposing McCarthy for the fraud he was could reverse their political slide in the aftermath of Hiss and other spy revelations, which had sapped confidence in the Democratic administration.

The investigation was an opportunity McCarthy had been advocating. In effect, Joe McCarthy would be tried by a panel of his peers—which is what he wanted. He was more convinced than ever that he could continue to dominate the news as he had for the last astounding month and, by playing on public fears of traitors, continue to build political support.

Two days after McCarthy had poked the tigers of the Senate and showed them to be toothless and clawless, the Senate adopted Resolution 231, authorizing "a full and complete study and investigation as to whether persons who are disloyal to the United States are or have been employed by the Department of State." Hearings were scheduled to begin in two weeks.

Majority Leader Lucas asked Tom Connally of Texas, chairman of the powerful Foreign Relations Committee, to head the investigation. Connally, a caricature of an old-style southern senator, with flowing white hair and florid speech, declined. When asked why, he was quoted as saying, "I have more important things to do than go to a skunk hunt." Lucas next turned to Millard E. Tydings of Maryland, one of the most powerful Democrats in the Senate establishment.

Vain and able, Tydings was a loyal Democrat but no party hack, and no liberal. He had opposed many New Deal reforms and after the 1936 election demonstrated his independence by publicly opposing FDR's attempt to pack the Supreme Court; he survived Roosevelt's attempt to purge him and other "defecting" Democrats from the Senate. As chairman of the Senate Armed Services Committee, Tydings had earned a reputation as a strong anticommunist and was known for his hard-line anti-Soviet positions. Politically, he seemed just the person to take on Joe McCarthy.

After twice rejecting urgent overtures from Senate leaders, Tydings finally accepted the job. He had been reluctant primarily because chairing the committee might take time from his reelection effort in the fall. But Tydings wasn't seriously concerned about his own political vulnerability. He was the overwhelming favorite to win in the race.

Millard Tydings was by far the most powerful politician in Maryland. No other public figure in the state had established a stronger political base or possessed such enviable credentials: World War I hero of trench warfare in France, where he rose from a machine-gunner Army private to colonel; member of the Maryland House of Delegates, then its Speaker; sponsor of the bill that created the present University of Maryland; member of Congress, where he served four years in the House before being elected to the Senate in 1927—and reelected every campaign since. Now, at the age of fifty-nine, twenty-three years after becoming a senator, he was at the peak of his political influence.

Within days of Tydings agreeing to head the investigating committee, Democratic confidence in exposing McCarthy was bolstered when it became known that he had been reading from the old Lee list instead of the new State Department dossiers he claimed to have.

It hadn't taken State Department security officials long to discover McCarthy's source. "Similar—perhaps identical— charges have been aired and thoroughly investigated before," Secretary of State Acheson told reporters in dismissing McCarthy's latest attacks. Truman, at another press conference, again denounced McCarthy's charges as false and continued to refuse to open the State Department's loyalty files, as McCarthy once more was demanding. The columnist Drew Pearson next reported more details of McCarthy's fraudulent use of the Lee list.

The story was out, though as usual the follow-up accounts didn't top the original page one headlines. Still, Democrats were convinced that this time they would crush McCarthy. No one was more confident than Millard Tydings, who held McCarthy in deep contempt. "Let me have him for three days in public hearings and he'll never show his face in the Senate again," Tydings boasted.

Chapter
TEN

The Network

We met "most discreetly."

Joe McCarthy didn't make it to the top by his wits alone. He reached his heights with the backing of an ever-expanding network of anticommunists.

This so-called McCarthy lobby was a highly diverse group, bound together by passionate opposition to Communism, but also by self-interest. It included conservative reporters, columnists, and radio commentators such as George Sokolsky, Westbrook Pegler, Fulton Lewis, Jr., Ralph de Toledano, and Walter Trohan; publishers such as those in the McCormick, Hearst, and Scripps-Howard chains; former Communists such as Whittaker Chambers, J.B. Matthews, Louis Budenz, and Freda Utley; political operatives such as Robert E. Lee of the Lee list; ultraconservative congressional Republicans in both House and Senate; representatives of Chiang Kai-shek's Nationalist China lobby; wealthy patrons such as Joseph P.

Kennedy and Claire Boothe Luce; militantly anticommunist Catholics such as New York's Francis Cardinal Spellman and Bishop Fulton J. Sheen; and an assortment of conspiracy-minded ideologues, true believers, and zealous right-wingers. Holding them together also was their connection to J. Edgar Hoover and his FBI.

Ed Nellor, a reporter with close ties to Richard Nixon from the Hiss case days and a dedicated conservative whom McCarthy hired from the *Washington Times-Herald* before setting out for Wheeling, described Hoover as McCarthy's "booster, backer, supplier of information." By the late 1940s, McCarthy and Hoover were going to the race track together, where they shared Hoover's private box, an invitation the FBI director apparently offered no other senator. Hoover also entertained McCarthy at his home. By the time of the Wheeling speech, Hoover and his closest aide, Clyde Tolson, were meeting with McCarthy and a former FBI agent named Don Surine for lunch, sometimes as often as once a week, at Harvey's Restaurant in Washington. "I tell you confidentially," Surine later told biographer Reeves, the four met "most discreetly," for Hoover would have been in trouble with the administration had news of the luncheons leaked out.* Surine added that Hoover was "very close to Joe."

---

*Surine, who deserves fuller treatment than I can provide here, was one of those fascinating behind-the-scenes operatives who could be cast in a lurid spy novel. Six foot four inches, lean, with the look of a "coiled spring," he was a "restless, relentless, perceptive, cold-blooded" operator with a disreputable past. He had been fired from the FBI after his relationship with a prostitute was uncovered during an FBI white slavery investigation. But he and Hoover remained close. The complete file of the remarkably revealing Reeves-Surine lengthy conversations, telephone

Surine, whom McCarthy hired a week before Wheeling upon Hoover's direct recommendation, became a key McCarthy operative. Hoover's FBI was the source for other McCarthy hires as well, and the FBI connection extended beyond McCarthy's personal staff: ex-FBI agents were sprinkled throughout Capitol Hill, often playing key roles on congressional committees investigating Communism as well as on congressional staffs. They exchanged information and worked together on political strategy to combat Communism.

For all his bravado, McCarthy could not operate without this network, and he was shrewd enough to know he needed it more than ever for the Tydings committee investigation. McCarthy began urgently gathering information that he could use to defend himself on his claims of subversion. His staff, headed by Surine and Nellor, moved throughout the capital, talking to sources, seeking new leads, examining old congressional hearing transcripts, reports, and documents in a Library of Congress room made available to them. In just two weeks, the gavel would bang down in the marbled Senate Caucus Room, opening the Tydings inquiry. They worked almost around the clock to prepare for that moment.

McCarthy sought Nixon's aid in examining the House Un-American Activities Committee's still-secret files. He attended a private strategy session of anticommunist leaders in the apartment of the ultraconservative Senator Styles Bridges of New Hampshire. Among those present were Nixon, Senator

---

interviews, and exchange of letters, covering several years beginning in 1977, are in the archives of the Wisconsin Historical Society. Also in those archives are the legal documents involving disposition of Surine's "white-slavery" case. So, too, are the files of the equally long and revealing exchanges between Reeves and McCarthy staffer Ed Nellor.

William Knowland of California, Lee of the list, and Senator Kenneth B. Wherry of Nebraska. A few weeks later, Wherry told a reporter the reason for that meeting. "Oh," said Wherry, the GOP's floor leader, "Mac has gone out on a limb and kind of made a fool of himself, and we have to back him up now."

Among others with whom McCarthy pleaded to give help for "the cause" was William Randolph Hearst, Jr. Later Hearst said: "Joe never had any names. He came to us. 'What am I gonna do? You gotta help me.' So we gave him a few good reporters." Some journalists in the network did more than offer tips and investigative information; they worked with Nellor to draft speeches for McCarthy and to prepare replies to his critics.

McCarthy also reached out to Boss Coleman in Wisconsin. Coleman had spent the week before the hearings in Washington, soliciting support in the capital among the Right, and then began a national fundraising campaign that targeted wealthy ultraconservatives. Money poured in.

During this period, McCarthy began traveling on weekends to the Westminster, Maryland, farm of Whittaker Chambers who, according to Nellor, "convinced and sustained" McCarthy's belief that America was in danger from internal spies. Chambers, Nellor added, became something of a philosopher for McCarthy, a "spell-binding" presence who "mightily impressed" him.* Accompanying McCarthy on these visits was his attractive twenty-five-year-old aide, Jean Kerr,

---

*Nellor's account notwithstanding, Chambers "detested" McCarthy. As Sam Tanenhaus writes in his definitive *Whittaker Chambers: A Biography,* Chambers refused to become a cheerleader for McCarthy, saying: "For the Right to tie itself in any way to Senator McCarthy is suicide. He is a raven of disaster."

"an extremely conservative Irish woman" who worked with Surine, Nellor, and others to provide McCarthy with research, writing, and advice.

By March 8, when Millard Tydings gaveled his committee to order, McCarthy was as prepared as he could be for a battle that would last, off and on, for nearly four months.

As in the Malmédy hearings, once again McCarthy blustered, bluffed, shouted, made misleading and outright false statements, and failed totally to prove his case to the satisfaction of any objective observer. He didn't document the existence of a State Department spy ring. He didn't clarify the discrepancies between his Wheeling and other speeches. He didn't produce the names of the eighty-one people on his loyalty list; not until March 20, exactly a month after his wild Senate performance, did he turn the Lee list over to the committee. Instead, he offered the committee nine new cases of supposed disloyalty, none of which he was able to prove, all of which were familiar to earlier anticommunist investigators. But his new cases generated more front page coverage.

When presenting his "evidence" to the committee, McCarthy promised not to hide behind Senate immunity. He pledged to colleagues that, "On the day when I take advantage of the security we have on the Senate floor, on that day I will resign from the Senate. Anything I say on the floor of the Senate at any time will be repeated off the floor."

The heart of McCarthy's defense, and the most sensational of his charges, came two weeks into the hearings. He announced to the press that he intended to unmask "the top Russian agent," the "boss" of Alger Hiss. He was prepared to "stand or fall" on the accuracy of his case against this "master spy and traitor." In an off-the-record session with reporters, he leaked the master spy's name, which instantly made the rounds in Washington, but wasn't published for fear of a libel suit.

Subsequently, before the committee (though never off the Senate floor) McCarthy named this "Soviet agent" as Owen Lattimore, an academic at Johns Hopkins University and an expert on Asia whom FDR had chosen in 1941 to serve as a political adviser to Chiang Kai-shek. In an extraordinarily charged moment, Lattimore appeared before the Tydings committee. In a ten-thousand-word prepared statement that took him nearly two hours to read aloud, Lattimore rebutted McCarthy's charges, assailed McCarthy's conduct as "unworthy of a senator or an American," and denounced McCarthy for "base and contemptible lies." He challenged McCarthy to repeat his accusations off the Senate floor, taunting him for failing to keep his promise to resign from the Senate if he declined to repeat in public charges he had made under the cloak of congressional immunity. "He has failed to do so," Lattimore said, "and he has not resigned."*

---

*In years to come Lattimore continued to be a target of anticommunists. In 1952 he was indicted on seven counts of perjury for telling a Senate internal security subcommittee that he had not promoted Communism and Communist interests. Three years later all charges in the flimsy case were dropped. The government abandoned its prosecution. Though he was never proven to have been a Soviet spy or agent, and nothing about him turned up in the Soviet Venona intercepts, Lattimore's reputation suffered greatly under continuous attacks of anticommunists. Eventually he moved to England.

Unembarrassed, McCarthy announced that he would produce a mystery witness who would testify that Lattimore had been a Communist Party member for several years. The witness was Louis Budenz, an active Communist in the 1930s and a one-time managing editor of the *Daily Worker.* Budenz had turned on the party and become a celebrated FBI informant; he was working with the Bureau for as much as eighteen hours a week. He was also a prominent—and highly paid—lecturer on the Soviet menace, a frequent star witness before congressional committees, and a key figure in the anticommunist network that supplied McCarthy with leads and lines of attack.

His appearance was a disaster. After testifying that he was told Lattimore was a member of a Communist cell in the late 1930s, and that he saw secret politburo reports written by Lattimore to other Communists, Budenz's credibility was shattered under questioning. Despite his long and vaunted relationship with the FBI and his claim that he was then working with the agency to compile a list of four hundred "concealed" Communists in the U.S., he admitted that he had not told the FBI about Lattimore's alleged party membership until a few weeks before, after he learned that the Tydings committee was investigating Lattimore and had been given a summary FBI file on him. Budenz further admitted that he had no first-hand knowledge of Lattimore's Communist membership, had never met him, and was unfamiliar with his allegedly subversive writings. Neither could Budenz explain why a transcript of a conversation that took place a year earlier between him and the editor of *Colliers* magazine showed that he had denied Lattimore was a Communist agent.

A critical moment in Budenz's testimony came when Edward P. Morgan, the committee's chief counsel, asked whether he considered Lattimore the top Soviet spy in the United States, as McCarthy had charged. "Well, to my knowledge, that statement is technically not accurate," Budenz replied. "I do not know, of course, the whole story, what other evidence there is, but from my own knowledge I would not say he was a top Soviet agent."

McCarthy backpedaled, then launched audacious counterassaults—in the hearing room, on the Senate floor, before clamoring reporters and audiences both in and outside Washington. As David Oshinsky points out, McCarthy's greatest asset came from outside the hearing room, in the country beyond the nation's capital.

Americans felt increasingly anxious about events at home and abroad from Communist traitors within to the prospect of a Soviet nuclear attack without. Their anxiety was instantly translated into primary election upsets that spring. In Florida, Senator Claude Pepper, a passionate New Dealer who had been close to FDR, was defeated by George Smathers in a bitter campaign. He was called "Red Pepper"—not for his red hair, but for his liberal views—a supposed friend of Stalin. In North Carolina, another liberal Democrat, Senator Frank Graham—formerly an admired university president—was defeated by Willis Smith after a vicious campaign in which Graham's moderate views on race were attacked and he was falsely accused of holding membership in eighteen Communist fronts.

Nationwide, states and municipalities enacted stern new anticommunist statutes and ordinances. This legislation eerily resembled that of the Red Scare during the World War I era. Professional wrestlers had to sign loyalty oaths in Indiana. A license to sell second-hand furniture was denied a man who had invoked his Fifth Amendment rights during a Communism inquiry in the District of Columbia. Communists were declared ineligible for unemployment benefits in Ohio. Pennsylvania barred Communists from receiving state aid—but made an exception for blind Communists. Every school district in Nebraska was required to inspect textbooks for foreign ideas and to set aside hours each week for the singing of patriotic songs. All Communists were ordered to leave Birmingham, Alabama. It was a crime for citizens to communicate with current or former Communists in Jacksonville, Florida. The death penalty was mandated for anyone seeking to overthrow the state government in Tennessee.

Joe McCarthy thrived in this atmosphere. As Oshinsky writes:

> Quickly people associated McCarthy with the hatred and the tension that gripped America. In three short months he had emerged as the nation's dominant Cold War politician—the new yardstick by which citizens measured patriotic or scurrilous behavior. Not since Franklin Roosevelt had a public figure been as clearly identified with the country's mood, or held as responsible for its excesses. The more Americans worried about the Russians, atomic war, loyalty oaths, or spies in government, the more they thought about Joe McCarthy. And the less certain they seemed about their own future.

Events in Washington reinforced these anxieties. In the third week of the Tydings hearings, Harry Truman was unable to restrain his anger during a news conference at his Key West vacation retreat when a reporter asked, "Do you think Senator McCarthy can show that any disloyalty exists in the State Department?" The president replied:

"I think that the greatest asset the Kremlin has is Senator McCarthy."

"Brother," a reporter said, "will that hit the front page tomorrow!"

Truman then poured gasoline on the fire.

Question: "Mr. President, would you like to name any others beside Senator McCarthy who have participated in this attempt to sabotage our foreign policy?"

Blunt as ever, Truman blurted out the names of Wherry and Bridges, two of McCarthy's most outspoken Senate Republican supporters.

Now the Republicans, led by Bob Taft, launched a fierce personal assault on the president, who had already been plummeting in the opinion polls. Truman, Taft railed, was guilty of a "bitter and prejudiced attack." The president had "slandered" McCarthy, "a fighting Marine who risked his life to preserve the liberties of the United States." As for the Kremlin's "greatest asset in America," Taft said it was "the pro-Communist group in the State Department." In a reference to Truman, Taft said removing this group would not be done by those who thought Communists were "red herrings."

Joe McCarthy wrapped himself in a martyr's cloak, depicting himself as a lonely fighter battling overwhelming odds against dangerous foes. It was a fight his friends had warned him against undertaking, he would say in speeches to his Senate colleagues and to the public: "They pointed out to me . . . that the road has been strewn with the political corpses of those who dared to attempt an exposure of the type of individuals I intend to discuss today." He said many people expressed to him "a deep concern for fear I may quit this fight." He wanted to assure these patriotic Americans that he would never surrender. "In the words of John Paul Jones," he exclaimed, "'I have just [*sic*] begun to fight.'"

He denounced all the "egg-sucking phony liberals" whose "pitiful squealing . . . would hold sacrosanct those Communists and queers" who had sold China into "atheistic slavery." He pledged to drive out the "prancing mimics of the Moscow party line in the State Department." Acheson and others were "dilettante diplomats" who "whined" and "whimpered" and "cringed" in the face of Communism. His critics were "dupes" of the Kremlin, spewing its "malignant smear."

Six weeks into the hearings, McCarthy went before the annual meeting in Washington of the American Society of Newspaper Editors and declared that he was being attacked in the press solely because he was exposing Communists and their agents. Of his journalistic critics, he told the editors: "Some write columns for your newspapers. It is your privilege to buy them; mine to ignore them." In the question and answer period after his address, this exchange took place: Q: "Senator, you have been accused of making statements on the Senate floor under immunity and you have been asked to make them on a public platform without that immunity. Will you do that?" McCarthy: "One of your questions is: 'Will you make the statement in public?' The answer is: 'No.' Number two, 'Are you going to resign?' The answer is: 'No.' OK?"

In this appearance before the editors, McCarthy called Acheson "completely incompetent." He then broadened his attack to include General George C. Marshall, perhaps the most revered American of the time. Marshall, he said, was a "pathetic thing" who was "completely unfit" for the high offices he had held. He had, McCarthy claimed, "boned up" for his earlier mission to China as secretary of state by reading the works of Owen Lattimore.

McCarthy was a star that spring at the Gridiron Club's annual white-tie, off-the-record dinner at which the capital's leading journalists lampooned the politics of the day by performing costume skits before an audience of the nation's top editors and publishers, major corporate executives, key White House, congressional, and diplomatic officials, and the president. McCarthy burst into the presidential ballroom of Washington's Statler Hotel carrying a toy machine gun, rifle, and sling shot, which he deposited before a baby's diaper. "I'll never let that go," he exclaimed of the diaper. "That's my cloak of immunity." Roar of laughter. Then, as the Marine Band struck up a Bert Williams tune, McCarthy sang:

> *Somebody lied,*
> *Somebody lied, dear, dear;*
> *Some say there is no evidence,*
> *While others say it's clear.*
> *Somebody lied, as plain*
> *as plain can be;*
> *Somebody's lied as sure as you're*
> *born—*
> *Somebody's falsified to me.*

Thunderous applause.

McCarthy was also winning the battle for public opinion. Each day, post office clerks delivered more burlap sacks of mail to his Senate office. The flood of mail, from all over the world, reached a rate of twenty-five thousand letters a day in 1950, and increased in years to come.

The mail was overwhelmingly pro-McCarthy. It even included a songwriter's attempt to celebrate this modern-day patriot. To the tune of *The Battle Hymn of the Republic,* verses to the ballad (mercifully unpublished until David Oshinsky discovered and wrote about it) went:

This is a land of freedom and when the Communists appear
They recognize a menace we must recognize and fear.
So get behind the movement of the modern Paul Revere.
His Truth is marching on.

Fall in line with Joe McCarthy.
Fall in line with Joe McCarthy.
Fall in line with Joe McCarthy
His truth is marching on.

Many letters contained cash and checks, totaling as much as a thousand dollars a day. Under Internal Revenue guidelines of the time, such money was termed a gift and thus tax free; no IRS reporting of the donations was required. The money accumulated; soon McCarthy's office was scattered with troves of cash. Some of the money McCarthy apparently invested in commodities or the racetrack. Other sums were used to hire more investigators. Willard Edwards of the *Chicago Tribune* remembered being in McCarthy's office and seeing McCarthy open envelopes and stuff cash into his pockets. McCarthy's staff eventually opened several bank accounts in which to deposit the cash. One account was reported to hold as much as $125,000.

———

By the middle of May, two months after the Tydings hearings began, it was clear Joe McCarthy was also winning the political battle. With each passing day, "traitors in government" became a more potent issue. James Reston of the *New York Times* captured the stakes involved when he interviewed Boss

Coleman that month. "The issue is fairly simple," Coleman told Reston, "and it was made by the newspapers. It is now a political issue, and somebody is going to gain or lose politically before it's over. It all comes down to this: are we going to try to win an election or aren't we?"

———

No longer was Millard Tydings the confident figure who boasted he would crush McCarthy after only three days of public hearings. Now, as Tydings witnessed the surge of public support for McCarthy and the accompanying polarization that swept Capitol Hill and the nation, he appealed privately to Democratic senators to speak out against McCarthy.

Freshman Democratic Senator William Benton of Connecticut called McCarthy "a hit-and-run propagandist of the Kremlin model." The veteran Dennis Chavez of New Mexico followed by condemning Budenz's trustworthiness. Most Democrats, though, maintained a safe silence. A disgusted Herbert Lehman later said, "Nearly all the senators did not lift a finger for two or three years."

Again privately, Tydings appealed to Truman for help. The president agreed, reluctantly, to make available to the committee the State Department loyalty files of cases McCarthy had cited in his February 20 Senate speech. The senators could examine them at the White House, but not make copies or take notes on their contents. As McCarthy well knew, studying the files would show how he had misrepresented them. He reacted in character. First he said that the files had been tampered with. Then, in a lurid speech composed in a hurried all-night session by Nellor and others, he laid out before the Midwest Council of Young Republicans a deeply conspiratorial account of what had been done to the files. Not only were they "phony." They had been "raped." As for the Tydings Committee, it was an "OPERATION WHITEWASH." (The caps are in the text of his speech.) He demanded that Truman summon J. Edgar Hoover and other top security officials to the White House. Have them compile a list of federal employees dangerous to the Republic, he commanded, then "tell them to study the list, use tough standards, cut them to fit the cloth of Communist treachery, and tell you who to fire. Take their word for it, Mr. President, not [Senator] McMahon's, not Tydings', not Earl Browder's [the American Communist Party's general secretary]."

ELEVEN

The Opposition

Paralyzed with fear.

In the terrible spring of 1950, a time of fears of nuclear war and treason, of demagoguery on a scale never before seen in America, of political cowardice and cynical opportunism, one bright moment briefly pierced the darkness.

On June 1, the Senate's only female member, the Republican Margaret Chase Smith of Maine, quietly moved down the aisle and began to address her colleagues. She was delivering, she explained, a speech she drafted that she called a "Declaration of Conscience," and was gratified that six fellow Republican senators* had "authorized me to announce their concurrence." She then delivered what, more than half a cen-

---

*New Hampshire's Charles Tobey, Vermont's George Aiken, Oregon's Wayne Morse, New York's Irving Ives, Minnesota's Edward Thye, and New Jersey's Robert Hendrickson.

tury later, remains one of the most remarkable political addresses ever heard in that often-mocked senatorial "cave of winds." Simply, directly, and eloquently it provided an impressive rebuke to Joe McCarthy and the dangers of McCarthyism. It was a true, and rare, "profile in courage."*

Margaret Chase Smith was then fifty-three years old. She was not among the leaders of the Senate. Her one claim to fame, though she never tried to capitalize on it, involved her gender. Two years before, she had become the first woman ever elected to the U.S. Senate. That fact was always mentioned in articles about her, coupled with another first: she was the first woman in the nation's history to serve in both houses of Congress. In 1940 she had succeeded her congressman husband upon his death, and went on to serve eight years

---

*In the spring of 2005, former Senate Majority Leader George J. Mitchell of Maine recalled the lesson of Margaret Chase Smith's courageous political independence as the Senate neared a vote on a proposal to unilaterally change Senate rules for confirming federal judges. Mitchell, a former federal judge himself, drew a parallel between Smith and the McCarthy era and the present embittered ideological Senate battle over redrafting its historic rules to permit the conservative Republican majority to prevail in its assault on the federal judiciary. "I am reminded," Mitchell said, "of the words spoken 55 years ago by Senator Margaret Chase Smith in her famous 'Declaration of Conscience' against the tactics of Senator Joe McCarthy, a member of her own party. 'I don't believe the American people will uphold any political party that puts political exploitation above national interest,' the senator said. 'Surely we Republicans aren't that desperate for victory. While it might be a fleeting victory for the Republican Party, it would be a more lasting defeat for the American people. Surely it would ultimately be suicide for the Republican Party and the two-party system that has protected our American liberties from the dictatorship of a one-party system.'"

in the House before winning her Senate seat in 1948. Smith was no bomb thrower, no ideologue, no seeker of publicity. She was just what she appeared to be: a moderate Republican from the Republican state of Maine, a backbencher, quiet, reserved, dignified in dress and manner. But she also possessed other character traits: a New Englander's flinty independence and integrity.

When McCarthy began making his charges about spies and traitors in the State Department, she at first believed her colleague "was on to something disturbing and frightening." As weeks passed she began to doubt her initial belief; but, she told herself, she wasn't a lawyer, and she didn't feel competent to judge all the accusations and countercharges. By the middle of May, however, she "began to wonder whether I was as stupid as I thought." McCarthy wasn't making sense. His charges didn't add up. She suspected they were overblown, or false. He might even be perpetrating a hoax on the Senate.

The more she watched and listened to McCarthy, the more disturbed she became. "Joe began to get publicity crazy," she told David Oshinsky years later. "And the other senators were now afraid to speak their minds, to take issue with him. It got to the point where some of us refused to be seen with people he disapproved of. A wave of fear had struck Washington."

It was against this backdrop that she decided it was time to speak out. Quietly, patiently, she drafted her statement and began to circulate it among Republican moderates. To gain their support, the speech could not be seen as a polemic; it had to strike an even balance condemning both Democratic failures of leadership and the present rise of McCarthyism. Her declaration did just that. It stated: "The Democratic administration has lost the confidence of the American people by its complacency to the threat of Communism at home"; it criticized the administration for its "mania for loose spending and loose programs"; and it expressed hope that voters would agree it was "time for a change and that a Republican victory is necessary to the security of this country."

This, however, did not mask her central target. Though McCarthy's name never appeared in her declaration of conscience, everyone understood who was being addressed, and whose tactics deplored.

"I would like to speak briefly and simply," she began, "about a serious national condition. It is a national feeling of fear and frustration that could result in national suicide and the end of everything we Americans hold dear."

She wanted to speak as briefly as possible "because too much harm has already been done with irresponsible words of bitterness and selfish political opportunism. I speak as simply as possible because the issue is too great to be obscured by eloquence. I speak simply and briefly in the hope that my words will be taken to heart. I speak as a Republican. I speak as a woman. I speak as a United States Senator. I speak as an American."

Carefully, deliberately she made her case: the character of the Senate had recently "been debased to the level of a forum of hate and character assassination sheltered by the shield of congressional immunity." The Senate had become a "publicity platform for irresponsible sensationalism"; for a state of "reckless abandon in which unproven charges" are hurled; for "vilification"; for "selfish political gain at the sacrifice of individual reputations and national unity"; for "the way we smear outsiders from the Floor of the Senate and hide behind the

cloak of congressional immunity and still place ourselves beyond criticism on the Floor of the Senate." It was time for
senators "to do some soul-searching" and "to weigh our consciences" on the manner in which "we are performing our
duty to the people of America—on the manner in which we
are using or abusing our individual powers and privileges."
The Constitution, she said, "speaks not only of the freedom of
speech but also of trial by jury instead of trial by accusation."
She could see little practical distinction between a criminal
prosecution in court and a character prosecution in the Senate "when the life of a person has been ruined."

Then she said:

> Those of us who shout the loudest about Americanism in
> making character assassination are all too frequently those
> who, by their own words and acts, ignore some of the basic
> principles of Americanism:
>   The right to criticize;
>   The right to hold unpopular beliefs;
>   The right to protest;
>   The right of independent thought.
>   The exercise of these rights should not cost one single
> American his reputation or his right to a livelihood merely
> because he happens to know someone who holds unpopu-
> lar beliefs. Who of us doesn't? Otherwise none of us could
> call our souls our own. Otherwise thought control would
> have set in.

The American people, she said, "are sick and tired of
being afraid to speak their minds lest they be politically
smeared as 'Communists' or 'Fascists' by their opponents."
The American people "are sick and tired of seeing innocent

people smeared and guilty people whitewashed." Americans were being "psychologically divided by the confusion and the suspicions that are bred in the United States Senate to spread like cancerous tentacles of 'know-nothing, suspect everything' attitudes."

Still speaking in a calm, quiet voice, she told her Republican colleagues she hoped their party would be returned to power—but not at the expense of replacing Democrats "with a Republican regime embracing a philosophy that lacks political integrity or intellectual honesty." In the words that are best remembered from her declaration, she said:

"I don't want to see the Republican Party ride to victory on the Four Horsemen of Calumny—Fear, Ignorance, Bigotry and Smear."

This was one of the few redeeming moments in the destructive tragedy of McCarthyism. In all the years since, the United States Senate has witnessed nothing to quite equal its example of courage, independence, and eloquence on an issue of transcendent national interest.

When she finished, her colleagues surrounded and congratulated her. Another Republican moderate, H. Alexander Smith of New Jersey, asked that his name be added to those who had endorsed her declaration.

Briefly, all too briefly, it seemed as if voices of reason might prevail, for Margaret Chase Smith's memorable call to conscience was not the only sign of Republican moderates' rising concern about McCarthyism that spring. Other Republican elders were becoming alarmed about the damage McCarthy's assaults were doing the nation.

Republican Henry L. Stimson, secretary of war under FDR and President William Howard Taft's long before that, had already added his great prestige to rebuke McCarthyism. Writing to the *New York Times* in defense of Dean Acheson, Stimson did not name McCarthy but left no doubt about the subject of his scorn. He wrote: "The man who seeks to gain political advantage from personal attack on a secretary of state is a man who seeks to gain political advantage from damage to his country." From Columbia University came another warning. Dwight D. Eisenhower, then the head of Columbia and two years away from his presidential campaign, cautioned that calling names was "a behind-the-iron-curtain trick." Americans, Eisenhower added, should not be suckered into calling anyone a Communist "who may be just a little brighter than ourselves."

Praiseworthy though such comments were, and admirable as Margaret Chase Smith's appeal to conscience had been, they did not signal the emergence of a political will to stop McCarthy—not by Democrats, not by Republicans, not by moderates in either party. As for McCarthy, he brushed aside Smith's words. He dismissed her and her co-signers as "Snow White and the Seven Dwarfs." Then he resumed his attack.

Within weeks, all but one of Margaret Chase Smith's co-signers dropped their public opposition to McCarthy, either by publicly signaling their support of McCarthy's anticommunist campaign or by their silence. The sole survivor was Wayne Morse of Oregon, and he subsequently left the Republican Party. "Joe had the Senate paralyzed with fear," Margaret Chase Smith wrote in her memoir, *Declaration of Conscience*. "The political risk of taking issue with him was too great a hazard to the political security of senators."

---

184 / **THE OPPOSITION**

On June 25, twenty-four days after Smith's speech, massive
North Korean Communist forces, backed by the Soviet Union
and Communist China, raced across the 38th parallel dividing
North and South Korea and began driving fleeing South Korean and American forces south toward the sea. The feared,
and predicted, hot war with Communism had begun. The
shock of war, and mounting casualties as U.S. forces retreated
pell-mell, temporarily pushed McCarthy off the front pages.
But not for long. Within days McCarthy launched another all-
out attack on Truman and the Democrats. On July 3, he
charged the State Department had "sabotaged" the Korean
aid program, and thus bore responsibility for the loss of American lives and looming disaster in Korea. Three days later he
said Dean Acheson must be removed.

It was in this context of sudden war without and alleged
treachery within that the Tydings committee began wrestling
with its final report. The time had long passed when Democrats wanted to keep the investigation going. Now Republicans wanted to keep the focus on McCarthy and his charges
right up to the fall election.

In the end, the Tydings committee, on a strict party-line
vote, approved a 350,000 word, 313-page final report. Joe
McCarthy, the majority report concluded, had perpetrated a
"fraud and a hoax . . . on the Senate." He had "stooped to a
new low in his cavalier disregard of the facts." His charges
"represent perhaps the most nefarious campaign of half-
truths and untruths in the history of this republic." The majority report added: "For the first time in our history, we have
seen the totalitarian technique of the 'big lie' employed on a
sustained basis. The result has been to confuse and divide the
American people, at a time when they should be strong in
their unity, to a degree far beyond the hopes of the Com-

munists themselves whose stock in trade is confusion and division."

The Tydings report was an unprecedented rebuke. More-over, it documented McCarthy's record of falsehoods and mis-representations point by point and case by case. Read now, it stands as a definitive document. In other times, perhaps, it would have put an end to McCarthy's demagoguery. The *Christian Science Monitor*'s Richard L. Stout wrote then: "Not before in this century have fellow senators denounced a colleague in such searing terms, and the question is raised whether expulsion action will be attempted." It was not. In-stead, McCarthy grew even stronger.

The impact of the report was considerably diminished by an announcement by J. Edgar Hoover. Whether by mere co-incidence, or a deliberate attempt to refocus attention on the prospect of Communist treason, Hoover chose the day the Tydings committee report was made public to announce the arrest of Julius Rosenberg on charges that he was the head of a spy ring and had transmitted atomic bomb secrets to the So-viet Union.

Coming after the Hiss, Fuchs, and other spy cases, the Rosenberg arrest confirmed the existence of an active, high-level Soviet spy ring in the United States. Within a month, the FBI had charged two others as members in that spy ring: Rosenberg's wife, Ethel, and his brother-in-law David Green-glass, a Manhattan Project technician.* Another suspect, Morton Sobel, was arrested while trying to flee to the Soviet

---

*Julius and Ethel Rosenberg were executed June 19, 1953. Green-glass, who testified for the government against his sister and brother-in-law, was sentenced to fifteen years in prison.

Union by way of Mexico. Here was proof to the public, it seemed, that as reckless and false as McCarthy's charges might be, he "must be on to something."

The shocking Rosenberg spy charges further inflamed the contentious atmosphere in Washington on July 20 as the full Senate began deliberating on whether to approve the Tydings recommendations.

What transpired was one of the most vicious debates in the history of the Senate, marked by profanities and Republican attempts to cut off the discussion and kill a vote on the report. Witnesses reported that Senator Wherry, the Republican's minority floor leader, was so enraged after spotting the Tydings committee's chief counsel, Edward P. Morgan, that the two men exchanged blows when they continued their heated exchange in the cloakroom off the Senate floor. Tydings spoke for more than two hours, defending the report with charts, documents, and photostats. His was not a dispassionate rendering, however. For three months, he said, he had "taken punishment from a colleague of mine who has used every epithet and every form of opprobrium and calumny to blackguard me . . . I have not returned the favor because I did not want to sink to that kind of behavior, even off the Senate floor." The time had come, however, to lay out the truth of McCarthy's behavior and charges.

Tydings became impassioned as he responded to Republican accusations, already hurled by McCarthy and Taft, that his report was a "whitewash" of Communism. In a climactic moment, Tydings turned and walked toward one of the most extreme of the Republican anticommunists, Indiana's William E. Jenner. In a speech a few days prior, Jenner had impugned Tydings' patriotism and minutes earlier had shouted across the Senate floor toward Tydings: "How can we get the Reds out of Korea if we cannot get them out of Washington?"

Trembling with rage, his voice cracking, Tydings pointed his finger almost in Jenner's face and said: "You know, I have been in some pretty tough places in my boyhood—on battle-fields where real men were killed. Perhaps the senator does not know that. When it is suggested that I would protect Communist spies in the country I love, I find—" Here his voice broke. For a moment, he could not speak. Then he said: "No, I cannot say here what I want to say."

Before returning to his desk, exhausted and soaking with perspiration, Tydings could not refrain from one last blast at his critics: "You will find out who has been whitewashing—with mud and slime, with filth, with the dregs of publicity at the expense of the people's love for their country. I ask the Senate: What are you going to do about it? I leave it up to your conscience."

On a straight party-line vote, the Senate then approved the Tydings report. Not a single Republican present voted for it.

———

The invective did not cease. Taft called the Tydings investiga-tion a "farce" and a "whitewash." Jenner, rising in the Senate, accused Tydings of "conducting the most scandalous and brazen whitewash of treasonable conspiracy in our history." His voice dripping with scorn, he said he didn't know Tydings "was such a brave and heroic man until he told us from his own itsy-bitsy lips yesterday, but I do know that there is an-other medal which probably will come to him. It will be very large, and emblazoned with a single name: 'Thanks, from good old Joe [Stalin], for a job well done.'" McCarthy attacked the majority report as "a green light to the Red Fifth column in the United States" and "a signal to the traitors, Communists, and fellow travelers in our government that they need have no fear of exposure." The Democratic majority who voted for the Tydings report had produced "a clever, evil thing to behold," McCarthy said. "It is gigantic in its fraud and deep in its deceit."

McCarthy was rebuked, but not rejected. From then until the November elections, he became the Republican Party's most tireless, sought-after, and effective campaigner, receiving more than two thousand speaking requests, double that of any other Republican senator. He carried his crusade against Communist "traitors" into fifteen states, making ever more inflammatory charges as he went. He escalated his charges that Truman-Acheson policies had permitted the loss of Nationalist China to the Communists; that their failures had created the "death trap" of Korea; that treason had imperiled the American future. By the end of August, McCarthy's speech about Korea before a gathering of the Military Order of the Purple Heart in Worcester, Massachusetts, was characterized in the local headlines: "Acheson Spilled Blood of Yanks, McCarthy Says." By Labor Day, after another McCarthy appearance before a patriotic group in Charleston, South Carolina, the local paper reported: "McCarthy Puts Acheson Into Molotov Class."

Everywhere he went, McCarthy drew passionate crowds. For McCarthy, the public's emotional response was intoxicating. To some, it was frightening. A McCarthy opponent, Milwaukee's Socialist mayor Frank Zeidler, watching with growing concern as a resolution hailing McCarthy as "a great American" was read before a wildly cheering Milwaukee crowd, said: "Joe has hit the ten strike. He's unbeatable now. He's a Northern Huey Long."

———

Nowhere did McCarthy put more effort, and more invective, into a campaign than in Millard Tydings's home state of Maryland. He was determined to destroy the committee chairman. To that aim, he dispatched his key aides—Jean Kerr, Don Surine, Ed Nellor among them—to help John Marshall Butler, a little-known Republican lawyer from Baltimore, defeat Tydings in his race for reelection. The McCarthy aides literally took over Butler's campaign, providing strategy, speeches, and themes. At McCarthy's suggestion, they employed one of his old tactics, mailing postcards seemingly signed by Butler to Maryland constituents. More than two hundred thousand were mailed, a feat accomplished through round-the-clock assistance of McCarthy's office staff and temporary workers hired by the Hearst Corporation. McCarthy raised large sums of money for Butler from right-wing contributors, many from Texas. Again he called upon the anticommunist network for help, and again it responded. Day after day, on page one and on the editorial page, the conservative *Washington Times-Herald* kept up a stream of anti-Tydings reportage, commentary, and cartoons. The day after the Senate adopted the Tydings report, for instance, the paper published a front page cartoon showing Tydings shaking hands with someone labeled a "Washington Communist." The next day, its page one headline blared:

Tydings Accused of Hiding Reds

Brazen Whitewash Charged by Jenner

From the editorial page came anti-Tydings columns by the conservatives Westbrook Pegler and George Sokolsky. One of Sokolsky's columns was headed: "Senator Tydings to Whitewash the Communists and Homosexuals in State Depart." A headline over another Sokolsky column read: "Tydings feels called upon to defend his whitewash of Commies."

McCarthy campaigned vigorously in Maryland, accusing Tydings of "giving the green light to the Russians," being a "Red coddler," and "protecting Communists for political reasons." By the eve of the election, McCarthy had coined a new term for all Democrats seeking office. They were "Commiecrats," Tydings worst of all.

In the most notorious act of a campaign later branded by a Senate investigating committee as "a despicable 'back street' type of campaign," McCarthy's staff put together a scurrilous anti-Tydings political tabloid that was distributed throughout the state in the days just before the election. The tabloid, produced with the help of *Times-Herald* publisher Ruth "Bazy" McCormick, was called *From the Record,* and set forth a series of false charges against Tydings. Among them was the claim that Tydings had "sponsored Owen Lattimore in a series of lectures on Communist Russia" and that his committee had cut back appropriations to arm the South Koreans and refused to investigate disloyalty in the State Department.

For dirty campaigning, though, nothing approached the McCarthy team's use of a composite picture showing Tydings apparently looking intently and pensively into the face of the American Communist leader Earl Browder. By reversing a 1938 photo of Tydings, cropping it, and placing it next to a current picture of Browder, a *Times-Herald* staff artist made it appear Tydings and Browder were engaged in intimate con-

versation. The two men had never met before Browder testified in front of the Tydings committee, and Browder was a
belligerent witness. They never appeared together, never exchanged pleasantries, never were photographed together. But
in the campaign tabloid they were linked as allies: a Commie-
crat and a Communist.

Millard Tydings' long political career ended that November 7. Despite the fact that seven of every ten Maryland
voters were registered Democrats, he lost by forty-three thousand votes. Tydings's defeat was the most dramatic upset that
fall, but he wasn't the only Democratic victim of anticommunism and McCarthyism. In Illinois, Democratic Senate Majority Leader Scott Lucas, who led the move to investigate
McCarthy, was defeated by Everett Dirksen in another campaign in which anticommunism figured. In Utah, the same
issue prevailed as Wallace Bennett defeated the Democratic
veteran Elbert D. Thomas. In California, Richard Nixon labeled his Democratic opponent, the incumbent Helen Gahagan Douglas, the "pink lady," resulting in Nixon's election to
the Senate.

As Marquis Childs assessed the new electoral landscape,
"In every contest where it was a major factor, McCarthyism
won." Surveying the new Senate makeup, the conservative
Republican Senator Herman Welker said were it not for Joe
McCarthy, seven of his new fellow Republican colleagues
would not be sitting in the chamber. It was, said another arch
conservative Republican, Maine's Owen Brewster, a triumph
for McCarthy and his "ism."

A political revolution was underway, and Joe McCarthy
was a central player in it. He immediately let it be known that
his anticommunist crusade was only beginning. "McCarthy

Plans Expansion of Red Exposures," the *Times-Herald* reported three days after the election. McCarthy quickly resumed his attacks on Truman, assailing the president's supposed "spurning of aid" to Nationalist China's Chiang Kai-shek that opened the way for the military menace of Red China now facing American forces on the Korean peninsula. Within three weeks, he was calling for Truman's impeachment.

In the wake of the election, McCarthy was attracting more attention—more adulation, more fear—than ever. The liberal columnist Doris Fleeson believed he was in a strong position to gain the Republican vice presidential nomination in 1952. How far he might go, no one could say, but as Margaret Chase Smith had feared, he was astride the "Four Horsemen of Calumny: Fear, Ignorance, Bigotry, and Smear," riding toward a victory of potentially great historical consequences.

TWELVE

The Demagogue

*I will have to blame some of the roughness in fighting
the enemy to my training in the Marine Corps.
We weren't taught to wear lace panties and fight
with lace handkerchiefs.*

—Joe McCarthy

Joe McCarthy was a demagogue, but never a real leader of
the people. His high public approval ratings notwithstanding, he wasn't even all that popular, except in the narrowest
sense of attracting a coterie of true believers and backers.
Even among them he was not viewed as *the* leader of the anticommunist cause, but rather a convenient figurehead behind
whom they could rally, a spokesman for their frustrations, suspicions, and hatred.

Better than anyone in his time, or perhaps in the entire
American experience, McCarthy represented what historian

Richard Hofstadter called "the paranoid style of American politics." McCarthy offered simple answers to complex questions. America's problems, its mistakes, its failures, could be explained by evil forces conspiring to do the country harm. "They" were responsible, all those sinister, hidden enemies plotting to destroy the nation. That there *were* enemies plotting to destroy America strengthened the plausibility of his message.

While he never approached the importance of a Hitler or a Stalin, McCarthy resembled those demagogic dictators by also employing the techniques of the Big Lie. Even in this, he wasn't original. Most of the defamatory phrases he used with loud and daily repetition had been commonplace for years among anticommunist crusaders: *bleeding heart liberals, liberal left-wing press, left-wingers, commies, comsymps, un-Americans, soft on Communism, fellow travelers, traitors within.* McCarthy used these words with such force, however, that he was able to persuade even those troubled by his tactics that he must be on to something.

At the same time, his intemperance, his bullying, his extreme language, and his taste for the jugular did pose a credibility problem. The great majority of Americans were neither ideologically driven nor certain what to make of the conspiracy theories he offered to explain America's dire condition. To allay public skepticism of him, McCarthy and his supporters mounted a counterattack.

An American Legion publication, noting criticism of him, assured readers that, "McCarthy's blunderbuss, loaded with rock-salt, birdshot, and nuts and bolts . . . is almost bound to bring down several important Reds and spies even though a few comparatively innocent people may get some rock-salt in their hides."

McCarthy was his own best advocate. In a typical speech before the Midwest Council of Young Republicans, he addressed public concerns that he was being too rough in his attacks:

> There are those who honestly say, "Oh, we think that you are on the right track, McCarthy, and we like the results you are getting, but we don't like your methods." Ladies and gentlemen, take my word for it . . . Either I have to do a brass-knuckle job or suffer the same defeat that a vast number of well-meaning men have suffered over the past years.

He then told his favorite anecdote, one he delivered before audiences hundreds of times. It was McCarthy's rationale for what he was all about, as well as his defense of his methods:

> When I was a small boy on the farm, mother raised chickens . . . We lived fairly close to the woods and weasels, snakes and skunks would steal the baby chicks from beneath the mother and kill them. One of the jobs which my brothers and I had was to dig out and destroy those killers. It was not a pleasant job and sometimes we did not smell too good when the job was finished. But the skunks were dead and the chickens were alive. A much more dangerous and smellier breed of skunk is now being dug out of Washington. And to those of you who do not like rough tactics— any farm boy can tell you that there is no dainty way of clubbing the fangs off a rattler or killing a skunk.

McCarthy, who began regularly referring to himself in the third person as public notice of him grew and his ego soared, was just the kind of patriot willing to take on the messy business of destroying the nation's enemies, however great the risk to himself. As he presented himself, and perhaps even believed himself to be, he represented an archetypal American: the intrepid cowboy going it alone against great odds to win the good fight. He was John Wayne at mid-century.*

If that meant applying brass-knuckles to the traitors, well, real Americans would understand. Americans lived in dangerous times, and they had to defend themselves.

———

More than any other event in the McCarthy story, an incident at Washington's exclusive Sulgrave Club on Tuesday evening, December 12, 1950, best exposed his brutality.

Drew Pearson, the widely read syndicated columnist, and his wife, Luvie, arrived at the club off Dupont Circle shortly after eight o'clock that night. They, and a hundred other guests, were attending a private dinner dance honoring, among others, James H. Duff, a lifelong Republican who had just been elected to the Senate after serving as governor of Pennsylvania.

Pearson disliked Washington dinner parties and hadn't wanted to attend. His wife had convinced him that as an old friend of the new senator and fellow Pennsylvanian, he should welcome Duff to Washington. Although Pearson was an outspoken liberal and a foe of Republican conservatives, he and Duff shared some political views. Duff, a big, bluff redhead, was a Theodore Roosevelt progressive with a strong streak of independence and a record of fighting for what today would be considered liberal causes. But for some reason Duff didn't even appear at the dinner in his honor, thus negating the sole

———

*Coincidentally, McCarthy and Wayne became close friends. Wayne, as one of the leading Hollywood conservatives, backed McCarthy with money and arranged patriotic rallies for him.

reason for Pearson's presence. Instead, the first person who greeted Pearson when he and his wife climbed the stairs to the ballroom, looking for Duff, was Joe McCarthy. Had Pearson known McCarthy would be among those invited, he never would have attended.

———

Drew Pearson was a day short of his fifty-third birthday, a slim, dapper man, with a long face, thinning dark hair, and a mustache familiar to the millions of readers who saw his picture each morning atop his nationally syndicated column, "Washington Merry-Go-Round." Countless other Americans knew his voice from his nationally broadcast radio program. Pearson was one of America's best-known personalities and one of, if not *the,* most feared journalists in America. He was a muckraker, and his column had been a staple of Washington's, and the nation's, life since the early 1930s.

Pearson had written positively about McCarthy's earliest Senate days, but turned increasingly critical of him and had the widest audience to make a case against McCarthy. It was Pearson (with the assistance of investigative material gathered by the *Madison Capital Times*) who publicized the $10,000 fee McCarthy received from Lustron Corporation for writing an article on housing; Pearson who exposed McCarthy's income tax problems, including his failure to pay taxes on $45,000 of his income during the three war years; Pearson who did some of the earliest work in making public the conservative network gathering around McCarthy, including key figures in the China lobby. Since the Wheeling speech, Pearson's drumbeat of McCarthy criticism had intensified. By the time of the dinner, he was the single source of anti-McCarthy material for most newspaper readers outside the capital and New York.

McCarthy had stewed for months as Pearson continued his near-daily commentary. In that time, Pearson himself had grown increasingly concerned about McCarthy's erratic behavior. There had been a nasty encounter at that year's Gridiron dinner. On seeing Pearson, McCarthy smiled, held out his hand, and said, "Someday I'm going to break your leg, Drew, but for the time being I just wanted to say hello." Pearson was so troubled by the incident that he recorded it in his diary with the conclusion: "I am more and more convinced that there is a screw loose somewhere." For his part, McCarthy was reported to have told friends that he wasn't sure "whether to kill Pearson or just to maim him."

It was with this history of mutual animosity that the two men met in the Sulgrave Club.

With what Pearson recalled as "mock effusiveness," all smiles and hearty cordiality, McCarthy sidled up to Pearson and began speaking in a low, taunting monotone. "I am going to make a speech about you on the Senate floor tomorrow, Drew," he told Pearson. "I am going to really tear you to pieces." Then, still smiling broadly, still seeming most affable, McCarthy told Pearson, "I am going to get you a drink."

McCarthy headed for the bar. Pearson later recalled, in a sworn one-hundred-forty-page deposition about that night,* that he was "so overcome in seeing Senator McCarthy" that

---

*Pearson's lengthy deposition was taken Sept. 25, 1951, in the U.S. District Court for the District of Columbia, as part of a $5.1 million suit against McCarthy he had filed that March charging McCarthy with three counts of assault and battery and slander. The suit dragged on for years, surviving a number of dismissal motions, but never came to trial and Pearson dropped it in 1956 after McCarthy's Senate censure.

he couldn't remember what kind of cocktail McCarthy brought him or whether he took a few sips of it. (Pearson seldom drank.) What he remembered vividly was the image of Joe McCarthy moving toward him, carrying two drinks, one of which he was spilling, before continuing in his hail-fellow manner his monologue about what he was going to do to Pearson on the floor of the Senate.

"I am certainly sorry to meet your wife here," Pearson said McCarthy told him. "I am going to feel awfully guilty" about the effect on her after what he was going to do to Pearson the next day. He was going "to rake the bejesus out of me." He was going to "take me apart . . . tear me apart . . . tear me to pieces." He was going to "take me to the cleaners." He said: "I am going to murder you."

Speaking in his threatening monotone, McCarthy said he had been doing a lot of research on Pearson, and had prepared his speech. He had already told the press to be sure to be there. He had his speech ready. Pearson should come to the press gallery and hear what he had to say. He was going to say things about Pearson on the floor of the Senate that he couldn't say in public.

Turning toward others in the room, he said in a loud voice: "Well, I certainly am sorry that Drew is here. This is a terrible thing because I am going to make a speech about him tomorrow."

Pearson, too shocked by this verbal assault to reply, finally turned away and began speaking with Senator Russell Long of Louisiana, Huey's son, and with Long's wife. Then dinner was served.

Luvie Pearson was seated across from McCarthy with Pearson far down their table. Pearson kept hearing McCarthy's loud voice, but couldn't make out what he was saying to his wife. Later that night, Pearson testified, Luvie told him: McCarthy kept repeating what he was going to do to you, "how I was a Communist, how he was going to prove I was a Communist, how when he got through with me she was going to divorce me."

The dinner, with breaks for dancing, lasted until nearly ten o'clock.

Twice, McCarthy got up from his seat, approached Pearson, and launched into the same taunting, increasingly menacing recitation of what he planned to do to Pearson in the Senate. "It was, in effect, if I may say so," Pearson later said in his deposition, "pretty much the way I have heard these Nazi or Gestapo inquisitions are carried on, just pounding home, pounding home, pounding home, trying to get under someone's skin, taunting about the fact that he could say anything he wanted to about me and he was going to do it. He had been working on me for months."

Pearson broke away, and began dancing. When he returned to his chair, McCarthy reappeared and pulled up a chair beside the columnist. He began again his insulting, badgering attack. Referring to Pearson's newspaper clients in Wisconsin, he said, "I don't see why they carry you up there," adding he was glad Pearson wasn't published in more papers because "you have hurt me some up there but I am going to hurt you more. I am really going to put you out of business . . . I am going to ruin you."

Once more, Pearson terminated the encounter and headed back to the dance floor. But when he returned to the table, McCarthy reappeared for a fourth time and resumed his litany, "repeating it, repeating it like a broken record."

Asked during his deposition by McCarthy's lawyer, the criminal attorney Edward Bennett Williams, who at the table might have overheard McCarthy, Pearson replied: "I was obviously not looking at the other end of the table when I had this maniac on my hands."

In this deposition Pearson tried to express how he felt under this extended barrage of threats from McCarthy: "It wasn't enough for him to upset my evening for me by telling me how he was going to murder me on the Senate floor with privilege the next day, say things that he couldn't say to me openly; it wasn't enough to announce that at the start; he had to come along and repeat it again and again and again, telling me how he was going to really take me over the hurdles, he was going to take me to the cleaners, he was going to ruin me, put me out of business. I wouldn't have anything left. It was at that time that I, in a very mild voice, asked him how his income case was coming along."

Asked by Williams exactly what he said to McCarthy, Pearson answered: "I said, 'Joe, how is your income case coming along?'" Pearson said he added: "When are they going to put you in jail?"

McCarthy leaped to his feet. "He said, 'You take that back.' He jumped up, put his thumb and index finger behind my nerves in the back of my cranium right here [indicates], gouged me as hard as he could, and says, 'You come out. We will settle this' . . . He didn't put his hand on my neck in any caressing form. He gouged me as hard as he could, so that an intense pain shot through my head and staggered me for a moment."

McCarthy pressed his challenge to a fight: "You are going to leave this place just as soon as you can. You will get out of here. Don't let me see you around here. You go on and get out."

"I started to get up," Pearson, a Quaker and a pacifist, said in his deposition. "Mrs. McCracken [the wife of a congressman] says, 'Don't be a fool. Sit down; he has been drinking, don't embarrass your hostess.' Congressman Bennet reached across the table. He is lame, he can't get up, but he reached across the table and held his hand out to me like this [indicating], said, 'Don't. Don't be a fool.'"

Pearson remained seated. Soon the nightmare of a dinner was over. Pearson headed downstairs to the men's cloakroom, retrieved his coat, and reached into his pants pocket for change for the hat check attendant.

"I had the money in my hand," he said. "I was about to pay the hat check boy, when McCarthy came up somewhat from the side and somewhat from behind—more or less from my right shoulder—pinned my arms down like this [indicating] in both his arms. No, I think he came around on my left. Yes, it was from my left, pinned my hands down, swung me around, and proceeded to kick me in the groin with his knee. I had this money in my hand; I started to put it back in my pocket. My wife says I am Scotch. He said, 'Keep your hands out of your pocket; no firearms, no guns,' I think he said, and I tried to get my arms loose. He kicked me a second time [in the groin], and we stood there, he saying, 'Take that back about my income taxes, take that back.' I said nothing. I tried to get away from him."

It was about that moment, Pearson said in his deposition, that "[newly elected] Senator Nixon came down and tried to push us apart."

"Let a Quaker stop this fight," Nixon exclaimed.

McCarthy would not back off. "I won't turn my back on that son-of-a-bitch," he shouted, as Nixon later recalled the moment to friends. "He's got to go first."

"First, he [Nixon] was not successful," in trying to separate them, Pearson said, "and then, as he did push us apart, McCarthy broke loose and swung on me with the flat of his hand. That was the incident."

Pearson, who was doubled over from McCarthy's kneeing, fell to the floor. He got up and left. In the account Nixon later gave, Nixon then escorted McCarthy out of the club. They spent the next half hour trying to locate McCarthy's car. He was so drunk he couldn't remember where he had parked it.

McCarthy showed no shame. In phone calls that same night to Urban Van Susteren in Wisconsin and Frank Waldrop, editor of the *Washington Times-Herald,* he boasted that he had just kicked Pearson "in the nuts." He told one of his aides, Ray Kiermas, how his blow had caused Pearson to jump "three feet in the air." McCarthy then requested that Ed Nellor leak the account that Fulton Lewis, Jr., the conservative commentator and supplier of tips and advice to McCarthy, told his Mutual Broadcasting System listeners in his national radio program the next night:

I have an exclusive news item tonight about Mr. Drew Pearson, the columnist and commentator. As you doubtless know, Mr. Pearson has been a long and bitter critic of Senator Joseph McCarthy of Wisconsin ever since Senator McCarthy made his charges against the State Department, which has always been a fertile source of news for Mr.

Pearson and his leg men—has been on the neck of the senator, so to speak—in his newspaper column and over the radio. Last night, Senator McCarthy was a guest at dinner at the very fashionable Sulgrave Club on Dupont Circle here in Washington and also a dinner guest at the same club was none other than Mr. Drew Pearson. During the course of the dinner Mr. Pearson got up from his table and walked over to where Senator McCarthy was sitting. Pearson leaned over and said something to the senator. I've not been able to find out yet just what it was. In any event, Senator McCarthy arose quickly, punched Mr. Pearson in the face and one witness says the blow lifted Mr. Pearson three feet off the ground, which frankly sounds a little extreme, but Joe McCarthy is an ex-Marine and very powerfully built individual. Senator McCarthy himself refused any comment to me tonight about the incident although he will have something more to say on the subject on the floor of the Senate tomorrow. Maybe—maybe the senator got the idea from Mr. Truman's letter to Paul Hume, the music critic whom the President threatened with a punch in the nose for criticizing daughter Margaret's singing. That's the top of the news as it looks from here.

———

Responding to reporters' questions about the brawl, McCarthy said, yes, after he saw Pearson trying to reach in his pocket he had "slapped" him, an instinctive move he had learned to guard himself against assassins. He declined to comment about reports that he had kneed Pearson twice in the groin. Pearson maintained an above-it-all stance, brushing aside McCarthy's punching power as "about as effective as his senatorial behavior." Nixon struck a statesman-like pose.

"Such foolishness," he said, "should not be bandied about in times like these." Privately, however, Nixon told a friend he had never seen anyone slapped as hard as McCarthy hit Pearson. "If I hadn't pulled McCarthy away, he might have killed Pearson," Nixon said.

For days to come, McCarthy gleefully recounted to numerous people what he had done to Pearson. He reveled in the publicity, and especially in the praise he received from political colleagues and the public. Twenty senators phoned his office to congratulate him. The conservative Republican Senator from Utah, Arthur Watkins, put his arm about McCarthy's shoulders in a Senate elevator and said: "Joe I've heard conflicting reports about where you hit Pearson. I hope both are true." According to biographer Thomas Reeves, a citizen from Missouri sent McCarthy an Elgin watch inscribed, "For combat duty on the 12th of December above and beyond the call of duty."

———

Before the Senate, and a packed Senate press gallery, McCarthy delivered the anti-Pearson speech he had promised. It employed all of his trademark techniques of character assassination—all protected from legal challenge by the cloak of Senate immunity.

As usual, McCarthy began by claiming he was taking great risks—dangers even—in exposing Pearson. Once again he quoted an unnamed fellow senator as having just warned him of the dire consequences of taking on Pearson: "McCarthy, don't do it . . . You will be merely inundated by the slime and the smear and he will go on every day polluting otherwise fine newspapers and poisoning the airwaves."

Nonetheless McCarthy had bravely decided to press on. Again portraying himself as a martyr, he said what happened to Joe McCarthy was unimportant; what mattered was exposing this "degenerate liar," this "sugar-coated voice of Russia" who protected "subversive elements" in Washington.

To McCarthy, Pearson was a "Moscow-directed character assassin," an "unprincipled liar and a fake," a man "of twisted, perverted mentality."

Even for McCarthy, this was an outrageous smear. Pearson's harshest critics knew him to be a strong anticommunist, and nothing in his background or record suggested he was in any way disloyal to America. None of this mattered to Mc-Carthy. In his diatribe, he stitched together a ten-year collection of criticism of Pearson from politicians who thought the columnist had unfairly attacked or maligned them. Later, he had these criticisms reprinted along with the text of his speech and distributed them to Wisconsin newspaper editors and others. This compilation wasn't the heart of his attack, however. That came at the end of his speech when he revealed the full measure of the revenge he had planned for Pearson, what he meant by his Sulgrave Club boast to "ruin" Pearson and leave him with nothing.

Standing on the floor of the Senate, immune from lawsuits, McCarthy offered citizens, editors, and broadcasters a remedy "to still this voice of international Communism," this evil that was Drew Pearson. He urged the editors to stop carrying Pearson's column. He called on "every loyal American" to threaten the sponsor of Pearson's radio broadcasts with an economic boycott if the sponsor didn't immediately cancel its underwriting of Pearson's program.

The Adam Hat Company was then sponsoring Pearson's program under a contract that set his compensation at five thousand dollars a week. "It should be remembered," McCarthy said, "that anyone who buys an Adams [sic] Hat—any store that stocks an Adams Hat—anyone who buys from a store that stocks an Adams Hat—is unknowingly and innocently contributing . . . to the cause of international Communism by keeping that Communist spokesman on the air."

With that, McCarthy doffed a gray Adam Hat and walked off the Senate floor.

———

Ten days after the Sulgrave incident, on Friday, December 22, the *Washington Evening Star* carried this page one headline:

Hat Company Refuses to Renew
Drew Pearson's Radio Contract

Boycott of Product Recently Asked
by McCarthy in Senate Speech

Buried inside that paper on page nine was a small story headed:

McCarthy Opposes Suggestion
to End Congressional Immunity

The Times-Herald reported the news of Adam Hat's cancellation of Pearson's radio contract more pithily, and with more punch:

Pearson Given the Heave-Ho by Adam Hat

The lesson was clear to all in both press and politics: cross Joe McCarthy at your peril.

PART FOUR

Prelude to Power

Chapter

THIRTEEN

Twenty Years of Treason

A conspiracy so immense and an infamy so black.

Throughout 1951 and 1952, with Republicans the minority in Congress, McCarthy kept making his headline-winning charges that America's leaders were guilty of treason. It was his prelude to power.

He attacked Truman's "no-win policy." Talking to reporters before addressing a meeting of furniture dealers in Milwaukee, he said of Truman: "The son of a bitch should be impeached." He implied that the president had been drunk when he sacked General Douglas MacArthur after hundreds of thousands of Red Chinese forces, blaring bugles and riding horses like the hordes of Genghis Khan, launched a devastating surprise attack on November 25, 1950, against U.S. lines in North Korea, sweeping all before them in what became the worst military retreat in American history. MacArthur, who had proclaimed "there is no substitute for victory," became for the right wing a symbol, a great military figure vanquished by the appeasement of Communism. McCarthy quickly offered a more sinister explanation for America's reverses. They were the result of "twenty years of treason."

McCarthy also accused Truman of acting under the influence of the "old Yalta crowd." He was a president "in name only," surrounded by Hiss and Acheson cronies who had "almost hypnotic powers over him." Acheson, the "Red Dean," was the real "heart of the octopus." He too must be impeached. McCarthy urged Acheson to seek asylum in the Kremlin.

Soon, McCarthy directed his attention to yet another administration leader: General George Catlett Marshall, often referred to then as "the greatest living American."

———

McCarthy promoted his attack on Marshall in advance to the press, and wrote all senators urging them to be present to hear him. His June 14, 1951, speech ran to some sixty thousand words.

He presented it as a scholarly review of the career forged by Marshall, then secretary of defense and before that secretary of state. Not long before, as the Army's chief of staff and FDR's principal military strategist, Marshall had emerged from World War II as the leading U.S. military figure of the era.

As usual, McCarthy delivered his attack under the cloak of congressional immunity. Also as usual, McCarthy claimed his speech, and an expanded paperback version of it published under his name (*America's Retreat from Victory: The Story of*

George Catlett Marshall), was entirely his own work. In fact, it had been written for him by others in the anticommunist network, and he was so unfamiliar with many passages that he stumbled over them while reading from the text. In years since, scholars have regularly cited one passage as evidence of the ludicrousness of McCarthy's claim to be its author. This was when he said: "I am reminded of a wise and axiomatic utterance . . . by the great Swedish chancellor Oxienstiern to his son, departing on a tour of Europe: 'Go forth my son and see with what folly the affairs of mankind are governed.'"

McCarthy resorted to his familiar rhetorical devices to explain his attack on so admired a public figure. Once again, he cited friends' warnings of the dangers of speaking out: "Don't do it, McCarthy," they said. "Marshall has been built into such a great hero in the eyes of the people that you will destroy yourself politically if you lay hands on the laurels of this great man." His supposed answer to "these well-meaning friends" was that "the reason the world is in such a tragic state today is that too many politicians have been doing only that which they consider politically wise—only that which is safe for their own political fortunes."

Not so Joe McCarthy. He knew that after unmasking such a towering American leader he would be savagely attacked by "all of the administration apologists and the camp-following of the press and radio led by the *Daily Worker*." He knew they would instantly scream: "the Big Lie," "irresponsible," "Congressional immunity," "etc. etc. etc." Yet here he was, once more bravely risking his career to expose a conspiracy aimed at destroying America.

McCarthy laid out his case for the "twenty years of treason" responsible for America's recent reverses: "The raw, harsh fact is that since World War II the free world has been losing 100 million people per year to international Communism: the "Yalta sellout"; the similar "Potsdam treachery"; the loss of Nationalist China; the failure to back Chiang Kai-shek's desire to unleash his troops against the Communists on the Chinese mainland; the Korean War "that Marshall had helped to produce."

McCarthy was not merely reciting old history, but painting "the complete, sinister, treacherous, traitorous picture." There were the spies and traitors who had enabled Russia to "acquire the technical secrets, the blueprints, the know-how to make the bombs with which the administration seeks to terrify us." The same "leftist-liberals who preached a holy war against Hitler and Tojo are today seeking accommodation with the senior totalitarianism of Moscow." While the Truman administration "preached a gospel of fear," Acheson and Marshall "expounded a foreign policy in the Far East of craven appeasement."

Above all was the fact that America's defense against life-and-death Communist threats rested in the hands of George Catlett Marshall, who was still the nation's secretary of defense.

Not only was Marshall's "mysterious" hand at work in all these disasters, his dark presence could be found in episode after episode from the outbreak of—indeed, even before—World War II. McCarthy even intimated that Marshall was complicit in Pearl Harbor because he allegedly authorized destruction of a "winds" message, intercepted from the Japanese, that could have prevented the sneak attack.

Marshall showed an affinity for Communists. He had marched "side by side" with Stalin in war and peace, and strenuously sided with Stalin's wishes for a "second-front" invasion of Europe in 1942 with "a vigor going far beyond the call of duty of a purely military adviser." Under Marshall's command, the U.S. Army had commissioned known Communists during World War II, protected Communists in the Army, and illegally attempted to destroy the Army's counter-intelligence files on subversives.

There was much more, all of it couched in as dark and conspiratorial allusions as have been directed against a major American figure. Finally, McCarthy said:

"How can we account for our present situation unless we believe that men high in this government are concerting to deliver us to disaster? This must be the product of a great conspiracy, a conspiracy so immense and an infamy so black as to dwarf any previous such instance in the history of man."

McCarthy closed with a long attack on Marshall's character and patriotism—typically leaving the clear implication that Marshall was a traitor or a Communist while never explicitly saying as much.

If Marshall were merely stupid, the laws of probability would have dictated that at least some of his decisions would have served this country's interests. Even if Marshall had been innocent of guilty intention, how could he have been trusted to guide the defense of this country further? We have declined so precipitously in relation to the Soviet Union in the last six years, how much swifter may be our fall into disaster with Marshall's policies continuing to guide us? Where will all this stop? This is not a rhetorical question; ours is not a rhetorical danger. Where next will Marshall's policies, continued by Acheson, carry us?

To those who thought his description of "so great a conspiracy" farfetched, McCarthy raised the specter of the decline and fall of great empires destroyed from within. This was America's fate, unless the public rallied behind McCarthy to end this treasonous conspiracy.

———

Editorial reaction to McCarthy's speech was the harshest he had yet received: "Berserk eruption . . . New outburst of . . . misstatements, misquotations, and vilification," *Milwaukee Journal;* "Sickening show of demagogic smear attacks," *Madison Capital Times;* "Innuendoes, half-truths, and deliberate misrepresentations," *Chicago Sun;* "Barker's hoopla . . . Same old hokum," *Washington Post;* "Character assassination," *St. Louis Post-Dispatch.* Even McCarthy characterized the press reaction as "extremely bad during the first few weeks."

Once again, McCarthy attacked. His critics were part of the "camp-following, left-wing" elements of the press who "editorialized in almost the same words as the *Daily Worker* and with equal viciousness." He claimed to be the victim of "deliberate distortion and suppression." His "carefully and thoroughly documented speech" hadn't smeared Marshall and misrepresented his record; on the contrary, it was the press that had smeared and misrepresented McCarthy by perverting what he had said. "I never even remotely promised to expose 'a conspiracy and an infamy so black as to dwarf any previous such venture in the history of man,'" McCarthy said piously, "but had merely promised to give a cold, documented history of one of the most powerful figures in American history."

Political reaction was far more muted—or marked by outright silence. Marshall declined all requests for comment. He never descended to McCarthy's level, never offered a single word in reaction to McCarthy or his speech.

In the Senate, a disgusted Margaret Chase Smith reintroduced her Declaration of Conscience, explaining: "What I said then is even more applicable today, particularly in view of the statements made in the past few days." It went nowhere. She had been suddenly removed from McCarthy's investigating subcommittee on expenditures at the beginning of the new Senate session in a typically brutal McCarthy maneuver.* Deliberately adding insult to injury, he replaced the veteran Senator Smith with the newly-elected freshman senator Richard Nixon. Again, the lesson was clear: Cross McCarthy, he'll get you. Don't, he'll reward you.

Most Republican moderates kept their silence. Communists in government was their party's issue. However they personally felt about McCarthy, they knew he would be their most formidable campaigner on that issue in the upcoming 1952 elections. Besides, there had been a marked change in mainstream Republican attitudes toward McCarthy.

Only months before, as William S. White reported for the *New York Times,* many Republican senators had "snubbed" McCarthy. "With a seeming casualness," they avoided public friendliness with him, going out of their way never to pass

---

*"McCarthy waited until the last minute to send notice he was eliminating me," Smith later wrote in her memoir. "He did it by having a member of his staff deliver to my office, after 6 p.m., a copy of a memo he had prepared for all Republican members. The door to my office was locked. McCarthy's staff member put the letter under the door." McCarthy's justification for removing her was that Smith lacked "proper investigative experience."

close to his desk and studiously not showing any sign of support. No longer was this so. "The desk of Senator McCarthy is not, these days, avoided very often by his Republican associates," White observed. "Senator McCarthy is, by any standard, the most politically powerful first-term senator in this Congress."

The fear that had enveloped the Senate was especially felt among Democrats. They had watched as McCarthy scored victory after victory, capped by the startling defeat of Millard Tydings. In Idaho and Utah, two other favored Democratic senators, Glen Taylor and Elbert Thomas, were defeated after McCarthy vigorously campaigned for their ultraconservative opponents, Herman Welker and Wallace Bennett. When Democrats held their first caucus after Congress's resumption in January 1951, White reported, there was "a general expression of fear that what had happened to Mr. Tydings could happen to any other man in the Senate."

"For whom does the bell toll?" one Democrat asked. "It tolls for thee."

The Democrats, with near unanimity, maintained silence after McCarthy's attack on George Marshall. They had initially considered confronting McCarthy during his speech, but ultimately they followed the advice offered by Connecticut's Brian McMahon, who had learned a hard lesson from the Tydings Committee investigation. Debating McCarthy was useless, he told the Democratic caucus, for it was impossible "to pin him down to the facts of the issue." The Democrats boycotted McCarthy's speech and literally stayed away from the chamber when McCarthy spoke. Their absence wasn't a strategic calculation that the best way to deal with Joe McCarthy was to ignore him; it was rather a sign of the deep fear of the political consequences of confronting him.

Four men then in the United States Congress went on to become president of the United States, and three of them were senators: John Kennedy, Lyndon Johnson, and Richard Nixon. From the House, Gerald Ford became vice president and then president. While one senator serving then, Prescott Bush of Connecticut, became the father of one president and grandfather of another, the Senate was filled with other men harboring presidential ambitions, and a number of them—including Estes Kefauver of Tennessee, W. Stuart Symington of Missouri, and Eugene McCarthy of Minnesota—became candidates. Among this group of would-be presidents, Minnesota's Hubert Humphrey became vice president and then lost to Nixon in one of the closest presidential elections ever. Of all those senators, the most powerful was Lyndon Baines Johnson of Texas.

Lyndon Johnson was a master tactician, a politician who knew as a puppeteer knows his marionettes how men were motivated, how they could be made to respond, how political groups reacted to pressure and blandishments, how ideas and measures and men were bought and sold. J. William Fulbright of Arkansas, later a thorn in LBJ's side on the issue of Vietnam, described to me how Johnson could work his will upon the political process: "He made the Senate function better than anyone. He pushed things around; he got things done. He was a hell of an operator . . . He was as dedicated to the practice of politics as any man I have ever seen. It was remarkable the attention he used to give to every bill—big and little—small and unimportant as they may be."

Yet Lyndon Johnson led the Democrats in strict public silence and a hands-off attitude toward McCarthy. Liberals repeatedly urged Johnson to take on McCarthy. In 1951, William

S. White, a fellow Texan and close personal friend, told how he urged Johnson, "Something, somebody, has got to stop this man McCarthy. You simply must put the Democratic Party on the attack against him." As Robert A. Caro writes in his biography of LBJ, "No help from Lyndon Johnson was forthcoming."

Caro explains Johnson's refusal to take on McCarthy: "The fight was one for which he had little stomach—for Lyndon Johnson had read not only the polls but the man, and he was very, very wary of the man. 'Joe will go that extra mile to destroy you,' he said privately." Caro quotes LBJ's closest aide, the fixer Bobby Baker, as hearing Johnson privately tell men he could trust: "Joe McCarthy's just a loudmouthed drunk. Hell, he's the sorriest senator up here. Can't tie his goddamn shoes. But he's riding high now, he's got people scared to death some Communist will strangle 'em in their sleep, and anybody who takes him on before the fevers cool—well, you don't get in a pissing contest with a polecat."

Johnson's most influential benefactors in Washington, including such leading New Dealers and former FDR associates as Tommy Corcoran and Ben Cohen, also urged him to lead the Democratic senators against McCarthy. The time wasn't right, Johnson always answered. McCarthy was too popular; Communism in government was too potent an issue; attacking McCarthy would only confirm to millions of Americans that Democrats were handmaidens of the Communist conspiracy McCarthy had uncovered.

When William S. White argued that McCarthy was "destroying civil liberties in this country," Johnson replied: "Bill, that's a good point, but let me explain something to you. If I commit the Democratic Party to the destruction of McCarthy . . . in the present atmosphere in the Senate, we will all lose and he will win. Then he'll be more powerful than ever."

So Lyndon Johnson waited . . . and waited . . . and waited. Years would pass before Johnson began to move against McCarthy, and then only behind the scenes.

The shame of that Senate, especially the shame of its leaders and moderates on both sides of the aisle, was expressed by historian Robert Griffith when he wrote that McCarthy's victories were made possible "only by the unwillingness of moderates to take a stand that might expose them to obloquy." Perhaps, Griffith added, "this was the key to McCarthy's continued power—not the ranting of demagogues, but the fear and irresolution of honorable men."

Griffith's explanation is as good as exists for why McCarthyism persisted for so long and remained unchecked by the very people society entrusted to protect them from such abuses.

———

One Democratic senator was bold enough to challenge McCarthy despite LBJ's policy of silence. William Benton had been appointed to the Senate in 1949 after Raymond Baldwin resigned to become a Connecticut Supreme Court justice; the next year Benton was elected to serve out the remaining two years of Baldwin's term.

Bill Benton was a remarkable figure, and deserves more attention than I can give him here.* He came to the Senate after a brilliantly successful business career and a distinguished

---

*The voluminous Benton Papers in the archives of the Wisconsin Historical Society are a gold-mine for capturing the essence of the McCarthy years, especially in documenting the extraordinary cloak-and-dagger political battles, including wire-tapping, surveillance, and illegal use of tax returns, waged then between both liberals and McCarthyites.

222 / TWENTY YEARS OF TREASON

record in academia and the government. In 1929, he and his partner, Chester Bowles, founded what became the world-famous advertising agency Benton and Bowles. Later, Benton—a former Rhodes Scholar and scion of Phi Beta Kappa "preachers, teachers, and scholars"—became vice president of the University of Chicago, working with his Yale classmate Robert Maynard Hutchins. He then became chairman of the board and publisher of *Encyclopaedia Britannica* and chief financial controller of the prosperous firm Muzak. In 1945 Truman appointed him assistant secretary of state, a post he held for two years while supervising the department's overseas information programs. His former partner, Chester Bowles, who went on to become ambassador to India and undersecretary of State in the Kennedy administration, was the Connecticut governor who appointed Baldwin to the state's highest court and then named Benton as Baldwin's interim Senate successor.

Benton did not fit well with the Washington of the early 1950s. He was a passionate, outspoken northeastern liberal, a millionaire, an intellectual, a challenger of the establishmentarian senatorial system, and not a man who suffered fools silently. His colleagues tended to dismiss him as not understanding the "culture of the Senate." Besides, he was an "ad man," hardly a credential for a true political player. But he was a master at understanding the mass media and public opinion, and he was convinced that McCarthy was a danger to the nation and must be stopped.

During the Tydings Committee investigation, it was Benton who called McCarthy a "hit-and-run propagandist on the Kremlin model." In succeeding months he watched as McCarthy's attacks claimed more victims, notably Ambassador

Philip C. Jessup, Truman's nominee for delegate to the United
Nations General Assembly. McCarthy accused Jessup, who as
Acheson's chief diplomatic troubleshooter as an ambassador at
large had long been a target of the Far Right, of being associated with "six Communist fronts" and of "following the Communist line" in foreign policy actions. Although Jessup was
never anything other than a highly respected and patriotic
public servant,* and though the Senate had confirmed him to
diplomatic posts five prior times, McCarthy's attacks prevailed.
The subcommittee considering Jessup's nomination declined
to approve him by a vote of three to two. The manner in which
two of the negative votes were cast underscored how fearful
the Senate had become. Both of the senators in question, as
Robert Griffith wrote, "affirmed their confidence in Jessup's
loyalty, honor, and integrity." Yet they voted against him. "He
is one of the most honorable men I know," declared moderate
Republican H. Alexander Smith, an old friend of Jessup's. Still,
Smith concluded, tortuously, that because Jessup had become
a "controversial figure," confirming him would "divide the
country at a time when above all else we need unity." Similarly, Senator Guy Gillette, a Democrat from Iowa, said Jessup
had been the target of "unfair and unprincipled attacks," but
he argued that Jessup should not be confirmed because those
attacks had destroyed public confidence in him.

---

*Thomas Reeves cites Jessup's impeccable background as including
his service in World War I, his commanding of an American Legion Post
in New York, his distinguished career as a lawyer, an author, and an international relations professor, and of his having "enjoyed the confidence of
such eminent public figures as William Howard Taft, Harlan F. Stone,
Elihu Root, Harry Guggenheim."

Benton was appalled by these McCarthy tactics, but he did not determine to take dramatic action until the first weekend that August, when he read the highly critical report of a Senate subcommittee that for months had been investigating McCarthy's role in the Tydings reelection campaign. The lengthy report was based on the testimony of virtually everyone involved, with one exception: McCarthy refused to appear, and the subcommittee never demanded that he testify.

Afraid that the report would be "filed and forgotten," Benton took unprecedented action. When the Senate resumed its session the next Monday, he introduced a resolution calling for an investigation by the Rules Committee to determine whether the Senate "should initiate action with a view toward the expulsion [from] the United States Senate of . . . Joseph R. McCarthy."

In the week after Benton's resolution was introduced, not a single senator rose to support it. Nor did any senator defend Benton publicly after McCarthy, speaking on the Senate floor, angrily denounced him as "Connecticut's odd mental midget" and said he had "established himself as a hero of every Communist and crook in and out of Congress." Still, unpopular though Benton's resolution was, it forced the Senate to act. It was referred to the Subcommittee on Privileges and Elections, where it began to wend its long, slow way through congressional procedure.

"Benton did what many other senators would like but never would dare to do," the *Christian Science Monitor*'s Joseph C. Harsch then wrote. "The fact is that the Senate is afraid of Joseph McCarthy. He is something its members don't understand." McCarthy, Harsch said, "seems to thrive on abuse. Anyone who has tangled with him has regretted it in the end." As for Benton's attempt to topple McCarthy, Harsch concluded, "This might look like David and Goliath, except that this David doesn't have a slingshot, or any other visible weapon. . . . The odds are 99 to 1 on the slugger from Wisconsin." Harsch was proved to be correct.

McCarthy accused the subcommittee charged with investigating him of "dishonesty" and linked some of its staff members to Communism, thereby discrediting its efforts. He charged that Benton had packed the State Department with a "motley, Red-tinted crowd"; had been "a clever propagandist" for years "paralleling the Communist Party line down to the last period, the last comma"; had taken "the megaphone for the Communist Party-line type of smear attack on me"; had given haven to "fellow travelers, Communists, and complete dupes"; had employed on his Encyclopaedia Britannica Films, Inc., eight writers with "a fantastic record of Communist activities"; and had set an example of "fraud and deception." If this weren't enough, he accused Benton of purchasing and distributing "lewd and licentious literature which has also followed the Communist Party line" and of buying "lewd art works and Communist-produced art works."

Finally, in a nationally telecast interview, McCarthy attacked Benton for "shouting and screaming to high heaven" about McCarthy's use of congressional immunity while Benton was using the same cloak to make charges against him. McCarthy had baited the hook; Benton swallowed it. Outraged, Benton took the Senate floor, compared McCarthy's methods to Hitler's, and offered to waive his congressional immunity. McCarthy immediately filed a two-million-dollar libel and slander suit against Benton, claiming that he considered his suit "a means of pinpointing the contest between America and the Communist Party."

McCarthy had no intention of following the suit to an end, nor did he believe he could win it. When his friend, fellow attorney Urban Van Susteren, told him he couldn't win two dollars in the case, McCarthy agreed, but explained that the suit would make Benton "sweat" and force him to spend money to defend himself. The suit dragged on for nearly two years; then, in 1954, just before it went to a court judgment, McCarthy dropped it. By then, Bill Benton had lost his Senate seat. Long before his defeat, Benton recognized that McCarthy had turned the tables on him.

"Instead of pursing McCarthy," he said ruefully, "I am the fellow who is being pursued."

McCarthy had taken another scalp; every senator understood the message. As *Newsweek* reported, while Democrats might fume at McCarthy, "he has them terrorized."

––––––

Harry Truman wasn't terrorized. The president launched his own characteristically blunt attack on McCarthy only days after Benton introduced his resolution. Speaking out against "lies and slander," the president decried the "wave of uncertainty and fear" gripping the nation. Of "scaremongers and hatemongers," he said: "Character assassination is their stock in trade. Guilt by association is their motto. They have created such a wave of fear and uncertainty that their attacks upon our liberties go almost unchallenged. Many people are growing frightened—and frightened people panic." He called on "every American who loves his country and his freedom" to "rise up and put a stop to this terrible business . . . [and]

take the lead against the hysteria that threatens the government from within."

Truman promised to make McCarthyism an issue in the next year's presidential election. "If Truman wants to make the fight against Communism—which he calls McCarthyism—an issue in the campaign, I will welcome it," McCarthy said. "It will give the people a chance to choose between Americanism or a combination of Trumanism and Communism."

Within seven months, with more than half a year to go before the 1952 election, Harry Truman announced that he would not be a candidate for reelection. He had sunk lower in the polls than any president before him. Nearly eight of ten Americans disapproved of the job he was doing. The hysteria and fears of which he had warned were not abating. McCarthyism was ascendant.

During 1952, which saw Dwight D. Eisenhower pitted against Adlai E. Stevenson in the presidential election, McCarthy's attacks grew wilder. He charged that the nation's leadership was "almost completely morally degenerate," described the president as "a puppet on the strings being pulled by the Achesons, Lattimores and Jessups," and said of the nation's then-majority political party: "The Democratic label is now the property of men and women who have . . . bent to the whispered pleas from the lips of traitors . . . men and women who wear the political label stitched with the idiocy of a Truman, rotted by the deceit of an Acheson, corrupted by the red slime of a [Harry Dexter] White."

Nothing stopped McCarthy. In speech after speech, he quoted anticommunists as alleging, without proof or names, that four hundred active members of the Communist Party held positions in the American press, radio, and motion picture industries. He turned on his congressional colleagues, claiming that "several U.S. representatives and senators have known Communists on their staffs"—without, of course, identifying the elected officials or the staff members. He called for the Missouri Democratic senator Thomas Hennings to disqualify himself from the investigation sparked by Benton's expulsion resolution because Hennings's St. Louis law firm represented the *St. Louis Post-Dispatch*, one of the newspapers that had "editorialized against my anti-Communist fight along the same lines as the *Daily Worker.*" He also attacked one of Hennings's law partners, John Raeburn Green, for representing an editor of the *Daily Worker* before the U.S. Supreme Court, and implied that Green was disloyal. Green, who had recently been cited by the *Journal of the American Bar Association* as exemplifying "what is pure and noble in our profession," had taken the case without fee to defend the right of free speech.

By then, Joe McCarthy possessed such power that, as one leading critic wrote, he "functioned for a time as a supplemental form of government in the United States." The testimony of two largely unknown congressional staff members offers a unique insight into what it was like to be in Washington then.

The first is Roy L. Elson, who had worked as a junior aide on Capitol Hill before returning to college to complete his education. When he returned to Washington in the early 1950s to act as an administrative assistant to one of the leading Democratic senators of the day, Carl Hayden of Arizona, he was startled to find the city he had known was gone. That

Washington had been a congenial place to work. While walking through the corridors of the only Senate Office Building then, people would stop and exchange pleasantries; there was a buzz of political chit-chat, discussion of issues, laughter. On his return, an unnerving quiet filled the same halls. "People wouldn't talk," Elson remembered. "There was a silence that was frightening. This guy [McCarthy] had really frightened people. There was something going on. You could feel the undercurrent. It . . . just scared the hell out of me. I'm still haunted by that period."

Heightening these emotions was the certain knowledge that this climate was accompanied by eavesdropping operations conducted by government investigators as well as those working on behalf of both conservative and liberal groups. Everyone knew, Elson remembered, that when you called an executive branch department someone would be taking down in shorthand everything you said. "I always went under the assumption, even back in the [19]50s, that there were no private conversations," he said. "If you wanted to have any, you better make sure you're outside somewhere, and even that wasn't safe. Someone was listening to your conversation if you were in any position of power."

Some senators confided to colleagues that they feared their mail was being read, their phones tapped, their files searched. Bill Benton was enraged to discover that McCarthy had obtained copies of his income tax returns, and was using them in the libel suit. So concerned was Benton that he had private phone lines bypassing the switchboards run into his hotel rooms. In return, liberals played the same dirty tricks on the McCarthyites. Benton's files reveal an extensive listing of what were clearly wiretaps, chronicling time, date, and duration of phone calls between such leading anticommunists as George Sokolsky, Westbrook Pegler, Fulton Lewis, Jr., and from McCarthy aides Surine, Kerr, and Nellor to Whittaker Chambers, William Randolph Hearst, Jr., Ralph de Toledano, Francis Cardinal Spellman, and many others in the conservative network.

Another Senate aide remembered all too painfully how McCarthy falsely accused him as a loyalty risk. Darrell St. Claire, whose forty-year Senate career was capped by service as assistant secretary of the Senate, had, while acting as chairman on the Loyalty Security Board of the State Department, cleared an employee who was the subject of twelve separate FBI reports. McCarthy's claim that St. Claire had declared a known Communist a non-security risk came when St. Claire was chief clerk of Senator Hayden's Rules Committee, and was prompted by McCarthy's erroneous belief that St. Claire had leaked critical information about him to the "leftwing press." Hayden defended St. Claire, saying his "name has been dragged into this dispute without any basis of fact at all." After this episode, Hayden took a lead in pursuing the McCarthy expulsion investigation.

Years later, having survived the McCarthy attack and spearheaded the transformation of the Senate staff system from patronage to professionalism, St. Claire recalled the fear McCarthy engendered. "He never really expected to be challenged in the arena that he selected for his politics," St. Claire said of McCarthy.

In another century, he would have been taken to the dueling ground and shot. He knew that the gamesmanship of the Senate was going to be his protection, and that the immunity of the Constitution would protect him. Therefore, he selected for his accusations a number of very small people. One I can remember worked in the Government Printing Office, probably had a job that paid him $2,000 a year, yet McCarthy denounced him because the man had been an immigrant out of Eastern Europe, and had some radical background. That put him on the front page of the *Daily News* and the man resigned. That's just like stepping on a snail. There was no reason for it.

What can you say about him? Robespierre? Ultimately he would send anybody to the guillotine just to get himself a headline.

———

Not all the abuses of McCarthyism were confined to the nation's capital, nor were all directly attributable to McCarthy. The virus of McCarthyism had spread to infect virtually all of American life. By the beginning of the fall semester of 1951, after nearly two years of McCarthyism, fears of Communism were imposing a crippling conformity on American campuses. "Misguided zealots shout 'Communist' at every college professor who ventures a new idea or selects a different text book," Jazzes H. Halsey, the president of the University of Bridgeport, told his students and faculty in that fall's convocation. "Pressure groups issue blanket condemnations of new curriculum developments, and State Legislatures conduct investigations about subversive campus activities. These are days of crises and on every hand we see numerous evidences of attempts to curb freedom of thought and freedom of expression . . . Social scientists have to be careful in their research work or in announcing their findings, and well qualified citizens hesitate to risk their reputations in government service."

Halsey noted that even Dr. Robert M. Hutchins, former leader of the University of Chicago, confessed he had become so intimidated by guilt-by-association charges that he refused to join any organization, "even one whose sole objective is merely to preserve and perpetuate Mother's Day in America." A survey of citizens on the Fourth of July in the old hotbed of liberalism, Madison, Wisconsin, showed how effective pressure to conform had become. Of one hundred twelve Madison citizens asked to sign a petition containing nothing but quotations from the Declaration of Independence and the Bill of Rights, all but one refused to sign. They feared the petition was a subversive document. They were afraid that if they signed it they would be called Communists.

Indeed, innocent Americans were accused of Communism and disloyalty throughout the country, on campuses,* in publishing houses, in private businesses, and at all levels of government activity. Many examples exist. I offer this one because it is my strongest personal memory of McCarthyism:

I was in high school in 1948 when my father, Malcolm Johnson, was writing his "Crime on the Waterfront" articles for the old *New York Sun,* exposing the organized crime reign of terror and murder on the waterfront. The articles attracted great attention, and the flood of anonymous calls threatening our family forced my parents to have an unlisted phone number for the rest of their lives. In public attacks, the head of the longshoremen's union, Joseph P. Ryan, repeatedly accused my father of being either a Communist or a dupe of the Commu-

---

*For a superb recounting of the fear and intimidation that swept America's universities, see Ellen Schrecker's *No Ivory Tower.*

nists and of relying on Communist sources for his newspaper exposé.

The articles were published at the same time that the first Alger Hiss trial was proceeding in the criminal courthouse near the *Sun* building across from City Hall. Headlines about my father's waterfront exposé and the Hiss trial competed for page one space each day, week after week. After the articles won the 1949 Pulitzer Prize, my father sold the movie rights to Hollywood and began expanding the articles—some two hundred in all—into a book. Then, early in January 1950, the *Sun* folded. As its star reporter, my father wrote his paper's obituary, then began looking for a job.

At the end of January, he signed a two-year contract with Hearst, his work to be distributed through King Features and Hearst's International News Service (INS). That spring, after completing his waterfront book, he began working for Hearst. By then, Hiss had been convicted and McCarthy had begun his rise after his Wheeling speech. Toward the end of the year, after rejecting several screenwriters' attempts to adapt my father's material into a movie, the Hollywood producers hired Budd Schulberg. My father was delighted. Schulberg's novel about F. Scott Fitzgerald's final days in Hollywood, *The Disenchanted,* had just been published to much acclaim, and his first novel, *What Makes Sammy Run?,* had become a classic in the early 1940s. His father was the major producer B.P. Schulberg, and Budd had a string of credits from well-received films. Schulberg became consumed by the waterfront project until he completed his final draft, on April 14, 1951, of the script for *Crime on the Waterfront,* as the screenplay was originally titled. This drew mention in the press.

234 / TWENTY YEARS OF TREASON

Some months earlier, another Hollywood writer had testified before the House Un-American Activities Committee
that Schulberg had been a Communist Party member at the
end of the 1930s after his graduation from Dartmouth. This,
coupled with news of Schulberg's work on the waterfront
movie, led Joe Ryan to write a classic guilt-by-association letter to William Randolph Hearst, Jr. Ryan's letter to Hearst,
who from New York was overseeing the Hearst editorial empire, was addressed to "Friend Bill." In it, Ryan wrote that the
script for an earlier version of the waterfront movie, which
had been "rejected by several of the large motion picture
firms," was written "by Budd Schulberg, who was, or had
been a member of the Communist Party." He added: "I understand now that the Monticello Motion Picture Corp. is
contemplating producing this picture in the near future, and
this Budd Schulberg has been mentioned recently by a motion picture artist, Richard Collins, as definitely a member of
the Communist Party."

Then Ryan wrote: "Knowing of the long fight that your father and yourself have waged against Communism, in every
form, I felt that I should call to your attention that Malcolm
Johnson is employed by International News Service and while
I do not expect him to change his identity, I believe he should
be in accord with the policies of his employer. Trusting that
you will understand the motive that has prompted me to write
this letter, it is in no spirit of criticism but just bringing the
facts to your attention."

Hearst immediately forwarded Ryan's letter to Seymour
Berkson, the chief executive of INS, with a penciled notation
about Ryan that read: "I know and rather like him personally.
Very anti-Commie."

My father replied to Berkson, who showed Hearst's letter to my father:

In general, I will say that this letter is typical of Ryan's tactics. Ever since my exposé of the New York waterfront and of his union in particular he has tried to smear me as a Communist or Communist sympathizer. He even tried it while I was on the *Sun*. But whatever else could be said of the old *Sun*, it could not be accused of being pro-Communist or of employing pro-commie writers.

The truth is that Ryan is understandably sore because I have attacked him and his union and will continue to do so, whether I work for INS or not. In print, over radio and television, and in lectures and public speeches I have accused Ryan of protecting racketeers, and I have proved it. I have charged that his union is racket-ridden and that he has appointed to key positions in the union known criminals and gangsters. Ryan is anti-Communist and as far as I am concerned that's the only good thing you can say about him. He has used his anti-Communism as a blanket defense of everything rotten in his racket union. He would have you believe that anyone who criticizes the union or his leadership is, per se, a Communist, Communist sympathizer, or tool of the Communists.

Everything I ever wrote or said about him has been documented, and supported by similar criticism by some of the most conservative newspapers in the United States, students of labor and, above all, by priests of Ryan's own faith, the Roman Catholic Church.

My newspaper articles, and later the book, were endorsed by these priests, by the District Attorney of New York, and by other officials. The book has received favorable reviews all over the country and from the Catholic press, which not even Ryan will dare to insinuate is Communist.

No, Ryan again is beating his favorite dead horse, and he knows it.

I do not know, of my own knowledge, whether Budd Schulberg is or was a Communist. Between you and me, if he is, or was, it will certainly hurt the prospects of our movie and that I shall regret for we had planned a hard-hitting, honest, documentary type of film. As for Ryan and Communism, I have always maintained that Ryan is one of labor's worst enemies and, consequently, the best friend the Commies could have because by his conduct of his union he gives the Communists real ammunition.

I do not question the right—or even the judgment—of Bill Hearst Jr., if he chooses to like Ryan personally. But I do say—and will say again and again—that Ryan heads one of the worst racket unions in the country; that he protects known racketeers and consorts with criminals. He's a lunkhead.

In words that evoke for me the climate of intimidation so many experienced, my father felt obliged to proclaim his loyalty: "My own political views are not secret. I am willing to take oath at any time that I am not, never have been, and never could be a Communist or a Communist sympathizer in any shape or form."*

---

*The travails of making the movie, which premiered as *On the Waterfront* in July, 1954, continued for three more years after Ryan had tried to get my father fired as a Communist. Thanks to Schulberg, who wrote at least seven more original scripts, director Elia Kazan (another young Communist in the 1930s), Leonard Bernstein, and the talents of a dedi-

My father was not fired; Berkson stood by him, and Hearst did not intervene—perhaps because by that time the New York Crime Commission had begun the investigation of Ryan that led to his union being expelled from the AFL-CIO for racketeering—the first such expulsion in the history of the trade union movement—and Ryan's eventual criminal conviction and prison term. But the episode remains for me an example of the fearful backdrop to a time when the careers and reputations of many were ruined by false accusations.

Joe McCarthy was treated as a hero at the 1952 Republican National Convention in Chicago that nominated Dwight D. Eisenhower for president. GOP strategists had continued to embrace McCarthy as a campaigner, arranging for him to

---

cated cast headed by Marlon Brando, Karl Malden, Lee J. Cobb, Rod Steiger, and Eva Marie Saint, some of the truths about the waterfront were told—and told despite attempts by Ryan's union to intimidate Hollywood from making a film they accused of being antilabor, anti-American, and created by current or former Communists. As for my father, all these years later I remain immensely proud to find among his papers a number of public speeches he made denouncing the tactics of McCarthyism, the first in October 1950, when he warned "that haphazard witch-hunts and smear campaigns threaten the loss of national liberty"; another in 1952, when he criticized "the increasing hysteria and the tendency to penalize any free expression of thought or of opinion"; and another later that year of 1952, when he warned that "a new malignancy, sometimes called McCarthyism, but always character assassination, the presumption of guilt by association and guilt before trial, is on the horizon. It is more dangerous even than Communism. It preys on ignorance and is promoted by men who do so for cold profit." In that address, he urged his audience to "sift through propaganda for facts and do not be swayed by false appeals."

238 / TWENTY YEARS OF TREASON

speak for Republican congressional candidates in no less than sixteen states. The convention elevated him onto an even grander public stage. From beginning to end, the convention was dominated by the attack theme of Communists in government who were protected by the "Democrat Party," as the GOP speakers then, and for years to come, termed the Democratic Party.

On July 9, a national TV audience watched as Walter S. Hallanan of West Virginia, temporary convention chairman and a friend of McCarthy's, stepped to the podium and introduced McCarthy amid a crescendo of cheers. Delegates began snake-dancing their way through the aisles waving red placards embossed with the names "Hiss," "Acheson," and "Lattimore."

Hallanan began:

> Ladies and gentlemen of the Convention, the Truman-Acheson Administration, the Communist press and the Fellow Travelers have all joined hands in a gigantic propaganda campaign to discredit and destroy an able and patriotic United States Senator, because he has had the courage to expose the traitors in our Government. [*applause.*] They have not succeeded and they will not succeed. The fact that Senator Joe McCarthy is the object of such violent hatred by Dean Acheson, the Alger Hiss gang, and the Owen Lattimore crowd is a badge of honor in the eyes of every patriotic American. [*applause.*] When anyone tells you that Joe McCarthy has recklessly slandered honorable American citizens ask that person to name one whose name has been unfairly besmirched. [*applause.*] One by one those named by him as bad security risks are being publicly exposed or quietly dropped from the rolls of the Federal Government.

[*applause.*] Let us make it clear to the country here today and now that we turn our backs on Alger Hiss but that we will not turn our backs on any man such as that fighting Marine from Wisconsin, whom I now present to this Convention, the Honorable Joseph McCarthy. [*prolonged applause.*]

Amid a cacophony of horns, cheers, and the strains of *On Wisconsin* and the *Marine Hymn,* a waving, smiling Joe McCarthy strode toward the podium, faced the cameras, the delegates, and the millions watching beyond the hall, and went into his by-now familiar twenty-years-of-treason litany against the "Acheson-Truman-Lattimore party." Referring to the number of American dead and wounded in Korea, he told the cheering delegates that loyal Democrats no longer had a party for their leaders had "squandered the blood of 110,631 sons of American mothers."

McCarthy had perfected his speaking style, worked out how to stir a partisan audience to a frenzy, learned when to pause for effect as he delivered shocking recitations of treason—and all in the ominous-sounding monotone that became his trademark. After making attacks on Truman's honor and patriotism, after declaring "the American people are through with you, Mr. Truman, and through with the Achesons, the Jessups, and the Lattimores," he reached the apogee of his oratorical thunder in four dramatically delivered sentences.

My good friends, I say one Communist in a defense plant is one Communist too many. [*applause.*]

One Communist on the faculty of one university is one Communist too many. [*applause.*]

One Communist among the American advisers at Yalta was one Communist too many.

And even if there were only one Communist in the State Department, that would still be one Communist too many. [*applause.*]

He left the convention hall an even more formidable national figure than he had been when he entered.

Chapter

FOURTEEN

Taking More Scalps

He exposed all those Communists.

There was a time, as the 1952 election year approached, when Wisconsin Democrats believed they could defeat McCarthy in his own reelection race. It proved another in a long list of Democrats' strategic miscalculations.

Days before the Wisconsin primary on September 9, the columnist Joseph Alsop toured Wisconsin sampling voter opinion about McCarthy. In Coon Valley, Wisconsin, Alsop entered a bar and struck up a conversation with the owner of the Coon Valley Ford dealership. He was going to vote for McCarthy, the car dealer said. Why? Alsop asked.

"He exposed all those Communists," said the car dealer.

"What Communists?" Alsop said. "Name one."

"Dean Acheson," the car dealer answered.

"Dean Acheson?" Alsop replied. "How do you figure *he's* a Communist?"

"If he isn't a Communist, how come he's in jail?"

McCarthy was nominated as Wisconsin's Republican senatorial candidate in a landslide, receiving 515,481 votes as compared to the 213,701 his closest opponent received. His total outnumbered the combined tally for all other candidates on the ballot—five Republicans and two Democrats: 435,492. Voter analysis, quickly reported to the nation at large, revealed the degree of McCarthy's hold on voters. Not only had Democrats crossed over to vote in the Republican primary; in large numbers those Democrats had voted for Joe McCarthy.

The magnitude of McCarthy's victory sent shock waves around the country but nowhere more so than in the editorial offices of the *Milwaukee Journal,* which had argued strongly against McCarthy's reelection. Once the returns had been tabulated, Paul Ringler drew the political lesson for Wisconsin and the nation in an angry editorial:

> This is not only appalling—it is frightening.
>
> It betrays a dulled moral sense, a dimmed instinct for truth, for honor, decency, fairness.
>
> It rewards falsehood, chicanery, deception, ruthlessness, the tactics of smear and fear, and contempt for the constitutional principles that safeguard American human and legal rights.

The political message of McCarthy's victory resonated to all levels of the electorate, not least to Republican strategists handling their presidential nominee. In order to carry Wisconsin, they concluded, Ike would have to ride on McCarthy's coattails.

Dwight Eisenhower had nothing but contempt for Joe McCarthy.

Decades later, General Andrew J. Goodpaster recalled vividly how Eisenhower struggled to control his temper when talking privately in the White House about McCarthy. Eisenhower's jaw would clench and a flush would rise from his neck to cover his face as the furious president said, "I'm not going to get down in the gutter with that man. I'm not going to take the presidency down into the gutter with that man."

Goodpaster, who was Eisenhower's staff secretary and defense liaison officer before becoming supreme allied commander in Europe and later still, West Point superintendent and commandant of the War College, knew the immense regard in which Eisenhower held George Marshall. Goodpaster had worked for Marshall and later still spoke of him in reverential terms. "What our country owed to Marshall is almost incalculable," he said, "and to have him vilified by the likes of McCarthy was absolutely horrible. And I know Eisenhower felt the same way."

At a Denver news conference on August 22, 1952, Eisenhower had exploded when reporters asked him about McCarthy's allegations of treason against Marshall. "There was nothing of disloyalty in General Marshall's soul," he said. "I am not going to support anything that smacks to me of un-Americanism . . . George Marshall is one of the patriots of this country . . . from the time I met him on December 14, 1941, until the war was over, if he was not a perfect example of patriotism and loyal servant of the United States, I never saw it. If I could say any more, I would say it, but I have no patience with anyone who can find in his record of service to this country anything to criticize."

An episode even more telling about Eisenhower's attitude toward McCarthy occurred late in the afternoon of October 2, the day before the two were to conduct a day-long whistle-stop swing through the Badger State. McCarthy requested that they meet in Eisenhower's hotel suite in Peoria, Illinois, saying he wanted to make a courtesy call on the general before their joint campaign appearances the next day.

Eisenhower, who had a famous but publicly concealed temper, had been grumping to aides for days that he didn't want to go to Wisconsin. He didn't want to meet McCarthy, either. Nonetheless, he agreed to the private meeting. Kevin McCann was one of two others present for the confrontation.

McCann was a longtime Eisenhower aide. He had served Ike in the Army, written speeches for him, helped write his book *Crusade in Europe,* and then gone with Ike when he assumed command of supreme allied headquarters in Europe in 1951. "I never heard the general so cold-bloodedly skin a man," McCann said of that hotel meeting. "He spoke with white-hot anger and just took McCarthy apart. The air turned blue—so blue I became embarrassed and finally had to leave." McCarthy's response? "He just grunted and groaned. He said damn little."

Immediately after, when William Lawrence of the *New York Times*—who would be covering the whistle-stop trip from onboard the train—asked McCarthy what had happened during his meeting, McCarthy replied: "We had a very pleasant conversation."

Eisenhower, however, planned to let the country know how he felt about McCarthy's tactics.

They were only seventy-four words in a single paragraph. Eisenhower directed a speechwriter to insert them in an address he would deliver October 3 in Milwaukee with McCarthy by his side. The brief paragraph read:

> Let me be quite specific. I know that charges of disloyalty have, in the past, been leveled against General George C. Marshall. I have been privileged for thirty-five years to know General Marshall personally. I know him, as a man and as a soldier, to be dedicated with singular selflessness and the profoundest patriotism to the service of America. And this episode [McCarthy's charges of treason] is a sobering lesson in the way freedom must not defend itself.

As William Bragg Ewald, Jr., an Eisenhower staff member, recalled, "Deliberately, intentionally, those words had been designed to slap McCarthy in the face in his own backyard. In his presence, Ike would disown the lie, the demagogic assault on Marshall, the ruthlessness of the senator's private anti-Communist crusade." The place of their delivery was carefully planned: the cavernous Milwaukee arena, filled with yelling McCarthy loyalists. There, Ike would deliver a speech that addressed the threat of Communism, but unlike McCarthy, Ewald said, Eisenhower would spell out "tough anti-Communism, no-nonsense anti-Communism, but anti-Communism moved by due process, that separated fog from fire, that respected civil liberties. It was anti-Communism smear-free. And it was anti-Communism that drew a sharp line around the region of McCarthyism."

The paragraph was in the speech text when Eisenhower

and his entourage, including McCarthy and leading Wisconsin Republicans, boarded their campaign train that day. On the train, a sharp debate began. Wisconsin officials argued strongly that the paragraph be taken out. Why needlessly antagonize Wisconsin GOP voters? Why pick a fight with a homegrown hero? Why risk defeat for the whole Republican state ticket? Why jeopardize Wisconsin's potentially crucial twelve presidential electoral votes? Finally, the advisers went to Eisenhower. He listened as they made their case.

"Are you telling me this paragraph should come out?" he asked.

"Yes," came the reply.

Then, the general's command: "Take it out."

Eisenhower, "the supreme organization man," as Ewald commented, "had bowed to his organization. And the organization had failed him."

What made matters infinitely worse was that William Lawrence had been leaked an advance copy of the speech text. On page one of the *Times* the next morning, Lawrence reported that the paragraph strongly defending Marshall in McCarthy's stronghold had been deleted—and he compounded this damaging news by writing incorrectly that McCarthy had persuaded Eisenhower to drop it during a private meeting between the two in Milwaukee's Perre Marquette Hotel before the speech. The great general, the Republican Party's new leader, had surrendered to McCarthy! McCarthy's expanding political power assumed near mythical proportions.

Bill Lawrence never disclosed his source about the supposed meeting in which Eisenhower caved in to McCarthy. Many close to Ike believed it was McCarthy himself. McCarthy was known at the time to be a principal source for

Lawrence, and using a news leak to advance himself—and strike back at Ike—was a typical McCarthy technique.

Eisenhower blamed his staff for arguing that he drop the paragraph, and blamed himself for being "mouse-trapped, bear-trapped," said Goodpaster. "I think Eisenhower took that to his grave." Adding to Eisenhower's anguish was his knowledge of the immense debt he owed Marshall, for it was Marshall who had backed him with President Roosevelt for the wartime promotion that placed Eisenhower in command of allied forces in Europe and paved the way to the presidency.

———

That November, Eisenhower won the White House in a landslide, and Republicans captured both houses of Congress. Twenty years after FDR's New Deal had reshaped the American political landscape, the era of continuous Democratic dominance had ended. A far more conservative period was underway. The actual margins of the Republican sweep in Congress were not that great: eight seats in the House, only one in the Senate. But there was no gainsaying that the Republicans were now solidly in control of the American government, nor was there any doubt as to how their victory had been achieved.

It had been an ugly, divisive campaign. McCarthy was not the only Republican leveling incendiary charges against the Democrats and their presidential candidate, Adlai Stevenson. Richard Nixon, Eisenhower's running mate, set the party's attack agenda at the GOP convention by promising to make Communist subversion "the theme of every speech from now until the election." He kept his word, maintaining Democrats were responsible for "the unimpeded growth of the Communist conspiracy within the U.S." and attacking what he called the Dean Acheson-George Kennan "cowardly college of Communist containment."

McCarthy sounded his twenty years of treason note across the country, drawing impassioned responses from crowds who turned out to hear him tell how he learned to do the dirty but essential job of killing skunks. Campaigning against Bill Benton, "the chameleon from Connecticut," he said Benton's Senate seat was "worth a hundred million dollars to the Kremlin on the floor of the United States Senate." At a rally in Bridgeport, the screaming crowd stunned Prescott Bush, father of George Herbert Walker Bush, and grandfather of then six-year-old George Walker Bush. Recalling the moment years later in an oral history interview at Columbia University, Prescott Bush said: "Well, we got down there, and the place is packed with standing room only. I never saw such a wild bunch of monkeys in any meeting I've ever attended. I went out on the stage with my knees shaking." When Bush mumbled a few words about his admiration for McCarthy's objectives but not his methods, the audience erupted. "With that," Bush said, "the roof went off with hisses and catcalls and 'Throw him out.' They booed and screamed at me. And Joe McCarthy got up, from across the stage, and he walked over and shook hands with me. I was taken aback by this friendly gesture, in view of all the booing going on. And he said, 'Pres . . . I want you to have dinner with me after the show's over.'"

On October 27, in the final days of the campaign, McCarthy made a nationally televised speech from the Palmer House in Chicago. Millions saw him viciously attack Adlai Stevenson, once saying "Alger—I mean Adlai," and at another moment calling Stevenson "Ad-lie," a derogatory mispronunciation McCarthy used throughout the campaign.

The popular radio commentator Elmer Davis was among those watching the speech. As he told listeners in his Hoosier twang the next day: "When I heard the applause for McCarthy last night an echo of memory seemed to give it an undertone: *Sieg Heil! Sieg Heil! Sieg Heil!*"

On election day, McCarthy could claim the scalps of four of the Democratic senators he had campaigned against, notably Bill Benton and Ernest W. McFarland, the Democratic Senate majority leader. McFarland, who had condemned McCarthy as a "character assassin" after McCarthy warned him that the Democrats were being made known as "a party of Communists and crooks," was defeated by the conservative Arizona businessman Barry Goldwater for whom McCarthy had spoken. (The two other Democratic senators who lost after McCarthy campaigned against them were Wyoming's Joseph O'Mahoney and Michigan's Blair Moody.) With these scalps added to the tally of McCarthy's senatorial victims, eight Republican senators could now be said to owe their seats to the "skunk-hunter." Some analysts would put the count one higher, with the ninth senator being a Democrat: John Fitzgerald Kennedy of Massachusetts.*

---

*In years since, political scientists have argued McCarthy's enhanced political power stemming from the 1952 returns was a myth. They cite voter analysis to show that Democratic senatorial candidates ran ahead of the national ticket in twelve of the non-Southern states in which McCarthy campaigned, and that McCarthy himself ran well behind the Wisconsin tally amassed by Eisenhower. At the same time, senators from both parties, the press, and the public were correct in believing McCarthy would wield even greater power in the next Congress—as he did. Whether myth or reality, the *perception* of McCarthy's growing influence made politicians even more reluctant to challenge him. He *did* emerge stronger than ever.

Old Joe Kennedy, the patriarch of his clan, was a staunch anti-communist and a strong supporter—financial and other-wise—of McCarthy. He invited McCarthy to his Palm Beach estate and to the Kennedy compound at Hyannis Port, where McCarthy socialized, went sailing, and played touch football with the family and even dated one of the daughters, Pat. More than anything else, Old Joe wanted his eldest living son, Jack, to become the first Catholic president of the United States.

A crucial step in fulfilling this goal was for Jack to move from the House of Representatives to the larger national forum of the U.S. Senate. In 1952, this meant unseating the highly favored Boston Brahmin Republican incumbent, Henry Cabot Lodge, Jr., who was then also serving as Eisen-hower's national campaign chairman. The last thing Old Joe wanted was for the popular Irish Catholic McCarthy to cam-paign against his son in a state with an Irish Catholic con-stituency estimated to number three-quarters of a million people. Old Joe appealed to McCarthy to stay out of Massa-chusetts that fall. What kind of inducements he made to Mc-Carthy remain lost to history, though there have been reports that he made a fifty thousand dollar contribution to McCarthy (and some McCarthy staffers discussed among themselves the belief that the payment was actually a hundred thousand dol-lars). Whatever the truth, despite appeals from Lodge, Mc-Carthy never campaigned in Massachusetts for his fellow Republican. In a hard-fought contest, Lodge lost by 70,000 votes while Eisenhower carried the state by 206,000. Was Mc-Carthy the difference? "Hell, half my voters in Massachusetts look on McCarthy as a hero," Kennedy later told Arthur M.

Schlesinger, Jr., in explaining his political rationale for not challenging McCarthy when they both served in the Senate.

————

On January 2, 1953, in the last hours of the last day of the 82nd Congress, the investigation sparked long before by Benton's resolution calling for the Senate to expel McCarthy ended with its submission of a final report.

Despite obstacles, the investigation had been kept alive by the determined prodding of Arizona's Carl Hayden, whose loathing for McCarthy stemmed not only from McCarthy's false charges against Darrell St. Claire but also from McCarthy's public attack on Hayden as "an old, blind, fuddy-duddy." According to Robert Caro, this assault led Lyndon Johnson to tell reporters: "Joe has made a lifelong and powerful enemy in Carl Hayden, and Carl is not a man who forgets easily."

The bipartisan report that the subcommittee presented after a year and a half investigation into Joe McCarthy's fitness to remain in the Senate dealt largely with McCarthy's complex financial affairs.

The record was damning. Even more so was the conclusion the report reached about McCarthy's repeated refusals to respond to the committee, or even to appear before it. His behavior reflected "a disdain and contempt for the rules and wishes of the entire Senate body, as well as the membership of the Subcommittee on Privileges and Elections." The record, it went on, "leaves the inescapable conclusion that Senator McCarthy deliberately set out to thwart any investigation of him by obscuring the real issue and the responsibility of the Subcommittee by charges of lack of jurisdiction, smear, and Communist-inspired persecution."

McCarthy reacted in character. The report marked "a new low in dishonesty and smear." He described the two Democrats on the subcommittee, Hayden and Missouri's Tom Hennings, as "left-wingers" and "lackeys" for the Truman administration. He was even more contemptuous of the sole Republican, New Jersey's Robert C. Hendrickson, calling him "a living miracle in that he is without question the only man in the world who has lived so long with neither brains nor guts."

There the report lay. Any action on the subcommittee's findings would have to come from a new Congress and a new administration in an even more highly charged political period.

Chapter

FIFTEEN

Junketeering Gumshoes

*And finally—across the seas—there occurred the vulgar
farce of McCarthy's audacious aides, Roy Cohn and
David Schine, hunting through American embassies for
signs, names, and faces of traitors.*

—Emmet John Hughes, *The Ordeal of Power*

Roy Cohn stepped off the elevator onto the eleventh floor of New York's Hotel Astor to find dozens of people milling outside the suite. Inside, he picked his way through a noisy crowd of men and women in formal dress until he reached the bedroom, and there, for the first time, he saw Joe McCarthy. McCarthy had shed most of his evening clothes and was standing in an undershirt, tuxedo trousers, with suspenders, and patent leather shoes. The two men were introduced. "My God, I'm glad to meet you—but you can't possibly be as good as everyone says you are," McCarthy said warmly. "I just want to find out what's public relations and what's real."

That was the way Roy Cohn and Joe McCarthy met.

————————

Cohn had been called by a Capitol Hill aide and told McCarthy wanted to see him. It was early December 1952, a month after McCarthy's reelection, seven weeks before Eisenhower's inauguration, at a time when McCarthy was plotting his next move as the 83rd Congress prepared to start its session under Republican control.

In recognition of McCarthy's greatly enhanced political stature, the Republican majority already had him slated for a powerful new role. He was to be chairman of the Senate's Government Operations Committee as well as chairman of its Permanent Investigations Subcommittee, with wide discretionary authority to investigate "the operations of Government activities at all levels." As chairman of both committee and subcommittee, McCarthy would operate with double the congressional funding from the previous year and the ability to significantly increase the size of the staffs.

The McCarthy aide had told Cohn over the phone that the senator would be in New York addressing a veterans' group. Could Cohn come by his hotel suite after the speech, say around eleven o'clock that night, so they could talk?

McCarthy took Cohn aside. Still surrounded by the throng of well-wishers, McCarthy began earnestly explaining why he had wanted them to meet. "You know, I'm going to be chairman of the investigating committee in the Senate," he said. A lot of people in Washington were trying to get him to ease off on the Communist issue. Don't jeopardize your strong political position by taking on new enemies, they advised him. Be sensible. Play it safe. Start investigating less controversial targets. Why not look at the Department of Agriculture, or the Library of Congress? Stay away from Communism for now. But that wasn't who he was, McCarthy went on. "I fought this Red issue," he told Cohn. "I won the primary on it, I won the election on it, and I don't see anyone else around who intends to take it on. You can be sure that as chairman of this committee this is going to be my work. And I want you to help me. I'm not sure in what capacity, but keep in touch with me."

The entire conversation lasted little more than three minutes, but Cohn never forgot McCarthy's energy and contagious spirit during this first encounter. "He was jovial, hearty, outgoing," Cohn later recalled. "He wanted to be liked, and he was liked."

———

Roy Cohn was twenty-five years old. Small, pale, with hooded eyes, black hair he wore slicked back and neatly parted on the right, and a faint scar from a childhood accident visible along his nose, "I was brash, smug, and smart-alecky," he later wrote of himself. "I was pompous and petulant." He was also brilliant, and extremely well-connected. His father, Albert Cohn, was a New York State Supreme Court justice and liberal Democrat who had backed FDR's New Deal and was friends with Herbert Lehman, the New York senator. Roy, after earning undergraduate and law school degrees from Columbia University in only three and a half years, began work in the New York District Attorney's office. Then, as a precocious prosecutor, he played a leading role in the Rosenberg spy trial and in cases involving Communist Party leaders.

Cohn came to McCarthy's attention through the anticommunist network where Cohn had already forged powerful allies, among them J. Edgar Hoover and the columnist and
family friend George Sokolsky. Cohn had accepted a position
as special assistant to the U.S. Attorney General in Washington, but the prospect of working with McCarthy presented
greater opportunities for an ambitious young man who had already made a mark fighting Communists.

A few days after meeting McCarthy, Cohn received a
phone call from Sokolsky, acting at McCarthy's behest. The
senator wanted him, perhaps as chief counsel. Then Sokolsky
called again. There was a complication: Old Joe Kennedy
wanted McCarthy to appoint his son, Bobby, as chief counsel.
McCarthy, Sokolsky told Cohn, was "anxious to 'do something' for Joe Kennedy because of their close friendship."
According to Cohn's and Sokolsky's account, McCarthy
persuaded Old Joe that because it was widely known that
Kennedy had contributed to McCarthy's reelection campaign,
it would be best to avoid the appearance of a quid pro quo.
Because of Bobby's limited legal experience, it would look
better to give him a lesser spot "at the beginning, then after
awhile he will be moved forward." Thus, when announcing
his new staff positions on January 2, 1953, in the closing hours
of the outgoing Democratic 82nd Congress, McCarthy said
the former FBI veteran Francis D. Flanagan would remain as
committee general counsel, and Robert Kennedy would be
Flanagan's new assistant. Kennedy immediately accepted the
position. Then McCarthy named Roy Cohn as the committee's chief counsel. Cohn was astounded at the confusion created by the divided roles: "I hadn't the faintest idea what it
meant."

Neither did Joe McCarthy. When reporters pressed McCarthy to explain the apparently conflicting roles—"Who is superior to whom? What does each title mean?"—McCarthy paused, grinned, spread his hands, and confessed: "I don't know." As Cohn later wrote, "And actually he did not. He kept Flanagan to placate Joe Kennedy. He made me chief counsel because he wanted me to direct the Communist hearings. But he had not figured out who was going to do what. I had my first hint of the chaos that was to prevail."

But Cohn had no reservations about taking the job. That night he was thrilled to attend a private Washington party in his honor that, as he later said, "will not be duplicated in my experience." The guest list was like a who's who of the anticommunist network now about to exercise even greater influence over American life. Among those celebrating Cohn's appointment were Richard Nixon, three weeks away from becoming vice president; J. Edgar Hoover; twenty United States senators; conservatives who would enter the White House with Eisenhower; and right-wing journalists such as Sokolsky. To Cohn, "It was heady wine, I don't mind admitting."

Two weeks later, even before the Eisenhower administration came to power on January 20, 1953, the McCarthy investigating subcommittee began the first of its executive session investigations into suspected Communist activity. Seated at the table with McCarthy were chief counsel Cohn and another twenty-five-year-old assistant, G. David Schine, whom Cohn had just named to the staff as "chief consultant." The subcommittee would conduct hearings behind closed doors for nearly two years. For the next fifty years, the executive session hearing records remained sealed; then in 2003, as America was about to launch the second front in its war on terror with the invasion of Iraq, Congress authorized their publication. Along with the intensely publicized public McCarthy hearings, these records tell a dark story in American political history. Decades later, it remains hard to believe that the events described in these private and public records happened.

During the two years it occupied the American center stage, the McCarthy subcommittee initiated four hundred forty-five "preliminary inquiries" and one hundred fifty-seven "investigations." Of these, seventeen became formal, televised hearings. McCarthy led most of those himself.

His purpose was never to develop information that would lead to criminal convictions. It was to expose Communists, fellow travelers, comsymps, pinkos—real or suspected. Most of all, it was to generate publicity for McCarthy's anticommunist crusade—and for Joe McCarthy. Viewed strictly on these grounds, the hearings, both private and public, were a spectacular success.

Once more, McCarthy's startling accusations dominated headlines—and not only in news flowing from the public hearings. During breaks in the private sessions, he would emerge to drop tantalizing hints to reporters about the subversion being uncovered behind the closed doors. Then he would dramatically return to press his search.

It mattered not that most of his and Cohn's vaunted investigations were, as historian Robert Griffith writes, "old and dusty, arising from charges and accusations dating back to 1946 and all well known to military intelligence and the FBI." Nor even that the investigations, however sensational their supposed revelations, failed to document McCarthy's charges of a vast Communist conspiracy threatening American society.

What mattered for McCarthy was that he now held a position further enabling him to exploit his charges. He renewed his assaults on his usual targets, principally the now Republican-led State Department.

McCarthy immediately began a widely publicized investigation of the department's loyalty and security files, seeking confirmation that knowledge of Communists and traitors was buried within them. He interrogated disgruntled file clerks about the "mess" the files were in, sowing suspicions about concealed subversives. He arranged to have his ally Scott McLeod named the department's overseer of security. A wave of firings ensued. The department and its new Republican leaders, headed by Secretary of State John Foster Dulles, reeled.

This furor produced dramatic daily headlines, as did McCarthy's assaults on the new president's power to conduct American foreign policy.

———

No sooner had Eisenhower taken office than two of his major foreign policy nominees, General Walter Bedell Smith and James B. Conant, were blocked by ultraconservative senators, led by McCarthy. Smith, Ike's World War II chief of staff and later U.S. ambassador to the Soviet Union and head of the CIA during the Truman administration, was nominated to become undersecretary of state. He was attacked for having defended one of McCarthy's State Department targets. Perhaps even worse, he had testified on behalf of Bill Benton in McCarthy's libel suit against the liberal Democratic senator from Connecticut. Conant, the president of Harvard University and a world-famous scientist, was nominated to become U.S. high commissioner to Germany. He represented everything the

McCarthyites hated: effete, elite, eastern intellectuals from liberal Ivy League bastions. McCarthy and other conservatives attacked Conant for holding opinions "contrary to the prevailing philosophy of the American people," and for having criticized public funding for parochial schools. Ultimately, both men were confirmed, but not before blood had been let and damage done to the president and to U.S. foreign policy.

Far more bruising was the confirmation fight over Eisenhower's choice to be the new U.S. ambassador to the Soviet Union, Charles E. "Chip" Bohlen.

As a career foreign service officer, Bohlen earned a reputation as the State Department's leading specialist on the Soviet Union, but passionate right-wing opposition to his nomination should have come as no surprise to the president. Bohlen was part of the Alger Hiss Yalta group that had sold out to Stalin, enslaved Eastern Europe, and led to the surge of Communism worldwide. Or so the Right argued. Bohlen *was* a major player at Yalta, and had served as FDR's interpreter with Stalin. His confirmation hearings were explosive. When Republicans attacked the "Yalta sellout," Bohlen coolly refused to go along with a blanket condemnation of the conference. He defended it. This enraged the McCarthyites, and especially McCarthy, who accused Secretary Dulles of lying about Bohlen's not having been a security risk. If Eisenhower saw Bohlen's entire security file, McCarthy thundered, he would instantly drop his nomination. McCarthy also employed his old tactic of smearing Bohlen as a homosexual— another false accusation.

Eisenhower had to twist arms. Two of the Senate's most respected members, the Republican Robert A. Taft of Ohio and the Democrat John J. Sparkman of Alabama (Adlai

Stevenson's vice presidential running mate in the last election), agreed to read the secret Bohlen security file in the White House. "There was no suggestion anywhere by anyone reflecting on the loyalty of Mr. Bohlen in any way," Taft said in reporting their findings, "or any association by him with Communists or support of Communism or even tolerance of Communism."

Bohlen was confirmed overwhelmingly, with a Senate vote of 74 to 13. A reporter asked Taft if this meant a break with McCarthy? "No, no, no," Taft quickly replied. Privately, he warned the White House against further antagonizing Republican conservatives: no more Bohlens, Taft said.

If McCarthy felt any diminution in support, he didn't show it. Two days later he brazenly announced that he had reached an agreement with Greek shippers—representing two hundred fourteen ships in all—to end their trade with Red China, North Korea, and Soviet bloc ports. This was a clear usurpation of the president's constitutional right to conduct foreign policy. Moreover, results of a meeting between Secretary Dulles and McCarthy strengthened the appearance that the administration was desperately attempting to appease McCarthy. Which it was. McCarthy agreed, Dulles reported afterward, that the execution of foreign policy rested solely with the president; nonetheless, Dulles praised McCarthy's actions as "in the national interest."

McCarthy's next act was even more audacious. He began investigating the State Department's overseas information program, including its libraries and the role of the Voice of America. Books and publications were removed from library shelves. Some were burned. McCarthy's staff began examining the department's films, radio, and television productions and promotional exhibits, looking for the taint of Communist influence. Again, the State Department attempted to appease McCarthy. Dulles issued a directive banning from its libraries books by "Communists, Fellow Travelers, et cetera"—then amended the directive with an even more sweeping order to withdraw works and periodicals containing "material detrimental to U.S. interests."

Not only were publications removed, or destroyed, but entire libraries were closed. Hundreds of employees were fired.

All this took place in the first two and a half months of the new Republican administration headed by a great wartime commander.

———

At around eleven o'clock in the morning on Tuesday, February 24, 1953, in the early weeks of the Eisenhower administration, Bob La Follette, then fifty-eight and working as a business consultant in Washington, left his office in the National Press Building carrying a briefcase. He told his secretary that he was going out and would call later. By then Joe McCarthy was, if not the most powerful politician in America, certainly the most feared. Already, McCarthyism was part of the language. Progressivism and the La Follettes were at best little-remembered names from a distant past in a dramatically different America.

No longer did La Follette look like "Young Bob;" his hair had turned almost completely gray, and he was suffering from numerous health problems including diverticulitis; mild diabetes; chronic neck, shoulder, and hip pains; and recurrent chest pains that had been diagnosed as probably stemming from coronary heart disease. None of these ailments, however, added up to a terminal illness.

Around noon, he phoned his wife Rachel from their home in Northeast Washington, asking her to leave a Red Cross meeting on Capitol Hill and meet him at their home. He was calm, and gave no explanation for the request. Half an hour later, she arrived home and, not finding her husband on the first floor, went upstairs. On their bed, she saw an empty pistol holster. Entering their master bathroom, she found La Follette's body sprawled on the floor. He was lying face up, one hand by his side, the other clutching a .22-caliber Woodman target pistol resting across his chest. A bullet had passed through the roof of his mouth and lodged in his brain. He had died instantly.

He left no suicide note, nor any kind of explanation for his death.

In the privacy of his family and among close friends, La Follette had at times exhibited deep depression. Family and friends recalled that he had become increasingly tormented by "an obsessive and apparently groundless fear of being called before McCarthy's committee." La Follette told friends that he was concerned he might be forced to testify about the steps he had taken to stamp out Communist influence on the congressional Civil Liberties Committee he had chaired. In fact, La Follette had quietly fired suspected Communists from his staff, and without going into detail had written about such Communist infiltration in a 1947 *Colliers* article.

Some people linked his death to his defeat by Joe McCarthy in 1946. As La Follette's biographer Patrick J. Maney was told, that defeat "ate away at him like a cancer and, coupled with an unrewarding job as a business consultant and with the destructive activities of his successor, McCarthy, heavily contributed to his depressed state of mind." La Follette may also have felt that he had failed his father by allowing his successor to reverse his legacy. Days after the suicide, Drew Pearson wrote that shortly before his death La Follette had expressed to friends at a social function his concern about McCarthy and "told how he never should have let McCarthy beat him, how he had let his father down." But all of this was speculation, and it all seemed a very long time ago when figures such as the La Follettes offered one vision of the American future and others, such as Joe McCarthy, a darkly different one. Now the public spotlight was shining on Wisconsin's McCarthy, not on Wisconsin's largely forgotten Young Bob La Follette.*

———

As McCarthy's contemptuous assaults on *his* State Department, *his* nominees, *his* policies, *his* right to lead America grew ever bolder, the president became increasingly furious beneath his grandfatherly public demeanor.

Ike's White House advisers were divided on how to deal with the Wisconsin demagogue. Some wanted the president to take him on publicly, others counseled a strategy of caution. The wisest course, they argued, was to avoid a political slugging match with McCarthy. Stay above the fray, act presidential, let others in the new Republican administration and congressional majority work quietly behind the scenes to pacify McCarthy and lure him back onto the team. Besides, while Republicans now controlled Congress, they had only a

---

*Some remembered La Follette, however. In Allen Drury's Washington novel *Advise and Consent,* Young Bob served as a model for the tragic main character, and John Dos Passos wrote movingly of him in *Midcentury.*

one-vote margin in the Senate; all the more reason not to antagonize McCarthy. Eisenhower chose that path—but at a great price that always comes with appeasement.

If Ike was not intimidated by McCarthy, he was extremely wary of McCarthy's influence with the Republican right wing, and worried that it could negatively affect his presidency.

Only weeks into his term, Ike responded to his brother Milton's appeal to "tear McCarthy to pieces," writing him privately, "You want me to make a martyr of McCarthy, and get the whole Senate to stand behind him because a president has attacked him?" That he would not do, Ike said. He was convinced, he told his brother, that the best way to handle McCarthy was not to give him "the publicity he craves." In the end, Joe McCarthy would self-destruct.*

Thus, Ike's strategy for dealing with McCarthy. For month after month, as he privately railed against new McCarthy outrages, the president would not even deign to mention the senator publicly by name. Others in the administration, notably Vice President Nixon and William P. Rogers, who became attorney general under Eisenhower and secretary of state under Nixon, met privately with McCarthy, held dinners, had cocktails with him on vacation trips to Florida, and encouraged him to be a team player. McCarthy invariably jovially agreed—and then launched another attack, and another. He widened his range of targets from the State Department to the Government Printing Office, the CIA, the Atomic Energy

---

*Years later, after the president's death, Milton Eisenhower said his brother "loathed McCarthy as much as any human being could possibly loathe another, and he didn't hate many people, but he felt McCarthy was a curse on the American scene."

Commission, and the defense plants producing weapons under contracts from the Defense Department. Finally, he targeted the U.S. military.

The president's diary entries reveal the inner battle he waged over how to deal with McCarthy, and his increasing turmoil and frustration.

April 1, ten weeks into his presidency, Ike to his diary:

"Senator McCarthy is, of course, so anxious for the headlines that he is prepared to go to any extreme in order to secure some mention of his name in the public press. His actions create trouble on the Hill with members of the party; they irritate, frustrate, and infuriate members of the Executive Department. I really believe nothing will be so effective in combating his particular kind of troublemaking as to ignore him."

In the same entry appears an astonishing statement that changes the impression I previously held of Eisenhower. He was becoming so frustrated with the obstructionism of McCarthy and other ultraconservatives, Ike confided to himself, that he was considering the formation of a new party bringing together all the sensible people in the great middle of American life.

Around the same time, Ike expressed his great irritation over McCarthy to a White House aide by saying he didn't want to run again in 1956 but would do so for only one reason—to defeat McCarthy. The aide, Bern Shanley, immediately recorded the president's confession in *his* private diary. A month later, Ike confided to his diary that he was aware of the terror that "McCarthy's calling names and making false accusations" had aroused in Europe, all to the detriment of the United States. At a Dartmouth commencement speech two weeks later, the president told the graduates, "Don't join the book burners."

On October 8, in the White House, he mused again about forming a third party in a diary entry to his private secretary, Ann Whitman. So furious was he over reactionaries trying to block his nomination of the Republican governor of California, Earl Warren, to be chief justice of the Supreme Court that he said: "If Republicans as a body should try to repudiate him, I shall leave the Republican Party and try to organize an intelligent group of independents, however small."

From the perspective of half a century later, Eisenhower made admirable statements from time to time—at press conferences or in formal addresses—articulating well the best American instincts for fair play, tolerance, and fundamental rights. "In all that we do to combat subversion," he remarked at one news conference toward the end of that searing first year, "it is imperative that we protect the rights of loyal American citizens. I am determined to protect those rights to the limit of the powers of the office with which I have been entrusted by the American people."

But Ike never issued the kind of clarion call that would challenge the nation to unite against the ravages of the senator. He never directly took on McCarthy. He continued to justify his policy of not challenging McCarthy publicly to his brother's repeated urging to take on McCarthy. In a passage that speaks as much to the twenty-four-hour, all-scandal TV news cycle of the America of the new millennium as it did to the America of McCarthyism, he wrote Milton in a tone of self-pity mixed with frustration: "Frankly, in a day when we see journalism far more concerned in so-called human interest, dramatic incidents, and bitter quarrels than it is in promoting constructive understanding of the day's problems, I have no intention whatsoever of helping promote the publicity value of anyone who disagrees with me—demagogue or not!"

Later, when Ike prepared his presidential memoirs at Gettysburg, a draft of his manuscript contained this passage:

> My brother, Dr. Milton Eisenhower, appealed to me to announce to the world that I strongly disapproved of all that McCarthy was doing and all that he stood for . . . [I] pointed out that if I were to attack McCarthy, as every instinct in me prompted me to do, I would greatly enhance his publicity value without achieving any constructive purpose. I was convinced that McCarthy's influence, such as it was, would be gone completely if he lost his headline value . . . In sheer political terms I was increasingly convinced that I would defeat him by ignoring him . . . I would not demean myself or the Presidency by getting in the gutter with him.

The public never saw this paragraph. It was deleted before publication, whether by Ike or his editors is unclear.

————

By early spring, McCarthy's investigation of the Voice of America had limped to an inconclusive end. McCarthy then dispatched his young aides, Roy Cohn and David Schine, on an eighteen-day search for Communists, suspected pro-Communists, or any subversive material housed by the State Department's overseas information collections in libraries and offices. On Easter Sunday, April 4, Cohn and Schine arrived in Paris to begin one of the most bizarre dramas in American history.

The two had met a year before when Cohn's former boss, U.S. Attorney Irving Saypol, invited them to lunch at a downtown Manhattan restaurant. Cohn and Schine were both twenty-five, ambitious, and from favored backgrounds, Schine even more so than Cohn. He was the son of Meyer Schine, a multimillionaire owner of a string of hotels and theaters. Not long after Schine graduated from Harvard, where his taste for luxury and a Cadillac standard of living had irritated class-mates, his father installed him as president of Schine Hotels, Inc. From their first meeting, Cohn and Schine struck up an intimate relationship. Soon they were cutting a swath through New York's best restaurants and nightclubs.

Physically, and it seems temperamentally, they were oppo-sites: Schine was tall, with wavy hair and "the build and the feature of a junior grade Greek god," as one magazine sketch gushed. To Richard Rovere, Schine was "sallow, sleekly coifed, and somnolent-eyed" in a "style that one used to asso-ciate with male orchestra singers." By contrast, Cohn was short (five foot eight), compact, and hyper. Schine, who didn't let his business responsibilities interfere with his taste for the good life,* admired Cohn's intellect, and considered him to be about the smartest person he ever met. Like Cohn, Schine wanted to become known as an investigator of Communists.

Schine's sole claim to expertise on the Communist men-ace was his production of a six-page pamphlet, "Definition of Communism." His father ordered it placed as prominently as the Gideon Bibles in his hotels' rooms. In it, Schine got wrong the dates of the Russian revolution, the founding of the Com-munist Party, and the start of the first Russian five-year plan. He misnamed Lenin, confused Stalin and Trotsky, Marx and Lenin, Kerensky and Prince Lvov. Yet later, as Ike's aide Ewald

---

*Schine's taste for good living included, while on the committee, sign-ing McCarthy's name to a letter to the Senate Rules Committee asking per-mission for himself and Cohn to have access to the "Senator's bath," a pool and steam room reserved exclusively for senators. His request was denied.

bitingly said, this pamphlet "stood as Exhibit A of author Schine's credentials as an authority on Communist ideology."

It made no difference to Cohn; after he named Schine the investigating committee's chief (and unpaid) consultant, they were inseparable. Cohn and Schine would fly from New York to Washington on Mondays, take adjoining rooms at the Statler Hotel, investigate Communists with McCarthy at private and public hearings on Capitol Hill on weekdays, and then fly back to Manhattan Friday nights for weekends of night clubbing at celebrity watering holes such as the Stork Club.

When Cohn and Schine departed for their swing throughout Europe that Easter weekend, their assignment from McCarthy was vague; they were on a mission, they explained to the press, to look into matters of "waste, efficiency, and loyalty."

Together, they formed a team that, as Rovere writes, provided a "ready-made plot for a gorgeous farce: two young Americans—a study in contrasts, like Laurel and Hardy or Rosencrantz and Guildenstern, with names memorably mated and advantageous for puns and rhymes—madly, preposterously bent on the ideological purification of the greatest government on earth."

As Rovere puts it, their trip:

was marked from beginning to end by comedy and at the end by devastation in the International Information Administration, by bitterness and anguish in every American embassy in Western Europe. This was no joke, but the trip was. Europe laughed its head off . . . There were such familiar fixtures of low comedy as a female secret agent who had once been the toast of Vienna, a contretemps that involved a platoon of diplomats involved in a search for a missing pair of pants, and an altercation denied by the prin-

Tail Gunner Joe, posing happily on August 16, 1946, beside his campaign poster after defeating Young Bob La Follette to become a U.S. senator.

© Bettmann/CORBIS

Old Bob La Follette campaigning for the presidency in Chicago in 1924 as the Progressive Party's candidate with his son Young Bob in the backseat. Library of Congress

Young Bob, posing for a publicity shot in 1938, after he and his brother launched the National Progressives of America (NPA) Party that year. Wisconsin Historical Society WHi-32459

Wheeling, West Virginia: McCarthy with head-table guests
before delivering his "I have here in my hand a list" speech on
February 9, 1950, which initiates the McCarthy era.
Courtesy of the Marquette University Archives

"You Mean I'm Supposed To Stand On That?"

McCarthyism:
Herblock of the
Washington Post
coins a phrase
that defines an
era a month after
Wheeling.
© The Herb Block
Foundation

No profiles in courage: Herblock portrays the timidity of senators and Eisenhower during the McCarthyism years.
© The Herb Block Foundation

The war hero at the peak of his powers: McCarthy gets medals for "heroism and extraordinary achievement" on December 29, 1952, despite the fraudulent claims made for his service record.
© Bettmann/CORBIS

The case of the doctored photo: Pvt. David Schine holds a portrait of himself with Army Secretary Robert Stevens (right) during the Army-McCarthy hearings on April 29, 1954.
© Bettmann/CORBIS, courtesy of the Marquette University Archives

McCarthy and Cohn: The senator and his young aide huddle during the Army-McCarthy hearings.
© Bettmann/CORBIS, courtesy of the Marquette University Archives

Court reporter Harold Miller displays transcripts containing 7,300 pages and two million words on the last day of the Army-McCarthy hearings, June 17, 1954.
© Bettmann/CORBIS, courtesy of the Marquette University Archives

"Have you no shame, Senator . . . " : Joseph Welch reacts in shock after
McCarthy attacks the loyalty of Frederick Fisher, a member of Welch's
Boston law firm, during the Army-McCarthy hearings.
AP/Wide World Photos

Awaiting judgment: McCarthy adjusts his glasses on the opening day of
senate censure hearings on September 1, 1954, two and a half months
after the disastrous Army-McCarthy hearings.
AP/Wide World Photos

The age of terrorism: Smoke still billows from Ground Zero ten days after the 9/11 attacks on the World Trade Center.
AP/Wide World Photos, Roberto Borea

President Bush, bullhorn in hand, stands beside firefighter Bob Beckwith amid World Trade Center rubble three days after the terrorist attack.
AP/Wide World Photos

A case for war: Secretary of State Colin Powell holds up a vial that he says could contain deadly anthrax while presenting evidence of Iraq's supposed weapons of mass destruction during testimony before the U.N. Security Council on February 5, 2003.
AP/Wide World Photos

Terror alerts: U.S. Attorney General John Ashcroft, with FBI
Director Robert Mueller beside him, spells out fears that the
United States faces a big attack from terrorists, on May 26, 2004,
without giving details of when, where, or how it might occur.
Reuters/Kevin Lamarque

Camp Delta, "Gitmo":
A U.S. soldier stands
guard on a tower at the
Guantánamo Bay, Cuba,
maximum security prison,
where charges of prisoner
abuse have been made.
Mark Wilson/Getty Images

cipals but believed by newspapermen and, in any case, firmly fixed in the legend in which Schine chased Cohn through a hotel lobby, swatting him over the head with a rolled-up magazine. The British correspondents who followed them quickly began chanting, "Positively, Mr. Cohn! Absolutely, Mr. Schine!"

The two spent forty hours in Paris, sixteen in Bonn, nineteen in Frankfurt, sixty in Munich, forty-one in Vienna, twenty-three in Belgrade, twenty-four in Athens, twenty in Rome, and six in London. Everywhere, they were followed by a throng of reporters whose dispatches mocked not only them but the good name of the United States of America.

Cohn and Schine's whirlwind hunt for subversion did not spark book-burnings in the State Department's libraries. That miserable work was already mainly accomplished under Secretary of State Dulles's directive to remove all Communist literature. To quote Rovere, "By the time Cohn and Schine got to the libraries, most of them had been thoroughly bowlderized."

Cohn and Schine were also on a hunt for traitors and subversives, though they seem not to have found any. However, American officials were so offended by their invasion that some were unable to refrain from making negative comments to reporters—a response that could, and did, ruin careers. In Frankfurt, Cohn charged that Theodore Kaghan, a senior official in the U.S. high commissioner's Public Affairs Division, had "once signed a Communist Party petition" in the 1930s. When Kaghan called Cohn and Schine "junketeering gumshoes," he was summoned home by the State Department—and fired.

One incident from their Frankfurt stopover speaks for

many other outrages that could be recorded. This came when the "gumshoes" wanted to inspect America House, as the U.S. cultural center in Frankfurt was called.

"Mr. Cohn and Mr. Schine arrived shortly after lunch, followed by a gaggle of reporters, creating a commotion in the normally subdued reading-room atmosphere of the cultural center," recalled the director, Hans N. Tuch, years later. "Mr. Cohn immediately asked where I had hidden the Communist authors in the library. I replied that, to the best of my knowledge, there were no Communist authors in the library. He then asked where I kept the Dashiell Hammett books. I led him to the shelf where *The Maltese Falcon* and *The Thin Man* were. He turned to the reporters and announced triumphantly that this was proof that there were indeed Communists represented in the American library."

They proceeded to the periodicals section. Cohn asked to see the anticommunist magazines. The director pointed out those he considered anticommunist, and showed Cohn the Jesuit magazine *America, Business Week, Time,* and *Newsweek.* Cohn dismissed *Time* by saying that the magazine was "a swear word to him."* He asked, "Did we have the *American Legion Monthly*?" the director remembered. "When I said no,

---

Time's approach to McCarthy provides an example of how coverage toward him shifted dramatically. Henry Luce, an old China hand and ardent backer of Chiang Kai-shek, started out sympathetic toward McCarthy, but by the spring of 1950 Luce changed his opinion. In a memo to his editorial staff then he wrote that "Communism has become too much . . . the scapegoat of everything that's wrong with us. The fact is, Communism is no longer a real issue, even indirectly, in America." He advised his staff that it was time to hit McCarthyism hard. Four months after the Marshall speech, *Time* published a major cover article on McCarthy entitled "Demagogue McCarthy," in which it judged McCarthy's record of

he countered that obviously we didn't have any anti-Communist magazines."

This "investigative" stop lasted exactly half an hour; then they were off again.

Before returning to the United States, Schine and Cohn interrogated some two hundred U.S. government employees of various rank, a number of whom they threatened to summon before the McCarthy committee, and claimed to have uncovered millions of dollars in waste and mismanagement. In their wake, they left embittered and demoralized career service officers, many of whom began making plans to leave public service rather than be subjected to such inquisitions again. They also left behind near-universal condemnation of their tactics by foreign officials and the foreign news media. Typical was the caustic commentary of the editorial page columnist of the *Financial Times* in London, who referred to Cohn and Schine as "these two brash young men," "scummy snoopers," and "distempered jackals." Though he wrote under the byline of "Observer," the author was widely known to be Viscount Bracken, confidant of Prime Minister Churchill and a former member of the Conservative government.

Years later, Cohn confessed that his trip with Schine was "a colossal mistake." But he never gave a hint of that conclusion when he returned to the United States.

---

uncovering Communists "miserable" and said "his antics foul up the necessary examination of the Truman-Acheson foreign policy." It quoted one source as saying of him: "He comes up with his tail wagging and all the appeal of a tramp dog—and just about as trustworthy." In *Time*'s judgment McCarthy was a crude, uncouth politician "with no regard for fair play, no scruple for exact truth." From then on, *Time* provided exemplary reports on all aspects of McCarthyism.

They were greeted by a crescendo of criticism. Cohn and Schine were a laughingstock, a rich target for lampooning in cartoons and editorials. On Saturday night, May 2, Ike and Mamie Eisenhower were honored guests at the annual dinner and stunt party of the Women's National Press Club. They appeared to enjoy a skit depicting two peripatetic sleuths censoring overseas libraries to the echo of, "Absolutely, Mr. Cohn; positively, Mr. Schine."

The next morning Cohn appeared on the NBC-TV show, *Meet the Press,* where he was uncharacteristically defensive and vague under sharp questioning. In answer to the first question, "Specifically, what was the purpose of this highly publicized trip to Europe that you and your assistant, Mr. Schine, took?" Cohn took umbrage at Schine being identified as "his assistant." "Mr. Schine," he said pompously, "is Chief Consultant for the Committee." As for the purpose of their trip, he gave nonresponsive answers: It was "to talk to a number of people over in Europe . . . to carry out a certain number of very specific assignments."

Question: What were those specific assignments, Mr. Cohn?

Answer: Well, the exact nature of most of them will have to come out at the public hearings of the committee. One has come out already with the revelation of the fact that a lecturer following the Communist line has been widely used by the State Department in our information service in Germany.

Question: Did you bring back proof he is presently a Communist or has Communist leanings?

Answer: I don't know whether he is or not, but we do know he has been lecturing in the United States Information

Centers, urging the adoption of the Soviet form of education . . . That didn't sound too much like the American way.

Asked the purpose of examining American libraries abroad, Cohn obfuscated. First of all, he began, the overseas programs "really aren't libraries," they are "programs to furnish information exposing Communism to people in foreign countries." The McCarthy hearings, he went on, "brought out the fact that a good many books by Communists and books following the Communist line were in use in this program . . . we looked at a number of these libraries to see whether or not the Dulles directive [to remove the so-called Communist literature] was being obeyed."

And what about the whirlwind nature of their excursion? Cohn was reminded that in the space of only four working days during their swing through Germany and Austria, he and Schine had interviewed one hundred thirty-seven government employees, and in half an hour processed twelve hundred employees of Radio Free Europe "to see if they were free of Communist taint." "How much could you learn from covering so much ground in so short a time?"

Again, Cohn's replies were nonresponsive. They hadn't gone to Europe with the intent of evaluating programs; they were "just gathering some facts which we will report to the committee." Their purpose was not to pass judgment, but to "carry out a certain specific number of assignments, talk to a certain number of people whose names we knew before we went, and check out a number of facts that had come to our attention over the months of investigation that preceded this trip."

What about the report that U.S. Ambassador to Great Britain Winthrop Aldrich had cabled Undersecretary of State Bedell Smith saying "Anglo-American relations were suffering seriously because of your trip?" Cohn was "quite sure there was no truth" in that account; he and Schine had had "a very pleasant talk with Ambassador Aldrich."

And why had the McCarthy committee earlier vigorously interrogated James Wechsler, editor of the then-liberal *New York Post,* who after being a young Communist in the 1930s turned into a strong anticommunist long before Cohn and Schine appeared on the scene? When he was in the Communist movement, Cohn said, Wechsler had written books, "some of which I believe are used in the State Department Information Program . . . We have been calling Mr. Wechsler and dozens of other authors whose books are in use in the State Department Information Program and who were, when the books were written, or are now connected with the Communist movement, and that's why Mr. Wechsler was called. As to what his present views and activities are, that is something I think the public will have to judge from his own testimony when that is made public."

Damaging as this intensely negative press coverage was to the reputations of Cohn and Schine—and McCarthy—it neither derailed nor deterred the McCarthy investigations. Even a public firestorm McCarthy triggered a month later failed to stem his determination to press on.

———

In June, McCarthy appointed J.B. Matthews as his committee's executive director. Matthews, formerly the House Un-American Activities Committee's key investigator, was one of the nation's most rabid anticommunists. He boasted of his ideological transformation, from being a member of more Communist-front organizations than any other American during his radical phase in the 1930s to his current role as the most zealous foe of Communism.

No sooner had McCarthy named Matthews to oversee his committee than an article by Matthews in the new issue of *American Mercury* magazine ignited intense controversy. Under the title "Reds and Our Churches," Matthews' first sentence was enough to stir heated denunciations. "The largest single group supporting the Communist apparatus in the United States today is composed of Protestant clergymen," he wrote. Amid a storm of criticism, McCarthy was forced to dismiss Matthews.

This didn't end the controversy. McCarthy's hiring someone like Matthews was too much for the three Democratic senators on the subcommittee. They strongly objected to McCarthy's exercising sole power to hire and fire subcommittee staff, a power the Republican majority had granted him. When Republicans backed McCarthy in using that authority, the three Democrats—senators John L. McClellan of Arkansas, Henry M. Jackson of Washington, and W. Stuart Symington of Missouri—announced they were resigning in protest from the committee. They would not return to the subcommittee until the next year.

Three weeks later, after almost literally coming to blows with Cohn, Robert Kennedy resigned. When doing so, he warned McCarthy that the subcommittee was "headed for disaster." Kennedy would return with the Democrats the following year as minority counsel.

———

McCarthy's actions six months into the Eisenhower era would seem to have been more than enough to spur the forming of a bipartisan front against him. Mainstream Republicans in the new GOP administration increasingly held negative feelings about him. Democrats were even more critical, as was, now, much of the national press. Yet no movement coalesced to curb McCarthy's ever-more outrageous assaults. If anything, McCarthy appeared more powerful than ever. His personal popularity was undiminished, and even seemed to increase. He still exerted a strong hold on the public, as the remarkable turnout for his wedding on September 29, 1953 demonstrated.

Waiting outside St. Matthew's Cathedral in Washington to cheer the senator and his bride, Jean Kerr, was a crowd estimated by police at three thousand five hundred. Private citizens broke into loud applause, and shouts of "Hi, Jeannie," when Kerr stepped from a limousine. McCarthy's arrival produced equally exuberant applause. Inside, nine hundred guests drawn from the top ranks of political and social Washington gathered in formal dress to witness the ceremony. Led by Vice President and Mrs. Nixon, the guest list included cabinet officers; members of Congress from both parties; three presidential advisers headed by Sherman Adams, the president's chief of staff; leading diplomats; and a plethora of celebrities, including the former heavyweight boxing champion Jack Dempsey. The Kennedy family was well represented, with Old Joe, Jack, Bobby, and Pat present. Eunice Kennedy, the oldest of the children, was one of Jean Kerr's bridesmaids. At the conclusion of the ceremony, the priest read from the altar a cablegram from Rome giving the Pope's "paternal and apostolic" blessings on the newlyweds. Only one negative note intruded: President and Mrs. Eisenhower didn't attend because of "other business," but the president sent McCarthy a personal letter of congratulations and well wishes, Ike's spokesman told the press.

———

Joe McCarthy's America produced the climate in which he flourished—and flourished despite growing public knowledge of the damage his tactics were inflicting. America was still frozen in the grip of the Cold War. An escalating arms race, and the launching of covert operations aimed at checking the spread of Communism worldwide by deposing or assassinating heads of state created even more anxiety among policymakers and the people. Americans confronted fears of nuclear war, Communism, spies, and traitors selling out their national interests. Everywhere a citizen then turned were reminders of how grim conditions had become. As the spy novelist John Le Carré wrote perfectly of those days, "the spies popped up like gray ghosts scurrying across the world stage." The U.S. Secret Service was so concerned about what it considered credible assassination plots that it doubled the number of agents assigned to protect Eisenhower's grandchildren. Americans were still dying in Korea, a conflict that remained a stalemate for half a century after an armistice was signed in the fall of 1953. In French Indochina (Vietnam), Communist forces were on the march, leading to the decisive fall of Dien Bien Phu, paving the way for France to lose its colony and creating a vacuum that the United States would soon fill. The Soviet Union appeared to be growing stronger militarily, and its pronouncements were more bellicose. In telecasts from Red Square, Soviet leaders paraded their expanding store of missiles and nuclear weaponry. And that spring, the electric chair execution of Julius and Ethel Rosenberg sparked world-wide demonstrations. Their deaths reminded Americans that atomic spies had, in fact, betrayed their country. (Whether they should have been executed for their crimes is a different matter. In my view, they should not have been.)

In the face of the prospect of an impending World War III, the Stanford Research Institute produced a handbook on nuclear war survival that seriously suggested citizens consider a "car body shelter." This entailed burying a car in your back-yard and installing plywood in one of its windows to form an entry hatch. The government created a cartoon character named Bert the Turtle, who encouraged children to "duck and cover" to protect themselves during a nuclear attack. Housewives were urged to keep their fallout shelters stocked with canned peas and non-perishable food.

The federal government also contributed to fears of an America infiltrated by subversives. Propaganda documentaries and films such as *Communism,* an Armed Forces Information Film, depicted Communists operating inside the U.S. In 1954 an effective conservative political campaign, playing on fears of "godless Communism," mandated the phrase "under God" be added to the Pledge of Allegiance. Similar fears led works with religious themes to top the nonfiction bestseller lists: the Bible was number one in 1953 and 1954, and other bestsellers included Norman Vincent Peale's *The Power of Positive Think-ing,* Fulton J. Sheen's *Life Is Worth Living,* Catherine Mar-shall's *A Man Called Peter,* Fulton Oursler and G.A.O. Armstrong's *The Greatest Faith Ever Known*—all offering an-tidotes to fears of impending Armageddon.

Popular culture reflected and capitalized on these Cold War fears. Movies with anticommunism themes included *I*

Was a Communist for the FBI and *I Married a Communist.*
During the peak of the McCarthy period, from 1950 through
1954, Americans watched Gregory Peck negotiate a delicate
deal with Communists as a CIA agent in West Berlin in *Night
People;* Clark Gable, in *Never Let Me Go,* a remake of an earlier anticommunist film, *Comrade X,* in which Gable also
starred; John Wayne in *Big Jim McLain* as a HUAC agent
battling Commies trying to seize control of the labor movement in Hawaii; and Ronald Reagan as an intelligence officer
who risks his life to enter a North Korean POW camp in
Prisoner of War. Popular books such as Mickey Spillane's
hardboiled thrillers depicted superspies combating, and eliminating, Reds.

Against this backdrop, McCarthy's greatly expanded investigations into suspected Communist activity commanded new
headlines, inspired new controversies, and attracted new con-
verts who believed he was fighting for them.

PART FIVE

Witch Hunts

Chapter
SIXTEEN

Inquisitions

*This is the era of the Armageddon—that final all-out
battle between light and darkness foretold in the Bible.*

—Joe McCarthy

F ifty-one years after England abolished the notorious star
chamber inquisitions, its American colonial subjects un-
derwent a similar ordeal in the Salem witch trials of 1692.
("Are you a witch? How long have you been in the snare of
the devil? Confess!") After ten months of trials, the death by
hanging of nineteen men and women, the crushing death of
another man, seventeen more deaths in prison, and the ruina-
tion of many lives, the governor of the Massachusetts Bay
Colony ordered the Salem trials ended. He instructed that
"reliance on spectral and intangible evidence no longer be allowed in trials."

Joe McCarthy's modern version of the star chamber inquisitions lasted for two years. There were no executions, though at least one witness committed suicide. Several witnesses were tried for contempt, and some were convicted, but each of these verdicts was overturned on appeal. In the end, not a single witness who appeared before McCarthy was imprisoned for perjury, contempt, espionage, or subversion, though many lost their jobs after McCarthy urged their employers to fire them for exercising their constitutional right against self-incrimination. When they finally passed into history, the McCarthy witch hunts left a legacy of fear and intimidation, a record of egregious misuse of the proper investigative role of Congress to right wrongs and check abuses of power, and a lasting stain on America's reputation for fair play and due process of law.

———

Before McCarthy became chairman, the Senate investigating subcommittee viewed its mandate primarily as looking into waste and corruption in the executive branch of government. McCarthy shifted this focus almost exclusively to alleged Communist subversion and exponentially expanded the number and pace of hearings.

In 1952, the year before McCarthy assumed the chairmanship, the subcommittee held six executive sessions. From January 15, 1953, to January 3, 1955, the final day of the 83rd Congress and the end of McCarthy's chairmanship, McCarthy held one hundred seventeen of them.

As McCarthy's hunt for subversives gained greater and greater momentum in 1953, Washington's atmosphere, laden with feelings of terror, rage, and helplessness enveloped the nation. McCarthyism was nearly immobilizing America, distracting the nation and destroying confidence in its institutions, schools, churches, government, press, military, and private and political leaders. Debate and dissent were stifled, making increasingly difficult America's ability to deal intelligently with vital questions of the day.

In retrospect, it's incredible to recall the depths to which McCarthyism descended and the damage it wrought. Reputations and careers were ruined, blacklists instituted, writers and artists threatened, film and stage productions closed down, university administrators and teachers intimidated, new loyalty oaths mandated. Boycotts were mounted against sponsors of radio and TV programs deemed insufficiently pro-American. Persons in public life could come under suspicion for having on their bookshelves a volume by Karl Marx. Public libraries were pressured to remove books thought subversive. Government employees took to receiving liberal publications in plain brown wrappers. Knowing the wrong people or contributing to the wrong organizations could result in being hauled before congressional inquisitors and losing one's job. The threat of being forced to testify in televised hearings inspired more fear. A congressional act barred distinguished visitors, including Nobel Prize winners, from entering the U.S. if they were believed to have expressed views considered un-American. Americans employing their constitutional right against self-incrimination were attacked as "Fifth Amendment Communists." Those regarded as insufficiently religious—and the devil take you if you were an atheist—were assailed as bordering on "godless Communism."

While the public focused on McCarthy's hearings, most of them televised, the greater share of the subcommittee's work was conducted behind closed doors. In McCarthy's first year as chairman, the subcommittee took testimony from three hundred ninety-five witnesses in executive sessions and staff interrogations, compared to two hundred fourteen witnesses in public hearings. It compiled 8,969 pages of closed-door testimony, compared to 5,671 from the public sessions. Transcripts of the public hearings were made available within months; the executive session transcripts were sealed and deposited in the National Archives, where they remained closed to the public for fifty years.

Out of the public's sight, the closed door hearings also enjoyed very little congressional oversight. Since many of the hearings took place away from Washington, usually on short notice in New York City, rarely were all members of the subcommittee present. By mid-1953, all three Democratic senators had resigned in protest, and the remaining Republican subcommittee members, with multiple other responsibilities in Washington, simply didn't attend. Contrary to the practice on other Senate committees, McCarthy became virtually the sole senator present—an unprecedented one-man committee. He continued his habit from speeches of referring to himself in the third person, as though he viewed himself as an "ism" rather than a person. Witnesses facing him were given the intimidating impression they were facing a "judge, jury, prosecutor, castigator, and press agent, all in one," as Erwin Griswold, dean of the Harvard Law School, then put it.

Army Counsel John G. Adams, who attended many of the executive sessions in 1953 and 1954, later observed: "It didn't really mean a closed session, since McCarthy allowed in various friends, hangers-on, and favored newspaper reporters. Nor did it mean secret, because afterwards McCarthy would tell the reporters waiting outside whatever he pleased." Witnesses had no chance to defend themselves against what Mc-Carthy told reporters and reporters had no chance to check the accuracy of his statements. General Telford Taylor, the American prosecutor of the Nuremburg war crimes trials of leading Nazis, charged McCarthy with conducting "a new and indefensible kind of hearing, which is neither a public hearing nor an executive session."

McCarthy responded to Taylor's charge by conducting an executive session into the general's loyalty. He also used closed hearings to settle scores with critics such as Edward Barrett, press spokesman for Dean Acheson and later dean of the Columbia University Graduate School of Journalism; and Edward Morgan, staff director of the Tydings subcommittee that had investigated McCarthy's Wheeling speech.

Even McCarthy did not appear at all of the hearings, however. In his absence, he gave Cohn free rein to conduct closed hearings as though he were a prosecutor before a grand jury rather than an impartial lawyer offering witnesses the opportunity for a full and fair hearing. He also permitted Cohn to allow Schine to ask witnesses questions, and even to preside over some executive sessions. Remarkably, at those times Cohn would deferentially address Schine as "Mr. Chairman." Others on the staff such as Don Surine also conducted badgering interrogations of witnesses.

Given the rapid pace and close scheduling of the hearings, and the chaos that habitually surrounded a McCarthy operation, the staff had little time to prepare. "No real research was ever done," Robert Kennedy later wrote. "Most of the investigations were instituted on the basis of some preconceived notion by the chief counsel [Cohn] or his staff members and not on the basis of any information that had been developed." Army counsel Adams also later wrote: "McCarthy ignored

Senate rules requiring a vote of other members every time he
wanted to haul someone in. He signed scores of blank subpoenas which his staff members carried in their inside pockets,
and issued as regularly as traffic tickets."

Witnesses repeatedly complained that subpoenas compelling them to appear were served on them just before the
hearings, often the night before or the morning of the hearing, making it all the more difficult for them to obtain legal
representation. Even if they found a lawyer, McCarthy didn't
permit their attorneys to raise objections or speak for them.

The hearings were mainly held in three locations aside from
Washington, one of them New York's luxurious Waldorf-Astoria
Hotel on Park Avenue, where Schine's father had a magnificent
suite. Schine not only made the Waldorf suite available to Mc-
Carthy's interrogators, he also made available his family limousine. McCarthy and his aides regularly used it to shuttle back
and forth from the Waldorf to the U.S. Courthouse at Foley
Square and to Fort Monmouth, New Jersey, where other
closed-door sessions were held. (The subcommittee also held
closed hearings in Boston and Albany.) When the sessions
ended, the Communist hunters would ride back to the Waldorf
in the limo. Schine's—and Cohn's—taste for comfortable living extended to Washington, where the subcommittee held
most of its hearings in Room 357 of the Senate Office Building,
now renamed the Russell Building. Rather than work out of the
cramped Senate subcommittee quarters, Cohn and Schine
rented more spacious offices in a private office building nearby.

Comfortable quarters and transportation notwithstanding, the hearings were an intense interrogation. McCarthy
had little respect for witnesses' Constitutional rights. He was
abrasive, hectoring—and, always, intimidating. Invariably,

witnesses were treated as though they were guilty before testimony was taken.

McCarthy, glowering toward the witness table, asked each person to answer two questions. "Are you now, or have you ever been, a member of the Communist Party?" And: "Do you now, or have you ever, belonged to any organization that is listed by the attorney general as subversive?" Those questions were a chilling reminder to witnesses that they had been summoned because they were under suspicion. McCarthy was out to get, or at least humiliate, them.

It mattered not if witnesses swore they had never joined the Communist Party, engaged in espionage or sabotage, associated with known or suspected Communists, or harbored subversive views—or even thoughts. They were held accountable for long-forgotten petitions they had signed a decade or more earlier; for having joined organizations that the attorney general later cited as Communist fronts; for having belonged to a union whose leaders were accused of being Communists; for being mistaken for a suspected Communist or Communist sympathizer with their same name; for having dated a Communist; or for belonging to a Great Books club that read Karl Marx, among other authors.

As Donald Ritchie of the Senate's Historical Office commented: "Seeking any sign of political unorthodoxy, the chairman and the subcommittee staff scrutinized the witnesses' lives and grilled them about the political beliefs of colleagues, neighbors and family members." Witnesses were questioned about incidents dredged up, accurately or not, from their college days. Some incidents dated back to the end of the 1920s or the early 1930s at the depth of the Great Depression, when witnesses might have attended campus protests attended by collegiate "radicals," written critically of college authorities in the school paper, or been quoted as expressing "admiration for the Russian idea."

When witnesses finished their testimony, often after hours—or days—of grilling, McCarthy's technique was to paraphrase their testimony and, as Ritchie noted, "give it a more sinister implication." He regularly informed witnesses of their right not to answer a question if doing so might incriminate them. Then he interpreted their refusal as an admission of guilt. He also regularly warned witnesses that if they *did* take the Fifth Amendment, conferring the right not to answer, they could be cited for contempt by Congress. If witnesses did not cooperate, McCarthy threatened them with indictment and jail. Witnesses faced a different problem with not "taking the Fifth": they were then required to answer all incriminating questions, and to name others as Communists or Communist sympathizers, as demanded by the interrogator. This led to the great controversy over witnesses being compelled to "name names."

In a typical exchange, McCarthy told one witness in a closed session:

> Do not just assume that your name was pulled from a hat. Before you were brought here, we make a fairly thorough and complete investigation. So I would like to strongly advise you to either tell the truth or, if you think the truth will incriminate you, then you are entitled to refuse to answer. I cannot urge that upon you too strongly. I have given that advice to other people here before the committee. They thought they were smarter than our investigators. They will end up in jail. This is not a threat; this is just friendly advice I am giving you. Do you understand that?

These words do not convey the fear McCarthy inspired as he questioned witnesses in his high-pitched, menacing monotone. Fear was the common denominator in these closed sessions, and even those brave enough to challenge McCarthy felt intensely apprehensive when they appeared before him. Many were simply terrified. Edward Barrett was one of the few witnesses with the nerve to bring up this factor. "I think you have many frightened witnesses, sir," he told McCarthy, "and I come here today as a frightened witness myself."

Aside from McCarthy's continuous browbeating of witnesses, a number of common themes that shed light on McCarthy and McCarthyism emerged from the now-public transcripts of the closed sessions. The records reveal repeated examples of witnesses being tarred with the McCarthyistic tactic of guilt by association and character assassination; of the obsessive hunt for homosexuals; of the hounding of noted writers, artists, and composers; of the tarnishing of the reputations of highly decorated military leaders; and, perhaps most contemptible of all, of the assaults on bewildered "little people" of no possible security threat who were unfortunate enough to become trapped in McCarthy's web.

THE KNOCK ON THE DOOR

Writers and artists offered a convenient target in McCarthy's assault on dissenters and the principle of freedom of thought and expression. He took dead aim on them, hauling into his hearings people with well-known leftist views who in no way could be called a threat to the republic. The McCarthy staff's mistreatment of them was typified by Howard Fast's experience of a knock on the door in the night.

Howard Fast, the author of *Citizen Tom Paine, Freedom*

Road, and *Patrick Henry,* was one of the prominent leftist writers who had taken the Fifth Amendment during a House Un-American Activities Committee hearing when asked whether he was a Communist Party member. When he appeared before McCarthy six years later in February 1953 as the first of many authors subpoenaed, Fast protested to McCarthy about the way his subpoena was served at night at his New York City home on West 94th Street:

> At about ten o'clock my bell rang. I opened the door. There was a young man there. He said he had for Howard Fast a highly secret communication from "Al."
>
> I said, "Al who?"
>
> He said, "Just from Al. Al said you would know me."
>
> I said, "Al who? I don't know any Al."
>
> He said, "Al. Are you Mr. Fast?"
>
> At that point, having no notion that there was a subpoena involved, having not been told that he was in any way an official, I said, "No."
>
> He said, "Well, I will wait for Mr. Fast."
>
> I said, "Wait outside." And I closed the door.

Fast was "highly suspicious and a little nervous and a little frightened." He returned to his bedroom, but was awakened three hours later.

> At about one o'clock in the morning following that, my bell rang. I went to the door. A voice said: "I am the assistant counsel for the House Committee on" or "for the Senate Committee on Operations, and I want to talk to you, Howard."
>
> I said, "My name is Mr. Fast."
>
> He said, "Okay, Howard. I just want to have a talk with you. Let me in."

I said, "I have no need to let you in. You cannot demand
that I let you in. I don't know you from Adam. Beat it."
He said, "No, I want to talk with you, Howard."
I said, "Beat it, or I will call the police."

Fast then called his lawyer, who advised him that he was
within his rights in refusing to open the door to someone at
that hour unless the person had a search warrant. He went
back to bed, and for the next half hour tried to sleep. "At about
1:30 there was a pounding on the door and a ringing of the
bell," he said, "which woke my children and terrified them in
the time honored Gestapo methods, and I came down there,
and here was this offensive character again, and this time for
the first time he stated that he had a subpoena with him."

Sneeringly, McCarthy interrupted. "Would you say they
were the GPU type tactics or NKVD type tactics also?" he
asked, referring to the Soviet secret police.

"I have read of these tactics in connection with the
Gestapo," Fast replied. "This is my choice of description, and
this action I find offensive and unworthy of any arm of the
government of the United States. I would have accepted service very simply and directly the following morning. There
was no need to go through that procedure."

When the McCarthy investigator had brought a policeman with him, Fast had opened the door and accepted
the subpoena. In the hearings, he took the Fifth again.* His
appearance developed no new information on Communists or
subversives, and led to no indictments or criminal proceedings.

---

*In his 1957 memoir, *Naked God: The Writer and the Communist
Party* (New York: Praeger), Fast said he joined the Communist Party in
1943 or 1944 and resigned from it in 1956.

ABUSE OF WRITERS AND ARTISTS

Without a doubt, Eslanda Goode Robeson was a Communist, and Joe McCarthy was hardly the first to suspect her of being one. Whether she posed a threat to the United States was another matter, and one McCarthy in no way documented. Her husband, Paul Robeson—actor, singer, and author—was perhaps the best known black American and made no secret of being a Communist in the 1930s and 1940s, though he was never charged with being a traitor to his country. Eslanda, also black, was the author of several books and had earned a Ph.D. in anthropology. Like her husband, she was never accused of treasonous activities. Thus McCarthy's purpose in compelling her testimony seems to have been to embarrass or intimidate her.

Her testimony was unusual not for the disclosure of any subversive activity, but for the way in which she claimed constitutional privilege to avoid saying whether she was a Communist. No sooner had Cohn begun the interrogation with the stock question, "Now, Mrs. Robeson, are you a member of the Communist Party?" than her reply confounded, then infuriated, first Cohn and then McCarthy. She answered: "Under the protection afforded me by the Fifth and Fifteenth Amendments, I decline to answer."

"The Fifteenth?" Cohn repeated.

"Yes, the Fifteenth," she said, "I am a Negro, you know. I have been brought up to seek protection under the Fifteenth Amendment as a Negro."*

---

*The 15th Amendment, ratified by Congress in 1870 five years after the Civil War and seven years after the Emancipation Proclamation freeing the slaves, held that no citizen can be denied the right to vote "on account of race, color, or previous condition of servitude."

McCarthy took over the questioning, saying, "The Fifteenth Amendment has nothing to do with it. That provides the right to vote." She replied: "I understand it has something to do with my being a Negro and I have always sought protection under it." She then tried to explain to McCarthy what she meant: "What confuses me a little bit about what you said—you see I am a second-class citizen in this country and, therefore, feel the need of the Fifteenth. That is the reason I use it. I am not quite equal to the rest of the white people."

The questioning continued with McCarthy pressing her again and again to answer whether she was a Communist.

Robeson: Under the protection of the Fifth and Fifteenth Amendments, if I can use it, I refuse to answer.

McCarthy: The question is: Do you feel a truthful answer would tend to incriminate you?

Robeson: I thought I had already [answered honestly].

McCarthy: You are being ordered to answer whether you feel a truthful answer will tend to incriminate you.

Robeson: I will have to consult my lawyer. I don't understand this. [After a brief break while she talked to her lawyer, she continued.] Now, once more, may I have the question?

McCarthy: The question is: Do you feel that . . . if your answer is a truthful answer, that might tend to incriminate you.

Robeson: I would not consider any other answer except the truth. I would certainly not be bothered with any untruthful answer.

McCarthy: I am going to make you answer that. We ask certain questions and if you feel the answer might tend to incriminate you, you are allowed to refuse to answer. Before granting you that privilege or right of refusing to answer, we must know from you very simply whether you feel a truthful answer might tend to incriminate you.

Robeson: I do not understand the truthful part. Certainly the answer would be truthful. Under any circumstances whatsoever it would be truthful. That is the reason you are confusing me.

McCarthy: The question is: Do you feel a truthful answer to the question of whether or not you are a Communist today would tend to incriminate you? You are ordered to answer that question.

Robeson: Under the protection of the Fifth and Fifteenth Amendments, I refuse to answer this.

McCarthy: The counsel is informed I am asking the full committee to cite the witness for contempt. She has refused to give us information and taken refuge under the Fifteenth Amendment.

Aaron Copland, composer of *Billy the Kid, Rodeo,* and *Appalachian Spring,* was a "fellow traveler" in the 1930s because, as he put it later in an oral history, "it seemed like the thing to do." But he never joined a political party, never thought of himself as involved with "radical causes," and testified before McCarthy that he had never been a Communist and wasn't at the time of his appearance. Still, he was compelled to testify because his name appeared on numerous petitions from groups later deemed either suspect or part of "Communist fronts" by the House Un-American Activities Committee. In 1940, after the Soviet invasion of Finland, he signed a letter asking President Roosevelt to back the Soviets by declaring war on Finland, though he had no memory of it thirteen years later.

More than that, what seems to have prompted McCarthy to summon Copland behind closed doors in May 1953 was a highly-publicized incident involving the composer and the Eisenhower inaugural ceremonies four months prior. In a brief news item announcing the inaugural concert program on January 18 in Constitution Hall, the *Washington Post* reported: "The master of ceremonies for the concert will be Walter Pidgeon, who will read *Lincoln Portrait*, by Aaron Copland, with accompaniment by the National Symphony." Two days before the concert, Copland's composition was removed from the program after a conservative Republican congressman, Fred E. Busbey of Illinois, objected to Copland's political affiliations. "The Republican Party would have been ridiculed from one end of the United States to the other if Copland's music had been played at the inaugural of a president elected to fight Communism," the congressman said.

News of the ban was condemned by fellow musicians, artists, and civil libertarians. Copland immediately protested, stating to the League of Composers, "I have no past or present political activities to hide. I have never at any time been a member of any political party: Republican, Democratic, or Communist . . . We are becoming the targets of a powerful pressure movement led by small minds . . . It is surely a sign of the times that a musical organization like our own should have become involved in an affair such as this." The ban stayed; Copland's composition was not performed. He then wrote the new president: "I am an American composer of symphonic music and the composer of a musical portrait of Abe Lincoln. I write to you because an incident occurred during the ceremonies attendant upon the inauguration of your administration too small to have come to your attention, certainly, but too large in its implications to be passed over lightly. If I did not think it transcended in importance my own personal stake in the matter, I would not be writing to you now." He never received a reply. The controversy continued. Bruce Catton, a Pulitzer-Prize-winning Civil War historian, writing a week after the inauguration in the *Nation,* told how the chairman of the arrangements committee had informed Copland that his work was being dropped "because we didn't want to do anything to bring criticism." Catton added: "So the Copland number was not heard, and if this in the end was something less than a fatal blow to the evil designs of the men in the Kremlin, it at least saved the assembled Republicans from being compelled to listen to Lincoln's brooding words: 'Fellow Citizens, we cannot escape history. We of this Congress and this Administration will be remembered in spite of ourselves.'"

It was against this backdrop that Copland received a telegram in New York at seven o'clock on a Friday evening, May 22, ordering him to appear before McCarthy behind closed doors the next Monday in Washington. After scrambling to obtain legal representation, Copland went to Washington. He discovered McCarthy's main interest to be who in the U.S. Information Agency had chosen Copland to represent the United States at functions abroad. By this time, thirty thousand volumes by those McCarthy considered Communist authors, as well as "subversive" works of music and art, had been removed from the State Department's overseas libraries. Not only had a blacklist of writers, composers, and artists been compiled; a "graylist," on which Copland's name appeared, contained one hundred forty persons yet to be cleared of Communist taint by McCarthy's investigators.

Copland attempted to explain to McCarthy why he had been chosen as one of the distinguished Americans to lecture overseas under State Department sponsorship despite the so-called Communist organizations with which the committee considered him associated: "Almost all of those affiliations have to do with sponsoring of something, the signing of protests, or the signing of a statement in favor or against something," he said, "and . . . I say in my mind they are very superficial things. They consisted of my receiving in the mail in the morning a request of some kind or a list of names, which I judged solely on its merits quite aside from my being able to judge whether that was a Communist front. I must say that when I first saw this list [from the committee] I was amazed that I was connected with this many things. I consider this list gives a false idea of my activities as a musician. It was a very small part of my existence. It consisted of my signing my name to a protest or statement, which I thought I had a right to do as an American citizen."

This explanation wasn't good enough for McCarthy. "There was nothing illegal about accepting employment in the [State Department] information program," McCarthy told him, "but we must find out why a man of this tremendous activity in the Communist fronts would be selected."

"May I reply on two fronts?" Copland said. "I was selected because of the fact that my employment as a lecturer had nothing to do with anything but music."

Still, this answer wasn't good enough.

"If you were a member of the Communist Party," McCarthy answered, "let's assume you were, and you were selected to lecture, you would be bound to try wherever you could to sell the Communist idea, wouldn't you?"

"No doubt," Copland said.

"So that," McCarthy went on, "I believe you and I would agree that in selecting a lecturer, even though they are an outstanding musician, before we put our stamp of approval on them we should find out whether they are a Communist or sympathetic to the Communist cause. Is that right?"

"Well, I would certainly hesitate to send abroad a man who is a Communist sympathizer or a Communist in order to lecture," Copland answered. But as for his own case, he tried to explain, he was primarily active in music organizations. "They are things which my whole life has been devoted to . . . That is why I think this list . . . would give a false impression of the situation—of myself as a man and as a citizen."

Although Copland only maintained a diary when traveling, the day after his hearing he felt compelled to record his impressions in his journal. Of McCarthy, he wrote:

> He seems to enjoy his position as if he was himself a spectator of his amazing rise to importance in the world political scene. Something about him suggests that he is a man who doesn't really expect his luck to hold out. It's been too phenomenal, and I suppose, too recklessly achieved. When he touches on his magic theme, the "Commies" or "Communism," his voice darkens like that of a minister. He is like a plebian Faustus who has been given a magic wand by an invisible Mephisto—as long as the menace is there, the wand will work. The question is at what point his power grab will collide with the power drive of others in his own party.

Copland's ordeal did not end with his testimony. For months, he remained under committee subpoena; he feared he would be recalled at any moment. His large legal bills took years to repay, and he found, as he told one friend, that his "sense of being pursued" had drained him emotionally. He also found his appearance before McCarthy had seriously affected his career.

His passport was lifted after the State Department informed him that its anticommunist policy prohibited the issuance of "passports to individuals under subpoena." Before being permitted to travel to a scheduled concert performance in Mexico, which did not require a passport, he was compelled to make a sworn statement to a notary: "Aaron Copland of Shady Lane Farm is not a Communist."

Not for several years after his testimony was his passport reinstated. In the interim, he repeatedly had to supply the Passport Office with affidavits from citizens testifying on his behalf and also to furnish evidence of his affiliation with "avowedly anti-Communist organizations." Thus, he was not permitted to perform at a number of international concerts to which he was invited.

At home, he found similar repression. Without explanation, the Hollywood Bowl canceled a Copland performance scheduled for March 1953. At the same time, the University of Alabama cancelled its invitation, which he had accepted, to speak and conduct at a composers' forum that spring. "I regret to inform you that the recent allegations of Communist sympathies on your part as set out on the Extension of the Remarks of the Honorable Fred E. Busbey . . . and inaugural concert affair in Washington make it inadvisable for us to have you as our guest," the university sponsors wrote.

The next January, the University of Colorado withdrew its invitation to Copland to be its Reynolds Lecturer. Appearances in Brooklyn were cancelled in 1956. A year later, the

American Legion attempted to kill his appointment as professor of music at the University of Buffalo. In 1960, long
after Joe McCarthy had passed from the scene, a Dallas Symphony board member cancelled a post-concert Copland
party after receiving anonymous cards protesting the composer's appearance.

———

Langston Hughes was one of America's best-known black
writers, and as with Howard Fast, some of his work had been
housed on the shelves of the State Department's overseas libraries. His poems and books of the 1930s expressed rage at
segregation and lynching, and called for what came to be
termed a generation later "the Negro revolution." He had
long been a target of anticommunists and, like so many others, feared being called by McCarthy.

He was ill, broke, and struggling to revise a children's book
in his third-floor New York study when late on a Saturday afternoon in March 1953, a U.S. Marshal appeared with a subpoena
demanding his appearance the next Monday in Washington.

Hughes rushed downtown to confer with a friend and attorney, Lloyd K. Garrison, great-grandson of the abolitionist
hero William Lloyd Garrison. "After I talked with Langston
for a few minutes," Garrison later recalled, "we both agreed
that he did not want to plead the Fifth Amendment. I called
up Roy Cohn in Washington, asking for a postponement.
Cohn was his typical rude, arrogant self: 'What does he need
an adjournment for? He's going to plead the Fifth, isn't he?'
I said, 'No, he's going to tell the full story.' Cohn was shocked.
'Oh, for God's sake!' he said." Unknown to the public, Cohn
and McCarthy *wanted* their witnesses to take the Fifth. They
didn't want those they subpoenaed to stand up to them.

On the advice of Garrison, who was unable to accompany him to Washington that Monday, Hughes wired McCarthy asking for a week's extension to arrange for legal representation and to prepare himself. He pledged to cooperate fully with McCarthy's committee. Monday morning he received a wire from Cohn: "YOU ARE DIRECTED TO APPEAR BEFORE THIS COMMITTEE AS SPECIFIED IN YOUR SUPOENA AT 2 PM TODAY. IF YOU FAIL TO DO SO CONTEMPT ACTION WILL BE RECOMMENDED." After borrowing money for his plane fare and hotel, Hughes headed to Washington.

His secret testimony illuminates the clashes and the anguish many like Hughes experienced at the peak of McCarthy's inquisitions. Despite his desire to avoid confrontation, when he appeared behind closed doors Hughes sparred vigorously with Cohn over the interpretation of his "radical" works praising Lenin and the "great Red flag rising to the strains of the *Internationale.*" After much parrying about his beliefs, with Cohn reading passages from poems and books to make ideological points, Hughes said he would like to explain himself as a writer.

"To give a full interpretation of any piece of literary work one has to consider not only when and how it was written," he explained, "but what brought it into being, the emotional and physical background that brought it into being."

He then offered an extemporaneous explanation of what it meant to be a black man in America: "I, sir, was born in Joplin, Missouri. I was born a Negro. From my very earliest childhood memories, I have encountered very serious and very hurtful problems. One of my earliest childhood memories was going to the movies in Lawrence, Kansas, where we lived, and there was one motion picture theater, and I went every afternoon. It was a nickelodeon. One afternoon I put my nickel down and the woman pushed it back and she pointed to a sign. I was about seven years old."

At this point, Cohn interrupted. This, clearly, was not what he wanted to draw forth from Langston Hughes. "I do not want to interrupt you," he said. "I do want to save time here. I want to concede very fully that you encounter oppression and denial of civil rights. Let us assume that, because I assume that will be the substance of what you are about to say. To save us time, what we are interested in determining for our purpose is this: Was the solution to which you turned that of the Soviet form of government?"

Hughes was steadfast. "Sir, you said you would permit me to give a full explanation."

Cohn replied: "I was wondering if we could not save a little time because I want to concede the background you wanted to describe."

"I would much rather preserve my reputation and freedom than to save time," Hughes said.

Cohn permitted him to continue.

"The woman pushed my nickel back and pointed to a sign beside the box office, and the sign said something, in effect, 'Colored not admitted,'" Hughes said. "It was my first revelation of the division between the American citizens. My playmates who were white and lived next door to me could go to that motion picture and I could not. I could never see a film in Lawrence again, and I lived there until I was twelve years old.

"When I went to school, in the first grade, my mother moved to Topeka for a time, and my mother worked for a lawyer, and she lived in the downtown area, and . . . being a working woman naturally she wanted to send me to the nearest school, and she did, and they would not let me go to the school. There were no Negro children there."

After describing more incidents of racial discrimination from his childhood, Hughes was interrupted again. "I think, Mr. Hughes, that would be adequate emotional background," Cohn said. Hughes didn't agree. "No, sir, that would not explain it all."

Finally, Cohn could take no more. "Mr. Hughes," he said, "you have belonged to a list of Communist organizations a mile long. You have urged the election to public office of official candidates of the Communist Party. You have signed statements to the effect that the purge trials in the Soviet Union were justified and sound and democratic. You have signed statements denying that the Soviet Union is totalitarian. You have defended the current leaders of the Communist Party. You have written poems which are an invitation to revolution. You have called for setting up of a Soviet government in this country. You have been named in statements before us as a Communist, and a member of the Communist Party.

"Mr. Hughes, you can surely tell us simply whether or not you ever desired the Soviet form of government in this country."

"Yes, I did," Hughes answered.

"The answer is yes," Cohn repeated. "I think if you were a little more candid with some of these things we would get along a little better, because I think I know enough about the subject so I am not going to sit here for six days and be kidded along. I will be very much impressed if you would give us a lot of straightforward answers. It would save us a lot of time . . . We are trying to find out which of these ['subversive' works] should be used in the State Department in its information program."

Hughes said he hoped his works would be included "to illustrate that we have freedom of the press" and "to show that we have a very wide range of opinion in our country."

His defiant attitude in the closed session created more difficulty for him, however. Two days later McCarthy called Hughes for a public televised hearing. This time, prior to going before the cameras, Hughes caved to McCarthy and Cohn. In return for less aggressive interrogation he agreed not to name names, but to retract some of his poems and harsher characterizations of American justice. His biographer, Arnold Rampersad, writes that Hughes did this because he was terrified his foundering career, sustained by loans from friends, would collapse. He was also said to have become disillusioned with the left and Stalin. After this, Hughes went out of his way to make sure his name was no longer connected with any of the "subversive" organizations on the attorney general's list. Months later, after being questioned by the FBI about being listed as a sponsor of the American-Soviet friendship group, he wrote that organization: "I would appreciate it very much if my name were removed from your letterhead and membership."

McCarthy's intimidation had won. Hughes was no longer as great an object of controversy as he had been before. His biographer writes: "Hughes had given in to brutish strength, not to moral or even constitutional authority, for such authority was clearly being abused. To cooperate with McCarthy . . . was to appear to endorse his cruelties. Hughes had come to his decision by recognizing that his choice was between two imperfections. He could defy [McCarthy] and destroy much of his effectiveness in the black world. Or he could cooperate, draw the disapproval, even the contempt, of the white left, but keep more or less intact the special place he had painstakingly carved out within the black community." Years later, Hughes made clear his feelings when he wrote: "Politics can be the graveyard of the poet. And only poetry can be his resurrection." In a poem published after his death he left a bitter testament about these days. Titled "Un-American Investigators," it reads in part:

> *The committee's fat,*
> *Smug, almost secure*
> *Co-religionists*
> *Shiver with delight*
> *In warm manure*

Decades later, in the 2004 presidential campaign, Democratic candidate John Kerry regularly quoted Langston Hughes's poetry about America in his speeches.

GUILT BY ASSOCIATION

Stanley Berinsky's mother had once been a member of the Communist Party. When this fact was discovered during a security investigation at Fort Monmouth, New Jersey, Berinsky was suspended from his civilian job at the Army Signal Corps and in 1953 ordered to appear before the McCarthy subcommittee. McCarthy, "The Chairman," led the questioning:

The Chairman: Let's get this straight. I know it is unusual to appear before a committee. So many witnesses get nervous. You just got through telling us you did not

know she [Berinsky's mother] was a Communist; now
you tell us she resigned from the Communist Party? As
of when?

Mr. Berinsky: I didn't know this until the security suspen-
sion came up at Fort Monmouth.

The Chairman: When was that?

Mr. Berinsky: That was in 1952.

The Chairman: Then did your mother come over and tell
you she had resigned?

Mr. Berinsky: I told her what had happened. At that time
she told me she had been out for several years.

The Chairman: . . . Well, did you ever ask her if she was a
Communist?

Mr. Berinsky: No, sir.

The Chairman: When you went to see her, weren't you curious? If somebody told me my mother was a Communist, I'd get on the phone and say, "Mother, is this
true?" . . . Did she tell you why she resigned?

Mr. Berinsky: It seems to me she probably did it because I
held a government job and she didn't want to jeopardize my position.

The Chairman: In other words, it wasn't because she felt
differently about the Communist Party, but because
she didn't want to jeopardize your position?

Mr. Berinsky: Probably.

The Chairman: Was she still a Communist at heart in 1952?

Mr. Berinsky: Well, I don't know how you define that.

The Chairman: Do you think she was a Communist, using
your own definition of Communism?

Mr. Berinsky: I guess my own definition is one who is a
member of the party. No.

The Chairman: Let's say one who was a member and
dropped out and is still loyal to the party. Taking that
as a definition, would you say she is still a Communist?

Mr. Berinsky: Do you mean in an active sense?
The Chairman: Loyal in her mind.
Mr. Berinsky. That is hard to say.

Forty-two civilian employees at Fort Monmouth were suspended. All but two were subsequently reinstated to their jobs. As far as can be determined, Berinsky was among those reinstated.

SETTLING SCORES

McCarthy used his hearings to settle scores, as he demonstrated by grilling Theodore Kaghan about Kaghan's widely publicized remark criticizing Cohn and Schine as "junketeering gumshoes." Kaghan explained his remark by telling McCarthy that he said it "because I thought they were going about a very serious business in a very superficial way," adding: "They came over there and by their activities I think reflected discredit on this committee and the Senate." McCarthy fired back by attacking Kaghan's patriotism: "I may say that, from the evidence before us ... the fact that you had books by Communist authors on the bookshelves, did nothing about it until the new State Department forced you to get them out, the fact that you lived with a Communist [during college in the 1930s] and attended Communist meetings, might justify almost anyone saying you had Communist tendencies, so that, so far, I do not think you have convinced us that they [Cohn and Schine] have done anything too wrong." Months later, in an article for *Reporter* magazine, Kaghan wrote that when he first learned his name had been mentioned in committee testimony as a security risk, he took it lightly. "I knew that I had been cleared for loyalty and security," he said, "and I waited for the

Department of State to send me some kind of instructions, advice, or information." The Department said nothing. He then learned his case was "under review." Then he was fired. Later, the Department cleared him of Communist sympathies. Kaghan became a United Nations correspondent and foreign affairs columnist for the then-liberal *New York Post.*

THE "LITTLE PEOPLE"

The prominent figures dragged before McCarthy's witch hunts—generals, writers, artists, composers, ranking government officials—were best remembered, but the private sessions offered more disgraceful examples. The transcripts were filled with heart-breaking accounts of the "little people" targeted by McCarthy. They were low-level workers, welders, grinders, clerks, messengers, many largely uneducated. Some spoke in broken English, some were union members who had signed some sort of protest paper they heard about from a family member or friend; the paper may, or may not, have expressed sympathy with a Communist philosophy. Nearly all were obviously bewildered and terrified. Many wound up being fired. For instance, everyone in General Electric's employ who took the Fifth when appearing before McCarthy's investigation of defense-related industries was fired. In one case, McCarthy ordered an immigration officer to be present when an alien of long standing in the United States took the Fifth Amendment. The alien was Cedric Belfrage, an author who wrote for Hollywood fan magazines, had been Sam Goldwyn's press agent, and who had traveled to the Soviet Union in 1936. After taking the Fifth, Belfrage was arrested on a deportation warrant, held on Ellis Island, and then deported to

Great Britain. Belfrage at least was known to prominent people; this was not the case of other "little people" who became McCarthy's victims.

Among these victims was Carl Greenblum, an Army Signal Corps civilian employee whose appearance offered a case study in how McCarthy could capitalize on a witness's emotions.

During a pause in a hearing, McCarthy dramatically informed the waiting press that a witness had broken down and cried after "some vigorous cross-examination by Roy Cohn." McCarthy added: "I have just received word that the witness admits that he was lying the first time and now wants to tell the truth." McCarthy melodramatically described this to the reporters as the "most important development" in his current investigation. He asked them not to identify the ashen-faced witness they had just seen leaving the closed hearing. Several newspapers, however, named Greenblum; shortly after, someone painted a hammer and sickle on his house. Greenblum told inquiring reporters about his appearance and McCarthy's claims, saying, "It's true that I broke down and they took me to another room and brought in a doctor and nurse." He explained that his mother had died two days earlier, leaving him emotionally unprepared to be questioned. "A few minutes later I sent word that I wanted to go back and tell my story from the beginning," he said. "That may have been interpreted to mean that I had been lying, previously, but that certainly was not the case."

Greenblum was fired. He sued the government, and five years later a federal district court ordered him reinstated to his job, ruling the Army had failed to give him adequate grounds for his dismissal.

McCarthy's investigators suggested John Sardella, a GE employee and member of the United Electrical Workers (UE) union, didn't deserve to live in the United States. His questioning from Cohn began:

Question: Do you consider yourself a good American?
Answer: Yes, sir.
Question: Do you want to contribute your money to an or- ganization which is giving to the Communist movement?
Answer: The only reason I belong to the organization is be- cause the organization is supposed to protect the work- ers, and that is the only reason I belong to it.
Question: You pay dues, don't you?
Answer: Yes, sir.
Question: How much dues do you pay a year?
Answer: $2.50 a month.
Question: How much a month?
Answer: $2.50 a month.
Question: Now, doesn't it bother you if part of that money is given by UE to the Communist Party? Doesn't that bother you?
Answer: How do I know they are Communists?
Question: I am asking you whether or not it would bother you if that money were going to the Communist Party?
Answer: Sure it would bother me if I know it went to the Communists, but the only reason I join the union is be- cause I figure the union is going to protect the working man, and that is the only reason I belong to it.
Question: Are there any other unions you could belong to?
Answer: No, sir.
McCarthy, interrupting: You are aware of the fact the UE was kicked out of the CIO because it was Communist controlled? Are you aware of that fact?
Answer: They weren't.

McCarthy: Did you hear that?

Answer: I read it in the paper.

McCarthy: I am not blaming you for the policies of the UE.
I know good, loyal people belong to the UE, but I
would like to find your attitude toward this Communist
controlled organization, however if you have got confidential clearance. Now, the time came when—

Sardella, interrupting: I tell you the truth, I don't go once
every three years to the union hall. That is how much
I am in the union.

McCarthy: There was a time when there was an election to
determine whether the UE would represent the workers or not. Did you vote in that election?

Sardella: When was that? I didn't get your right question?

McCarthy: Do you recall when there was an election to determine whether or not the UE would be the bargain-
ing agent for the people at GE?

Sardella remembered. Replying to McCarthy's question,
"Do you think a Communist-controlled union is the type of
union you want representing you?" Sardella answered: "Well,
the way I feel about it is this, sir, it wasn't there when I went
to work and it is the only union I know, and it represents us,
and it is the way I feel about it, to help me whenever I need
a little help; if anything happens to the job or anything like
that, that is what I belong for."

Before McCarthy dismissed him, he lectured Sardella that
anyone who belonged to an organization kicked out of the CIO
because of Communist control, and who exhibited the attitude
he had, should not be handling secret material. Sardella was a
"pretty lucky fellow to be in this country," McCarthy said, to
which Sardella replied: "I done my share and everything, and
I was in service as much as anybody else." He repeated: "I

have done my share, and I never done anything against the country, and I never intend to do anything against the country. I will do my best, and—"

McCarthy cut him off. As he dismissed him, he made one last threat:

"If you decide that you were not telling the truth about signing the Communist petition, contact the counsel and we will let you change your story, and have a handwritten expert examine it, and if we find that you signed that, as you apparently have, your case will submitted to the Grand Jury for an indictment for perjury, and I would suggest that you get yourself a lawyer."

———

Harold K. Briney, who did airbrake work at Westinghouse Air Brake Company, testified that he didn't know whether he had secret clearance and that he wasn't a Communist now, but took the Fifth when asked whether he ever had been. McCarthy asked him: "If you were ordered to commit sabotage by the Communist Party in case of war with Communist Russia, would you obey those orders?" Briney replied, "I would not. I would protect this country against anyone." Westinghouse fired him.

———

Vachlav Lofek, nearly sixty-one, spoke in broken English, had a hard time understanding the questioning, and clearly was fearful of losing his job as a messenger for the then-Communist Czech embassy in New York. The only apparent explanation for his having been summoned is that his job required him to carry documents from the Czech delegation at the United Nations to the Czech embassy.

The questioning was first led by Cohn and then concluded by McCarthy.

Question: Are you a citizen of the United States?

Answer: That is right.

Question: Naturalized?

Answer: Yes, sir.

Question: In what year?

Answer: 1937, in January.

Question: What is your employment at the present time?

Answer: Employment, I work for?

Question: Where do you work?

Answer: In the Czech delegation . . . to the United Nations.

Question: Are you a Communist?

Answer: No, sir, I never been.

Question: Are you a Communist at the present time?

Answer: No.

Question: You work for the Communist government?

Answer: Yes, I do.

Question: Do they make a practice of employing people who are not Communists?

Answer: I don't know, but they never asked me to join, or anything.

Question: Are you sympathetic to the Communist regime in Czechoslovakia?

Answer: No, sir.

Question; Are you opposed to it?

Answer: Well, just nothing. I don't say nothing.

Question: I don't want to know if you say nothing. Are you in favor of or opposed to the Communist regime in Czechoslovakia?

Answer: I don't like the way they do. It is now is there anymore.

Question: Pardon me?

Answer: I don't like the way they do.

Question: You mean in Czechoslovakia?

Answer: That is right.

Question: You are opposed then?

Answer: That is right.

Question: To the Communist government in Czechoslovakia?

Answer: That is right.

Lofek explained that he didn't like the way the Communists "treat the people, like they took the property away from them, you know, that is what I think because they did it for my sister, my brother-in-law, you know." Asked whether these family members were still living in Czechoslovakia, he said both were dead, which prompted McCarthy conspiratorially to ask: "Natural deaths?" "What is that?" Lofek asked, to which McCarthy replied: "They were not killed by Communists? They died natural deaths?" "Yes," Lofek said. "My sister had a stroke." Not satisfied, McCarthy asked whether they were members of the Communist Party in Czechoslovakia. "No, never as far as I know," came the answer. "My brother was against them. Always against them. And my sister, she never know nothing about politics because she was old."

Cohn resumed the questioning, wanting to know about Lofek's Communist employers at the embassy.

Question: Do they know you are opposed to them up there?

Answer: I don't know. They never ask. No, I never tell it.

Question: What kind of work do you do?

Answer: I am mostly like a messenger. I have to go all around. They need something. I have to go and get it.

Question: Do you ever carry papers back and forth?

Answer: Papers, like the United Nations papers. I go to the headquarters and pick them up and bring them to the

office and when they sort them they tell me to mail
them, you know, I send them back, you know, what
they want to Czechoslovakia.
Question: What is your salary?
Answer: $200 a month.

The questioning continued, with Cohn and later McCarthy
expressing doubt that the embassy had never asked Lofek
whether he was a Communist. McCarthy pressed the point,
asking about Lofek's American family, about whether he ever
attended Communist meetings, joined the party, had dinner at
the home of Communists in the embassy; all were answered in
the negative. Then he asked whether Lofek had ever worked
for a U.S. government agency. "No," he said, "only once I
worked for the Post Office but in the, you know, Christmastime
two months, like that, you know, when they were busy."

"It seems rather unusual," McCarthy said, still clearly un-
convinced he didn't have a Communist before him, "that the
Communist delegation would hire an American who was
against Communism."

"They don't know about that," Lofek told him. "They
don't know. You see, if I tell them, I am finished with the job,
you know. And the job sufficient for me, like I am an old guy,
you know, and it is not hard, so that is why I am trying to keep
it as long as I could."

McCarthy finally ended the questioning, saying: "I don't
think we will want you back but consider yourself under subpoena in case we want to call you."

"Yes, if you want to, then I am willing," Lofek said. Then
he confessed to a great concern. He might lose his job, because "the only thing is I got to tell the boss because, you
know, he wants to know . . . that I go [before McCarthy]."

McCarthy was not interested. "That is all," he told him. Then he added, in a note of cavalier disregard: "If you are discharged, let us know. Understand, there is nothing we can do about it if you are, but let the committee know if you are fired, will you?"

The hearing record is silent as to what happened to the old messenger.

HUNT FOR HOMOSEXUALS

McCarthy and Cohn took it as their mission to search for, and have fired, all homosexuals in the government. Page after page after page of the transcripts consisted of witnesses being grilled about their sexual preferences, while McCarthy and Cohn dropped numerous innuendoes about homosexuality to other witnesses.

McCarthy's attitude toward homosexuals was shown when he questioned a State Department personnel officer about whether a homosexual had been promoted.

McCarthy: Is it your position that the promotion board should not know that this man is a queer, that they should be allowed to go ahead and promote him, even though he is a homo, hoping that you might catch his homosexuality in some later check by some other department? Is that your testimony?

Witness: No, sir, that isn't it.

McCarthy: Why did you, in your department, think that you should keep the homosexuality of an individual from the promotion board? On what possible theory would you want to hide the fact that this man was a homo?

If anything, Cohn was even more abusive in his consistently ruthless questioning of witnesses about homosexuality. Cohn's behavior toward witnesses exposed a breathtaking hypocrisy. Roy Cohn was himself a homosexual who died of AIDS in the mid-1980s.

The questions asked of a United Nations economist, Dimitry Varley, were typical of the interrogations taking place behind closed doors. McCarthy dramatically told reporters after this session that the committee had heard testimony from a "high official" of the UN who admitted to friendship with Communists and to having contributed to organizations on the attorney general's lists of Communist fronts. Yet inside the hearing room the interrogation produced virtually nothing to prove a case of subversion or espionage, and Varley, a twelve-thousand-dollar-a-year American UN employee, was by no definition a "high official." When Cohn and McCarthy exhausted their search for evidence of subversion, the hearing became an investigation of possible homosexuality and a police morals case.

Cohn: Is it your testimony that you've never been arrested?
Varley: That's right, sir.
Cohn: What do you think, the records of the New York Police Department are, forged? . . . Isn't it a fact that you were found by members of the New York City Police Department in the men's room [on] Fifty-something Street and Lexington Avenue on December 29, 1941, arrested on a morals charge, and that you pleaded guilty and paid the fines, or you were given the alternative of a fine or jail sentence and you paid the fines, not only for yourself but for the other man who was

taken in along with you, a man named Leonardo Boronek? Isn't that a fact?

Varley insisted "this is not a fact," and attempted to explain, saying, "I was never arrested and I was never convicted on a morals charge."

This triggered an intense exchange between Varley and Cohn, with McCarthy taking over at times and interjecting with several threats that Varley would go to jail because of his testimony. At one point, after Varley asked McCarthy, "May I say how I remember what happened?" McCarthy cut him off with a curt: "No, you answer my questions. I may say that if the policemen's testimony is correct, you have perjured yourself about three times now. You can keep on if you want to, or you can tell us the truth."

The "truth" was that twelve years prior Varley had been picked up by policemen in the men's room, taken with the other man to a magistrate's court, told by the officers that the magistrate would settle the matter, ultimately charged with "loitering," fined fifteen dollars, and released. He paid the other man's fine because, he testified, "I felt sorry for the guy" after he said he had no money.

No evidence of either man engaging in a homosexual act in a public men's room was introduced, and none whatever of espionage or subversion. Nonetheless, McCarthy continued to interject such remarks as, "Mr. Cohn, I want this transmitted to the U.S. attorney, a clear case of perjury." At another point, McCarthy took over the questioning, going back over questions repeatedly asked and answered:

McCarthy: Have you ever been found guilty of a morals charge?

Varley: No, sir.

McCarthy: No?

Varley: No, sir.

McCarthy: Have you ever pleaded guilty on a morals charge?

Varley: No, sir.

McCarthy: You never have?

Varley: No, sir.

McCarthy: You never have been either convicted or pleaded guilty to any charge involving morals?

Varley: No, sir.

McCarthy: Your answer is no?

Varley: That's right.

McCarthy: You are sure of that?

Varley: I am sure of that, sir.

McCarthy: Mr. Cohn, we want the magistrates' record and the policemen in here who arrested him before he was found guilty. This is a clear case of perjury.

Cohn: What do you think you were picked for by the policemen at the time you were taken down to court in the policemen's car? Didn't they tell you?

Varley: It was a charge of loitering.

And there the matter ended: a case of suspected but unproven homosexuality involving an insignificant figure who had nothing to do with jeopardizing the security of the United States. Despite McCarthy's repeated threats, no charges of perjury were brought against Varley.

———

The case of Eric L. Kohler offered a more serious, and damning, example of McCarthy and Cohn's determination to expose and humiliate homosexuals. It is a story both poignant and cruel, starkly told in forty-four pages of testimony ex-humed from the once-sealed files.

Kohler was an accountant with a record of honorable gov-ernment service that included high positions with the Ten-nessee Valley Authority before World War II, wartime service with the Office of Emergency Management War Production Board and the Petroleum Administration for War, post-war service as financial adviser to Truman's secretary of Agricul-ture, and the post of controller of the Economic Corporation Association. He also was president of the American Account-ing Association, a visiting professor at several universities, and the author of the highly regarded *Kohler's Dictionary for Ac-countants*. At the time he testified, Kohler had not been a U.S. government employee for three years. The ostensible purpose for summoning him behind closed doors, just twelve days after Eisenhower became president, was a comment about Communism he made years before.

"Now, Mr. Kohler, have you yourself ever expressed any admiration for the Soviet form of government?" Cohn asked. When Kohler answered, "I don't think I have, no. I hope I haven't," Cohn pressed on. What about expressing admiration for the Russian idea? Years before, Kohler explained, he did express admiration for the way the Russians were appealing to consumers to rebuild their economy. "That is the only thing I was referring to," Kohler explained. "I certainly was not sub-scribing to any Russian ideology. I never have and never will."

Now Cohn got to the real purpose of summoning Kohler: "Let me ask you this, Mr. Kohler. You are a homosexual, are you not?"

After brief fencing, with Cohn hammering at him to an-swer the question directly, Kohler said: "I am perfectly willing to admit that I am, for the purposes of your private record here."

Kohler then appealed to McCarthy, saying that he was in sympathy with the purposes of McCarthy's investigation and that "I don't want to seem to be in a position of compromising my own case . . . because one who is accused of such a thing never gets anywhere denying it." He would be happy to discuss his personal situation with McCarthy in confidence. McCarthy wasn't buying. "The only reason we are concerned with this," McCarthy said, "or the principal reason, is because it [homosexuality] appears to make a man a bad security risk."

Kohler again appealed to McCarthy's better instincts. "Let me say this also, senator: In making this inquiry as to that [homosexual] condition, I think it is very easy to do a man irreparable harm, because agents can go to his friends and try to find out from them if they have any information on the subject. Now, as a matter of fact, something like that has been done in my case. It is very sad."

"I think not by this committee," McCarthy said.

"Well, I think it has been," Kohler replied.

Cohn quickly demonstrated the truth of Kohler's claim. He dramatically displayed to the witness, and the committee, an old two-page handwritten letter of Kohler's describing a sexual encounter years before with a "Bill" who headed a unit of the Budget Bureau during World War II. Cohn demanded Kohler concede that this flatly contradicted Kohler's testimony that he didn't know of any homosexuals "who have been or are now employed in the United States government." After Kohler responded, "I don't think that proves that he was a homosexual," Cohn amended his earlier question to ask whether "you know of any persons who have engaged in homosexual practices who have been or now are employed in the United States government.

"Certainly this Bill is one?" Cohn prompted.

Kohler conceded the point: "Well, he has been, yes."

"What is Bill's name?" Cohn next demanded.

"Must I say that, Mr. Chairman?" Kohler appealed to McCarthy. "I would like to protect him. He is a very fine citizen, and he has done a lot of good for his country."

Question: Is he employed in the government now?
Answer: No, he is not in the government now.
Question: Not in the Army or in the State Department?
Answer: No.
Question: What is he doing now?
Answer: He is teaching at the present time.
Question: Where is he teaching?
Answer: Mr. Chairman, should I state? It is getting closer and closer—

McCarthy cut him off. He ordered Kohler to answer, explaining, "If we find any [homosexuals] are in government, we will contact their superior, and if they are handling classified material we will insist that they be discharged." That neither "Bill" nor Kohler had been a government employee for years and neither had ever been accused of being a security risk didn't seem to matter.

Kohler, still appealing to McCarthy's sense of decency, delivered a heartfelt plea that the committee not do damage to this person. "The reason I made the statement I did or asked the question is because I have an extremely high regard for this man, and he is an up and coming economist, and he is developing a new theory that has won considerable acclaim in his field, and he has considerable free time which has been given to him by the school to develop this idea, and he is writing a book at the present time. He and I wrote a memorandum at the end of the war period which . . . won a prize, and has to do with the contribution accounting made to the war effort.

"I am willing to state his name, but I hope that he is not disturbed in this process. I would hate very much to have anything to happen to him, for the reason that he has got a great contribution to make, and he is making it."

Then Kohler made a mistake, at least by McCarthy's terms, by saying of "Bill" that, "Now, his life at the present time, so far as I know, is completely normal."

McCarthy snapped: "You see, Mr. Kohler, what you have just said there indicates the danger of having anyone with this, what I refer to as an affliction or mental aberration, handling secret work, and it shows how much they will be disturbed by having this known, and it shows—"

This time Kohler interrupted: "That is my estimate."

McCarthy: "And it shows how easily they could be blackmailed into giving out secret information." He then ordered Kohler to give names of Bill and the college where he was presently employed, and to specify the position Bill had occupied in the government and the time he had left public service. Kohler reluctantly provided the details. As it turned out, most of Bill's service had taken place eight or more years earlier. Neither Kohler nor Bill was involved in current government projects or in the handling of "secret work."

This wasn't the end of it. McCarthy raised a number of his adversaries' names, including former Senator Bill Benton, asking whether Kohler "knew them well." More questioning ensued about prior homosexual relations dating back years.

Cohn introduced letters and diaries the committee had obtained; then he and Surine subjected Kohler to vigorous grilling about other people Kohler had known, prompting this exchange between Cohn and Kohler:

Question: Did you have a friend named Jack?
Answer: Yes.
Question: Did he keep a diary?
Answer: He kept one, yes . . .
Question: Was this man Jack ever employed by the United States government?
Answer: No. He was killed; a boy.
Question: What is he doing now?
Answer. He is dead. He was killed in an automobile accident.
Question: When?
Answer: About two or three years ago.
Question: And where?
Answer: Out in Oak Park.
Question: Oak Park where?
Answer: A suburb of Chicago.
Question: Can you fix the date of the accident?
Answer: No, I can't.

It turned out that Jack was sixteen years old when he died; that despite Kohler's attraction toward him, they never had a homosexual relationship; and that Cohn had confused him with someone with a similar name who had worked for the government—but whom Kohler had not known.

Even this did not end Kohler's ordeal. Later, Surine insisted on revisiting the letters Kohler wrote describing Jack. "Must we go into this again?" Kohler pleaded. "The point at issue is your credibility," Surine told him, "and therefore I feel that we should go into it."

The entire tale was told again, with clearly prurient relish as Surine read aloud embarrassing passages. In the end, the interrogators proved nothing about the relationship between a dead youth with no government connections and a former civil servant who honorably left public service years before his private life and reputation were defamed by McCarthyism and the hunt for homosexuals.

For the rest of his life, Kohler maintained a quiet presence—so quiet that colleagues at Chicago's Roosevelt University, where he continued to serve as a trustee for fifteen years until his death in 1986, knew nothing about his secret appearance or his sexual preference. "Eric Kohler was one of the most conservative people I knew," Rolf Weil, Roosevelt's president from 1964 through 1988, told Lynn Sweet of *The Chicago Sun-Times* after Kohler's testimony was made public in 2003. All Weil knew about Kohler's private life was that he was a bachelor.

TARNISHING THE UNIFORM

By the fall of 1953, as his first year as chairman was drawing to a close, McCarthy focused more and more intensely on possible Communists within the armed services—and specifically the Army. He summoned civilian employees from clerks to security guards—and then expanded his target to include uniformed personnel. He demanded that the military provide personnel files of witnesses he interrogated, then that it provide the names of those responsible for giving the witnesses security clearances, and then the compulsory appearance of members of various loyalty boards. Under orders of Eisenhower, who invoked the constitutional doctrine of executive privilege, these people were not permitted to testify. By September, McCarthy's charges were growing more extreme. For instance, he accused the Army's chief intelligence officer, Major General Richard C. Partridge, of being "completely incompetent for his job."

All of this set the stage for McCarthy's announcement in October that he had uncovered new evidence of a spy ring operating out of the Army Signal Corps' engineering laboratories at Fort Monmouth, New Jersey.

It was not a new story; the FBI and the House Un-American Activities Committee had looked into it, particularly since Julius Rosenberg had worked at Fort Monmouth a decade prior, and had not developed any leads. In fact, McCarthy and his staff had manufactured what they claimed as their new evidence, a letter from FBI Director Hoover to the chief of Army intelligence, accusing thirty-five scientists, engineers, and technicians at Monmouth of subversive activities. The letter they cited was actually a truncated version of a 1951 Hoover letter that made no specific allegations of espionage or subversion. But McCarthy plunged ahead. Acting on information supplied by Cohn, he cut short his honeymoon that fall and raced back to launch his highly publicized investigation, one to which he committed virtually his entire staff. At stake, he claimed, was nothing less than defending the United States against attack from foreign enemies.

McCarthy transformed the old Monmouth story into an intensely publicized and showy trial of subversion, claiming to have uncovered a situation with the "earmarks of extremely dangerous espionage" that might infest the entire Signal

Corps. Rosenberg's wartime spy ring that stole radar secrets from the Monmouth laboratories was still operative. There appeared to be a link to Alger Hiss. An important witness "broke down and agreed to tell all he knew about spy rings." All this McCarthy conveyed breathlessly to reporters before rushing back inside his closed-door committee room.

Chapter
SEVENTEEN

The Case of Private Schine

*It is one of the few things I have seen [Roy Cohn]
completely unreasonable about. He thinks Dave should be
a general and work from the penthouse of the Waldorf.*

—Joe McCarthy, in a phone call to the Secretary of the Army

A t 3:28 P.M. on October 27, 1953, Robert Ten Broeck
Stevens, Eisenhower's new secretary of the Army, picked
up the private phone in his Pentagon office. Roy Cohn was
calling from New York, and not for the first time.

They had been in constant communication, in person and
by telephone, in the months since the new administration had
come to power, and even more so in recent weeks as Mc-
Carthy focused more and more on the Army. Now Cohn
briefed Stevens on where things stood from McCarthy's
standpoint and the need, as the investigating subcommittee
saw it, to obtain security and loyalty board documents and
other Army records.

Their conversation, which was pleasant in tone, ended with Cohn raising a sensitive subject, one he identified as dealing with "our young friend." Stevens well knew who Cohn meant: G. David Schine. In Cohn's view, Schine's case had become even more urgent. The next Tuesday, November 3, Schine was to be inducted as a private in the United States Army.

———

In July, Schine's draft board had reclassified him from 4-F because of a previously slipped disc, to 1-A. That he now faced induction after initially being classified physically unfit for active duty was what could be called a case of Drew Pearson's revenge: after learning of Schine's 4-F classification, the columnist had called Schine's draft board and demanded that his case be reopened. It was. Doctors reexamined Schine. This time they found him physically able to serve.

Since then, McCarthy and Cohn had worked diligently behind the scenes on Schine's behalf, trying to get him an officer's commission or to find some other way for him to avoid service. They made one appointment after another with officials in the armed forces. All were unsuccessful. First the Army, then the Air Force, then the Navy rendered a negative judgment. Schine did not qualify for a direct commission. The possibility of naming Schine the subcommittee's "chief consultant" to the Army was also raised, and rejected as unworkable.

This didn't stop McCarthy and Cohn, and it certainly didn't stop Schine from directly lobbying the secretary of the Army.

By then, McCarthy and his young aides had established a close relationship with the fifty-four-year-old Army secretary, who was doing his best to keep McCarthy from attacking the Army. Stevens met with them in New York; invited them to one of his private clubs, the Merchants Club, where he extended dining and barroom privileges to McCarthy; jovially told Cohn how he wanted to have lunch with "you boys"; entertained the three men at dinner; was, in turn, invited to be a guest at social gatherings in the Schine family's Waldorf suite; and extended them the use of his plane for flights back to Washington.

Schine pleaded his case with the secretary in a number of phone conversations. Invariably, Schine would make a remark about "a personal matter" affecting him, adding that "time was running out." The secretary knew exactly what these references were concerning, as he had taken a call from Schine in his Pentagon office only a week before Cohn's October 27 phone call.

Stevens had told Schine he was sorry he had missed seeing him the day before, when Stevens and his new Army counsel, John Adams, made an inspection tour of the Fort Monmouth base, where McCarthy was conducting his hearings. Then Stevens addressed Schine's personal matter: "I have reviewed the whole situation with Mr. Wilson [the secretary of defense]," he told Schine, "and it adds up to this: neither he nor I can see an appropriate way to avoid the basic training. We feel that is almost a must in the situation as it exists. And after going over the situation three times now insofar as you are concerned, it is my honest conviction that that is the wise thing to do, Dave. And having done that, I think there is an excellent chance that we can pick you up and use you in a way that would be useful to the country and to yourself." He added: "Just what that would be, I don't know. I can't define it now because I haven't got to that point. But it's something on my mind, and one that I would make every effort to carry out. I personally would like to arrange it . . . that you would come into [the] Army or military establishment in such a way that you would use the knowledge and ability you have in certain fields."

There matters stood until Cohn phoned the secretary a week later.

"I have got two ideas in my head," Cohn told the secretary. "The main thing I am concerned about, since nothing else apparently can be done, since we are in the middle of this thing here [the Monmouth investigation], we would like him around for a while."

He suggested that Schine be furloughed from the Army for a few weeks so that he could continue working for the committee. Then Cohn raised his other idea: getting Schine a job with the CIA, a subject he and Stevens had previously discussed. "I am thinking of this again," Cohn explained. "Have you given it any further thought?"

"No," the secretary said. "It was more or less on ice until you and Dave brought it up again."

"For a while anyway it might be a good idea," Cohn continued, "because with us going into the [Monmouth] shop over there with such intensity, it might avoid embarrassment all around. I talked to Joe and I talked to Dave, and they would be willing. The question is, could the people over there [CIA] pick him right away?"

Accommodating as ever, Stevens replied: "Do you want me to talk to [CIA director] Allen Dulles?" Then, after a slight pause: "I think I might do it."

The next morning, at 8:15, the secretary of the Army called on the director of Central Intelligence. Twenty-four hours later, he reported back to Cohn, still in New York, by phone. He had bad news about the CIA: They couldn't use Dave; they wanted people for a long period of service, and they had a policy against taking men eligible for the draft.

Cohn persisted. Couldn't something be done for Dave once he was drafted? "I can probably do a better job on that than [the CIA] could," Stevens reassuringly told him. "Now, on the furlough business, it would be possible to make him available in the New York area for a couple of weeks at the beginning of his service period."

There it stood. Numerous private phone conversations had failed to resolve the problem facing G. David Schine.

————

They weren't *really* private phone conversations.

Every time the secretary of the Army's private phone rang in his Pentagon office, the words transmitted over the line were heard not only by the secretary but also by a balding young man, usually wearing a bow tie, sitting just outside the secretary's office door. He was John J. Lucas, Jr., the secretary's appointments clerk and a career civil servant. Listening on another phone, the receiver cradled against his shoulder, Lucas recorded every word in Gregg shorthand in his stenographic notebook. He was "fast, accurate, and meticulous," and had been recording all telephone conversations with secretaries of the Army since 1949. The result was, as Eisenhower aide Ewald later described it, a historical "gold mine" buried in untranscribed notebooks—"a rolling contemporaneous record of thousands upon thousands of words spoken by and to the secretary, day by day, minute by minute, month after month." If Lucas left his desk to go to the bathroom, attend to other office duties, or take a vacation, one of his assistants took his place and continued the unbroken shorthand record of everything said over the secretary's private Pentagon line.

The White House impounded these documents as the Army-McCarthy hearings began in April 1954, in order to keep them from being subpoenaed by McCarthy. They were maintained under lock and key, then returned to the Pentagon and kept in locked file cabinets, before finally being removed to the Nebraska home of an Eisenhower aide, Fred Seaton. After his death in the early 1980s, Seaton's widow donated them to the Eisenhower presidential library in Abilene, Kansas, where William Bragg Ewald, Jr., discovered and used them in his book, *Who Killed Joe McCarthy?*

————

Bob Stevens was nothing if not honorable. Tall and trim, with thinning gray hair, a ruddy complexion, and a ready smile, he exuded decency and good intentions. He was one of the favored Americans who formed what came to be called, inadequately, the establishment. The heir to a New England textile business founded a century and a half prior by a Yankee ancestor, Nathaniel Stevens, he moved effortlessly among the upper rungs of American society, a multimillionaire WASP with all the credentials for success: schooling at Andover and Yale; directorships on major boards such as General Electric, General Foods, and New York Telephone; a director and ultimately chairman of the Federal Reserve Board of New York; chairman of the influential Business Advisory Council (predecessor to the present Business Roundtable); membership in a number of exclusive clubs and a trustee of such prestigious institutions as the Rockefeller Foundation and Roosevelt

Hospital; plus a fine home in New Jersey, a rented mansion in Washington, D.C., and a ranch in Montana. Over the decades, Stevens served his country in a number of capacities. He interrupted his Yale studies to serve as an artillery lieutenant during World War I. Before Pearl Harbor, he volunteered for a special Army command and staff school course at Fort Leavenworth, Kansas, emerging from World War II as a decorated colonel.

Bob Stevens was a patriot, a believer in public service and in the basic trustworthiness of those he dealt with professionally. This was the patient, even-tempered, self-effacing—and, yes, utterly naïve and bumbling—man whom Dwight Eisenhower chose as his secretary of the Army. His credentials and distinguished record aside, he proved to be singularly unsuited for the job. His story demonstrated that good intentions were not enough when dealing with Joe McCarthy. Nor, as Stevens's experience made clear, did a policy of appeasement produce anything more than new abuses and demands for further concessions.

Stevens kept misjudging McCarthy and Cohn. For weeks, then months, as McCarthy's assaults against the Army grew more outrageous, Stevens continued to believe that he could placate McCarthy by appealing in private to a fellow public servant's sense of honor and duty. He would meet with McCarthy and accommodate him as much as possible. He would even defend McCarthy to critical, perhaps more cynical, but realistic administration officials, who tried to warn the secretary about McCarthy's true character.

Snatches drawn from transcripts of Stevens's phone conversations in this period tell a sad story of trust misplaced and supposed friendship abused.

September 9, 1953. The day before, during a closed hearing, McCarthy had torn into the Army's legislation liaison office head, Major General Miles Reber, during a closed hearing for refusing to turn over classified security documents, saying: "Don't give me that General . . . I can't conceive that the president, who is elected on a platform of opposition to Communism, would whitewash those who are responsible." After this blast, William P. Rogers, then the deputy attorney general, called to see how Stevens was holding up.

"How are you getting along with Jumping Joe?" Rogers, a far savvier and tougher political figure than Stevens, asked the secretary.

Stevens naïvely replied:

"To be honest, perfectly well. Yesterday I was willing to give way on several things, but on major things like the Executive Order of the President, we'll stand tight and see."

September 10. Stevens to the Defense Department's general counsel, Struve Hensel, who called to ask uneasily about the Army's response to McCarthy's continuing demands and attacks:

"I was just beginning to turn this over in my mind, and I was wondering whether it would make any sense to go up there [New York] and see Joe and the staff and see what it is they want and get the thing back on the track."

Six days later, Stevens did go to New York and met privately with McCarthy the next morning at breakfast in the Schine's Waldorf suite, then returned to the Pentagon.

September 17. Fred Seaton, a former Republican senator and Nebraska newspaper publisher who had just been named the Defense Department's assistant secretary for legislative and public affairs (and was later an Ike White House aide and secretary of the interior), phoned Stevens to ask about his New York meeting with McCarthy. "I couldn't help being curious about your own appraisal of the situation the other day in New York," Seaton said.

"I still continue to have my fingers crossed," Stevens told him, "but so far the thing has gone along surprisingly well. I followed along the lines we discussed the other day . . . I agreed to give him the names of the people that reviewed that one case [dealing with someone suspected of homosexuality] . . . I refused, of course, on the loyalty files and things of that kind."

The secretary added, even more naïvely: "Joe was definitely pleased with the conference; so I felt I had accomplished quite a bit. I feel that at the moment he is very strong for the Army and the way we are operating with him."

By mid-October, with the headline-catching Fort Monmouth hearings underway and McCarthy smelling political pay dirt in them, Stevens went back to New York to attend a closed-door hearing. He took McCarthy, Cohn, and Schine to lunch at his club, then attended an expansive dinner party hosted by Cohn in a private dining room at the Waldorf; the next morning, Schine picked him up in the family limo and took him to the hearing. Back in Washington, Stevens took a call from an Army undersecretary, Earl Johnson, a Wisconsin native who invited Stevens to a dinner with Wisconsin governor Walter Kohler, Jr. and McCarthy and his new wife, the former Jean Kerr. "I call him your senator, you know," Stevens amiably told Johnson, saying of the dinner with McCarthy, "I think it would be a good thing to do."

Stevens fairly gushed as he volunteered how his relationship with McCarthy was going: "The Army is getting along fine with Joe. He is getting headlines and is entitled to them. Fundamentally, he has been fine with us."

October 28. Shortly after Stevens told Cohn the CIA wouldn't take Schine, Fred Seaton, clearly growing more concerned about McCarthy's assault on the Army, called to stiffen the secretary's resolve not to give in to McCarthy's demands for classified material. It was a "matter of fundamental principle," Seaton told Stevens, adding: "I don't want the public to think we don't have [a] loyalty review unless McCarthy says we should have." Don't worry, the secretary assured him, "I am just going to tell Joe no in a nice way."

Seaton wasn't entirely persuaded. "I think you have another thing," he warned Stevens. "If Joe gets into this situation, you pay hell in getting anyone to serve on those boards."

"We can order them to serve," Stevens, apparently taken aback, replied.

Pathetically, Stevens added: "Joe never fails . . . to tell [reporters] how much he thinks [of] the way we have gone about this thing and the way we are trying to clear it up."

Stevens remained convinced that he would be able to get McCarthy to stop his destructive assaults on the Army. To no avail, of course: McCarthy's public remarks about Communist penetration of the Army, and his private bullying of uniformed witnesses, became even more abusive. The looming final collision between the senator and the Army became more inevitable.

———

As ordered, G. David Schine was inducted into the Army on November 3, and, as promised, the Army secretary immediately gave him a fifteen-day assignment on temporary duty to the McCarthy committee investigations being held in New

York. If the Army secretary thought that would end his problems over the new private—and with McCarthy and Cohn—he was quickly disappointed. The pace of the confrontation only quickened as Stevens found himself embroiled in even more bitter disputes with McCarthy over the hearings, and with Cohn over Schine. Still, Stevens tried to appease McCarthy. He invited McCarthy and "the boys" to lunch with him at the Pentagon to discuss the investigations—and, presumably, Schine's future.

November 7. Saturday, shortly after noon, a few days after the Pentagon luncheon, McCarthy phoned Stevens and asked the secretary whether Schine could at least be excused from Army duty on weekends, saying, "Roy . . . thinks Dave should be a general and work from the penthouse of the Waldorf."

Three days later, Schine reported to Fort Dix to begin his basic training. Immediately Cohn began what became a constant stream of calls to the commanding general of the base, requesting that Schine be granted not only weekend passes but weeknight passes as well. Cohn's ostensible reason: so-called committee business that required Private Schine to be in New York.

The pressure was relentless. Cohn, accompanied by a former FBI agent who was now a member of the subcommittee, visited the commanding general of Fort Dix the day after Schine's arrival and asked to see Schine. He was allowed. The next day the general received a call from a committee member requesting that Schine be given a weekend pass. Granted. Two days later Schine received another pass to visit with Joe and Jean McCarthy and Cohn—and with Secretary Stevens, when Stevens's plane carrying them landed at nearby McGuire Air Force Base. Photographs were taken. More passes followed: for visits to New York; for Christmas and New Year's holidays; for a trip to nearby Trenton, where the committee was holding another hearing. In just under his first month in the Army, Private Schine, the new draftee, received sixteen phone calls from committee members, was visited by them eight times at the base, got four weekends and five week nights off, was relieved from KP after Cohn protested, and was excused from drill to place or receive two hundred fifty long distance calls. He and Cohn resumed their round of dinners and night-clubbing in the city.

This special treatment did not go unnoticed. Press reports quoted other Fort Dix recruits as saying Schine was living there "like a visiting dignitary," including wearing non-issue boots and a fur-lined hood.

It was finally too much for the commanding general. On December 4, General Cornelius Ryan declared that henceforth weekends would start at noon on Saturdays instead of Friday nights. Four days later, on December 9, in a phone call to Army Counsel John Adams, General Ryan said, as Adams reported, "the matter of the handling of Private Schine was completely out of hand, that the soldier was leaving the post nearly every night, that he had been seen in Trenton on business which was obviously social and in no way connected with the committee." Ryan's request to rule out weeknight passes altogether for Schine was approved. This triggered an instant and violent protest from Cohn to Counsel Adams, who phoned his boss, the secretary, on December 9 to report that: "Roy said to me this morning, 'The Army has doublecrossed me for the last time . . . The Army is going to find out what it means to go over my head.' I said, 'Is this a threat?' He said, 'It is a promise, and I always deliver on my promises.'"

Adams also told Stevens that McCarthy now was reversing himself on Schine and wanted him assigned to New York after completing only eight of the compulsory sixteen weeks of basic training, perhaps then transferring to West Point, where he could investigate textbooks for pro-Communist material. (Subsequently, Adams raised the possibility of Schine being assigned to Fort Gordon, Georgia, to be trained as an Army criminal investigator. Initially, Cohn thought the idea promising, but after grilling Adams—how many days would Schine be there? Would he have to live on the base? Whom should Cohn call to get "Schine off"?—he pronounced it "completely unacceptable" because the location was so far from New York.)

Adams then relayed to Stevens an explicit threat Cohn had made regarding McCarthy's investigation of the Army: "Roy says, 'We are never going to stop. Joe will deliver, and I can make Joe do what I want.'"

Cohn launched a barrage of abusive phone calls to Adams, one of which lasted for an hour and fifteen minutes. Dutifully, the counsel passed their contents on to Stevens.

As John Adams summarized it at the time, "The sustained violence of telephone abuse which I took . . . is hard to describe. The obscenities and vituperative remarks which Cohn used to describe the secretary of the Army, the Army itself, and our treatment of McCarthy, Schine, and Cohn, cannot be recorded or publicly repeated." Over and over during this period, Cohn accused the Army of double-crossing him by not giving Schine a direct commission, as allegedly promised; for not assigning Schine to New York City; for cutting back Schine's availability on evenings and weekends. "The most consistent remark which he made," Adams says, "was that the

Army was requiring Schine to eat [obscenity] [as Adams wrote] because he worked for the McCarthy committee. He repeated this at least thirty times during this telephone conversation [of December 9] and at least a hundred times during the eight weeks during which we were discussing the Schine situation."

In other calls, Cohn threatened to show the country how shabbily the Army was being run. He named military officers and civil servants he promised to "ruin." On one occasion, Adams noted that Cohn "attacked me with unusual violence even for Cohn, and told me he would teach me what it means to go over his head." When Adams asked Cohn: "Roy, what will happen if Dave gets an overseas assignment?" The answer was quick and startling: "Stevens is through as Secretary of the Army." "Oh, come on now, Roy," Adams replied. "Can that stuff. Really, what's going to happen if Schine gets an overseas assignment?"

"We'll wreck the Army," Cohn told him. "We have enough stuff on the Army to have an investigation run indefinitely. We'll smear you over every newspaper in the country. The Army will be ruined."

Cohn proceeded to unleash a stream of even more abuse: "Dave gets out of Camp [sic] Dix tomorrow," he said. "The day he's gone we're going to start in on [Commanding General] Ryan . . . He'll be ruined before you know it for the lousy rotten unfair way he's let Dave be treated . . . We are going to ruin him, and then we're going to wreck the Army if you pull a dirty, lousy, filthy [obscenity] double-crossing like that [sending Schine overseas]. I wouldn't put it past that lousy doublecrossing Stevens."

McCarthy himself warned Adams, during a nighttime meeting at McCarthy's home, "not to take on Roy" because Cohn has "very powerful connections with various . . . [right wing] newspaper elements, including Sokolsky and Pegler," who would write articles harmful to the Army. On another occasion a McCarthy staff member recommended that Adams deal privately with Sokolsky in order to pacify McCarthy. "I had better talk to Sokolsky because Sokolsky 'had a capacity for getting very angry if he were not consulted when he thought he should be,'" Adams was told. "'George is the only means you have got of getting back in good with Joe.'"

Sokolsky, in fact, directly lobbied Stevens on behalf of Schine and McCarthy during an hour-long visit at the Pentagon. Stevens, still naïve, told his counsel during another phone conversation: "I had a good visit with him [Sokolsky] . . . although I am not exactly clear why he came in. I sort of thought he was on a mission . . . He talked about Dave [Schine] quite a bit and maybe his idea was to find out whether anything could be done for Dave . . . He said he knew Joe very well, and I made note of his phone number."

Adams replied: "We might get Sokolsky to see if we can get him [McCarthy] to back off."

———

While this drama was unfolding behind the scenes day by day, other major events, both public and private, were shaping the final showdown between McCarthy and the Army—and, most critically, between McCarthy, the Eisenhower administration, and the president himself. But McCarthy continued to have his say, and it was increasingly critical of the president.

On November 19, during a presidential news conference,

a reporter asked the president how significant an issue the exposure of Communists in government in the previous Democratic administration would be in the upcoming congressional elections of 1954. Ike said he was "certainly trying" to see that those investigations were being conducted "without doing injustice to any individual, because I don't believe we can afford to destroy inside what we think we are protecting from the outside."

Then he said: "Now, I hope this whole thing [the hysteria caused by the search for Communists] will be a matter of history and of memory by the time the next election comes around." He added, again sounding a note of honorable concern, "I don't believe we can live in fear of each other forever, and I really hope and believe that this administration is proceeding decently and justly to get this thing straightened out."

Once more, the president's words were admirable, if passive, and once more they had no effect on checking Joe McCarthy. They only emboldened him. McCarthy quickly launched an all-out attack, not just on the "treason" of the Truman administration, but on the weakness of the Eisenhower administration toward Communism.

The trigger for McCarthy's attack was a typically strong remark by Harry Truman accusing the new administration of embracing "McCarthyism." This provided McCarthy with another opportunity to win the kind of national audience he craved. He instantly demanded the TV networks give him free air time to reply to Truman's attack. Once more, as they had done previously with McCarthy, the networks cravenly bowed to him.

On November 25, 1953, little more than a year after Eisenhower was elected president, McCarthy began his nationally televised remarks by lashing his old target, Harry Truman, whose administration, he said, had been "crawling with Communists." Then he shifted his focus from Truman to Ike: "A few days ago, I read that President Eisenhower expressed the hope that by election time in 1954 the subject of Communism would be a dead and forgotten issue. The raw, harsh, unpleasant truth is that Communism is an issue and will be an issue in 1954 . . . I would . . . like to remind those very well-meaning people who speak about Communism not being an issue that Communism is not isolated from other great evils which beset us today."

Even more audaciously, McCarthy next took aim at the Republican Party, attacking what he called "the failure of my party . . . to liquidate the foulest bankruptcy of the Democrat Administration." That was, among other Democratic sins, permitting "continuation of trade with countries who do business with Red China."

He also said, ominously: "It is time that we, the Republican Party, liquidate the bloodstained blunder of the Acheson-Truman regime."

It required no shrewd analysis to decipher his message: after a year in office, the Eisenhower administration had failed to eradicate the "treasonous" acts of the Truman administration and was even abetting them.

"Sheer fascism," Jim Hagerty, Ike's press secretary, wrote in his diary that night after watching McCarthy's nationally televised performance.

In his own secret diary entry that night, C. D. Jackson expressed horror at what he saw as McCarthy's declaration of war on Eisenhower. Jackson, a key White House aide, viewed McCarthy's brazen attack on Eisenhower as an attempt "to establish McCarthy as Mr. Republican ... to establish Mc-Carthyism as Republicanism, and anybody who didn't agree was either a fool or a protector of Communism."

To Jackson, the thrust of McCarthy's reasoning suggested a "Wonderful syllogism—I am the only rooter-outer of Communists; there are still Communists in government . . .; this government [is] headed by Eisenhower; therefore, unless Eisenhower roots them out my way, he is a harborer of Communists."

It wasn't long before McCarthy was adding another year to his delineation of treason. It was no longer only "twenty years of treason" imperiling America; it was now "twenty-one years of treason."

McCarthy's speech ignited an intense debate among presidential advisers. Some, such as C. D. Jackson, wanted the president to take on McCarthy in a nationwide address; others continued to counsel caution, citing again the one-vote margin Republicans held in the Senate. The appeasers won; but counterforces were beginning to form at the highest levels within the administration.

By January 1954, as the second year in Eisenhower's term began, changes on Capitol Hill were affecting McCarthy. The Democratic members who had walked off the investigative committee in protest five months prior had returned. Flexing their muscles, they won the right to choose their own minority counsel and to have a say in the hiring of McCarthy's staff, the subpoenaing of witnesses, and the scheduling of hearings. They picked the returning Robert Kennedy as their counsel. Despite their more confrontational stance, however, the Democrats still weren't ready to wage an all-out public war with McCarthy. Nonetheless, a convergence of Republican and Democratic political forces was beginning to form.

Army Secretary Bob Stevens continued to cling to his belief that he and McCarthy would reach an agreement that would satisfy both the senator and the Army. One of Stevens's phone calls illuminated the secretary's cast of mind about McCarthy even at this late date. On January 12, 1954, Republican senator H. Alexander Smith of New Jersey, where the Monmouth hearings were underway, called.

"Is Joe behaving?" Senator Smith asked.

"I would say so," Stevens replied. "I have never had any trouble myself at all with Joe. His general counsel there is not the easiest fellow to deal with. I guess you know Roy Cohn?"

"Yes," Smith said. "He is terrible."

Nine days later, on January 21, Attorney General Herbert Brownell, Jr., convened a top-level meeting at the Justice Department. Army Counsel Adams—but not Stevens—was instructed to attend. When Adams arrived, he was surprised to find an imposing group of most senior presidential advisers present. Among them were Deputy Attorney General Bill Rogers, United Nations Ambassador Henry Cabot Lodge, and the most influential of all, Sherman Adams, the president's chief of staff.

Brownell asked Adams to brief them on everything that had taken place with McCarthy. Adams recited a chapter-and-verse account of McCarthy's demands that he be given the testimony of witnesses in earlier loyalty board hearings and other national security documents that the president had ordered classified. He also related McCarthy's abusive behavior, laying out in detail the endless intercessions of Cohn on behalf of Private Schine and the extraordinary threats Cohn had made against the Army.

Sherman Adams instructed Counsel Adams to begin compiling a detailed written chronology of these events, with appropriate transcribed records of conversations. Acting on Bill Rogers's suggestion in an earlier phone call, Adams had also begun talking to Democratic senators on the McCarthy committee. After describing Cohn's actions with regard to Schine, Adams received the same advice from the wily Democratic senator John McClellan of Arkansas: keep a written record.

––––––

Against this backdrop of clandestine strategy meetings, McCarthy had once more commanded the full attention of the public with his claims of having uncovered the Army's treasonous actions in promoting and protecting a Communist.

The case involved an Army dentist named Irving Peress, commissioned in October 1952 during the height of the Korean War. A year later, in October 1953, as McCarthy was targeting the Army at Fort Monmouth, Peress was promoted to the rank of major through the normal provisions of the Doctor Draft Law upon which he had entered the service. He was then stationed at Camp Kilmer, New Jersey. The next month, the armed forces bureaucracy discovered that Peress had declined to answer questions about his political beliefs when he was drafted. He had, in fact, been a member of the left wing American Labor Party. When this knowledge surfaced, on January 18, 1954, the Army ordered Peress discharged within ninety days.

When facts about the "pink dentist" were leaked to McCarthy he summoned Peress, who took the Fifth. After McCarthy demanded that he be court-martialed, Peress requested his discharge be made effective immediately. It was. McCarthy then demanded to know "who promoted Peress,"

insisted he be given all the names of those in the Army involved in Peress's discharge, and renewed his old demand for
all service security records involved in the case.

When Major General Kirke B. Lawton, in command at
Fort Monmouth, appeared before the committee, he told Mc-
Carthy he was prohibited by executive order from providing
specific details of the number of security risks reported from
his installation to Washington. "I would love to tell you," he
said, "but I honestly feel that . . . you can get it so easily another way."

McCarthy erupted.

> May I say, General, if you honestly feel you would be vio-
> lating a rule, I would not want to put you between two
> fires: of being in contempt of this committee or being sub-
> ject to a court martial for having violated the presidential
> directive. For that reason I am not going to order you to an-
> swer the question. I would like to make it very clear for the
> record that I think it is ridiculous to the point of being lu-
> dicrous to think that an Army officer cannot tell the Amer-
> ican people how many Communists or disloyal people he
> has gotten rid of. I may say that all of the evidence of infil-
> tration by Communists and subversion of the Army has
> caused the Army to drop to a rather low point in the esti-
> mation of the American people, and it is bad for this coun-
> try. It would be a good thing if the American people could
> learn that we have someone someplace who is kicking the
> Communists out.

He then made a contemptuous remark about how poorly
he thought Eisenhower was protecting the nation's security as
commander-in-chief:

I know how many security risks you have been working on, and how many cases of subversion; and if the President of the United States wants to continue to operate under a rule which is going to keep the facts in the dark, that is all right. I may say I do not blame the president on this. I do not think he has any conception of the fact that Army officers will come before a committee and refuse to give this testimony . . . If I may risk being boresome by repetition, I think it is the most fantastic and it is the most unbelievable situation that I have ever heard, to think the people cannot hear facts about whether or not you are cleaning house.

McCarthy grew even more abusive when Lieutenant Colonel Chester T. Brown, the assistant chief of staff at Peress's Camp Kilmer base, declined to answer a question about the promotion of the dentist, saying, "I cannot answer that question. It is classified."

After Cohn asked whether the colonel had submitted a questionnaire to his superiors about the case, the colonel said, "I am not permitted to tell you, sir."

McCarthy tore into the colonel:

On what grounds? May I say something to you, sir, and to the others of you officers. I will listen to Communists refuse to answer; I will listen to no Army officer protecting a Communist, and you are going to answer these questions or your case will come before the Senate for contempt and I intend to shove it all the way through. I am sick of this, sick and tired of it. This whole case is the greatest scandal I ever heard. Somebody in your command—and yours, general [referring to General Lawton]—has been protecting a man guilty of treason. We are going to find out who.

Answer the question, and you are going to be ordered to answer it.

The colonel stood his ground. "I will have to refer the committee, with regret, to special Regulation 380-320-10, paragraph 43, which states: 'The disclosure of the nature, sources or even the existence of counterintelligence information to persons mentioned in such report or to any other persons not normally entitled to such information, may be made only when specifically authorized by the assistant chief of staff, G-2, Department of the Army, or higher authority.' Under that regulation—"

McCarthy blew up: "I do not recognize that as authority to refuse to answer this question. You will be ordered to answer."

Again the reply: "I respectfully must refuse to answer."

"All right," McCarthy snapped. Turning toward Army Counsel Adams, who was seated beside the witness, McCarthy lashed out not only at the witness and Adams but at the Eisenhower administration:

"And I want you to know, John, that I am sick of this. These cases are going to be made public. I am going to let the public see you, sir—see what your new administration, John—is doing, protecting and covering up Communists."

He turned back to the colonel and accused him of having lied when he said earlier that Adams had not instructed him to withhold the information. "I would suggest you tell the truth, colonel," McCarthy said. "I am telling the truth, sir," the colonel answered. "You say that Adams did not advise you?" "No, sir," the colonel continued, "I quoted the regulation and he agreed with me."

Furious, McCarthy again addressed Army Counsel Adams in an increasingly embittered exchange:

> McCarthy: Mr. Adams, will you stand and raise your right hand? You are more than a lawyer, you are a government employee. I am ordering you, Mr. Adams, to be sworn, because you are also an employee of the government.
>
> Adams: Mr. Chairman, I respectfully request the opportunity not to appear as a witness before the committee.
>
> McCarthy: That will not be granted.
>
> Adams: I appear as a representative of the secretary of the Army at your invitation, sir.
>
> McCarthy: You are here as an employee of the government, Mr. Adams, and I intend to order you to be sworn. You are now ordered to stand up and be sworn.
>
> Adams: Mr. Chairman, may I request the opportunity to get instructions from the Secretary of the Army?
>
> McCarthy: You may.
>
> Adams: That will take some time, and I probably cannot accomplish it this afternoon in time before the conclusion of the hearing.

Now McCarthy directly accused the colonel of lying. Adams protested that the colonel was telling the truth. McCarthy responded dismissively: "If you are going to testify, Mr. Adams, you will be sworn."

McCarthy then ordered "the room completely cleared of everyone except the witness."

He didn't mean, as it turned out, that Cohn and his other staff members would exit. Instead, after Adams left, the colonel sat alone before the committee without counsel. The grilling of the colonel continued, with Cohn taking the lead: "Colonel, is this your own decision, or have you received advice and instructions from superiors? If it is your own decision, it is an awfully bad one."

"It is my own decision based on the regulations," the colonel replied.

Another McCarthy committee member, Harold Rainville, Senator Dirksen's administrative assistant on leave to the committee, asked McCarthy whether he could "make a statement." McCarthy agreed, and Rainville proceeded to threaten the colonel with the loss of his job.

Question: Who pays your salary, colonel?

Answer: The United States government.

Question: Where do they get the money from?

Answer: From Congress.

Question: Then the paymaster is the guy that is in charge of you, and you ought to realize that you don't even have a job if this man decides that there is going to be no appropriation for the Army. I mean, don't you realize that the Senate—

Answer: I cannot see that that has a bearing on it, sir.

Question: That certainly has a bearing on it. That statement says that you can only give the information to authorized people. Who creates your job? Who promotes you? The president of the United States cannot promote you unless the Senate agrees.

Answer: That says when specifically authorized by the assistant chief of staff, G-2, the Department of the Army, or higher authority.

Question: And what higher authority is there than the guy who raises your dough?

At that point Cohn intruded, and unintentionally demonstrated the haste with which the committee operated.

Question: Have you requested authorization from higher
     authority?
Answer: I have not.
Question: Why?
Answer: I have not had the opportunity. I only knew I was
     coming here at 5:30 last night.

Minutes later McCarthy attacked Brown in a most vicious and insulting manner:

Colonel, may I say to you that this committee has a very difficult job, a job of digging up traitors," McCarthy began. "We have been finding some, such as Peress, with the complete wholehearted opposition of men like yourself, men who give no cooperation at all, men who like yourself are responsible for covering up the facts so that we cannot find out who has been placing Communists in the Army and keeping them there. For your information, I want you to know that this is something we are going to have to bring to the attention of all the American people. I want them to see our Army officers sitting here, refusing to give the facts about traitors and spies, saying that if they tell us about these traitors, about those spies, if they let the senators know, that that will endanger the security of the nation.

I think, may I say this, that any man in the uniform of his country, who refuses to give information to a committee of the Senate which represents the American people, that that man is not fit to wear the uniform of his country. And in my opinion he is in the same category, colonel, as the traitor whom he is protecting. I just want to make that very clear to you, so you know it will be made very clear to the American people.

McCarthy then threatened the colonel: "I am going to ask the Senate to have you cited for contempt for failure to give information which the committee is entitled to, relying upon a phony order." He also suggested the colonel would face a perjury charge because, as McCarthy put it, "frankly, colonel, I do not believe you are telling us the truth."

McCarthy brought this extraordinary star chamber proceeding to a close by asking the colonel the name of his commanding general. "General Zwicker, sir," the colonel said, adding of Zwicker: "He reminded me I could not answer any questions with regard to classified matters in this case."

Immediately, McCarthy summoned Zwicker to appear behind closed doors that afternoon. An Army medical officer, Captain W. J. Woodward, told McCarthy after Colonel Brown left the room that Zwicker "came into the hospital yesterday complaining of some vague chest pain over the heart area, that actually radiated like angina pain. We have had two electrocardiograms on him." Asked whether being forced to testify could endanger Zwicker's health, the captain told McCarthy that "would depend, senator, on how upset he gets."

Nonetheless, Zwicker was summoned to testify an hour later. McCarthy told the medical officer he would be permitted "to sit beside [Zwicker] and if you see he is getting disturbed, if you will let us know, we will act accordingly."

———

When he appeared before McCarthy on February 18, 1954, General Ralph W. Zwicker was one of the U.S. Army's most admired officers. A West Pointer, class of 1927, he testified wearing a chest full of decorations for heroism on his military blouse: the Silver Star, the Legion of Merit with Oak Leaf Cluster, the Bronze Star with two Oak Leaf Clusters, the British Arrowhead for distinguished service. During World War II he had served with great gallantry at Normandy and in northern France, the Ardennes, the Rhineland, and central Europe. Ironically, it was Zwicker who first blew the whistle on Peress that fall, and who subsequently concurred in the decision to remove Peress from the Army. But Zwicker was also bound by existing executive orders not to provide classified security information to the investigating subcommittee.

Zwicker reiterated as much when the now thoroughly furious McCarthy confronted the ailing general, seated without counsel, behind closed doors that afternoon. After Zwicker explained that he could not furnish the classified records sought by the committee because the president had ordered such files classified, McCarthy brutally tore into the general. "Don't be coy with me, general," he raged, "don't try to give me that doubletalk." He continued his assault, saying, "General, let's try and be truthful" and, "I am going to keep you here as long as you keep hemming and hawing." His tirade continued with one insulting remark after another: "I mean exactly what I asked you, general, and nothing else. Anyone who has the brains of a five-year-old child can understand that question."

Finally, McCarthy repeated the assault he had made hours before on Colonel Brown:

Then, general, you should be removed from any command. Any man who has been given the honor of being promoted to general and who says, "I will protect another general who protects Communists," [which Zwicker never said] is not fit to wear that uniform, general. I think it is a tremendous disgrace to the Army to have this sort of thing given to the public. I intend to give it to them. I have a duty to do that. I intend to repeat to the press exactly what you said.

When he dismissed Zwicker, McCarthy threatened, "You will be back here, general," and then announced that Zwicker would be ordered to appear in public session after the subcommittee's weekend break. That night, in a speech in New York, McCarthy called Zwicker's afternoon testimony "a disgraceful performance" and warned the secretary of the Army by name that he should "take a new look at the top of the team to see whether this type of coddling of Communists will continue."

Joe McCarthy thereby triggered the events that finally resulted in the Army-McCarthy hearings. He set the stage even more dramatically by ordering that General Zwicker's closed-door testimony be made public four days later. Even many of McCarthy's most ardent supporters were appalled. In an editorial, the *Chicago Tribune* warned McCarthy that he should learn to "distinguish the role of the investigator from the role of avenging angel." Clearly, McCarthy was so blinded by his sense of power and mission that he didn't appreciate how the Eisenhower administration and the American public would react to his attack on a valorous officer who had served his country with distinction.

———

The top ranks of the Army reacted, privately, with fury. By the morning after Zwicker's closed-door testimony, Secretary

Stevens had heard from a livid General Matthew Ridgway, then the Army's chief of staff and a hero of Korean combat operations. Stevens phoned Zwicker to tell him he had "no intention of leaving you out in left field and I wanted to give you a vote of confidence." But he also told Zwicker, weakly, that he didn't know what he could do about the general being called back in open session. "I deeply resent such comments as Senator McCarthy made to you yesterday," he said. "I understand he has called you for one of his TV shows on Tuesday. Whether or not that will take place we don't know . . . We will have to work this out and make some sense out of a serious situation."

General Zwicker was fighting mad. Pointedly, but respectfully, he let Stevens know how he felt—not only about his situation, but also about the reputation and honor of the Army. "Mr. Secretary," he said, "I feel if that is not done, it is going to make a great deal of difference to the Army because if any other officer's character is impugned as mine was yesterday and the officers in the Army ever get an inkling of the fact that . . . higher authority [is] doing nothing to refute those statements, I feel that the loyalty of officers to the Department of the Army is going to vanish."

Speaking personally, Zwicker said, he didn't intend to stand still in the face of the things McCarthy had called him, "because he called me everything you can imagine in the book."

At Stevens's order, Counsel Adams phoned Bill Rogers at Justice to inform him that the Army secretary "has just about reached the point where he . . . [is] not going to permit [either officers or civilians] to appear . . . and put up with this sort of treatment."

Rogers's reply was instantaneous: "That's okay with Justice."

The political and military ranks were closing. Stevens, braced by the green light from Justice, accompanied Adams on private rounds of first the Democratic, and then the Republican members of McCarthy's committee. A consensus resulted: the public hearing on Zwicker would be put off and the Army would not permit further witnesses to appear. This was duly reported through "sources" in the next day's *New York Times.*

———

If Bob Stevens still harbored questions about the true character of Joe McCarthy, they were resolved the next day, Saturday February 20, during the Washington's Birthday weekend.

Honorable as ever, Stevens phoned McCarthy to tell him of his meetings with both Republican and Democratic members of the committee and of his decision that "because I was so upset by the reports I had on the executive appearance of General Zwicker . . . that I just felt in fairness to the officer corps of the Army that I had to do something about it."

The McCarthy who answered him was not the politician who in their private meetings had thrown his arms around Stevens's shoulder and with smiles and jokes told him what great friends they were and how much McCarthy admired him. The politician Stevens now confronted was the thug, the dirty fighter, the groin kicker.

McCarthy began by offering gratuitous advice. "The best thing you can do is not follow in the old tradition of the previous administration," he told the secretary. "I think you have got a wonderful opportunity here, Robert, to either set the course for a housecleaning [or] to try to cover up, as has gone on before. That will be impossible, I guarantee you . . . Let me ask you this: Is it your position that you are going to try to keep from us the names of the officers who protected these men [referring to the Peress case]?"

Stevens answered: "I am going to try to prevent my officers from going before your committee until you and I have an understanding as to the abuse they are going to get—"

McCarthy erupted.

"You are not going to order them not to appear before my committee. Just go ahead and try it, Robert. I am going to kick the brains out of anyone who protects Communists. If that is [your] policy . . . , you just go ahead and do it. I will guarantee you that you will live to regret it . . . I don't give a damn whether an officer is a general or what he is, when he comes before us with the ignorant, stupid, insulting aspect of those who appeared, I will guarantee you that the American people will know all about it."

He wasn't covering up Communists, Stevens protested. McCarthy bullied on. Was he refusing to let his officers testify? he asked. Was that what he had told the other committee members? "Yes," Stevens said.

In a last burst of rage, McCarthy said: "Consider yourself subpoenaed for 10 o'clock Tuesday morning." Then he slammed down the phone on the secretary of the Army.

This incident became page one news after Stevens returned a phone call that afternoon from James Reston of the *New York Times*. Reston had heard about the clash with McCarthy. During their "for background only" conversation, Stevens confirmed it. He then issued a press release denouncing McCarthy's treatment of General Zwicker and defending the "loyal men and women in our Army." If

McCarthy requested that the secretary appear before him, he would do so, the news release stated. The Reston story, the Stevens press release, and the publication of the Zwicker testimony all appeared on Monday February 22, Washington's Birthday. In liberal circles, and in much of the press commentary nationally, Bob Stevens was treated as a hero. At last someone had emerged to put a stop to McCarthyism. The secretary began working on a strong statement he intended to deliver to the McCarthy committee when he answered McCarthy's subpoena.

After Stevens's long ordeal of trying to work with McCarthy, things finally seemed to be headed in the right direction for the secretary and for the Army. Stevens was still polishing and strengthening his statement the next day, Tuesday February 23, when one of his military aides received a phone call from the ultraconservative Republican Senator Karl Mundt, a member of the McCarthy committee. It was urgent, Mundt informed the aide. He was to tell the secretary that "tomorrow we are setting up a lunch at the Capitol for him and the Republican members of the committee—McCarthy, Dirksen, Potter, and me. And no one else is to know."

———

About 12:45 the next afternoon, Wednesday February 24, the day Bob Stevens's world would collapse, aides in his Pentagon office noticed that the secretary had left without informing them. He had taken his limousine to the Capitol, gotten out on the Senate side, ridden the elevator upstairs, and headed toward Room P54, the office of Senator Everett Dirksen, where Dirksen and the Republican committee members, including McCarthy, were awaiting him for their "secret" meeting.

When Stevens arrived, he was surprised to find a crowd of reporters milling in the hallway near Dirksen's office. As a White House aide later noted in his diary, the secretary of the Army should have turned on his heel and left. He did no such thing. Like a lamb led to slaughter, Bob Stevens opened the door and entered. He was alone, without a lawyer, without any witness of his own to testify about what would take place over the next two hours in what became known as the "Fried Chicken Lunch," because of the fried chicken the Republican senators served the secretary.

McCarthy raged at Stevens for refusing to permit Zwicker to testify in open session, for not furnishing the committee the names of all those involved in the promotion and honorable discharge of Peress, and for making what McCarthy called an end run around him by going to the other committee members. Stevens tried to defend himself. He insisted that McCarthy make a public pledge not to abuse other witnesses as he had Zwicker. McCarthy adamantly refused.

At some point, the idea of reaching a mutual understanding of the future ground rules emerged. With moon-faced Karl Mundt sitting at a typewriter, surrounded by McCarthy and his fellow conservative senators, they began drafting an agreement.

After a number of attempts, and with numerous changes, Stevens agreed to a final text of what the group called a "Memorandum of Understanding." Under its terms, Stevens would make a commitment to remove any known Communists from the armed services, provide all names sought in connection to the Peress case, and permit Zwicker and others to testify in open session if still requested by the committee. The statement made no mention of courteous, fair treatment for witnesses. Stevens and the senators agreed that they would not talk to reporters about what had taken place in the meeting.

The deed was done and the doors opened. A horde of reporters and photographers rushed inside. There, facing the news people, was a scene of political harmony. Seated on a couch beside a beaming McCarthy, hemmed in by the other senators, was the hapless secretary of the Army. Flashbulbs popped. When reporters asked Stevens whether Army witnesses would be beaten up in the future when going before McCarthy, Stevens stuck to the agreement they had reached inside the room. "No comment," he answered. Then he headed back to his Pentagon office, without even a copy of the agreement he had just signed. Stevens believed, or tried to convince himself, that he had struck an acceptable compromise with McCarthy and the Republicans conservatives. He was "fairly pleased" with the results, he said in a phone call to Vice President Nixon upon returning to the Pentagon. Nixon, tricky as ever, had worked behind the scenes to set up the ambush without the knowledge of top Eisenhower White House and Pentagon officials. To Pentagon reporters who asked him whether Army witnesses would continue to be abused in the future, Stevens replied he "had every reason to believe" they would not. To his staff, he maintained that he had protected Army personnel from further abuse.

Then the bubble burst. News reports coming over the wires into the Pentagon accurately characterized what had occurred as a complete capitulation by the Army to McCarthy. Fred Seaton, one of those present in the secretary's office on his return, began reading the news reports—then read, and reread, the text of the agreement reproduced over the wires. He was stunned. As Stevens's office meeting ended,

Seaton quietly told the secretary at the door, "Bob, you've been had."

————

The reaction was unsparingly negative, both publicly and privately. Yet Stevens seemed incapable of seeing his humiliation. At 5:10 P.M., forty minutes after his Pentagon staff meeting had ended, the secretary returned a call from UN Ambassador Henry Cabot Lodge. Lodge wanted to offer thoughts about strengthening the secretary's forthcoming statement before the McCarthy committee.

"Cabot, the hearing is off. Did you know that?"

"No," the incredulous Lodge answered.

"I . . . went up and had lunch at their request with the Republican members of the committee."

"All of them?"

"Yes. We were there a long time, and finally worked out a memorandum of agreement."

Stevens defended himself, saying "I went along, and [if] it will break out again . . . I will say, 'We did it your way last time. This time we will do it mine.'"

Lodge issued a warning. "Between you and me," he said, "[this] is all preliminary to an attempt to destroy the president politically. There is no doubt about it. He [McCarthy] is picking on the Army because Eisenhower was in the Army, and it is not the end of this. You have got to be prepared to live with it, you know." Lodge added: "I know these guys, and I know how their minds work. And the same crowd that supported Senator Taft at the convention in 1952 are all now revolving around Joe. And this is basically an attempt to destroy Eisenhower."

368 /

Lodge revealed that he knew about the chronology Army Counsel Adams was preparing about the McCarthy-Cohn abuses. Referring to Schine, he said: "You have that documentation there about Boy S, and I think you ought to get that in shape . . . for publication."

"We are doing that," the secretary replied.

"That would be a devastating thing," the UN ambassador said. Then he hung up.

———

For hours, Stevens refused to acknowledge the damage done. But as more news reports filtered into his home that night, reality began to sink in. He became despondent. Family and friends tried unsuccessfully to reassure him. At ten o'clock that night, he phoned Eisenhower press secretary Jim Hagerty and told him he wanted to issue his statement condemning the McCarthy committee's treatment of witnesses and then resign. "Cool it overnight," Hagerty told him. They would discuss it in the morning. Hagerty noted in his diary: "We were sure dumb. Someone let Stevens walk right into a bear trap, and now I'll have to work like hell to get him out of it. What a job!"

The morning brought more dismal news reports. On the front page of the *New York Times,* alongside a picture of a beaming Joe McCarthy seated next to a glum Bob Stevens, the headline told the story of a great humiliation:

Stevens Bows to McCarthy
At Administration Behest;
Will Yield Data on Peress

The London *Times* reached back in history for its analogy: "Senator McCarthy this afternoon achieved what General

Burgoyne and General Cornwallis never achieved—the surrender of the American army." McCarthy's quote in the *New York Times* regarding Stevens was less elegant: "He couldn't have given in more abjectly if he had gotten down on his knees." As Eisenhower aide William Bragg Ewald, Jr. later wrote of Bob Stevens, "He had gone into that meeting a national hero, he came out a national joke."

––––––––

Those closest to the president rallied desperately to repair, if possible, the damage. At 2:13 P.M. Stevens took a call in his Pentagon office from General Lucius Clay, perhaps the closest to Ike of all the military officers and advisers. He had succeeded Ike as commander of allied forces in Germany at the end of the war and had maintained a critical personal role ever since. Clay was credited as the person who finally persuaded Ike to run for president.

"I got the dope," Clay told Stevens, "that Sherman Adams and the group were all set to battle, and then I read the papers. Have they let you down from above?"

Yes, Stevens said, he had been let down by top GOP political figures—some in the White House who privately backed McCarthy in a split with other Ike aides, but most in Congress, who said "the Republicans shouldn't be squabbling among themselves." That paved the way for his meeting with McCarthy and the other committee members. But, the secretary quickly added, he hadn't been let down by "the Boss," meaning Eisenhower. "The president wasn't in it in any way shape or form."

Well, Clay went on, the president was being credited "all over the country with having run out on you." Then he said:

"I personally think this has hurt the party one hell of a lot . . . I have a right to go to the Boss and tell him what I think at least once, and I have never used it yet; and this is an issue on which I am prepared to use it."

Clay hung up, and immediately called the president.

"I heard about this fracas just this morning," Eisenhower told his old friend and counselor. "I feel the Army must go down and admit administrative error [about Peress] and [then not] give an inch . . . [Stevens] is now in a state of shock and near hysteria. He made an error in agreeing quickly."

Clay agreed. "They were too smart for him," he said. Eisenhower agreed. "He is too honorable."

An extraordinarily charged, and candid, exchange then took place between these two old warriors.

Clay: "This thing [gave an] initial impression that you instructed Stevens to settle this thing."

Eisenhower, clearly stung: "Nothing could be further from the truth."

Clay then suggested McCarthy posed a direct threat to the president: "This fellow [has] got too powerful—people [are] scared to do anything about him. I'm willing to bet he has information on honorable discharges [for Communists] while you were chief of staff."

Eisenhower, outraged at the thought, snapped back: "[McCarthy] could never be able to prove there was anything where I authorized [a subversive an honorable] . . . discharge."

But Ike recognized the political danger and McCarthy's overweening ambition: "[He has] made speeches calling all Democrats traitors, knowing that that will defeat us in the long run because we must have Democrats to win [in Congress]. Consequently, he will go around and pick up the pieces. He's crazy if he believes that."

In his diary, Jim Hagerty recorded Eisenhower's responses to Clay's warnings about McCarthy. "President very mad and getting fed up," he wrote. "It is his Army and he doesn't like McCarthy's tactics at all." Then, he quoted Ike as having said: "'This guy McCarthy is going to get in trouble on this . . . I am not going to take this one lying down . . . my friends tell me it won't be long in this Army stuff before McCarthy starts using my name instead of Stevens's. He is ambitious. He wants to be president. He's the last guy in the world who will ever get there if I have anything to say.'"

In a burst of activity, presidential aides, assisted by Eisenhower, began drafting a response to McCarthy that Stevens would be instructed to read later that afternoon from the White House. At five o'clock, with a watchful Hagerty standing nearby and other top Pentagon officials there to show support, Stevens read to reporters a strong statement that finally, after months of temporizing and appeasing, drew a line between the Eisenhower White House and Joe McCarthy.

"I shall never accede to the abuse of Army personnel under any circumstances, including committee hearings," the secretary read from the prepared statement. "I shall never accede to them being browbeaten or humiliated. I do not intend for them to be deprived of counsel when the matter under consideration is one of national interest to me as secretary, as was the case with General Zwicker."

When reporters asked whether the president backed the statement, Hagerty answered: the president endorsed Stevens's words one hundred percent.

The next morning, believing his honor had been saved, Bob Stevens phoned Lucius Clay to thank him "for getting in when the going was tough." Clay murmured, "That is the only time I am worth a damn." Before ending their brief conversation, the old general offered a final word of advice to the still-beleaguered secretary of the Army: "I would let that Adams story [about Schine and Cohn] leak out," he said.

———

Thirteen months after Dwight D. Eisenhower entered the White House, his presidency hung in the balance. In the political world of Washington, if not in the country, everyone knew it.

For the first Republican president coming to power since the 1920s, it had been Joe McCarthy, not the president, who had dominated the political scene. Eisenhower seemed on the defensive, if not in retreat. The Wisconsin senator had cowed the Democrats, intimidated Republican moderates, forged a strong alliance with GOP congressional conservatives, won the headlines, framed the debate, and now, dramatically, forced the capitulation of the United States Army. For Eisenhower, the commander in chief of that Army, another defeat at the hands of McCarthy could prove crippling. The political world watched to see how Eisenhower would react. His weekly news conference was scheduled for the morning of March 3.

On March 1, the columnist Walter Lippmann captured the conflict between the president and the senator. Writing in the *Washington Post* of McCarthy's "totalitarianism . . . his cold, calculated, sustained, and ruthless effort to make himself feared," Lippmann said McCarthy had become "a candidate for . . . the dictatorship of the Republican Party." Two days later, and only a few hours before the ten thirty Eisenhower news conference, readers of the *Post* found the influential Alsop brothers issuing a stark warning to the president. "If the president permits just one more appeasement of Senator Mc-

Carthy," they wrote, "he can say goodbye to his own authority in his administration, his party, and in the Congress."

As for himself, the president had his blood up. He was still unwilling to attack McCarthy by name or "get down in the gutter with that guy."* But he had let his most senior aides and advisors know that he intended to make a strong statement, one that equated the methods of McCarthyism with the methods of Communism. The president's draft statement *did* make that comparison, saying in words clearly directed at McCarthy that "only under tyranny is error equated to treason" and that "people who import such methods into our free country are helping Communism, not hurting it." However when Vice President Nixon learned of the comparison, he feared the damage that could result on Capitol Hill among Republican conservatives. So Nixon asked for, and received, a copy of the draft which Hagerty had been working on, and sent it back after toning it down. In an accompanying memo to Hagerty, Nixon explained his objection. He wrote, "Such a statement . . . would cause Eisenhower and the party more trouble than he or his White House staff and liberal friends . . . could imagine."

Nixon prevailed. Ike's statement was not the ringing condemnation of McCarthyism that the political world had been

---

*Privately, Ike expressed even more rage at McCarthy and McCarthyism. To his diary, he confided: "McCarthy is grabbing the headlines and making the people believe he is driving the administration out of Washington." To his close friend William E. Robinson, then publisher of the mainstream Republican *New York Herald Tribune,* he expressed his anger in a confidential letter in which he vented his frustration at the "hidebound reactionaries" and the "reactionary fringe of the Republican Party that hates and despises everything for which I stand."

led to expect. "The Department of the Army," Ike began, "made serious errors in handling the Peress case, and the Secretary of the Army so stated publicly, almost a month ago. The Army is correcting its procedures to avoid any such mistakes in the future. I am completely confident that Secretary Stevens will be successful in this effort."

The tone was moderate, reasonable, and neither indignant nor angry. No subordinates, he said, should violate their principles or "submit to any kind of personal humiliation when testifying before congressional committees." But at the same time, "we can be certain that" members of Congress "will respond to America's convictions and beliefs" in regard to their "sense of justice and fair play."

When he finished, Joe Alsop, one of more than two hundred journalists present, turned to Willard Edwards of the *Chicago Tribune* and said, "Why, the yellow son of a bitch!" Edwards, a confidant and private political adviser to McCarthy, was stunned, too, by the president's most temperate statement. In fact, Edwards was alarmed because he knew McCarthy had been preparing a slashing rebuttal to the expected Eisenhower blast. Edwards raced from the White House to Capitol Hill to warn McCarthy to soften his reaction. He was too late. By then, McCarthy had spoken before reporters in his office. "If a stupid, arrogant or witless man in a position of power appears before our committee and is found aiding the Communist Party, he will be exposed," McCarthy said. Then he attacked the president. "Apparently," he said, "the president and I now agree on the necessity of getting rid of Communists."

This statement may have been McCarthy's ultimate political mistake, for by using the deadly word *now*, he bluntly said he believed that until that moment Dwight David Eisenhower, the great World War II general and thirty-sixth president of the United States, had been protecting Communists.

Later that day, acting on Edwards's advice, McCarthy issued a correction to his statement that eliminated the poisonous word *now*. Once again, it was too late. The damage had been done. From that moment, the president let it be known to his staff and administration officials that he intended to wage all-out war on Joe McCarthy, albeit a war fought behind the scenes and one in which the president never showed his hand.

———

Whether Joe McCarthy understood how critically he had hurt himself with the president and his administration is an open question. The evidence suggests that he didn't fully realize how his fortunes were about to turn.

In a nationally televised address the next day, Adlai Stevenson, with his usual gift for the felicitous political phrase, made a barbed attack, in which he defined the yawning split in the Republican Party between the moderate Eisenhower wing and the ultraconservative McCarthy one. Speaking of the Republicans, Stevenson said: "A group of political plungers has persuaded the party McCarthyism is the best formula for political success." Then, employing Lincoln's famous house-divided analogy to make a contemporary political point, the 1952 Democratic presidential candidate said: "A political party divided against itself, half McCarthy and half Eisenhower, cannot produce national unity."

McCarthy was enraged, and demanded national network air time to respond to Stevenson's attack, clearly assuming that as in the past the networks would grant his request. This time, however, he was blocked. Eisenhower privately let the networks know that he wouldn't hear of McCarthy giving that speech. Stevenson's attack, he said, was on the Republican Party, therefore the party should answer it. He picked Nixon to make the response on national TV.

Arriving in Miami on a trip, McCarthy learned of the choice of Nixon and reacted in fury. In remarks to reporters, he threatened the networks if they should reject him. "The networks will grant me time or learn what the law is," he snarled. But Dick Nixon, not Joe McCarthy, was the one who went on national TV. And when Nixon spoke, he not only defended the Republican Party, but figuratively stuck a knife into McCarthy.

Displaying his gut-fighter technique, Nixon savaged Stevenson and the Democrats for being soft on Communism, but he also took a slice out of McCarthy. "Some people think Communist traitors should be shot like rats," the vice president said. "Well, I'll agree they're a bunch of rats, but just remember this: When you go out to shoot, you have to shoot straight, because when you shoot wildly it means that the rats may get away more easily, you make it easier on the rat, but you might hit someone else who's trying to shoot rats, too."

Without mentioning McCarthy by name, but leaving no doubt of whom he spoke, Nixon said: "Men who have in the past done effective work exposing Communists in this country have, by reckless talk and questionable methods, made themselves the issue rather than the cause they believe in so deeply."

From then on, McCarthy privately referred to the vice president as "that prick." For McCarthy, Nixon's speech was a

signal of what now became the administration's all-out opposition to him. In his diary, Hagerty noted the president was
now "dead set [on] stopping McCarthy—a pimple on the
path of progress." Ike, he added, was determined "to fight
him from now on in."

———

Within seven days of Eisenhower's March 3 news conference,
the final combat lines between the president and the senator
were drawn. By then, Army Counsel Adams had leaked
copies of his explosive summary of the Cohn-Schine case to
selected reporters and columnists across Washington. At the
same time, higher level officials led by Fred Seaton were
rushing to complete a starkly declarative narrative of the
events—citing times, dates, and conversations—which they
intended to release publicly.

Secretly, both Republican and Democratic members of
McCarthy's investigating committee were briefed about Cohn
and Schine. The most moderate Republican Senator in the
McCarthy committee, Charles Potter of Michigan, a World
War II veteran who had lost his left leg at the hip and his right
leg below the knee, was tagged to receive a copy of the Army's
documented case against Cohn. Potter was told that Democrats knew about the report and were clamoring to see it. He
was urged to take it to the other Republicans so they could
act before the public explosion occurred. Potter did as suggested: on March 9 he briefed Dirksen, Mundt, and the others, who reacted with alarm. Everyone agreed that Cohn
must be fired. Next, Potter confronted McCarthy, who reacted as might have been expected. He tore into Potter, refused to fire Cohn, and threatened Potter that he would, as

William Bragg Ewald, Jr., put it, "loose the dogs of the right wing press on Potter himself."

But McCarthy's support was clearly crumbling. In the Senate that day, Republican Ralph Flanders of Vermont made a most rare and derisive public attack on McCarthy. Flanders, having lunched days before at the White House with his fellow Vermonter Sherman Adams, Ike's chief of staff, belittled McCarthy's record of fighting Communism. McCarthy, he told his fellow senators, "dons his war paint, goes into his war dance, emits his war whoops, goes forth to battle and proudly returns with the scalp of a pink Army dentist." That night, Ike wrote Flanders a note of thanks. "America," he said, "needs to hear from more Republican voices like yours."

America soon heard from the deep, resonant voice of its most famous TV journalist. That same night, Edward R. Murrow devoted the entire broadcast of his widely followed *See It Now* CBS-TV show to Joe McCarthy. It became a signal event, not only for what was said but even more for who said it.

Murrow was an institution, one of the most admired Americans to emerge from the World War II era, when his radio broadcasts from London, beginning with the blitz, stamped him upon the consciousness of the country. He had an unmatched reputation for integrity and courage. Now, for half an hour, millions of Americans coast to coast were introduced to his portrait of Joe McCarthy, demagogue.

Upon what meat does Senator McCarthy feed? Two of the staples of his diet are the investigation (protected by immunity) and the half-truth ... We cannot defend freedom abroad by deserting it at home. The actions of the junior Senator from Wisconsin have caused alarm and dismay amongst our allies abroad and given considerable comfort to our enemies. And whose fault is this? Not really his. He didn't create this situation of fear; he merely exploited it, and rather successfully. Cassius was right: "The fault, dear Brutus, is not in our stars but in ourselves."

Murrow's clipped, understated style, and his eloquent indictment of McCarthy, left a powerful impression on the nation. The broadcast drew the heaviest response of phone calls and telegrams in CBS's history.

———

The next day, March 10, McCarthy learned of the impending release of the Army's documented case against him and Cohn. In a Pentagon phone call, he protested to Fred Seaton. From what he had heard of the report, it told only one side of the story—and a false one at that—McCarthy said. He had his own side, documented in black and white. It told a far different and more damaging tale about the Army, Secretary Bob Stevens, and Chief Counsel John Adams. McCarthy won a promise that his side, too, would be made public.

Days later, while the American press devoted front page headlines and TV bulletins to the Army's accusations of blatant pressures and threats by Cohn to gain special treatment for Private Schine, McCarthy released his own extensive chronology, supposedly maintained over the months, in the form of eleven documents from his committee's staff. They purported to be a point-by-point rebuttal of the Army charges, and included memos of conversations and statements allegedly made in private meetings. In McCarthy's telling of the controversy, the Army tried to "blackmail" him into stopping his exposure of Communists in the Army by holding Private Schine as a "hostage." Stevens, according to the McCarthy records, tried to stop McCarthy's investigation by promising to give details of subversion and homosexual rings operating in the Air Force and the Navy. Cohn also entered the fray, and vigorously denied having made the statements of which he was accused.

The two accounts were in direct conflict. Clearly, one side was not telling the truth. The issue was too explosive to be covered up or ignored. Only one solution presented itself. Congress would have to investigate. After tense consultations and much internal disagreement about the details and logistics, an agreement was reached. The McCarthy committee would conduct the investigations. For obvious reasons of conflict of interest, McCarthy would not chair the hearings but would be permitted to question witnesses. The hearings would be open—and televised. Work began on the delicate task of naming independent outside counsel to conduct the case for the Army, and for McCarthy and Cohn.

Chapter

EIGHTEEN

Point of Order!

*He complained bitterly of being interrupted . . .
and yet he came charging in on every one else's
testimony time and again with his "Point of order,
Mr. Chairman, point of order."*

—Roy Cohn, on Joe McCarthy

Joseph Welch was talking to a widow about a will in his Boston law office when he was interrupted by a phone call from an old friend calling from a New York pay phone "on an extremely sensitive subject."

After excusing himself from his client meeting, Welch resumed the phone conversation. He listened intently as Bruce Bromley, formerly an appeals court judge in New York and now a leading lawyer with Cravath, Swaine & Moore, made a most mysterious request: that Welch fly from Boston to New York, go to a specific room in a private club at a prearranged time, and there meet someone who would be waiting to talk with him. Bromley would be there to introduce them.

Welch agreed. When he walked into the private New York City club room, he found Bromley seated beside Thomas E. Dewey.

Tom Dewey, the short man with the little mustache who had made presidential runs against first FDR and then Truman, was then fifty-two, still Governor of New York, and still one of the most powerful figures in the mainstream, progressive wing of the Republican Party.

Dewey was not personally close to Eisenhower, but he had been instrumental in placing a number of key figures in leading positions in Ike's administration. Among those who had worked for Dewey, either in his gangbusting days as New York's district attorney or during his governorship, and had gone to Washington were the new attorney general, Herb Brownell; his chief deputy, Bill Rogers; and Jim Hagerty, Ike's press secretary. Now, as the administration began searching for a counsel to represent the Army in the case against McCarthy, the insiders turned to Dewey for advice on the selection.

Though he didn't know Joseph Welch, Dewey trusted Bruce Bromley, whom he had earlier appointed to the New York State Court of Appeals. It was Bromley who recommended Welch to Dewey, and Dewey, after their meeting, who recommended Welch to the Eisenhower administration.

————

Joseph Nye Welch, a senior partner in the old and distinguished Boston firm of Hale & Dorr, had impeccable credentials: Phi Beta Kappa, Harvard law school, for twenty-five years head of Hale & Dorr's trial department, and recognized nationally as an eminent courtroom lawyer. He was then sixty-three years old and exhibited the mannerisms and appearance of a nineteenth century New England gentleman lawyer. He dressed most properly, and conservatively, with trademark bow ties, elegant custom-made three-piece suits, and button-down Oxford shirts; worked at a stand-up desk; wrote out everything for his cases in long hand; and was given to dropping old-fashioned sounding phrases (things were "delicious"; he was feeling "weary") in conversation. He was wry, under-stated, and witty, with a puckish sense of humor and a self-deprecating gentle manner that masked what Roy Cohn later described as "an unerring instinct for the jugular."

On April 2, Welch traveled to Washington to meet Secre-tary of the Army Stevens, and the Defense Department offi-cials Fred Seaton and H. Struve Hensel. Accompanying Welch from Boston was a junior partner, James St. Clair,* and a younger Hale & Dorr lawyer, Frederick G. Fisher, Jr., both Harvard law graduates whom Welch held in the highest regard.

After meeting with the Pentagon officials and Stevens, Welch met his Hale & Dorr lawyers for dinner in their hotel and then, as previously agreed, joined Seaton and Hensel in the cocktail lounge to discuss their handling of the case. Welch raised the question of whether his legal partners would be personally vulnerable to an attack by McCarthy. "Boys," Welch told St. Clair and Fisher, "we're in the midst of a law-suit that is different from anything you've known . . . even the

---

*Twenty years later, St. Clair played a leading role in another historic drama as lead counsel to Richard Nixon in Nixon's impeachment battle.

lawyers will be on trial. If there is anything in either of your lives that might be embarrassing to you, it better come out."

"Jim, do you know of anything about yourself?" he asked St. Clair. No, St. Clair told him.

"How about you, Fred?" Welch asked Fisher.

Fisher *did* have a problem. While at Harvard in the 1940s, he explained, he had joined the National Lawyers Guild, one of the organizations listed by the House Un-American Activities Committee as "subversive." Not only that, he had organized a Guild chapter with someone named Greenberg, who turned out to be a Communist Party official. He had never been a Communist himself, Fisher said, and had joined the Guild primarily as a way to meet other lawyers. He had resigned his membership in 1950 after learning of the connection between the Boston chapter and the Communist Party.

Shaken by this news, the men finished their drinks and reconvened upstairs in Welch's suite.

In his unpublished account of the episode, which he later made available to biographer David Oshinsky, Fisher described how, with "several bottles of whiskey on hand," they "engaged in a discussion of the problem raised by my past associations . . . Everyone agreed that the matter would certainly come out at the hearing. The only controversy was whether the damage to the Army's case would be more severe if I left than if I remained."

The Boston lawyers, Fisher recalled, believed that he "should return to Boston as soon as possible," and so did he. Moreover, Welch and St. Clair asked Seaton and Hensel to relieve them from the case.

The Defense officials strongly disagreed. While they were unsure about Fisher's participation, they were adamant that

Welch and St. Clair remain as the Army's lawyers. After an intense discussion, the men agreed to seek the advice of Jim Hagerty and to rely on his judgment.

Hagerty was attending a private dinner given by another White House staffer at the Sulgrave Club when he received a message from Fred Seaton asking if he could come immediately to Hensel's Georgetown home, where the group had reassembled.

Hagerty and his wife rushed to Georgetown where, in an upstairs room, Hagerty, the Boston lawyers, and the Defense officials huddled over the Fisher problem. After listening to Fisher's account of joining the Lawyers Guild and then resigning, Hagerty at first saw no problem. He told Fisher that he could guarantee him the support of a friend in the White House—the president. But when Fisher explained that he had helped establish a Guild chapter with the assistance of a known Communist organizer, Hagerty let out a groan. That was "a different story"; that would give "McCarthy an opportunity to brand Fisher as Red and smear-up Army defense," as Hagerty wrote in his diary later that night. He was sorry, he said, but there was no alternative. Fisher was soon on the midnight sleeper train to Boston.

The next day, April 3, the Army held a news conference to announce that Welch, assisted by St. Clair, had been retained as its counsel.

Two weeks later, in a move to protect against a possible McCarthy attack, wily Joe Welch broke the story about Fisher's earlier connection with a Communist. The *New York Times* reported on April 16 that Frederick Fisher, a second assistant counsel to the Army, had been relieved from the case "because of admitted previous membership in the National

Lawyers Guild, referred to by Herbert Brownell, the attorney general, as 'the legal mouthpiece of the Communist Party.'"

The story, buried on page sixteen, attracted little attention and virtually no follow-up. Six days later, as the Army-McCarthy hearings began, it seemed to have been forgotten.

———

From March 11, when the Army's chronology of McCarthy and Cohn's pressuring them dominated the news, until the hearings began on April 22, Joe McCarthy traveled extensively to rally his supporters. In Chicago, before a roaring throng on St. Patrick's Day, he compared himself to St. Patrick, who "drove the snakes out of Ireland, and the snakes didn't like his methods either." In Milwaukee, he donned the mantle of a patriotic crusader, saying, "I'm fighting for America now." In Oklahoma City, he promised an all-out battle against the forces of Communism, drawing cheers when he declared, "I didn't start this fight, but I guarantee you that I'll finish it." In Houston, he stirred memories of immortal heroes, and produced more roars of approval, when he said, "Luckily . . . there were no Fifth Amendment Texans at the Alamo." In New York, before six thousand members of the police department's Holy Name Society, he received what he called the greatest reception of his life after he attacked "Pentagon politicians" who gave honorable discharges to Communists while letting American POWs rot in Red China's jails. When Cardinal Spellman walked across the stage to shake his hand, the crowd rose to its feet, wildly cheering and whistling in what one press account called a spontaneous tribute to a hero.

McCarthy never lost his rock-solid admirers, but the emotions he stirred in them were deceiving. For the first time since he had burst from political obscurity four years earlier, McCarthy's overall popularity was steadily declining. He was losing the great moderate middle, a group not motivated by ideological extremes or identities, the majority of the American people. Throughout 1954, the Gallup Poll tracked a precipitous drop. In January, Gallup found fifty percent viewed him favorably as opposed to only twenty-nine percent unfavorably. By April, when the hearings began, his unfavorable rating had risen to forty-six percent compared to thirty-eight percent favorable. Half a century later, a considerable bloc of Americans still bear allegiance to McCarthy's memory and remain devoted to his anticommunist (or, now, anti-liberal) cause. But by August 1954, Joe McCarthy was finished as a political force. By then, fifty-one percent of the public viewed him unfavorably while his favorable numbers had dropped to thirty-six percent. While some thirty percent of the people remained loyal to him, his plummeting poll numbers had finally emboldened politicians in both parties to oppose him. The Army-McCarthy hearings alone did not bring about his fall, but they were central in it.

———

Contrary to myth, the Army-McCarthy hearings did not represent the final rendering of judgment by political leaders on Joe McCarthy and McCarthyism. The hearings were a disorganized shambles, both legislatively and politically. In many respects they showed the American system at its most ineffectual—or its worst. They were not judicious, either as a trial—which they were not—or as a fact-finding enterprise. They did not resolve questions the public wanted answered about the reality of the Communist threat and the extent of high-level traitors, but instead were dominated from beginning to end by irrelevancies. They did not strip McCarthy of his chairmanship or his seat in the Senate. They did not hold the Army accountable for its acts of appeasement and special favors, or hold McCarthy and Cohn accountable for the attempts to intimidate the military that had brought about those favors. They did not render a decisive verdict on McCarthy, Cohn, and Schine. They did not even stop McCarthy's plans to launch greater Communist witch hunts, though in the end, time and circumstances did curtail those investigations. And they certainly did not present any profiles in courage, with the notable exception of Joseph Welch.

Yet, despite all these failures, the hearings were a landmark in American history. They were consequential, and they stamped indelible images in the public mind. A decade after they ended, lawyer and author David T. Bazelon said of the hearings that they represented a moment when "the television camera, for the first time, acted as an independent force in our history."* It was television that distinguished the hearings; television that gave them such power; television that, as

---

*The explosive growth of television that played a critical role in McCarthy's rise can be seen in the following figures: when McCarthy spoke at Wheeling, there were only 98 TV stations and 3.7 million TV sets in the nation, contrasted with overwhelming radio dominance of 2,029 stations and 93 million radio receivers. At that point, 94 percent of American families had at least one radio in the home. By the end of 1950, there were 10 million TV sets and 106 stations broadcasting in 65 cities. By the Army-McCarthy Hearings in 1954, when McCarthy's TV appearances became more important than newspaper coverage of him, the number of TV sets had more than tripled, to 35 million, with 413 stations broadcasting in 273 cities.

Bazelon said, proved in the end "to be a superb vehicle for the exposure of personality, motive, method, character—which were indeed the 'real' issues of the case and the stuff of a new form of political drama."

Only one other televised spectacle had come as close to fixating the public, and the televised Kefauver hearings on organized crime in 1951 neither lasted as long nor reached anything like the total audience of the Army-McCarthy hearings. In the half century of the television age since then, only three news events rivaled the impact of the Army-McCarthy hearings: the four days from John F. Kennedy's assassination to his funeral in 1963; the Watergate Committee hearings of 1974 that led to the impeachment vote against Richard Nixon and Nixon's forced resignation as president; and the horrifying scenes of carnage and wreckage from the terror strikes in 2001 that ushered in our new Age of Anxiety.

Television enabled the American people to see the real Joe McCarthy, live and unfiltered—snarling, blustering, abusing, bullying, giggling, threatening, lying, filibustering—for thirty-six days, from the third week of April through the second week of June. It was a public drama that consumed the nation's attention for one hundred eighty-eight hours, with thirty-five witnesses and forty-two exhibits that resulted in two thousand nine hundred seventy-two recorded pages, or two million words, of testimony.

It was a drama seen by what then was the largest television audience in history. An astonishing eighty million Americans, of a total population of slightly more than one hundred fifty million, were estimated to have seen at least some part of the hearings. As David Oshinsky later wrote, surveys showed that during the hearings' first week, two-thirds of all household TV sets were tuned to them. Department stores reported a sharp drop in daytime customers; sales of TV sets soared; and other news events were almost completely overshadowed. Among the events downplayed were the fall of Dien Bien Phu in French Indochina (Vietnam) on May 7 and, ten days later, the U.S. Supreme Court's *Brown v. Board of Education* ruling outlawing public school segregation.

Nor was television the only medium that devoted total attention to the hearings. Newspapers, magazines, radio broadcasts, and editorial columns were filled with reports on them. The *New York Times* published a dozen pages of testimony daily. To Walter Lippmann they were "our national obsession," driving all else out of public attention. "Only McCarthyism is much on people's minds," he wrote.

———

While the public formed its own picture of Joe McCarthy based on the images on the TV screen, it did not see everything.

By this point, McCarthy was in the midst of a prolonged physical and mental breakdown. His drinking was verging on being out of control. By 1952 his closest friend, Urban Van Susteren, observed that McCarthy was regularly getting drunk in the evenings. By then, too, he was trying to conceal his drinking. "Van," he would say, "do you have any milk?" Then, as Van Susteren later told biographer Thomas Reeves, "when your back was turned, he would spike it with undetectable vodka."

McCarthy was drinking at night, in the morning, and during the day, consuming at least a bottle of liquor daily. He was also exhibiting signs of paranoia. When meeting with friends or acquaintances in his Washington home, he would caution them to lower their voices. "The walls have ears," he would say, referring to wire taps. By the time of the Army-McCarthy hearings, he feared an assassination attempt and had taken to carrying a gun wherever he went, including Capitol Hill. One night that spring, chairman of the Republican National Committee, Leonard Hall, making a private visit to McCarthy's house, was startled when Joe opened his front door with a pistol in his hand.

Troubling as these signs were, no hint of them surfaced in the press. Though McCarthy had put on considerable weight, he appeared as energetic as ever. He seems to have approached the hearings with supreme confidence that, once again, he would turn the tables on his enemies and emerge as powerful as before, if not more so.

And why not? This was the forum he knew best, one that played to his strengths, and McCarthy had succeeded in guaranteeing that he would be the dominant figure. It was his committee, after all, and though he had stepped down as chairman, he had handpicked the pliant Idaho conservative, Senator Henry Dworshak, to take his place as a committee member. He had also demanded, and won, the right to cross-examine witnesses, vote on committee procedures, and testify himself. And unlike many of his fellow Republicans who fought for private, closed-door hearings, McCarthy wanted them to be public—and televised. Once again, Joe McCarthy was poised to act as advocate, juror, and judge.

———

In the opening minutes of the Army-McCarthy hearings, Mc-Carthy established the behavior that he would continue throughout all the televised hours that followed. Army Secretary Stevens had just told the committee that before testifying to the circumstances behind the efforts to get Private

Schine "preferential treatment," he wanted "to make two general comments: First, it is my responsibility to speak for the Army. The Army is about a million and a half men and women, in posts across this country and around the world, on active duty and in the National Guard and Organized Reserves, plus hundreds of thousands of loyal and faithful civil servants—"

The loud monotone voice of McCarthy suddenly filled the marbled Senate Caucus Room.

"Mr. Chairman," he called out, "a point of order." This was the parliamentary procedure by which an objection was raised as to whether proceedings were in violation of the rules.

"Senator McCarthy has a point of order," the acting chairman, Republican Karl Mundt, responded in what would become the hearings' refrain.

"Mr. Stevens is not speaking for the Army," McCarthy said. "The committee did not make the Army a party to this controversy, and I think it is highly improper to try to make the Army a party. Mr. Stevens can only speak for himself."

Ignoring the fact that he had led the assault on the Army, McCarthy then cast himself its *protector*, while making it seem that Stevens was on trial, saying: "All we were investigating has been some Communists in the Army, a very small percentage, I would say much less than one percent. And when the secretary says that, in effect, 'I am speaking for the Army,' he is putting the 99.9 percent of good, honorable, loyal men in the Army into the position of trying to oppose the exposure of Communists in the Army . . . I think it should be made clear at the outset, so we need not waste time on it, hour after hour, that Mr. Stevens is speaking for Mr. Stevens and those who are speaking through him." He added: "I may say I resent very, very much this attempt to connect the great American Army with this attempt to sabotage the efforts of this committee's investigation into Communism."

From then on, day after day, week after week, McCarthy disrupted the hearings with his loud calls for a "point of order, Mr. Chairman, point of order."

Of all the critics of McCarthy's performance no one captured the essence better than Roy Cohn, who in his 1968 memoir, *McCarthy*, wrote:

> He complained bitterly of being interrupted . . . and yet he came charging in on every one else's testimony time and again with his "Point of order, Mr. Chairman, Point of order." He used the words so often that they were taken up by countless comedians and had a vogue as a national catchphrase. His language toward his opponents was often less than parliamentarian. He was verbally brutal where he should have been dexterous and light; he was stubbornly unwilling to yield points where a little yielding might have gained him advantage; he frequently spoke before thinking of the effect of his words; he was repetitious to the point of boredom.

———

For those who had paid attention to McCarthy's rise to power, much of what appeared during the Army-McCarthy hearings seemed a replay of his past behavior and tactics. His language was, as usual, laced with insulting remarks about witnesses resorting to "phony" and "lying" testimony. "Can't you and I both agree, colonel," he said to one Army witness, "that the average person . . . in this television audience, and they are the jury in this case, can't help but get a completely false impression in this case—can't help but get a completely false impression from these phony charts—and that is completely dishonest, colonel. Isn't that true?" The colonel's succinct response, "No, sir, it is not true," failed to deter him. He retold his "Indian Charlie" story, never understanding how damning the advice to fight dirty would sound to ordinary Americans.

When challenged, or when a witness's reply was damaging to his case, McCarthy raised the Red Flag, launching into a monologue about how the witness was unwittingly, or not, aiding the cause of the Communists McCarthy was patriotically trying to expose. After an exchange with Army Secretary Stevens that did not suit McCarthy, he referred to the testimony of Earl Browder, U.S. Communist Party chief, and linked it to Stevens's testimony. "Does that mean I'm a Communist, Senator?" Stevens shot back. "That's awfully funny, isn't it, Mr. Secretary?" a sneering McCarthy responded. "That's terribly funny. I've made it very clear to you at all times that I felt you are anti-Communist. I've also made it very clear to you that I thought you were very naïvely and unintelligently anti-Communist. You know that, Mr. Secretary?"

His bullying and rudeness were, to those who had not seen him in action, shocking. "Oh, shut up," he shouted at one point to one of his fellow senators. He even treated Karl Mundt, his fellow Republican conservative, with contempt. When Mundt once had the temerity to overrule McCarthy on a point of order, McCarthy immediately snapped, "I can assure you there'll be no interruptions unless I think it's of importance." At another point, he interrupted the chairman with a curt, "Oh, be quiet, Mr. Chairman." When Mundt attempted to assert control of the hearing by saying, "The Chair has the floor to determine whether or not Senator McCarthy is speaking to a point of order," McCarthy erupted: "Mr. Chairman, may I suggest, I'm getting awfully sick of sitting down here at the end of the table and having whoever wants to interrupt in the middle of a sentence."

McCarthy and his staff resorted to other techniques they had employed successfully in the past, even introducing a doctored photograph and a faked letter purportedly from J. Edgar Hoover.

The photograph seemed to dramatically back up Mc-Carthy's contention that Army Secretary Stevens and Private Schine had established a close relationship during Schine's service. The picture showed Stevens and Schine standing alone, side by side. In the next day's hearing, Welch made a sensational charge: the photo had been altered. "I have the photograph which was offered yesterday in evidence," Welch told the committee, holding the photo up to the TV cameras. "I would like now to offer the picture that I have in my right hand as the original, undoctored, unaltered piece of evidence."

Welch's photo showed Stevens and Schine standing with two other Army officers. Initially McCarthy accused Welch of making "a completely false statement that this is a group picture. It is not." As McCarthy began to bluster, though, he was interrupted by Ray Jenkins, the independent counsel hired by the committee to represent him and Cohn, as well as the committee.

Jenkins was angry. He called Cohn to testify, and sharply interrogated him about the picture and the circumstances by which he, Jenkins, had received it. Addressing Cohn, he said sternly: "I ask you whether or not you told me you had documentary evidence in the form of a photograph of Mr. Stevens and Mr. Schine [alone] corroborating your statement to me that Mr. Stevens requested his photograph to be taken with Schine?" Cohn was rattled. "I told you, sir, . . . that as far as I knew that we had a picture of Mr. Stevens and Private Schine." Jenkins hammered at him. "Was that original the photograph introduced yesterday, delivered to me by you or a member of your staff, prior to my cross-examination of the secretary?" Again, Cohn was defensive and at first unresponsive. Jenkins kept pressing. "Was anything ever said to me up to this time, about any person being cut out of that photograph?"

Finally, after more stumbling, Cohn admitted that a member of his staff had seen a third person in the photo "but thought that person had no relevancy . . . and that the picture wanted was the picture of Stevens and Schine [alone]." Therefore, the third (and fourth) person was cut out of the print submitted to Jenkins—and, through him, to the committee and the American people.

Still angry, Jenkins called the staff member to testify about the photo. "Did I say anything about cutting out . . . any individual[s], mister?" he snapped. "No, sir," he was told.

Welch then questioned the staff member. Holding forth the doctored photo, he demanded to know where it had come from. When the witness professed not to know, Welch said, amid much laughter, "Did you think this came from a pixie? Where did you think this picture that I hold in my hand came from?" When Welch was told "I have no idea," McCarthy interrupted the interrogation and asked the committee reporter to reread Welch's question.

> Reporter: Question: Did you think this came from a pixie?
> McCarthy, addressing Welch: Would counsel, for my benefit, define—I think he might be an expert on this—the word "pixie"?

Welch: I should say, I should say, Mr. Senator, that a pixie
is a close relative of a fairy. [*laughter.*] Shall I proceed,
sir? Have I enlightened you?

McCarthy: As I said, as I said, I think you might be an authority on what a pixie is.

More laughter. But the dark humor quickly faded when
Welch questioned Cohn about the photo. He forced Cohn,
who at first pleaded far-sightedness, to examine the photo
more closely and then to concede it was indeed a group picture. In an attempt to match Welch's wit, Cohn, who had
been present when the photo was taken, remarked that another officer in the picture, a Colonel Bradley, "had a good
steak dinner after this. Maybe he was anticipating it." To
which Welch quickly replied, "Well, now, if Bradley is feeling
good about a steak dinner, Schine must be considering a
whole haunch of beef, is he not?"

The laughter that swept the committee room was too
much for McCarthy. "How long, Mr. Chairman—Mr. Chairman—" "Do you have a point of order?" Mundt cheerfully
asked.

Yes, it's a point of order. How long must we put up with this
circus? If the counsel, the counsel is trying to elicit information, good. If he is looking for a laugh from the audience, then don't talk about any physical defects of my chief
counsel [referring to Welch having commented on Cohn's
remark about his nearsightedness]. It's so, so indecent, so
dishonest. I'm not talking about any physical defects that
Counsel Welch may have. I do not intend to. Let's get down
to the issues, Mr. Welch. Each minute, Mr. Chairman, may
I point out, each minute that we waste here is wasting a
vast amount of manpower, very important manpower I

think. The manpower of eight senators and the heads of our military establishment.

Laughter aside, the case of the doctored photo dealt McCarthy and Cohn a heavy blow, as did a second highly charged incident involving falsified evidence—this supposedly a classified letter written by J. Edgar Hoover. In this incident, Welch called one of Hoover's aides to testify about the letter's authenticity after McCarthy claimed it was an original from the FBI. When the aide appeared, he read a letter from Attorney General Brownell stating that "Mr. Hoover has examined the document and has advised me that he never wrote any such letter."

Welch zeroed in on the witness and, employing some of McCarthy's favorite language, asked: "So far as you know, this document in this courtroom sprung by Senator McCarthy is a perfect phony. Is that right?" McCarthy leaped to his defense, framing the issue as a matter of his principled insistence on protecting his patriotic informants, telling Welch and the committee that "I will not under any circumstances reveal the source of my information, which I get as chairman of the committee." Once more, he tried to use the specter of Communism as his trump card. "Now," McCarthy said, "one of the reasons that I have been successful . . . in exposing the, uh, Communism is because the people who give me information from within the government know that their confidence will not be violated. There is no way on earth that any committee, any force, can get me to violate the confidence of these people."

McCarthy thereby blundered into a trap set by Welch.

"Senator McCarthy," the lawyer said, "when you took the

stand you, of course, understood you were going to be asked about this letter, did you not?"

"I assumed that to be the subject," McCarthy answered.

"And you, of course, understood you were going to be asked about the source from which you got it," Welch continued.

McCarthy hedged. "I never try to read the minds of the senators for what they will ask me," he replied. Then Welch startled him by asking, "Could I have the oath that you took read to us slowly by the reporter?" The oath, Welch said, "included a promise, a solemn promise by you to tell the truth, comma, the whole truth, comma, and nothing but the truth. Is that correct, sir?"

McCarthy was defiant. "Mr. Welch, you are not the first individual who tried to get me to betray the confidence and give up the names of my informants. You will be no more successful than those who tried in the past—period."

Welch, his manner almost sorrowful, persisted. "I am only asking you, Sir," he said, "did you realize when you took that oath, that you were making a solemn promise to tell the whole truth to this committee?"

McCarthy, visibly angrier, replied, "I understand the oath, Mr. Welch."

"And when you took it," Welch continued, mildly, "did you have some mental reservations, some Fifth or Sixth Amendment notion that you could measure what you will testify to?"*

McCarthy was indignant: "I don't take the Fifth or Sixth Amendments."

---

*The Sixth Amendment guarantees citizens a speedy and public trial by an impartial jury.

Welch pressed on. "Have you some private reservation, when you take the oath, that you tell the whole truth, that lets you be the judge of what you will say?"

No sooner had McCarthy said, "The answer is there is no reservation about telling the whole truth," than Welch pounced.

"Thank you, sir," he said, springing the trap. "Then tell us who delivered the document to you."

A hush settled over the hearing room. Then McCarthy said sharply, "The answer is no. You will not get that information."

Welch wasn't finished. "You wish then to put your own interpretation on your oath and tell us less than whole truth?"

McCarthy, deftly snared, resorted to bluster. "Mr. Welch," he said, "I think I made it very clear to you that neither you nor anyone else will ever get me to violate the confidence of loyal people in this government who give me information about Communist infiltration. I repeat, you will not get their names, you will not get any information which will allow you to identify them so that you or anyone else can get their jobs. You can go right ahead and try until doomsday."

This was too much for some of McCarthy's fellow senators. Democrat John McClellan of Arkansas suggested to McCarthy that he was acting as though he were above the law. "You're saying what you'll do and what you'll not do," McClellan said in his flat Arkansas twang. "I tell you, senator, that I will not set myself up above and apart from the law. I'm going to conform to it. Now you do as you please."

This precipitated a sharp exchange between the two senators, with McCarthy accusing McClellan of trying to put him in jail, and McClellan, scowling and leaning forward toward McCarthy, replying: "I don't care if you stay in or out. No one's afraid of you out anymore than they would be in, as far as I know. But the point I'm making, Joe, and you know it, we've reached the crossroads in this thing, and we're entitled in the course of these hearings now to have this thing settled if there's any way to settle it."

The questions about McCarthy's use of supposedly classified material as well as his refusal to answer questions under oath were never resolved by the committee, but the damage was done.

One of the most contentious issues in the hearings that has continued in decades since to stir controversy in clashes between presidents and the Congress is the access to classified information. During the hearings, Eisenhower—invoking the doctrine of executive privilege—claimed the right to keep his aides from testifying, as well as the right to deny the committee access to classified information, the release of which the president deemed detrimental to national security. Presidents since, notably Nixon during Watergate, Reagan during Iran-Contra, and George W. Bush during the presidential commission hearings into the 9/11 terror attacks, have also asserted this privilege, sparking intense political battles in each case.

Not surprisingly, during the Army-McCarthy hearings, McCarthy swept aside the constitutional questions involved and publicly encouraged federal workers to break the law by giving him classified material in order to "save the land."

A telling exchange between McCarthy and McClellan foreshadowed controversies to come, and demonstrated McCarthy's belief that he could act above the law.* McCarthy

---

*U.S. Code, Title 18, made it a crime to furnish classified information to unauthorized persons.

praised those who violated the law by providing him classified documents, saying: "I want to compliment the individuals who have placed their oath to defend the country against enemies—and certainly Communists are enemies—above any presidential directive."

McClellan instantly replied: "I don't know of any oath that any man took for loyalty to his country that requires him to commit a crime."

McCarthy's response constituted a radical new doctrine. "As far as I am concerned," he said, "I would like to notify those two million employees [of the federal government] that I feel it is their *duty* to give us any information which they have."

McClellan responded, "If this theory is followed . . . then you can have no security system in America. It will destroy it totally and irrevocably if all who have information give it out indiscriminately."

When Eisenhower heard of McCarthy's appeal to employees of the executive branch to violate the law, his temper flared and he began pacing behind his desk in the Oval Office. Jim Hagerty quoted him as saying:

> This is nothing but a wholesale subversion of public services. McCarthy is making the same plea of loyalty to him that Hitler made to the German people. Both tried to set up personal loyalty within the government while both were using the pretence of fighting Communism. McCarthy is trying deliberately to subvert the people we have in government, people who are sworn to obey the law, the Constitution, and their superior officers. I think this is the most disloyal act we have ever had by anyone in the government of the United States.

Ike then instructed Hagerty to draft a statement under his name and release it to the public, which Hagerty did. The statement read, in part: "The executive branch of the government has the sole and fundamental responsibility for the enforcement of our laws and presidential orders. That responsibility cannot be usurped by any individual who may seek to set himself above the laws of the land to override the orders of the President of the United States to federal employees of the executive branch of the government."

Unequivocal as the statement was, it did not mention Joe McCarthy by name. Whether because of principled conviction or fear of the political consequences of confronting McCarthy, Ike still refused to get into the gutter with him.

———

Even McCarthy, despite his confidence, realized the hearings were not going as he had hoped. Welch was emerging as the real public hero, time and again deflecting legitimate criticism of the Army and turning it against McCarthy and Cohn. By mid-May, Republicans on the committee were growing increasingly eager to end what had become a debacle for them and their party—a point that was urgently made to them by GOP leaders nationally and backed by polling data showing damage to Republican prospects in the upcoming fall elections. McCarthy complained that the hearings—the Welch "circus," as he put it—were diverting his attention from pursuing the truly critical problem of the Communist threat. He publicly raised the peril America faced from "the vast number of Communists working . . . with a razor, if you please, poised over the jugular of this nation."

After a month of hearings, Everett Dirksen led the Republican senators on the committee in proposing that the public portion be brought to a quick conclusion with the final appearances of the two principal opponents, McCarthy and Stevens. Any remaining sessions could be conducted in private, away from the TV cameras. Then, they agreed, McCarthy could resume his chairmanship and conduct his planned hearings into Communist penetration of the American defense industry.

McCarthy and Cohn were all for it, as were the Pentagon and especially the Army, whose officials who felt airing of the Private Schine affair had damaged the uniformed services. Welch also agreed. Aside from the three Democratic committee members who formed a minority, only two people were opposed: Bob Stevens and Dwight D. Eisenhower.

Stevens, so pliable previously, was now determined that the full story of McCarthy and Cohn's abuses be told, in public, on television. It was a matter of fundamental fairness, he maintained. As for the president, he privately stood by Stevens as a point of personal honor, but he also feared closed hearings would enable McCarthy to make false headline-garnering charges that would further damage the Army, to which he had devoted his life.

The deciding vote on the seven-man committee belonged to Karl Mundt. But the acting chairman had tied his hands by agreeing at the start that the hearings would not be halted prematurely if any of the principals objected on grounds of fairness. Stevens so objected. Mundt was obliged to vote with the Democrats. The hearings, open and on TV, continued for more than a month.

———

Of all the strange aspects of the hearings, the strangest was the failure of the committee to call Private G. David Schine to testify. It was Schine, more than anyone, who precipitated the events; Schine whose special status struck the most negative chords among the public. He did appear, briefly, wearing his private's uniform, to identify himself in the doctored group photograph. But he was never interrogated or asked to give sworn testimony about the controversial events that swirled around him. On this, too, the committee was sharply split along partisan lines, with Democrats wanting him as a witness and Republicans, especially Cohn, strongly opposed. The hearings did, however, lay out the damaging material in the Army's chronology of the Schine case, and revealed harmful new information about the private.

The nation heard how Schine left the drill field to place and receive numerous long-distance calls; paid other soldiers to clean his rifle; didn't ride in a truck with the other men but walked to training; patronizingly told the commanding general that he had come to Fort Dix to "reorganize the Army along modern lines"; and threw his arms around Secretary Stevens's shoulders, complimenting him pompously on the good job he was doing getting Communists out of the Army, suggesting he could help the secretary further by becoming his personal assistant. McCarthy, under sharp questioning by Senator Henry M. Jackson, a Democrat from Washington, stammered when asked to explain not only Schine's credentials but also what Schine *did* for the investigating committee.

"I think you have testified, senator," Jackson said to McCarthy, "that Mr. Schine had spent considerable time . . . dealing with the problems of psychological warfare."

"That is correct," McCarthy answered, "It has been more or less his hobby . . . He submitted a plan to the State Department. Roy says he has a copy of it here in case you would like to see it."

This was a mistake by McCarthy, who had not read the so-called Schine Plan. Robert Kennedy, the Democratic counsel, had—and had provided devastating background questions for Jackson that made a mockery of Schine. As with his error-ridden treatise on Communism, this three-page document was filled with bromides. "The broad battlefield is the globe," Schine wrote, "and the contest is for men's souls. We can fill their bellies, as we must, but man does not live by bread alone. We require of the free peoples of the world, their hearts, their consciences, their voices, and their votes."

As Jackson read aloud from the Schine document, laughter filled the room. McCarthy, squirming, said, "Mr. Jackson, apparently you think this is amusing."

"Let's turn to 'periodicals,'" Jackson said, citing a "Schine Plan" passage. "He has 'Universal Appeal—pictures, cartoons, humor, pin-ups.'"

McCarthy protested that "pictures and cartoons can have an important place in any information program."

"I am directing the question to pin-ups," Jackson replied, drawing more laughter.

"As to pin-ups, I don't know," McCarthy said.

"We can all laugh on that one, I think, Senator," he was told.

Moments later, Chairman Mundt came to McCarthy's rescue by gaveling that day's hearing to a close. Immediately after, an enraged Cohn headed straight for Kennedy. As Cohn later described their confrontation, Kennedy snapped, "Don't threaten me. You've got a [expletive] nerve threatening me." As they squared off for a fistfight, others intervened. "Since touch football and mountain climbing are not my long suits," Cohn wrote, alluding to Kennedy's well-known activities, "I was probably the gainer in the stopping of the fight."

Though the committee never put Schine on the stand for extended testimony, they did summon his "girlfriend" as a witness in one of the closed-door sessions. Had it been televised, Iris Flores's executive-session appearance would have produced another wave of national laughter, and more humiliation for Schine.

She was called in an attempt to document the Army's charge that Schine had "misused his pass privileges for feminine entertainment when he was supposed to be on committee business." Flores, described as a "stunning young brunette," was the person to whom Schine had made several phone calls a day during his Fort Dix duty, and had also traveled back and forth with Schine in his family's limousine from her New York apartment to the Army base. Her long-sealed testimony reads like a parody of the gum-chewing Judy Holliday in *Born Yesterday*.

Sworn in as a witness, Flores gave her occupation as "an inventor." Was she employed? No, she said. "I sold an invention to I. Newman and Company, and it has to do with brassieres and it is a gadget and DuPont has been working on it, a man from DuPont, and a brassiere designer for them. I have been working closely with them for working models. We hope to bring it out in a few months." I. Newman and Company, she explained, was a girdle company, and she was developing "a brassiere shaper," or a "plastic bra." As for Schine, he and she had "a great friendship" that has "always been proper."

She was vague about how many times they had dined while he was at Fort Dix, because, she said, it was always "very late at night because he was always busy with things to do, and [with] Roy Cohn . . . He always seemed so terribly tied up with all kinds of things." On New Year's Eve, for instance: "At

Cohn's house he was always so terribly, terribly tied up, so terribly, terribly busy . . . He would get terribly involved with Mr. Cohn in New York." And how many times had Schine called her while he was at Fort Dix?

> I have thousands of calls all day and I don't just remember. He is a very quiet boy and he doesn't like night clubs and this business of newspapers is ridiculous. He likes—if he dines quietly it is very quiet, and [it] was always dinner. After all, one has to eat, you know. That was the only time I saw him, very late, after he had completed his business, but he always was very busy, so he told me . . . late in the evening after he had completed what he had to do with Mr. Cohn. There were always dinners with people he had to work with. He called me to tell me this on the telephone. I understand these things. I understand people have to work. I work very hard myself.

By the time the committee heard public testimony from John J. Lucas, Jr., the bow-tied appointments clerk who recorded all of Stevens's Pentagon office phone conversations, poisonous feelings had developed between McCarthy and the Democratic senators, particularly W. Stuart Symington of Missouri. The rancorous partisanship that now enveloped the committee became clear in a divisive closed-door session four days later, in the first week of June.

During the public hearing, Lucas told the committee about a conversation between Stevens and Symington on February 20, just after McCarthy's attack on General Zwicker. Though they belonged to different political parties, Stevens and Symington were old friends, both World War I veterans, both Yale graduates, both independently wealthy, and both devoted to the professional military corps. Before his election to the Senate, Symington had served for three years as the first secretary of the Air Force, and before that, in the Pentagon. Now, in their recorded call, Stevens laid out for Symington what had happened to Zwicker, and said that he "did not intend to have this abuse of our professional officer corps continued." He also said that he had decided not to permit Zwicker to appear before the McCarthy committee, and reported how McCarthy had angrily ordered him to testify in a few days. Symington advised Stevens not to testify, and suggested that he seek the private counsel of Clark Clifford, one of the top political strategists of the Democratic Party, and, like Symington, a Missourian.

When McCarthy learned of this exchange, he charged that Symington had allowed Clifford, "one of the top aides of President Truman, to run the show." He demanded that Symington recuse himself from the committee, accusing his fellow senator of having "got Clark Clifford to mislead a fine, naïve, not too brilliant Republican Secretary of the Army." Then he theatrically demanded that both Symington and Clifford be subpoenaed to testify under oath.

It was a bluff, a smoke screen by which he sought to divert attention from the damaging phone conversations that had proven so devastating for both him and Cohn. Symington, in response, said he had recommended that Stevens speak to Clifford only after Stevens appealed to him for help, and dismissed McCarthy's demands as "just another diversion."

Emotions simmered until the committee next met and, behind closed doors, received another blast from McCarthy. He threatened to extend the hearings indefinitely by calling, and recalling, a succession of witnesses; he "would not consent" to any "limitation of the witnesses" unless his latest demands were met. It was another bluff, for by then Stevens was the only principal—McCarthy included—who had not agreed to bring the hearings to a conclusion. In fact, in addition to Symington's testimony, McCarthy wanted the committee to set "a definite cut-off date, so we can get back to the Communist issue."

McCarthy's latest tactic set off an extraordinary exchange.

"Here is the thing about these hearings that begins to somewhat appall me," Welch said, shedding his mild-mannered persona behind closed doors. Directly addressing McCarthy, he continued: "Looking at you, Senator McCarthy, you have, I think, something of a genius for creating confusion, throwing in new issues, new accusations, and creating a turmoil in the hearts and minds of the country that I find troublesome. And because of your genius, sir, we keep on, just keep on, as I see it, creating these confusions. Maybe I am over-impressed by them. But I don't think they do the country any good."

Welch then turned to the full committee and delivered an eloquent extemporaneous statement.

> Now, Mr. Chairman, I think it is quite clear that this hearing cannot actually resolve and solve some of the things that have been presented in it, to wit, the constitutional issues, as I view them, that can only be revealed to the public, and thought about, and settled in the course of the next year or five years or ten years or our lifetime . . . As to the personal conflicts here of who is saying what, I hesitate to say this but as a lawyer it would seem to me that neither side is

bound to have a 100 percent clear-cut victory in that. That is going to be left in some kind of balance from the way the committee looks and acts, and probably the way the country reacts. It follows that from the viewpoint of the United States of America, that I think we do no good in continuing the hearings beyond the point that Mr. Jenkins has suggested.

McCarthy could not resist a response to Welch's criticism. "Mr. Welch made a statement that I want to comment on," he remarked. "He said Mr. McCarthy had a genius for creating confusion. I assume by that he means a genius for bringing out the facts which may disturb the people."

Then McCarthy renewed his demand that both Symington and Clifford testify under oath. The Democrats quickly agreed to summon Clifford, but now the Republicans objected. McCarthy dropped that line of attack, and turned back to Symington.

"I will make a deal with you," Symington told him. "I will go on the floor of the Senate and make a speech, and then I will take the stand, see, and I will go under oath and let this committee examine me, if you will make a speech and if you will go on the stand on the charges you never answered in 1952.* There is your deal, and I will make it with you right now." Symington also promised to make the deal live on television, if McCarthy wished.

---

*The charges stemmed from the original Benton resolution to expel McCarthy from the Senate that later formed the basis for the highly critical Hennings hearings that rendered harsh judgment on McCarthy.

Symington had called McCarthy's bluff. McCarthy blustered, but didn't take him up on his offer.

Their exchange became more vitriolic, with reciprocal accusations of lying and dishonesty, until Everett Dirksen interjected a motion to adjourn, which quickly received a Republican second. "Mr. Chairman," Dirksen called out in his mellifluous tones, "I respectfully suggest there is a motion to adjourn, which is not debatable."

Symington stayed on the committee, Clifford was never called to testify, and the American people never learned how viciously partisan the hearings had become.

Chapter

NINETEEN

_____

"Have You No Shame, Senator?"

*Until this moment, Senator, I think I never gauged
your cruelty or your recklessness.*

—Joseph Welch to Joe McCarthy

L ate in the afternoon of June 7, after the committee adjourned from another long session, Roy Cohn and Joe
Welch walked out of the hearing room together. "There's a
little matter I'd like to talk to you about sometime," Welch
said. "I think you're the sort of person to whom I can talk off
the record."*

---

*This account comes from Cohn's memoir. Welch, who intended to
write his own memoir, never got it done before his death and did not mention this episode in a *Life* magazine article he wrote that summer.

414 / "HAVE YOU NO SHAME, SENATOR?"

"Coincidentally," Cohn replied, "there is something I would like to talk to you about privately."

"Well, then," Welch answered, "let us make that sometime now."

They spotted an empty committee room down the hall, entered, and shut the door.

Welch wanted to talk about Fred Fisher, Cohn about further questioning of his own draft status, to which Welch had briefly alluded when Cohn testified several days earlier. "Mr. Cohn," Welch had asked Cohn then, "there have, I think, been some articles published about you and your draft status, of which you are probably aware, are you not?" Cohn had answered: "Sir, I would say articles have been published about me on just about everything, yes, sir." Before further pursuing the question, Welch had said he hoped Cohn would "consult your file, or bring it to the stand with you, so you can reel it off to us, what your whole story has been."

Avoidance of military service—an issue that, like so many in the McCarthy story, keeps reappearing to this day—was a matter of potentially acute embarrassment to Cohn, especially if it came to light amid the case of Private Schine. Cohn was of draft age at the end of World War II. Though he was initially classified 1-A, he gained a reprieve when a family friend secured him an appointment to West Point, which he never entered; then, two days before a peacetime draft law took effect in 1948, Cohn enlisted in the National Guard—a practice that then, and later during the Vietnam War, enabled many to avoid combat. At the least, Cohn wanted to forestall the airing of this background.

Welch, for his part, was anxious to avoid McCarthy or Cohn raising Fred Fisher's membership in the National

Lawyers Guild or Fisher's connection with a Communist organizer at the time. He had reason to worry. Though Welch had leaked the fact of Fisher's membership before the hearings began, McCarthy on several occasions since had approached Welch and his assistant, James St. Clair, with a threat to tell "the Fisher story" on national TV.

Now, alone behind closed doors, Welch told Cohn that while as lawyers they had their respective jobs to do, "nevertheless we don't have to hurt each other unnecessarily while we're doing it." He paused, then asked, "Do you want to go first or shall I?" Cohn spoke first. While he was not a draft dodger, he said, he acknowledged that "the matter would be personally embarrassing to me." He asked about his draft status: "Do we have to go into it?" Welch presented the Fisher situation. He offered what he called a "trade," then spelled out "my *quid pro quo:* If you will omit any reference to the Fisher case, I will not return to the topic you want me to stay away from."

They sealed their deal with a handshake. "That night," as Cohn wrote in his memoir, "I went to Senator McCarthy's home and gave him a full account of my conversation with Welch and the agreement into which I had entered. *McCarthy approved the trade* [italics in original]."

Two days later, though, McCarthy would lose his temper one time too many and, as Cohn wrote, "blurted out the story of Fisher case," with irreparable harm to himself.

———

The voluminous record of the Army-McCarthy hearings, public and private, is filled with dramatic moments. But nothing in the transcripts comes close to the confrontation that unfolded on June 9 toward the end of another long hearing day.

With what Cohn later described as his "deceptive gentleness," Welch set out on a cross-examination of Cohn intended to expose the fraudulency of the McCarthy claim that the hunt for Communists countered a new and mortal threat to the United States, a peril especially posed by Communist infiltrators in America's defense industry. Welch began a series of quickly delivered but mild-sounding questions by asking: "Mr. Cohn, what is the exact number of Communists or subversives that are loose today in these defense plants?"

"The exact number that is loose, sir?" Cohn replied.

"Yes, sir."

"I don't know."

"Roughly how many?" Welch continued.

"I can only tell you, sir, what we know about it," Cohn answered.

"That is one hundred thirty, is that right?" Cohn agreed. Welch pushed on.

When Cohn said, "I am going to try to particularize for you, if I can," Welch told him in an urgent tone: "I am in a hurry. I don't want the sun to go down while they are still in there, if we can get them out."

"I am afraid we won't be able to work that fast, sir."

How many plants were these Communists in, Welch asked, and where were they located? "Reel off the cities," he implored Cohn.

"Would you stop me if I am going too far?" Cohn asked.

"You can't go too far revealing Communists, Mr. Cohn," the Boston lawyer told him. "Reel off the cities for us."

Cohn, sounding increasingly defensive, listed a number of cities: Schenectady, N.Y.; Syracuse, N.Y.; Rome, N.Y.; Quincy, MA.; Fitchburg, MA.; Buffalo, N.Y.; Dunkirk, N.Y.; another at Buffalo, N.Y.; Cambridge, MA.; New Bedford, MA.; Quincy, MA.; Lynn, MA.; Pittsfield, MA.; Boston, MA.

"Mr. Cohn, you not only frighten me," Welch said, "you make me ashamed when there are so many in Massachusetts." When others laughed, Welch added, "This is not a laughing matter, believe me. Are you alarmed at that situation, Mr. Cohn?"

"Yes, sir; I am."

"Nothing could be more alarming, could it?"

"It certainly is a very alarming thing."

Then Welch said, even more urgently, "Will you not, before the sun goes down, give those names to the FBI and at least have those men put under surveillance?"

Cohn was flustered. He began stammering. At this point, a clearly furious McCarthy interrupted.

"Mr. Chairman, let's not be ridiculous," he said. "Mr. Welch knows, as I have told him a dozen times, that the FBI has [been given] all of this information. The defense plants have the information. The only thing we can do is to try and publicly expose these individuals and hope that they will be gotten rid of. And you know that, Mr. Welch."

No, Welch said sorrowfully, "I do not know that." He continued to ask: "Cannot the FBI put these one hundred thirty men under surveillance before sundown tomorrow?"

Cohn then made an admission that undercut the premise of the McCarthy investigations: that they were providing new evidence about Communist infiltrators and traitors not known to the government. "Sir," Cohn said, "if there is need for surveillance in the case of espionage or anything like that, I can well assure you that Mr. John Edgar Hoover and his men know a lot better than I, and I quite respectfully suggest, sir, than probably a lot of us, just who should be put under surveillance. I do not propose to tell the FBI how to run its shop. It does it very well."

"And they do it, don't they, Mr. Cohn?" Welch asked.

"When the need arises, of course."

"And will you tell them tonight, Mr. Cohn," Welch pressed on, "that here is a case where the need has arisen, so that it can be done by sundown tomorrow night?"

"No, sir; there is no need for my telling the FBI what to do about this or anything else," came the reply from an even more flustered Cohn.

Welch's examination continued: "Mr. Cohn, tell me once more: Every time you learn of a Communist or a spy anywhere, is it your policy to get them out as fast as possible?"

"Surely, we want them out as fast as possible, sir."

"And whenever you learn of one from now on, Mr. Cohn, I beg of you, will you tell somebody about them quick?"

Now Cohn began pleading with Welch to appreciate the limitations upon him. "I work for the committee here," he said. "They know how we go about handling situations of Communist infiltration and failure to act on FBI information about Communist infiltration. If they are displeased with the speed with which I and the group of men who work with me proceed, if they are displeased with the order in which we move, I am sure they will give me appropriate instructions along those lines, and I will follow any which way they give me."

Welch, displaying his talent for the deadly thrust, said: "May I add my small voice, sir, and say whenever you know about a subversive or a Communist spy, please hurry. Will you remember those words?"

This pushed McCarthy over the edge. His familiar cry of "Mr. Chairman, Mr. Chairman" filled the room.

Mundt, as usual, asked, "Have you a point of order?"

"Not exactly, Mr. Chairman," McCarthy answered. "But in view of Mr. Welch's request that the information be given once we know of anyone who might be performing any work for the Communist Party, I think we should tell him that he has in his law firm a young man named Fisher whom he recommended, incidentally, to do work on this committee, who has been for a number of years a member of an organization which was named, oh, years and years ago, as the legal bulwark of the Communist Party, an organization which always swings to [denounce] anyone who dares to expose Communists."

Millions watching saw a look of what Cohn himself later described as "horror" cross his face. As *Time* magazine reported the scene: "Roy Cohn grimaced toward McCarthy, shook his head, and his lips seemed to form the words, 'No! No!'"

The cameras captured Cohn hurriedly scribbling a note, which was handed to McCarthy from one congressional page to the next. It read: "This is the subject which I have committed to Welch we would not go into. Please respect our agreement as an agreement because this is not going to do any good."* McCarthy paused to read the message, and later during his long and ultimately destructive remarks acknowledged he understood it, saying, "I know Mr. Cohn would rather not have me go into this." But he charged ahead, launching a classic McCarthy smear of both Fisher and Welch.

---

*Welch kept his part of the agreement with Cohn and never brought up Cohn's draft status in the hearings.

"I certainly assume that Mr. Welch did not know [this] of this young man at the time he recommended him as the assistant counsel for this committee," McCarthy said in that by-now familiar contemptuous monotone, "but he has such terror and such a great desire to know where anyone is located who may be serving the Communist cause, Mr. Welch, that I thought we should just call to your attention the fact that your Mr. Fisher, who is still in your law firm today, whom you asked to have down here looking over the secret and classified material, is a member of an organization, not named by me but named by various committees, named by the Attorney General, as I recall, and I think I quote this verbatim, as 'the legal bulwark of the Communist Party.' He belonged to that for a sizable number of years, according to his own admission, and he belonged to it long after it had been exposed as the legal arm of the Communist Party.

"Knowing that, Mr. Welch, I just felt that I had a duty to respond to your urgent request that before sundown, when we know of anyone serving the Communist cause, we let the agency know. We are now letting you know that your man did belong to this organization for, either three or four years, belonged to it long after he was out of law school."

Nothing could stop McCarthy now. He was doing what he instinctively did when challenged—striking back, brutally, viciously, unfairly.

"I don't think you can find anyplace, anywhere, an organization which has done more to defend Communists—I am again quoting the report—to defend Communists, to defend espionage agents, and to aid the Communist cause, than the man whom you originally wanted down here at your right hand instead of Mr. St. Clair," he continued.

"I have hesitated bringing that up, but I have been rather bored with your phony requests to Mr. Cohn here that he personally get every Communist out of government before sundown. Therefore, we will give you information about the young man in your own organization. I am not asking you at this time to explain why you tried to foist him on this committee. Whether you knew he was a member of that Communist organization or not, I don't know. I assume you did not, Mr. Welch, because I get the impression that, while you are quite an actor, you play for a laugh, I don't think you have any conception of the danger of the Communist Party. I don't think you yourself would ever knowingly aid the Communist cause. I think you are unknowingly aiding it when you try to burlesque this hearing in which we are attempting to bring out the facts, however."

Through this assault, Welch sat slumped back, his hands over his face. Finally, he spoke up, saying, "Mr. Chairman." But before he could speak, Mundt interrupted to say: "Mr. Welch, the Chair should say he has no recognition or no memory of Mr. Welch's recommending either Mr. Fisher or anybody else as counsel for this committee."

Mundt then announced, "I will recognize Mr. Welch."

McCarthy would not give way. "Mr. Chairman," he said, "I will give you the news story on that."

Welch attempted to regain the floor. "Mr. Chairman," he said, "under these circumstances I must have something approaching a personal privilege."

"You may have it, sir," Mundt told him.

His voice husky, tears welling in his eyes, Welch tried to get McCarthy's attention. "Senator McCarthy," he began, "I did not know—"

McCarthy, smiling broadly, turned away from Welch and whispered gleefully to an aide. "Senator," Welch said sharply, "sometimes you say 'May I have your attention?'"

McCarthy ignored him. He continued smirking and talking to his aide. "I am listening to you," he said, his face still turned away. "I can listen with one ear."

"This time I want you to listen with both."

"Yes," McCarthy said, still turned away.

"Senator McCarthy, I think until this moment—"

He was interrupted by McCarthy's aside to an aide: "Jim, will you get the news story to the effect that this man belonged to this Communist-front organization? Will you get the citations showing that this was the legal arm of the Communist Party, and the length of time that he belonged, and the fact that he was recommended by Mr. Welch? I think that should be in the record."

"You won't need anything in the record when I have finished telling you this," Welch said, for the first time forcing McCarthy to face him. "Until this moment, Senator, I think I never really gauged your cruelty or your recklessness. Fred Fisher is a young man who went to the Harvard Law School and came into my firm and is starting what looks to be a brilliant career with us."

The hearing room was deathly still now.

When I decided to work for this committee I asked Jim St. Clair, who sits on my right, to be my first assistant. I said to Jim, "Pick somebody in the firm who works under you that you would like." He chose Fred Fisher and they came down on an afternoon plane. That night, when he had taken a little stab at trying to see what the case was about,

Fred Fisher and Jim St. Clair and I went to dinner together. I then said to these two young men, "Boys, I don't know anything about you except I have always liked you, but if there is anything funny in the life of either one of you that would hurt anybody in this case you speak up quick."

Fred Fisher said, "Mr. Welch, when I was in law school and for a period of months after, I belonged to the Lawyers Guild," as you have suggested, senator. He went on to say, "I am secretary of the Young Republican's League in New-ton with the son of Massachusetts' Governor, and I have the respect and admiration of the twenty-five lawyers or so in Hale & Dorr."

I said, "Fred, I just don't think I am going to ask you to work on the case. If I do, one of these days that will come out and go over national television and it will just hurt like the dickens."

So, senator, I asked him to go back to Boston.

Little did I dream you could be so reckless and cruel as to do an injury to that lad. It is true he is still with Hale & Dorr. It is true that he will continue to be with Hale & Dorr. It is, I regret to say, equally true that I fear he shall always bear a scar needlessly inflicted by you. If it were in my power to forgive you for your reckless cruelty, I would do so. I like to think I am a gentleman, but your forgive-ness will have to come from someone other than me.

McCarthy, no smiles now, called out loudly, "Mr. Chairman."

"Senator McCarthy?" Mundt answered.

"May I say that Mr. Welch talks about this being cruel and reckless," McCarthy said. "He was just baiting; he has been baiting Mr. Cohn here for hours, requesting that Mr. Cohn, before sundown, get out of any department of government anyone who is serving the Communist cause. I just give this man's record, and I want to say, Mr. Welch, that it has been labeled long before he became a member, as early as 1944—"

This time it was Welch who interrupted McCarthy. "Senator," he said, "may we not drop this? We know he belonged to the Lawyers Guild, and Mr. Cohn nods his head at me. I did you, I think, no personal injury, Mr. Cohn."

"No, sir," a stricken-looking Cohn replied.

"I meant to do you no personal injury, and if I did, I beg your pardon," Welch told Cohn. Turning back to face McCarthy, he added words that became engraved in the American memory:

"Let us not assassinate this lad further, senator. You have done enough. Have you no sense of decency sir, at long last? Have you left no sense of decency?"

Even then, McCarthy was incapable of recognizing the damage he was inflicting on himself. "I know this hurts you, Mr. Welch. But I may say, Mr. Chairman, on a point of personal privilege, and I would like to finish it—"

"Senator, I think it hurts you, too, sir," Welch cut in.

McCarthy blundered on.

I would like to finish this. Mr. Welch has been filibustering this hearing, he has been talking day after day about how he wants to get anyone tainted with Communism out before sundown. I know Mr. Cohn would rather not have me go into this. I intend to, however. Mr. Welch talks about any sense of decency. If I say anything which is not the truth, then I would like to know about it. [quoting from a document before him] "The foremost legal bulwark of the Communist Party, its front organizations, and controlled unions, and which, since its inception, has never failed to rally to the legal defense of the Communist Party, and individual members thereof, including known espionage agents."

Now, that is not the language of Senator McCarthy. That is the language of the Un-American Activities Committee. And I can go on with many more citations. It seems that Mr. Welch is pained so deeply he thinks it is improper for me to give the record, the Communist front record, of the man whom he wanted to foist upon this committee. But it doesn't pain him at all—there is no pain in his chest about the unfounded charges against Mr. Frank Carr [one of McCarthy's staff members]; there is no pain there about the attempt to destroy the reputation and take the jobs away from the young men who were working in my committee.

And, Mr. Welch, if I have said anything here which is untrue, then tell me. I have heard you and every one else talk so much about laying the truth upon the table that when I hear—and it is completely phony, Mr. Welch, I have listened to you for a long time—when you say "Now, before sundown, you must get these people out of government," I want to have it very clear, very clear that you were not so serious about that when you tried to recommend this man for this committee. And may I say, Mr. Welch, in fairness to you, I have reason to believe that you did not know about his Communist-front record at the time you recommended him. I don't think you would have recommended him to the committee, if you knew that. I think it is entirely possible you learned that after you recommended him.

Once more, Mundt interjected. Speaking as chairman, he repeated that he did "not believe that Mr. Welch recommended

Mr. Fisher as counsel for this committee, because [I have] through this office all the recommendations that were made." Mundt didn't recall that any of the recommendations "that came from Mr. Welch," included "Mr. Fisher."

McCarthy couldn't drop it. "Let me ask Mr. Welch," he said, adopting his most inquisitorial manner. "You brought him down, did you not, to act as your assistant?"

Welch had the last word. "*Mr.* McCarthy," he said, "I will not discuss this with you further. You have sat within six feet of me, and could have asked me about Fred Fisher. You have brought it out. If there is a God in heaven, it will do neither you nor your cause any good. I will not discuss it further. I will not ask Mr. Cohn any more questions. You, Mr. Chairman, may, if you will, call the next witness."

"Are there any questions?" Mundt asked the committee. There were none. For what seemed like a long time, not a sound was heard. It was as though everyone present, and by extension everyone watching on television, had been holding their breath. Now, suddenly, the room was rocked by spontaneous and thunderous applause.

The hearing was adjourned. Joseph Welch, close to tears, his face grim, walked slowly, almost painfully, from the room. McCarthy followed. He too looked grim, his face flushed. Far too late, he recognized that he had been hurt. What he didn't know was to what extent. His closest allies and aides knew, however. Sitting near him during the hearing was one of his most loyal assistants, Ed Nellor. "I got physically ill," Nellor said of witnessing McCarthy's implosion. A similar reaction came from McCarthy's staunchest friend, Urban Van Susteren, who watched the hearings from his Wisconsin home. "It made me sick," Van Susteren told biographer Thomas

Reeves. As for McCarthy, some sense of how profoundly damaging his encounter with Welch had been seemed to affect him after he emerged into the Senate hallway, where he was immediately surrounded by people. "What did I do?" he murmured. "What did I do?" The answer was that he had destroyed himself.

PART SIX

Judgment

Chapter

TWENTY

Belling the Cat

The Senator is out of order.

Two days after the Welch-McCarthy confrontation, Ralph Flanders, the elderly Republican senator from Vermont, precipitated the final acts against McCarthy. In a scene captured live on television, Flanders strode dramatically into the Army-McCarthy hearings and deposited a piece of paper on McCarthy's desk. It was an announcement stating that later that day Flanders would introduce a Senate resolution calling for McCarthy's censure. McCarthy glanced at it and sneeringly dismissed it. After that hearing, when reporters asked him to comment on the Flanders move, McCarthy said of his fellow senator, "I think they should get a man with a net and take him to a good quiet place."

It was clear to all who watched that McCarthy's power was rapidly diminishing. Even before the Democrats won back both houses of Congress that November and he lost his chairmanship, McCarthy had run head-on into political reality. Republican Senate leader William Knowland, fearing a greater political and public backlash, blocked McCarthy's plan to begin new investigations out of Washington. McCarthy's committee also revolted and demanded that Roy Cohn be fired. Cohn, under intense Republican pressure, saved the GOP further embarrassment by resigning on July 19.* Other McCarthy aides transferred from the committee staff to McCarthy's personal one. In the meantime, the brewing confrontation between McCarthy and the Senate gathered momentum.

After years in which both Republicans and Democrats failed to summon the courage to deal with McCarthy, the political climate had changed. Even before the November midterm election results, Republicans feared McCarthy had become a major political liability. Their loss of Congress confirmed these fears and proved crucial in compelling both sides finally to act. Yet even the election returns probably would not have been sufficient without a triggering event. It took a Re-

---

*Cohn never held another government position. During his subsequent career as a private attorney, he continued to spark controversy, and was frequently reprimanded for unethical conduct. In 1964, 1969, and 1971 he was tried and acquitted on charges of conspiracy, bribery, and fraud. Just before his death from AIDS in 1986, he was disbarred. Schine, after completing Army service as a military policeman in Germany, spent the rest of his life in Hollywood as a movie producer, winning an Academy Award for *The French Connection.* He married a winner of the Miss Universe contest. In 1996 Schine and his wife died in the crash of a small plane piloted by one of their sons in California. Conspiracy buffs had a field day, suggesting the crash was caused by subversive forces.

publican willing to stand up and bell the cat. That person was
Flanders of Vermont.

———

Ultimately, the Flanders resolution passed into the hands of a
select bipartisan committee forged by the consummate
wheeler-dealer, Lyndon Johnson.

LBJ imposed tight party discipline, suppressing attacks
on McCarthy or the Republican Party to ensure that Democrats could not be accused of partisanship. Working with
Republican leader Knowland, LBJ saw to it that respected,
conservative senators—mainly from the South and West—
sat on the select committee. None of the men Johnson chose
could be accused of harboring liberal ideologies. Heading
the committee was the conservative Republican from Utah,
Arthur V. Watkins, a devout Mormon elder. Joining him were
two other conservative Republicans, Frank Carlson of Kansas
and Francis H. Case of South Dakota. They sat alongside
three Democrats: John C. Stennis of Mississippi, Sam J.
Ervin, Jr., of North Carolina (destined, like Jim St. Clair, to
play a historic role a generation later in Nixon's impeachment), and Edwin C. Johnson of Colorado, a close confidant
of LBJ's. The committee began hearings on August 31, in the
closing weeks of the midterm election campaigns, and continued during a lame duck congressional session after the
elections.

Watkins established the rules for the hearings and set the
tone for these conservative pillars of the Senate. He permitted no television coverage, brooked no interruption, and insisted upon absolute discipline and order. Watkins and the
other senators were determined not to allow the hearings to

become another circus with McCarthy acting as ringmaster—as Watkins made clear toward the end of the first session.

Until that moment, McCarthy, who had fidgeted visibly as he struggled to contain himself during the initial testimony, had refrained from his usual disruptive tactics. Finally, he could sit still no longer. He grabbed the microphone from his attorney, Edward Bennett Williams, and began to shout, "Just a minute, Mr. Chairman, just a minute—"

Watkins would have none of it. "The senator is out of order," he ruled as he struck down his gavel. "We are not going to be diverted by these diversions and sidelines." He hammered down the gavel again. "We are going straight down the line." Again, he cracked down the gavel. Then he adjourned the hearing for the day.

A reporter witnessing this put-down of McCarthy described it as "the gavel crack heard around the world."

For McCarthy, it was a stunning rebuke, one he had not previously experienced. Racing to appear before the reporters and photographers assembled outside the hearing room, he sputtered, "I think it's the most unheard of thing I've ever heard of." But he had been corralled. He would be kept tightly in check throughout the hearings.

By happenstance, the first day of the censure deliberations was also the day the McCarthy investigating committee rendered its "verdict," if it could be called that, on the Army-McCarthy hearings. It was strictly a party-line affair. The Republican majority cleared McCarthy of charges of bringing "improper influence" on behalf of Private Schine. The Democratic minority castigated McCarthy and Cohn for "inexcusable actions." As a serious coming to terms of the many abuses that had occurred, the final report was virtually useless; but a judgment had already been rendered in the court of public opinion. The hearings, poor as they were as an exercise in political accountability, had altered history.

Now the focus shifted to the infinitely more difficult task of the entire United States Senate deciding whether to censure one of its own. Senators had been censured only four times before, the first in 1811, the most recent in 1929.

The Watkins committee had before it more than forty charges of misconduct against Joe McCarthy. The offenses ranged from alleged financial transgressions dating back to the Lustron affair; to lying about his military record and wounds; to a pattern of abusive behavior toward colleagues and witnesses; to misuse of senatorial investigatory processes and the power of subpoena; to acts of perjury and fraud committed by his aides in falsifying documents McCarthy used to counter Army charges; to potentially illegally mishandling classified material. The list of transgressions even included an assertion that McCarthy's entire anticommunist crusade was a fraud perpetrated to deceive the public. "He has posed as a savior of his country from Communism," this passage read, "yet the Department of Justice reported that McCarthy never turned over for prosecution a single case against any of the alleged 'Communists.' (The Justice Department report of December 18, 1951.) Since that date not a single person has been tried for Communist activities as a result of information supplied by McCarthy."

Beyond this, in the wake of the Army-McCarthy debacle, the public was watching to see what judgment, if any, the senators would render on McCarthy—a fact of which the Watkins committee was acutely aware. "We realize the United States Senate, in a sense, is on trial," Watkins said in his opening remarks, "and we hope our conduct will be such as to maintain the American sense of fair play and the high traditions of dignity of the United States Senate under the authority given it by the Constitution."

Noble words, to be sure, but no less so than those uttered in the four earlier official investigations into McCarthy's conduct, none of which resulted in formal action to stop him.

In the best analysis of the Watkins committee, Robert Griffith writes: "The committee denied all the familiar props for his earlier performances. There was no audience to play to and no antagonist to harass and intimidate. There was no drama, no hovering specter of a foreign conspiracy. There were only six stern men and Joe."

Calmly, deliberately, the committee worked their way through the charges against McCarthy. They whittled them down until finally, on September 27, the committee of "six stern men" recommended in a unanimous report that McCarthy be censured on two counts: First, for contempt of the Senate, for refusing to appear in 1952 before the special subcommittee handling former Senator William Benton's original move to expel him. Second, for his abuse of General Zwicker, which the committee found "reprehensible."

In the end, the second count was dropped as a sop to the McCarthyites; in its place was one charging McCarthy had abused the Watkins committee by equating it with Communism. In both these counts, the word "censure" was eliminated. Instead of being "censured," McCarthy would be "condemned." The hard-line McCarthy bloc of some twenty Senate conservatives also fought to offer McCarthy a way out, attempting to negotiate a deal in which all charges would be dropped if he agreed to apologize to the Senate. Friends in

both parties urged him to take the deal. McCarthy, a battler
to the end, refused to apologize.

When senators entered the chamber on November 8 to
begin debate on the final Watkins Report, they found placed
on each of their desks a twenty-page pamphlet of anti-
McCarthy articles culled from the *Daily Worker.* As the *New
York Times* reported on its front page the next day, the far-
from-subtle cover sheet was pink. It bore the words: "Official
Communist Party Line on Senator McCarthy." Ergo: a vote
against McCarthy was a vote *for* the Communists.

The Senate debate was passionate and bitter, marked by
shouted exchanges and muttered obscenities (carefully deleted from the official *Congressional Record*). McCarthy's opponents found themselves the target of coordinated attacks
from right-wing zealots; the volume of hate mail exceeded
anything in the memory of senators. One senator, the scholarly J. William Fulbright of Arkansas, who had cosponsored
the Flanders Resolution, read into the *Congressional Record*
some of the letters he had received. "Red Skunk," one of
them began. "You are not fit to clean Senator McCarthy's
shoes. Hope you are struck by God." Another read: "I am an
ex-Marine who fought in the South Pacific to open this nation
to the commie Jews that Hitler did not kill? You are one of the
phony pinko punks connected with Lehman, Morse, Flanders
and Bennett." Fulbright was also called a "louse," a "coward,"
a "dirty Red," and a "jackass."

McCarthy had long encouraged such attacks, not only by
referring to Fulbright on the Senate floor and in hearings as
"half-bright," but also by accusing him of being a do-good
liberal who was soft on Communism and thus unpatriotic.
His attacks intensified after Fulbright, earlier that year,

became the only senator to vote against appropriating more money for the McCarthy committee investigations. In return, Fulbright, who had nothing but contempt for McCarthy, played a leading behind-the-scenes role in bringing together moderate Republicans and Democrats. Among those with whom Fulbright worked closely in coordinating the political strategy against McCarthy was former Senator Benton, who never stopped working to marshal public and political anti-McCarthy forces. The final Watkins Report was filled with names of senators who had opposed McCarthy during the previous investigations into his behavior: Hayden, Hennings, Gillette, Hendrickson.

Not surprisingly, after being held in check during the committee deliberations, McCarthy resorted in the floor debates to tactics he knew best. He depicted himself as a martyr who was in danger of being silenced because he dared to be America's "symbol of resistance to Communist subversion." In an invective-filled Senate speech, he said he was now the victim of a "lynch-bee." As for the Watkins Committee, it was part of a Moscow-directed conspiracy. It had "imitated Communist methods," relied on "Communist lawyers," and become the "involuntary agent" of the Communist conspiracy. The Communist Party, "a relatively small group of deadly conspirators, has now extended its tentacles to the most respected of American bodies, the United States Senate," and made one of the Senate's own committees—Watkins's—"its unwitting handmaiden."

This was red meat for the ultraconservatives. McCarthy's speech brought the right-wing extremist William Jenner of Indiana to his feet, where he roared approval. "The strategy of censure," Jenner shouted, "was initiated by the Communist conspiracy."

The Watkins committee members reacted angrily. John Stennis of Mississippi accused McCarthy of pouring "slush and slime" on the Senate. Sam Ervin of North Carolina told his colleagues they should not merely censure McCarthy; they should expel him. Watkins denounced McCarthy's speech as an attack on the Senate itself and asked his colleagues: "Do we have the manhood in the Senate to stand up to a challenge of that kind?"

As the roll call vote neared, the viciousness of the attacks escalated. On the eve of the vote, Fulbright read aloud to his Senate colleagues from a letter saying the liberal Senator Herbert Lehman, one of McCarthy's most outspoken opponents, should be deported to Germany and "given the gas treatment." Its author, a Texas oilman named G. G. Gurley, said Fulbright should be deported with Lehman. Gurley called Fulbright a "Jew-dealer" for standing with Lehman, who was Jewish, against McCarthy. "If they like Russia better than they like our form of government, they should be deported," Gurley told a reporter who phoned him for comment after Fulbright read his letter. "I like a hundred percent American like McCarthy," he said, adding: "I agree with the fellows who say we've had twenty years of treason."

Even as the senators prepared for their final debate on the censure resolution, an armored truck carrying one million eight hundred sixteen signed petitions opposing the censure was on its way to Washington. There it would be met by a retired rear admiral, John G. Crommelin, who then presented the petitions—part of a pro-McCarthy conservative campaign called "Ten Million Americans Mobilizing for Justice"—to Senate leaders.

Leading off the debate late in the afternoon of December 1, 1954, was the Republican moderate Prescott Bush of

Connecticut, father and grandfather of future presidents. Bush, reflecting the consensus of northeastern Republicans, was outraged by McCarthy's attacks on the Watkins committee and on its chairman, whom McCarthy had called, among other things, "a coward." Bush, his voice shaking with emotion, told his fellow senators, "If I ever saw a brave and noble Senator, Arthur Watkins is that man . . . I will not walk away from this floor and leave him standing with a tag of coward." Bush was the first to announce he would vote against McCarthy, a stand that drew condemnation from far right Republicans, who accused Bush of having made up his mind prematurely. The debate continued.

The next day, moments before the votes were to be cast, Lyndon Johnson finally broke his long public silence on Joe McCarthy. "Each of us must decide whether we approve or disapprove of certain actions as standards of senatorial conduct," he told the Senate. "I have made my decision." Referring to McCarthy's language toward his Senate colleagues, Johnson said it did not belong in the *Congressional Record*. It would be "more fittingly inscribed on the wall of a men's room."

Finally, on December 2, 1954, amid catcalls and bitter laughter from die-hard McCarthy supporters, the senators rendered their verdict.

By sixty-seven to twenty-two, the United States Senate voted to condemn Joe McCarthy's conduct for having been "contrary to Senate tradition."

This final act of political judgment might seem inevitable in retrospect. It wasn't. There was enough intrigue and high-stakes, behind-the-scenes maneuvers in the days leading to the final vote to provide grist for a host of Washington potboilers. Though McCarthy had lost forever the support of the American majority, he retained the passionate backing of bitter-end Republican conservatives who had fought a last-ditch battle to save him. The final vote reflected that ideological division: every Democrat present and voting, forty-four in all, plus the sole Independent (and former Republican), Wayne Morse, voted against McCarthy. By contrast, Republican senators were split down the middle, twenty-two for and twenty-two against. Right-wing forces stayed with McCarthy, the more progressive eastern GOP wing opposed him. Only three senators failed to vote: McCarthy himself; Alexander Wiley, his fellow Republican from Wisconsin; and the single absent Democrat, John Fitzgerald Kennedy of Massachusetts.*

Nor did the judgment take place without more dramatic encounters and fierce in-fighting, both public and private. No sooner had the votes been tallied than the bitter-enders launched an effort to discredit the proceedings and diminish the meaning of what had taken place. The right-wing Republican Styles Bridges arose to inquire whether the word "censure" appeared in the resolution on which the senators had just voted. If so, it was incorrect. There hadn't been a censure. Vice President Richard Nixon, then presiding, hurriedly struck the word "censure" from the title, making it read: "Resolution relating to the conduct of the Senator from Wisconsin, Mr. McCarthy."

More jeers from the bitter-enders, who took this as a sign that McCarthy had been only minimally rebuked. At this

---

*At the time of the vote Kennedy was hospitalized for back surgery stemming from his World War II PT-109 injuries. His aides later claimed he would have voted for censure, but he neither paired his vote with another senator nor had his vote recorded with the secretary of the Senate.

point, Fulbright, the former Rhodes Scholar, university president, and professor of law, asked the parliamentarian to provide a dictionary. He read to his colleagues the definition of both "censure" and "condemn." Censure: *strong or vehement expression of disapproval.* Condemn: *to pronounce an adverse judgment on; express strong disapproval of; censure.* They were synonymous. Case closed.

The Senate's condemnation left many of McCarthy's transgressions unanswered. It was not close to being definitive. But it was enough to inflict a fatal blow.

TWENTY-ONE

Oblivion

There he was—right across the hall. Nobody went near.

—Dorothye G. Scott, Senate aide

Pathos is not a word one associates with Joe McCarthy, but there was a pathetic quality to his fall from power. That the fall came, in large measure, from his self-destructive miscalculations and personal misbehavior only contributed to its enormity.

McCarthy was not given to introspection. He was incapable of seeing how grievously his Senate rebuke had damaged him, especially following his disastrous televised performance during the Army-McCarthy hearings. Even after all this he was not necessarily through. He still held his Senate seat, was still only in his mid-forties, still retained a passionate following, still was determined to press ahead with accusations of traitors within.

Yet McCarthy made one last horrendous mistake. On December 7, 1954, five days after the Senate vote, he recklessly attacked President Eisenhower.

The final collision between Ike and McCarthy had been building for some time. What triggered it was the president's inviting Senator Watkins, chair of the censure hearings, for a forty-five-minute visit to the White House the day after the Senate vote against McCarthy. The president instructed Press Secretary Hagerty to tell journalists that he had congratulated Watkins for a "very splendid job." Eisenhower had previously invited Joseph Welch and Senator Flanders to the White House and congratulated them for their respective roles against McCarthy, but those were private events that went unreported. The Watkins invitation was a media event designed to let the American public know how the president felt about McCarthy.

Acting against the strong advice of such close conservative allies in the Senate as Karl Mundt, McCarthy responded with a speech that figuratively drove a stake into his own political heart. From the floor of the Senate, he apologized to the American people for having endorsed Eisenhower for president.

"During the Eisenhower campaign," he said, "I spoke from coast to coast promising the American people that if they would elect the Eisenhower administration that they could be assured of a vigorous, forceful drive against Communists in government. Unfortunately, in that I was mistaken. I find that the president, on the one hand, congratulates senators who hold up the work of our committee, and, on the other hand, urges that we be patient with the Communist hoodlums who as of this moment are torturing and brainwashing American uniformed men in Communist dungeons."

Then he said: "There has been considerable talk about an apology to the Senate for my fight against Communism. I feel that, instead, I should apologize to the American people for what was an unintentional deception on them"—supporting Ike.

Despite the overwhelming condemnation his attack on Eisenhower received, McCarthy was so self-deluded that even then he believed he could rise again. He considered running against Eisenhower in the 1956 presidential election either as the Republican nominee or as a third-party candidate. Whether he was seduced by the mirage of massive grassroots support for him, or because of his relative youth,* McCarthy seriously convinced himself of his electability. He even sent Donald Surine to take a private sounding of leading Republican figures to assess his prospects for the 1956 Republican primaries.

The results were devastating. Surine reported to McCarthy that only three percent of GOP leaders would openly support him. Politically, Joe McCarthy was finished. Personally, he began his long descent into oblivion.

———

In his memoir, Roy Cohn described McCarthy as "dispirited and bewildered" when the new, Democratic-controlled Congress convened barely a month after the Senate rendered its vote of condemnation. "He would sit at home in the evenings

---

*At forty-six, McCarthy was then the same age as Ulysses S. Grant when Grant became the youngest person elected president to that point. Theodore Roosevelt was forty-two when he became president through an assassination in 1901, and in 1960 John F. Kennedy, at forty-three, became the youngest elected chief executive.

and talk endlessly about the immediate past," Cohn wrote of his boss. "Jean, always loyal, was bitter against the political forces that had combined to pull her husband down. She sought above all to restore his confidence. It was difficult, because that winter after the censure there was no fight left in Joe McCarthy."

McCarthy's morale grew far worse. More and more McCarthy withdrew from public notice. He missed Senate proceedings, stayed away from his office, and, as Cohn described it, "took to late rising and sometimes spent the day gazing into the fire in his living room and watching television soap operas." When close friends phoned him, he often refused to take their calls. He would sit, a drink in hand, awash in bitterness and self-pity. Occasionally, with a renewed burst of energy, he would rouse himself to launch another attack on the Communist conspiracy—and on Eisenhower. But time, health, and his political standing worked against McCarthy.

Though still in play, the issue of Communism was ebbing. Gaining in strength was a new conservative alliance between southern Democrats and staunch anticommunist Republicans. Now the attack was on the liberal excesses of the new Supreme Court, led by Eisenhower-appointed Chief Justice Earl Warren, with its support for school desegregation, civil rights, and civil liberties, and its reversal or modification of a number of Cold War national security and loyalty judgments spawned by hysteria over the perceived domestic threat of Communism. For a time, McCarthy was an eager participant in this new ideological battle, working with such arch southern segregationists as Mississippi's James Eastland—who, along with many others, considered the Warren Court's rulings part of a Communist conspiracy to destroy states' rights and usurp the powers of the Constitution.

At one point, while chairing the Senate Internal Security Subcommittee, Eastland asked, "What other explanation could there be except that a majority of the Court is being influenced by some secret, but very powerful Communist or pro-Communist influence?"

McCarthy, then serving on the subcommittee, answered: "It is impossible to explain it. Either incompetence beyond words, Mr. Chairman, I would say or the type of influence you mentioned."

They went on to say:

> Eastland: You have heard one Communist after another come before this committee and take the position that the Communist Party was just another political party; in fact, that is the Communist line, is it not?
>
> McCarthy: That is strictly the Communist line.
>
> Eastland: Is that not the line that the Chief Justice of the United States takes?
>
> McCarthy: Unfortunately, yes, Mr. Chairman . . . In their book Earl Warren is a hero. Now, I do not accuse Earl Warren of being a Communist, not even remotely. But there is something radically wrong with him. And I think it is extremely unfortunate that he was confirmed as Chief Justice.

These ideological arguments became more intense with each passing year. They played a major role in the historic shift that saw Democrats lose their electoral base in the South to a conservative Republican bloc that rose there with Barry Goldwater in the mid-1960s, crested with Ronald Reagan in the 1980s, and continued into the twenty-first century under George W. Bush. "Had the censure vote come a bit later, or the Cold War and civil rights cases a bit sooner, a formidable alliance of McCarthyites and Dixiecrats could easily have emerged," concluded David M. Oshinsky. But in this, too, poor timing and his personal demons prevented Joe McCarthy from achieving greater power.

———

On Sunday, April 28, 1957, twenty-nine months after he had been condemned by the Senate, McCarthy was admitted to Bethesda Naval Hospital, diagnosed as "seriously ill."

He had been in and out of Bethesda several times in the previous months, strapped down, confined to an oxygen tent, suffering from the d.t.'s (delirium tremens). The public was never informed about many of those admissions, the reasons for his hospitalization, or the reality of his physical condition. The truth was that McCarthy's drinking had grown out of control. It became so serious that friends who hadn't seen him for some time were shocked to encounter his listless appearance, his vacant look, his shaking hands.

During a trip to Appleton nearly a year before, McCarthy had startled friends by saying he had nightmares of snakes leaping at him. Urben Van Susteren was so concerned about his deteriorating condition that he talked to McCarthy's wife, Jean. He suggested to her that he take McCarthy on a trip to "dry him out," but added he was worried that Joe might become violent. She confessed she knew McCarthy's liver was severely damaged and, in the account Van Susteren gave biographer Thomas Reeves, Jean then called Joe's physician in Washington and put Van Susteren on the phone.

How much alcohol was McCarthy consuming? the doctor asked. At least a quart a day, Van Susteren told him. The doctor said two-thirds of McCarthy's liver was gone. He would die in a short time if he didn't stop drinking.

The next morning, Van Susteren confronted McCarthy. He had been talking to McCarthy's doctor, he began. Joe blew up. "Who the hell do you think you are butting into my life?" he shouted before becoming more abusive. Van Susteren, angry himself, pointed to a bottle of whiskey on the table, shoved it toward Joe, and told him to "empty it and die without further disgracing yourself and your family." McCarthy replied, "Kiss my ass."

McCarthy's heavy drinking was not a new phenomenon. It had been an open secret in Washington from his earliest days. His Senate colleagues and his aides, reporters and photographers, congressional employees and Capitol policemen, all knew. Not a word about it appeared in print.

In his early days, McCarthy had not been a mean or destructive drunk. Those who knew him then, from Senate colleagues to low-level Senate aides and Capitol employees, found him charming and good-natured no matter how much he drank.

As years passed, however, McCarthy's personality seemed to change. Recalled Pat Holt, long-time chief of staff of the Senate Foreign Relations Committee, "He had a much more outgoing personality [in his early years in the Senate] than he had later. McCarthy later developed a persecution complex and became very withdrawn, but in the early years he was a very outgoing fellow."

––––––––

After his condemnation by the Senate, McCarthy became a leper among most of his peers. They left the floor when he began to speak, turned away from him in the cloakroom, ignored him in the dining room.

For McCarthy, more crushing than being shunned by his

colleagues, so many of whom he held in contempt, was the loss of the audience he craved most—the press, his ticket to the public, his passport to power. No politician had demonstrated greater skill in courting the press, or a greater ability to overcome political opposition by manipulating the media. That ended after the vote to condemn him. For years, as the McCarthy spell enveloped the nation, the Senate press gallery in Washington had established signals to alert reporters that McCarthy was taking the floor to speak. At the shout, "McCarthy's up," reporters would stampede into the gallery to scribble down McCarthy's every word. When McCarthy rose to speak a few weeks after his censure vote, a gallery attendant rushed to summon reporters with the familiar, "McCarthy's up." Not a single reporter stirred. The most newsworthy figure in American politics was no longer news. His slide into almost total obscurity was swift, and startling.

"It was fascinating to watch the effect . . . of censure on McCarthy," said Francis R. Valeo, the secretary of the Senate.

I don't know whether it was a consequence of what happened in the Senate, or whether events just happened to coincide with a personality disintegration, but when McCarthy was in his heyday he used to have dozens, literally dozens, of reporters following him wherever he went. He took the Senate censure vote as being ridiculous, and of no meaning at all; it had no effect on him whatsoever. He found it laughable that they'd even try to stop him . . . But after the censure vote, from then on it was interesting to see the transition that took place. The press no longer followed McCarthy. He'd write these enormous tracts, [but] nobody would be on the floor to hear them anymore. He would run them up to the press gallery personally and say,

"Boys, look at this one. I've got some real hot stuff here."
And they'd say, "Oh, yeah? Okay, Joe, lay it on the table."
It was that kind of thing, and gradually the spotlight
ceased to shine on him. As it ceased to shine on him, he
shriveled more and more in every respect, physically along
with everything else. He was heavy on alcohol at that point
toward the end. He more and more lost interest in what
was happening. Or I should say, people lost interest in
McCarthy.

———

More than one person who knew McCarthy during this period spoke of how utterly lonely he seemed. In one episode,
in December 1956, just four months before McCarthy was
admitted to the naval hospital in Bethesda, he entered a Senate elevator that contained Lee Williams, the top assistant to
Senator Fulbright, Williams's wife, and some of Fulbright's
Arkansas constituents. At the peak of his power, McCarthy
had singled out Fulbright for special scorn and attack. But
though McCarthy knew what position Williams and his boss
had taken against him, he seemed eager to talk. "I'm Joe Mc-
Carthy," he said to those who had never met him. He was
carrying an armful of Christmas presents—intended, he explained, for his wife and the weeks-old girl they had just
adopted, with the help of Cardinal Spellman, from a New
York foundling hospital. He was about to mail the presents to
where his wife and daughter were staying in Arizona.

As McCarthy talked, he put the presents down on the elevator floor and then reached inside his overcoat to a suit
pocket to retrieve a gold oval picture frame. It held a photograph of his daughter. McCarthy was still proudly showing it

around when the Arkansans got off the elevator. The doors closed and McCarthy rode on alone.

————

On Thursday, May 2, 1957, four days after he entered Bethesda Naval Hospital, authorities announced that Joe McCarthy had died at 6:02 P.M. of what they described as "acute hepatitis," a liver disease. A hospital spokesman, briefing reporters, said McCarthy's death "followed several weeks of illness at his home." In fact, McCarthy died of cirrhosis of the liver after a much longer period of decline. He literally drank himself to death.

That day, when a reporter asked Dean Acheson for his re-action to news of Joe McCarthy's death, the former secretary of state referred the reporter to the classics. Quoting from Diogenes Laertius, he said: *De mortuis nil nisi bonum.* Then he helped the reporter with the Latin translation: "Of the dead, nothing but good."

Drew Pearson got the news in New York that night when one of his staff members called him. "In some respects, I am sorry to see him go," Pearson wrote in his diary. "He caused this nation all sorts of pain and setbacks in the field of foreign affairs. But toward the end I couldn't help but feel sorry for him. He was a very lonesome guy. All the glamour that once surrounded him was gone. The newspaper men who had once hounded him wouldn't pay any attention to him any more. He used to carry press releases through the Capitol and try to hand them to newsmen. They were polite. They accepted the press releases but that was all."

In a spirit of both compassion and hypocrisy, McCarthy was given a hero's farewell. Not surprisingly, the effusive tributes he received obscured darker truths about his life and times. They also diverted attention from the circumstances of his death and the reality of the life he had led for two and a half years after being condemned by the Senate. But the outpouring of emotion and praise, followed by the elaborate near state funeral he received, testified that even in death Joe McCarthy possessed a remarkable power.

———

For two days his body lay in state in a funeral home a block from the White House. A Marine honor guard, whose ranks were ceremoniously changed every half hour, stood watch over his coffin. A continuous stream of mourners filed through the viewing room, more than two thousand the first day and even more the second. As they neared the open casket where McCarthy lay dressed in a dark blue suit and gray tie, a crucifix resting in his hands, some wept, some prayed. One woman murmured to others approaching the casket, "People were a little bit late showing how they felt. Here we are— flags at half staff, even at the White House."

A phalanx of Marines, flanked by Marines with rifles raised in salute, escorted McCarthy's flag-draped casket from the funeral home to St. Matthew's Cathedral. Waiting outside the cathedral were several hundred mourners led by Vice President Nixon and a host of McCarthy's admirers, associates, and Senate colleagues. Roy Cohn was present. So was John F. Kennedy, whose own funeral would be held there just six years later. Inside, thirty-nine priests, followed by fourteen monsignori wearing their purple robes, took their places in the sanctuary. Archbishop Patrick A. O'Boyle officiated over a solemn pontifical high requiem mass. Those present heard

Monsignor John K. Cartwright eulogize McCarthy as someone who played "a role which will be more and more honored
as history unfolds its record." Monsignor Cartwright also said:
"Not everybody saw from the beginning, and many still do not
see, that the threat of Communism is domestic as well as foreign, civil as well as military . . . Millions of people now see
the truth, which was only perceived by hundreds before this
man gave his testimony. To do this required a magnificent
heart of courage such as has been needed at every time for
those who saw ahead."

From there, the cortege made its way to the plaza on
Capitol Hill. Several hundred more people gathered there,
watching silently as the casket was carried up the steps, past
more Marines posted on either side, to the main entrance of
the Senate wing. It was the first time in seventeen years that
a senator had been honored by a funeral service held in that
chamber.

On the Senate floor where they had condemned him, Mc-
Carthy's colleagues heard their chaplain, the Reverend Dr.
Frederick Brown Harris, deliver a florid tribute describing
McCarthy as one in whose heart "there burned the bright
flame of patriotism pure and undefiled." No critical words
were uttered by colleagues who had either cowered before
him in fear or despised him. An unreported incident, however, bespoke the true feelings of many senators.

One of the rules of the Senate allowed McCarthy's widow,
Jean, who was with him when he died and became the passionate keeper of his flame, to have McCarthy's casket transported from Bethesda Naval Hospital to lie on the Senate
chamber floor before it was taken to the funeral home to await
the formal services in the next few days. "There was his casket

in there on the Senate floor," remembered Dorothye G. Scott, an administrative assistant to the secretary of the Senate,

> and nobody went near the place. It was right across the hall from me, across from the secretary's office. Nobody! Nobody went in all day long. I think that was kind of cold . . . I was thinking of the difference for Senator Lucas, the former Majority Leader [whose casket also was permitted to lie there], the little honors, the flowers that spoke for it. And Senator McCarthy lying there all day long and nobody going near the place. I remember that very well. There he was—right across the hall. Nobody went near.

Publicly, the honors accorded McCarthy continued. Accompanied by the Marine honor guard, twenty-one senators, the ten Wisconsin members of the House of Representatives, Robert F. Kennedy, and McCarthy's family and friends, McCarthy's body was flown to Appleton. There, thirty thousand people gathered to pay him a final tribute. They packed St. Mary's Catholic Church, spilled outside onto the grounds, and lined the streets for a mile to his burial site on a bluff overlooking the Fox River. Joe McCarthy was home. His life story was over, but not his place in history.

PART SEVEN

Legacy

Chapter

TWENTY-TWO

The Politics of Fear

*Between 1950 and 1954 the politics of the possible
were also the politics of fear.*

—Robert Griffith, on the McCarthy Era

By the time I arrived in the nation's capital as a young reporter in 1957, Joe McCarthy had been dead for three months. Already, he was relegated to a mere footnote to a troubled era. People seldom mentioned him, and if they did it was usually to tell a sad story about his decline during his final years.

His sudden, early death, and a certain feeling of pity for his long fall from the pinnacle of power, prompted people to say in later years in Washington that Joe McCarthy wasn't such a bad fellow after all; that despite his bluster, he was gregarious and friendly; that, no matter what his offenses, his intentions were good. Senator Fulbright, whom I came to know well, never changed his views. He never thought of McCarthy in any kindly light. In the closing hours of the Senate censure debate, he had described McCarthy as "having the greatest contempt for the human personality of anyone I have ever seen." Years later, in recalling McCarthy, he would describe him to me as "a very ugly fellow . . . I never saw him exhibit any humor, particularly about himself."

Whatever McCarthy's personal qualities, McCarthyism in one form or another outlived the man. Its impact on our politics, and on the way Americans view their leaders and their government, has been profound. It continues to this day, and we are still forced to come to grips with it.

———

Of Joe McCarthy it can be said that fear made him possible, partisanship was responsible for his rise, and politicians, press, and public shared the blame for failing to check his abuses, which damaged countless individuals and brought shame to the United States.

Joe McCarthy became a symbolic agent of reactionary change at a pivotal moment when the United States began shouldering the burdens of post-World War II leadership amid the anxieties of the atomic age and the new Cold War. It was his ability to play on those fears that made McCarthyism such a potent force, and so difficult to counter. But McCarthy was the beneficiary, not the leader, of the anticommunist movement that wrought a political revolution in America.

Formidable and wide-ranging though McCarthy's public support was, he never would have achieved such prominence had he not received the encouragement of his party, including the Republican leaders of the Senate. Years before Mc-

Carthyism, those leaders were cynically seeking to capitalize politically on the specter of Communism. If this meant impugning the patriotism of their opponents and encouraging people such as Joe McCarthy in his anticommunist crusade, so be it. Their tacit approval, even outright advocacy, of McCarthyism was a shabby chapter in the history of the Republican Party.

Yet McCarthy's Republican Party was far more moderate—even liberal and progressive—than the present Republican Party. Over the decades, a more rigidly ideological Republican Party has emerged, forged by many of the forces that McCarthy unleashed or harnessed. Out of McCarthyism came the modern conservative movement and the former liberals turned neocons who exercise their greatest intellectual and political influence today—as seen in the major role they played in making the Bush administration's case for preemptive war against Iraq. McCarthyism was a major factor in the rise of the radical Right and the polarization that plagues American life, pitting group against group and region against region, sowing cynicism and distrust, and manipulating public opinion through fear and smear. The so-called culture wars that afflict our public discourse are another of McCarthy's legacies, as is the continuing demonization of liberals, the national press, and others whose values are not those of "real" and "patriotic" and church-going Americans. (Prominent conservatives who dared question the wisdom of the rush to war in Iraq were also accused of being unpatriotic and of supporting America's enemy.)

President Eisenhower, that good and decent man who understood and despised everything McCarthy stood for, in the end was proven correct by following a strategy of ignoring

McCarthy and waiting for him to self-destruct. But this tactic permitted McCarthy to inflict even more damage through his witch hunts during the first two years of Eisenhower's presidency. Think what a difference it would have made had Ike, with his immense prestige and personal popularity, rallied Americans against McCarthy through an Edward R. Murrow type of address to the nation.

As for the Democrats and McCarthyism, with all but a few exceptions they deserve no laurel wreath and certainly no medals for courageous action. Like the Republicans, they were afraid to challenge McCarthy directly and operated out of petty political considerations. They believed they could profit from McCarthy's excesses by pointing out that he was a Republican problem, not a Democratic one—theirs, not ours. He was, of course, an American problem.

The Democratic Party that emerged from the McCarthy years has grown increasingly fearful of accusations of being weak on defense and soft on, first, fighting Communism and, now, fighting terrorism. And with good reason. Over the decades Democrats have been targeted by political attack campaigns that employ the same defamation and distortion tactics used in the McCarthy years, campaigns that smear opponents with charges of being un-American, unpatriotic or, as the nation witnessed again during the 2004 presidential election campaign, of giving "aid and comfort" to America's enemies. These kinds of assaults produced the Nixon presidency's enemies lists, and divided America. They have become standard to this day, and the nation has paid a heavy price for them.

The polarization of society to which McCarthyism contributed was compounded by the embittered legacy of Vietnam. During the Vietnam era, some antiwar protestors heightened public rancor with their burning of American flags, their contemptuous treatment of those who wore their nation's uniform, their taunting denunciation of police officers as "pigs," their justification of violent means, their distrust of authority, and their embrace of "radical" political action. They thereby demonstrated they were as capable of true-believer dogmatism as their right-wing counterparts who had supported Joe McCarthy. As the 2004 election demonstrated disturbingly, these societal fault lines still exist in America.

Extremism—and the suspicion and hatred it engenders—may be Joe McCarthy's most lasting legacy. No sooner had McCarthy died than extremists began claiming that he had been murdered, "killed," "tortured," "crucified." The ultra-right-wing editor William Loeb blamed McCarthy's death on Ike, "that stinking hypocrite in the White House." Then he attributed McCarthy's death to a Communist conspiracy. Editorializing in his Manchester, New Hampshire *Union Leader*, Loeb wrote: "McCarthy was murdered by the Communists because he was exposing them. When he began to arouse the United States to the extent of the Communist conspiracy in our government, in our schools, in our newspapers, and in all branches of American life, the Communist Party realized that if it was to survive and succeed in its conspiracy to seize control of the United States it had to destroy McCarthy before he destroyed the party."

Eisenhower, Chief Justice Earl Warren, and CIA Director Allen Dulles were all labeled Communists by the John Birch Society, a national organization established the year after

McCarthy's death to combat the supposed continued infiltration of Communists into American life. Backed by wealthy conservatives, the society grew rapidly from its original eleven members into a membership of close to one hundred thousand and an annual income of five million dollars by the early 1960s. The society argued that in order to combat the threat of Communist subversion, the United States must become as conspiratorially-minded as the Communists. Later, the John Birchers moved their national headquarters from Massachusetts to McCarthy's hometown of Appleton, where it still operates.

In our time, the perpetuation of conspiracy theories continues to affect American politics and public attitudes.° In McCarthy's day, his self-serving show diverted the public from understanding the reality of the Communist threat, internal as well as external. Liberals tended to dismiss it as a figment of the right-wing mentality, conservatives to see it as explaining all U.S. failures. Such rigid ideological polarization prevented the American people and their leaders from uniting to fashion sensible policies to deal with the genuine problems of Communism—and do so without permitting hysteria to create abuses of civil liberties and destruction of careers and reputations. These fissures in American life hardened the ideological extremes, weakened the middle where consensus lies,

---

°A prime example of this mind-set is Ann Coulter's *Treason,* published in 2003, which depicts McCarthy as the hero of the age and of having been a victim of liberally-motivated attacks. Coulter argues that America's current problems stem from fifty years of liberal, Democratic treason. That her book became a national bestseller testifies to the continuing depth of such conspiratorial thinking in American life.

worked against true bipartisanship in the national interest, and made more difficult meaningful public discussion of complex critical issues. They still do—now more than ever.

Most troubling about McCarthyism is what it says about the institutions, especially the political system and the press, that are supposed to protect the public from demagogic abuses—and what it says, too, about how sorely the public requires such protection. For these and other reasons, although McCarthy and the leading players of his time—Truman and Acheson, Eisenhower and Nixon, the Kennedy brothers and LBJ, Cohn and Schine, Stalin and Mao—have long since passed from the scene, McCarthyism remains a story without an ending.

Chapter

TWENTY-THREE

Parallels

*History teaches that grave threats to liberty often come
in times of urgency . . . The World War II [Japanese-
American] detention camp cases and the Red Scare
and McCarthy-era internal subversion cases are only
the most extreme reminders.*

**—Supreme Court Justice Thurgood Marshall, in *Skinner v.
Railway Labor Executives' Association*, 1989**

*We've cleared whole forests of paper developing procedures
for these tribunals, and no one has been tried yet. They just
ended up in this Kafakaesque sort of purgatory.*

**—The Pentagon's deputy general counsel for intelligence,
speaking in October 2004**

T he parallels between past and present raise the oldest of
democratic dilemmas: how to safeguard the nation's security without jeopardizing its liberties. They tell a terrible,

and terribly familiar, story: how fear can produce abuses that damage individuals and dishonor America in the name of making both safer. During the McCarthy era, the profiling of people perceived as national security threats became commonplace. Then, suspected Communists were profiled— artists, Jewish scientists and intellectuals, and foreigners— and subjected to imprisonment or blacklisting. Today, another type—Muslim males—has been subjected to profiling, resulting in massive detention "sweeps" eerily similar to the dragnet arrests that grew out of the Great Red Scare hysteria in the aftermath of World War I.

The ground was still smoldering around the World Trade Center site and part of the Pentagon when the Justice Department, with its leader, Attorney General John Ashcroft, aggressively setting the administration's ideological tone, sought expanded powers to investigate terrorists on American soil. The result, the USA Patriot Act, made changes in more than fifteen federal statutes and had an especially profound impact on Muslims, as it permitted indefinite detention without trial.

On November 9th, 2001, under authority of an Ashcroft directive, federal and other law enforcement officials were ordered to search out and interview Muslim and Arab men between the ages of eighteen and thirty-three who had legally entered the United States on nonimmigrant visas in the past two years. (This came after Ashcroft ordered the FBI to launch a nationwide sweep of Muslim men suspected, however tenuously, of links to terrorism.) The government's November search list was compiled solely on the basis of national origin; all those selected came from countries the U.S. had linked to terrorism. An American Civil Liberties Union (ACLU) report tells what happened next:

> Unannounced, the FBI descended upon thousands of Arabs, Muslims, and South Asians at their workplaces, homes, universities, and mosques. Although called "voluntary," the interviews were inherently coercive and few felt free to refuse. The FBI agents, sometimes accompanied by immigration officials, asked questions about sensitive activities protected by the First Amendment such as religious practice, mosque attendance and feelings toward the United States.

The second round of Ashcroft-ordered sweeps began in March 2002, when the Justice Department announced that three thousand more Arab, Muslim, and South Asian men legally in the U.S. as visitors or students would be called in for questioning. The federal government asked local police to assist in this dragnet. While these interrogations were taking place, hundreds more Arab and Muslim men continued to disappear into detention as a result of the original roundup.

In June 2002, after Ashcroft announced the implementation of NSEERS, the National Security Entry-Exit System, a third set of regulations and requirements were enforced as counterterrorism measures. One of the most ambitious aspects of this program was called "Special Registration." To quote an ACLU study published in February 2004, "Sanctioned Bias: Racial Profiling Since 9/11":

> In a massive operation reminiscent of the Nazi's requirements for Jews living in Germany and countries under German occupation, all male nationals over the age of fifteen

from twenty-five countries were ordered to report to the government to register and be fingerprinted, photographed and questioned. With the exception of North Korea, all targeted countries are Arab and Muslim. Despite the fact that the government gave no individualized notice for this poorly publicized requirement, all those who failed to register were made vulnerable to deportation and criminal penalties.

The ACLU denounced the plan as a thinly veiled effort to trigger discriminatory deportations of immigrants. In one year, the Special Registration program registered 83,310 foreign nationals, placing 13,740 into deportation proceedings. Included in the Patriot Act were secrecy provisions that allowed courtrooms to be closed during immigration proceedings in which Muslim immigrants faced detention and deportation. Lawyers representing detained Muslim immigrants were unable to learn whether evidence against their clients had been obtained under the act's provision granting government agents the power to conduct secret surveillance. As the ACLU noted, "Not a single one of these individuals was ever publicly charged with terrorism," adding:

> The human costs of our government's ethnic profiling policies are incalculable: hard-working, law-abiding men suddenly finding themselves shackled hand and foot, held incommunicado in solitary confinement for months at a time; families separated; homes and businesses lost; and lives turned upside down. For many, the greatest loss of all was the bitter discovery that their adopted country, which promised freedom and opportunity, no longer wanted them.

The exact number of men picked up under the PENT-TBOM (Pentagon/Twin Towers Bombing) sweep after 9/11 is not known. The United States Justice Department simply "stopped reporting the cumulative totals after the number reached approximately 1,200," an official told the department's own investigators, "because the statistics became confusing." The best estimate, compiled three years later through exhaustive investigation by the ACLU and other civil rights groups, is the one cited by author David Cole: five thousand. In the Great Red Scare dragnet, occurring under orders of Attorney General A. Mitchell Palmer in the wake of the terrorist bombings of 1919, at least five thousand foreign nationals were rounded up and imprisoned. More than eighty years later, in the wake of 9/11, an estimated five thousand foreign nationals were imprisoned under orders of Attorney General John Ashcroft. Of those detainees, not one was convicted of a terrorist crime.

"What's the record there? Zero convictions for terrorism," Professor Cole of Georgetown University Law Center, and author of *Enemy Aliens: Double Standards and Constitutional Freedoms in the War on Terrorism,* told Ray Suarez of the *NewsHour with Jim Lehrer* immediately after the 2004 election. "So I think you see a roundup of exactly the same size, if not larger than the Palmer raids—with the same results. With the Palmer raids they found no actual terrorists. And the same thing is true here with respect to the foreign nationals who were targeted."

Of Ashcroft, Cole said: "This is an attorney general who treated dissent and criticism as if it was treason, who launched the largest campaign of ethnic profiling we've seen in this country since World War II, who . . . treated judicial review and congressional oversight as inconvenient obstacles to getting the job done. I think John Ashcroft essentially repeated the Palmer Raids. I think you can call them the Ashcroft Raids."

———

The multiple, often brutal, abuses suffered by aliens thrown into high security U.S. prisons in the wake of the 9/11 attacks cannot be categorized as a parallel with the McCarthy era. They were far worse than anything that happened then. These abuses led to a yearlong investigation by the U.S. Justice Department's Office of the Inspector General (OIG). The language in the Inspector General's final report is measured, the tone judicious, but the documented facts are devastating.

Not surprisingly, the results of the OIG's investigation* attracted little notice, for they were made public as United States armed forces were invading Iraq in April 2003. I didn't obtain and read the report until a year later. By then, prison abuses in Afghanistan and at the U.S. Guantanamo Bay base in Cuba as well as the horrific incidents at the Abu Ghraib prison in Baghdad had been revealed—at least some had been exposed. Toward the end of 2004, the International Red Cross disclosed new evidence that it said was "tantamount to

———

*The September 11 Detainees: A Review of the Treatment of Aliens Held on Immigration Charges in Connection with the Investigation of the September 11 Attacks, Office of the Inspector General, U.S. Dept. of Justice, April, 2003. Investigators interviewed such top officials as the Attorney General, the FBI director, the head of the Immigration and Naturalization Service, and the director of the Bureau of Prisons, as well as many others.

torture" of prisoners held in Cuba; additional details of mistreatment of prisoners, not only in Iraq, Afghanistan, and Cuba, but in other nations, have continued to surface. These more recent revelations documented cases in which U.S. intelligence services handed over prisoners to officials of other nations where torture routinely occurs.

In studying the year-old Justice Department document, which is more than two hundred pages long, plus extensive appendices and glossaries, I was startled to discover not only the similarities between domestic and international prison abuses in the aftermath of 9/11 but also, as I've noted, how strikingly they resembled the abuses that took place during the first Great Red Scare. I was startled, too, by how much they reflected the mind-set of the McCarthy era.

Even as the domestic dragnet was taking place, an extraordinary new system of justice bypassing the federal courts, constitutional guarantees of due process, and the Geneva Conventions stipulation on the humane treatment of prisoners of war was being imposed in utmost secrecy from the highest levels of the United States government.

Not until a week before the presidential election of 2004, and more than three years after implementation of the new system, did the public learn that a small group of senior White House officials considered their plan, as the *New York Times* reported, "so sensitive that [they] kept its final details hidden from the president's national security adviser, Condoleeza Rice, and Secretary of State Colin Powell . . . It was so urgent, some of those involved said, that they hardly thought of consulting Congress." Under this plan, the American military was given the power to detain indefinitely foreigners suspected of terrorism and to prosecute them as "enemy combatants" in tribunals not used since 1942 in World War II. A presidential order, signed by Bush in the White House on November 6, 2001, with virtually no public attention, said that "enemy combatants" such as those imprisoned at the U.S. Guantanamo Bay base in Cuba could be denied basic guarantees of American justice: the right to a lawyer; the right to a public trial; the right to remain silent; the right to a presumption of innocence; the right that one's guilt be proven beyond a reasonable doubt. As written, President Bush's order on November 13, 2001, allowed for closed trials—trials in which a simple majority could sentence a defendant to death. No provisions existed to permit the accused to appeal such a sentence either in the United States, in a foreign country, or in an international forum.

At the time of the *Times*'s article, however, the prisoners continued to languish in jail. The paper quoted the Pentagon's former deputy general counsel for intelligence, Richard Shiffrin, as saying: "We've cleared whole forests of paper developing procedures for these tribunals, and no one has been tried yet. They just ended up in this Kafkaesque sort of purgatory."

This purgatory was the fate, too, of those detainees thrown into prisons inside the United States immediately after 9/11. Prisoners were denied access to lawyers, and held incommunicado under an unprecedented—and quite likely unconstitutional—"communications blackout" order. They were forbidden from making or receiving phone calls, and from sending or receiving mail. Family members were prevented from knowing where, or even if, loved ones were being held, often for weeks or longer after they had been picked up. In many cases, relatives and attorneys attempting to visit detainees were told by prison authorities "that the detainees were not housed" there "when, in fact, the detainees were in the facility." Investigators were told by "several Department officials" that "it soon became clear that many of the September 11 detainees had no immediately apparent nexus to terrorism." One ranking government attorney told investigators "that after reviewing the files of these detainees it was 'obvious' that the 'overwhelming majority' were simple immigration violators and had no connection to the terrorism investigation."

Days, and weeks, passed before the detainees were told what—if any—charges were brought against them. This was after they had been designated persons "of high interest," "of interest," or "of undetermined interest" to terrorism. These broad, vague new FBI categories were applied haphazardly, investigators found. For similarly long periods of time, they were forbidden from making phone calls or receiving visitors or mail.

But although by far the greater number of those picked up ultimately were found to have no connection with terrorism generally or with the attacks on the World Trade Center and the Pentagon specifically, under a new "hold until cleared/no bond" policy, all prisoners were lumped together as guilty until proven otherwise. Investigators were unable to learn the origins of this policy—which apparently was never committed to writing—though investigators suggest the policy emanated "at least" from the attorney general. Whatever its origins, it was "clearly communicated" by "a number of high Justice Department officials" to INS and FBI field officials, "who understood and applied the policy." As a consequence, many detainees were not released until months had passed.

For example, investigators examining a sample of prisoners at the U.S. Bureau of Prison's Metropolitan Detention Center in Brooklyn, New York, determined it took FBI headquarters an average of one hundred seventeen days to clear a detainee of any connection to terrorism. It took, on average, another twenty-four days for the facility to be informed by the FBI that a prisoner had been cleared. One detainee entered on October 4, 2001. Two and a half months later, he was cleared by the FBI. One hundred nineteen days after that, he was released from prison. Another prisoner was incarcerated on November 5, 2001. More than six months later, on May 16, 2002, the FBI officially determined he was of "no investigative interest" in regard to either the 9/11 attacks or terrorism in general. Due to an "internal FBI admin[istrative] error," the Bureau of Prisons did not receive FBI notification that he had been cleared until June 13, 2002. He was released that afternoon—seven months after his arrest.

Investigators heard credible allegations that prisoners were slammed against walls and doors, kicked in the side and groin, beaten, dragged across floors by their handcuffed arms or by their necks by guards who also frequently stepped on the chains between their ankle cuffs, causing severe injuries. At least one prisoner was thrown into a cell naked without a blanket. Racial slurs and threats by guards were common: "You will feel pain." "Someone thinks you have something to do with the World Trade Center, so don't expect to be treated well." "You're never going to get out of here." "You're going to die here."

This was happening not in Cuba, Afghanistan, or Iraq, but in the United States. But the public knows even less about these domestic abuses than the ones that had occurred in military prisons overseas.

Prisoners often were not provided adequate medical care or clothing, or even toilet paper or toiletry articles. Cells were illuminated with bright lights around the clock, leading prisoners to suffer from sleep deprivation, "exhaustion, depression, stress, acute weight loss, fevers, panic attacks, rapid heart beat, and reduced eyesight." Guards routinely banged on cell doors in the night, ordered prisoners to "shut up" while they were praying, and interrupted afternoon prayers by conducting a "stand-up count" each day at four P.M. In general, investigators concluded, prisoners were subjected to "prolonged confinement . . . sometimes under extremely harsh conditions."

The OIG report includes many case studies detailing appalling treatment suffered by prisoners. In one of the most disturbing, a prisoner was beaten repeatedly; he was pepper sprayed; his eyes were blackened such that the lids swelled shut; and he was compelled to use a wheelchair after being left with a permanent limp. When he protested to guards that he was unable to get out of his bed, they brought a dog from their canine unit into his cell and told him that if he didn't get up as ordered by the next day they were "going to let the dog loose."

The Justice Department report laconically concludes its account of this incident: "Officers told us that it is not unusual to make rounds with dogs, including in the SDU [Special Detention Unit] area, but denied that they threatened to use the dogs on the detainee."

This incident at a Passaic, New Jersey, prison occurred more than a year before Americans were horrified to see photographs of American soldiers using dogs to intimidate terrified Iraqis at the now-infamous Abu Ghraib prison. In one of the report's refrains, the Justice Department investigators state: *The OIG's Investigations Unit investigated the incident and presented the evidence to the Civil Rights Division, which declined criminal prosecution. The OIG is currently conducting an ongoing administrative investigation of the matter.*

But this was no isolated incident. In concluding that "the evidence indicates a pattern of physical and verbal abuse" in the prisons the inspector general's office investigated, the report also chronicles an official cover-up of abuses. Hundreds of videotapes showing detainees in their cells and being moved to other prison locations were destroyed. These tapes were supposed to be maintained "indefinitely," but that policy was "revised." Consequently, the report reads, "videotapes that could have helped prove or disprove allegations of abuse raised by detainees were not available." This circumstance made it all the more difficult to prosecute. Another reason cited for the failure to prosecute was "the scarcity of medical records documenting injuries and the lack of evidence of serious injuries." Without access to such material, the U.S. Attorney's Office for the Eastern District of New York and the Justice Department's Civil Rights Division were forced to decline criminal prosecutions.

Frustrated in its efforts to obtain concrete evidence that could produce criminal sanctions, and despite the conviction that "there is evidence supporting the detainees' claims of abuses," the Inspector General's office was forced to treat most of the cases as "an administrative matter."

No one was held accountable. The day after the damning report was made public, Attorney General Ashcroft was asked to respond to its shocking allegations of abuse. "We make no apologies," he said. That was that.

———

In addition to deporting more foreign nationals, the U.S. has barred more foreigners from entering. In Joe McCarthy's time, the nation paid a price for denying entry to distinguished scientists and technologists, as well as eminent writers and artists, because of misplaced concern over their political backgrounds or connections. Those refused visas included people with skills needed to develop missiles for the military. In our time, visas have been denied to writers and artists as well as to talented scientists who could redress a new "brain drain" in the United States. Moreover, the Patriot Act required that U.S. colleges and universities monitor their foreign students and scholars to determine that each student was "sufficiently engaged in course studies to dispel suspicion of terrorist activities." Schools were also required to maintain databases about their international students to ensure compliance with these new regulations. For foreign students getting an America visa, these new regulations have created what Harvard's Joseph S. Nye, Jr., called "a nightmare of red tape," a situation in which "horror stories abound." Ever since 9/11, he said, the hassle of getting visas has deterred many foreign student applicants, contributing to "major enrollment declines" at leading research institutions, to the detriment of the nation. "In an effort to exclude a dangerous few," Nye wrote in the *New York Times,* "we are keeping out the helpful many." This time the immigration barriers were erected because of fears not of Communism but of terrorism.

Most of the visa abuses attracted little public note. A few involving celebrities such as the singer Cat Stevens did spark attention. On September 22, 2004, three years after 9/11, Stevens was detained on "national security grounds" after his Washington-bound flight from London was diverted and ordered to land in Bangor, Maine. The singer, who had taken the name Yusuf Islam after converting to the Muslim faith, had posted on his Web site numerous statements opposing terrorist acts, had criticized the 9/11 attacks, and had donated a portion of his music royalties to families of the September 11th Fund. Other than its statement claiming "some relationship"—unspecified—between Stevens and with terrorist activity, the government offered no information as to why he had been singled out. "We are getting a little tired of this kind of Kafkaesque treatment of people, where vague allegations are made and actions are taken against individuals and organizations," said Ibrahim Hooper, spokesman for the Council on American-Islamic Relations. American Muslim leaders, he said, "need to know where the allegations are coming from. I don't think we want to be in a situation where people are denounced by anonymous government officials and labeled as terrorists and that's it—everybody says, 'OK, we don't need any more information.'" Comics had a field day. David Letterman: "President Bush says he's very excited about Cat Stevens. He says it's proving we're winning the war against singer/songwriters." Jay Leno: "Cat Stevens, who is also known as Yusuf Islam, he was denied access into the United States . . . His flight was from London, and it was diverted to Maine. Well, thank God he wasn't allowed in the United States, huh?"

Another telling incident, taking place shortly before the 2004 presidential election, was relegated to an inside page of the *Washington Post.* Some fifty Muslim scholars had filed into a classroom on George Mason University's Arlington campus, Carole Murphy reported, to hear the keynote address for their three-day conference on Islam and modernity. They had to watch the keynote on DVD because their speaker, Tariq Ramadan, could not attend. Ramadan, who had visited the U.S. dozens of times and has denied ever endorsing terrorism, had been given a work visa five months prior so he could become the Henry R. Luce Professor of Religion, Conflict, and Peace Building at Notre Dame's Kroc Institute of International Peace Studies. But to Notre Dame's dismay, the visa was revoked under a section of a new security measure barring entry to foreigners using a "position of prominence . . . to endorse or espouse terrorist activity." "We very much want him here, " said a Notre Dame spokesman after Ramadan was denied entry to the U.S., "and we are holding the position open." In her report on Ramadan's keynote address in absentia to the Muslim scholars, Murphy wrote: "His moderate words sounded like the kind of message U.S. officials would applaud. He urged a serious dialogue on the 'universal values' shared by Islam and the West, and added, 'We should not blame the West for our problems.'"

———

The denial of visas is the least of the problems arising from the fearful aftermath of 9/11 and the heavy-handed, if well-intentioned, attempts to implement security measures at our nation's borders. Numerous abuses involving foreign students, ordinary tourists, and business visitors have occurred, and most of them have either gone unreported, or been buried in brief news accounts. Not until mid-August 2004 did the U.S.

Department of Homeland Security announce a change in its policy governing the treatment of foreigners from twenty-seven industrial nations, including Britain, Germany, and Japan, and only after stories about abuses affecting those nationals were, as the *New York Times* reported, "splashed on television shows and in newspapers in Britain, giving what [Homeland Security] Commissioner Robert Bonner . . . described as a 'black eye' to the United States' reputation."

People from the industrial nations do not require visas to enter the United States for visits of up to ninety days. Numerous travelers from Britain—America's most steadfast ally in the military operations in Iraq—told of being detained, searched, placed in hand and ankle cuffs, and denied the opportunity to call husbands, wives, or lawyers because of, as U.S. officials conceded, "'minor, technical' violations of immigration," such as having overstayed their visit. "Typically," Commissioner Bonner added, "these individuals were handcuffed during the time they were transported to and from detention. In other words, they were treated as criminals." When asked how many travelers had been subjected to such detention and mistreatment, Bonner could not give a figure except to say "the number was significant."

British journalists and distinguished authors were among those ensnared, unaware that they were required to obtain visas under one of several categories that applied to journalists, authors, and students. Journalist Elena Lappin, writing in the *New York Times,* told how upon arriving at Los Angeles International Airport she was denied entry to the United States, detained, handcuffed, body searched, fingerprinted, photographed, interrogated for four hours, and held overnight in a detention cell. Twenty-six hours after landing, she was sent back to England. A month before her ordeal, the award-winning British novelist Ian McEwan was detained after telling immigration officials who questioned him in Vancouver that he was on his way to Seattle to give a speech. He was denied entry for thirty-six hours. The British consulate, an immigration lawyer, two members of Congress, and sponsors of his widely-publicized lecture had to intervene before INS granted McEwan a business entry visa. He began his speech by thanking the Department of Homeland Security "for protecting the American public from British novelists."

Untold numbers of Americans have also run afoul of the new security systems while passing through the nation's airports. Because their names are similar to those of suspected terrorists, they have been placed on security "watch lists." Most of these incidents attract no public attention, and the person entrapped finds it hard to have his or her name removed from the list. That was what happened to Jan Adams and Rebecca Gordon, two middle-aged peace activists who were pulled off a flight while en route to visit relatives in Boston, questioned by authorities for hours before being released, and never told why they had been detained except for a vague mention that they might be on an FBI "no-fly" list. After turning to the ACLU for help, they began the time-consuming process of suing the government to find out more about such no-fly lists. Prominent Americans as well as obscure citizens have found themselves caught in the same bureaucratic net.

Two of many examples: In the fall of 2004, the Republican chairman of the House Transportation and Infrastructure Committee, Don Young of Alaska, became the latest member of Congress to be stopped, interrogated, and mistaken for a terror suspect when he arrived at the Anchorage airport for his usual flight to the nation's capital. Ironically, Young's committee oversaw the Transportation Security Agency that implemented the flight watch list policy. After being held for two hours, Young was also detained in Seattle when he tried to check in for his connecting flight to Washington. One of the most familiar congressional figures, Senator Edward M. Kennedy of Massachusetts, was also stopped from boarding a U.S. Airways shuttle from Washington to Boston in August 2004, questioned, and required to identify himself because his name appeared on the terror suspect list. After a flurry of phone calls, Kennedy was able to fly home—but the same thing happened on his return flight to Washington. As Kennedy related to colleagues on the Senate Judiciary Committee, he had to make three phone calls to Homeland Security Director Tom Ridge to get his name stricken from the list. And that process took several weeks. Far less prominent figures—ministers, students, and members of the American military, among documented cases—had no such influence, or luck.

———

As in McCarthy's day, the press's record in holding the government accountable has been, at best, mixed and, at worst, an abdication of its responsibility as the public's watchdog to check government abuses of power. Too often, as in the McCarthy days, it has accepted without challenge the official government position,* acting as a cheerleader instead of a

———

*In 2004, the nation's two most influential papers, the *New York Times* and the *Washington Post,* in highly critical analyses of their coverage of the government's WMD claims, published scathing examples of their failures to alert the public to the weakness, and falsity, of the government's stated positions during its "rush to war" in Iraq—but this self-criticism came more than a year after combat operations had begun.

critic. Too often it has operated under a specious standard of objectivity that treats conflicting political claims as equal by "balancing" polemical assertions—giving each side the same weight without attempting to determine the truth of either and without calling attention to often flagrant misstatements and outright lies. It's "he says/she says," and thank you viewers/readers for letting us give you their contrary, often false, opinions without any assessment of their accuracy.

As in McCarthy's days, Congress too often has failed to protect the people. Members of both political parties gave the president a virtually free hand in implementing new security measures, and turned a blind eye to legitimate concerns about the danger of civil rights abuses arising out of these laws and regulations.

A classic example of this political abdication of governmental oversight came in the hasty passage of the Patriot Act—an act hardly any member of Congress read before it became law. Under the Patriot Act, the government was given new power, as a civil rights consortium put it, to "read your medical records, screen your credit card bills, search your home or business without telling you, patrol your Internet use, wiretap your phone, spy on you and your house of worship, examine your travel records, inspect your bookstore purchases, snoop on your library records, [and] monitor your political activities."

On October 2, three weeks after 9/11, one of the first mentions of the words "Patriot Act" came in a *Washington Post* article by Dana Milbank. "House Bill Would Expand Federal Detention Powers," the headline read. As Milbank reported, the House was preparing to consider the bill in only a week's time. The same day, the *New York Times* and the *San Francisco Chronicle* reported on negotiations between the House and Senate to craft antiterrorism legislation that would also address concerns about civil liberties. Nonetheless, with one notable exception, little in the initial coverage alerted the public to the potential dangers posed by congressional haste to pass the Patriot Act.

That exception came on October 7, when Patty Reinert, writing from Washington, informed readers of the *Houston Chronicle:* "As lawmakers vote this week on a scaled-back version of the Bush administration's anti-terrorism package, civil libertarians from the left and right warn that Americans still face an unprecedented invasion of privacy that won't necessarily make them any safer than they were Sept. 11." This assessment drew hardly any response—or congressional action. Reinert's article also contained a warning from Nadine Strossen, president of the ACLU: "This legislation is moving through Congress very rapidly, and we need to be careful." Again, no reaction.

A LexisNexis computer search of stories printed in the next four days, produces *no coverage* about the Patriot Act or its Senate counterpart, the USA Act. Then, on October 12, anyone concerned about the implications of these fast-track antiterrorism laws awoke with a surprise on their doorsteps— if, that is, they subscribed to the *Washington Post.* The *Post* reported that shortly before midnight, in a near-unanimous vote, the Senate had passed the USA Act, giving the Justice Department most of the provisions it wanted. The *Post* quoted Senate Judiciary Committee Chairman Patrick J. Leahy, a Democrat from Vermont: "Despite my misgivings, I have acquiesced in some of the administration's proposals because it is important to preserve national unity in this time of crisis and to move the legislation process forward."

Only one senator voted against the bill. "This is one of the ridiculous things they do in Washington," said the lone dissenter, Senator Russell D. Feingold, a Wisconsin Democrat. "They want to intimidate people . . . A number of my colleagues said they thought I was right on the merits but felt they had to vote for it anyway." Feingold had little hope that provisions in the bill would be overturned: "The problem is that these things tend to go only in one direction."

That day the House Republican leadership scrapped the compromise bill reporters had been covering and passed a hastily-drafted version of the Patriot Act similar to the Senate's administration-friendly USA Act. In an editorial printed a few days later, the *Washington Post* assailed the House Republican leaders' action as "a mockery of the normal legislative process." The paper noted that the vote had been forced "on a major anti-terrorism bill that had been anonymously written only the night before and that not even members of the Judiciary Committee had had more than a fleeting chance to read."

A disgusted Representative David R. Obey, also a Wisconsin Democrat, called the revised act "a backroom quick fix," and added: "Why should we care? It's only the Constitution."

On October 26, six weeks after the 9/11 attacks, President Bush signed the USA Patriot Act, an acronym for the official title of the four-hundred-thirty-two-page antiterrorism legislation: *Uniting and Strengthening America by Providing Appropriate Tools Required to Intercept and Obstruct Terrorism Act.*

Two weeks after signing the Patriot Act into law, President Bush issued an order authorizing use of military tribunals for suspected terrorists. For the next three years, as Americans, their elected officials, and the press focused on terrorist alerts at home and military action in Afghanistan and Iraq, occasional news stories reported concerns that the Patriot Act and other presidential executive orders were infringing on civil rights and liberties. The ACLU, for instance, said the Patriot Act threatened Americans' First, Fourth, Fifth, Sixth, Seventh, and Eighteenth Amendment rights.

In 2003, one story briefly attracted attention. Librarians were shredding records in protest of Patriot Act provisions that empowered the FBI to subpoena library patrons' records with court permission and to prevent record keepers from telling anyone, including the person targeted by investigators, about the government search. "When I'm reporting to the [library] board, in my standard oral report to the board," the director of the Santa Cruz, California, Public Libraries, Anne Turner, told the *Sacramento Bee,* "I say we've not been contacted by the FBI in the last month. The month I don't say it, the board will know I *have* been contacted because, of course, I'm not allowed to tell them."

Under this part of the act, libraries and bookstores were directed to produce "tangible things" such as the titles of books an individual had purchased or borrowed, along with names of individuals who had purchased or borrowed certain books. For American librarians, this requirement propelled them into dark places not normally associated with card catalogues and the Dewey Decimal System. And for Americans with longer memories, it recalled the days of Cohn and Schine racing through libraries in search of dangerously "subversive" and un-American material, seeking to ban and burn books and periodicals.

"Sneak and peek" provisions were only one aspect of the Patriot Act that civil liberties groups found alarming. The law also authorized law enforcement to trace the telephone calls or e-mail of people who were not suspected of a crime, and authorized the power to launch investigations of American citizens and permanent legal residents in order to question them about such actions as writing a letter to the editor or attending a rally.

Expressing dissent, or publicly criticizing the president, also could bring legal consequences. In February 2003, Andrew O'Connor, a former public defender in Santa Fe, New Mexico, was arrested by city police officers for questioning by Secret Service agents in Albuquerque. He was on an Internet chat room when someone reported him as saying "Bush is out of control." A similar incident occurred during the 2004 presidential campaign, when the director of the Nebraska branch of the ACLU, Tim Butz, filed a complaint against the Nebraska State Patrol, charging a state trooper and an FBI agent had harassed him after he presented a film critical of the Patriot Act at a community college in North Platte. After showing the film, *Unconstitutional: The War on Our Civil Liberties,* to about seventy-five citizens, Butz was confronted by two troopers and told he "shouldn't come out to these small towns and scare people and stir things up." The local sponsor for the screening was the North Platte Bill of Rights Defense Committee.

Incidents like these, and the concerns of public librarians, led five states and three hundred seventy-three communities across the nation to pass resolutions calling for a complete or partial repeal of the Patriot Act. The resolutions went nowhere. Congress did not act.* Against a backdrop of leaders cynically playing upon public fears through scenes of distant battlefields and terror alerts at home, concerns over civil liberties were eclipsed by feelings of anxiety. Neither did the press sufficiently examine the Patriot Act—either through follow-up stories that documented the ways in which the new law was working, or through reports that placed the latest repressive acts in the historical context of the Alien and Sedition days, the Great Red scare, or McCarthyism. Fear of terrorism, and the "fog of war" that gripped the U.S. after the invasion of Iraq, ruled the day.

————

The manipulation of public opinion continues—as does a true-believer mentality that led officials to make a grievously flawed case about Iraq's supposed weapons of mass destruction into a license for war and an atmosphere in which dissent, however mild, is not allowed. The American band, the Dixie Chicks, whose three members are from Texas, were riding the crest of popularity when they were chosen to sing the national anthem at the Super Bowl in January 2003. Then, during a concert appearance in London, the lead singer expressed mild criticism of the president because of the invasion of Iraq. "Just so you know," she said, "we're ashamed the President of the United States is from Texas." This remark led to national protests, the use of a thirty-three-thousand-pound tractor to

————

*The House of Representatives, acting despite the threat of a White House veto in June 2005, voted to restrict investigators from using the Patriot Act in bookstores and libraries. Unless the Senate followed suit, however, with similar legislative action, these Patriot Act provisions remained in force.

destroy Dixie Chicks CDs; boycotts of their scheduled appearances and the sale of their CDs; lawmakers in South Carolina passing a resolution requesting the singers apologize directly to South Carolinians before being permitted to appear at an upcoming concert in the state; the banning of Dixie Chicks music on forty-two stations controlled by the Milwaukee-based Cumulus Broadcasting; and the televangelist Jerry Falwell denouncing them for saying "unacceptable things about their president."

Evidence of a national state of mind that punishes people for speaking out by labeling them as unpatriotic, or even as traitors, is all around us: from repressive policies promulgated from Attorney General John Ashcroft's Justice Department office in the first Bush administration; to more governmental pronouncements on secrecy; to assertions of new governmental powers to combat terrorism; to political exploitation of fears of terrorism to gain, or expand, political power.

Even before the "new kind of war" in the Persian Gulf, secrecy in the George W. Bush administration was the greatest in any presidency in my lifetime. It has grown more so since. As we've seen, secret trials, drumbeat tribunals, the holding of suspects without formal charges, the denial of citizens' rights to counsel or even to speak to family and friends after their incarcerations, and the vast expansion of the power of the state to eavesdrop on citizens all have been taking place—and now, not half a century ago. Consider, as only one example, the Total Information Awareness program developed out of the Pentagon. This secret project was described as "an experimental system . . . that seeks to scan information on billions of electronic transactions performed by millions of people here and abroad each day, analyze them, and flag suspicious activity for possible investigation."

When news of the project surfaced, it was critically per-
sonified as an Orwellian Big Brother. Reinforcing this impression was the logo the Pentagon had fashioned for the project.
Underneath the motto *scientia est potentia* (knowledge is
power): a human eye, embedded in the peak of a pyramid,
scanning the globe. In the face of public criticism, the Pentagon announced first that it was redesigning the creepy logo,
and later that the project itself was being scrapped.

Nor was this the only secretive project the Pentagon had
been developing. During post-9/11 U.S. combat against
Taliban forces in Afghanistan, a shadowy propaganda unit,
funded by millions of taxpayer dollars and bearing the equally
Big Brotherish name of *Office of Strategic Influence*, had
been created. Its mission was to foster favorable public reactions among U.S. allies and to cultivate disinformation among
foes. A principal method of achieving its goals was the plant-
ing of false news stories in the press. When this propaganda
effort was disclosed, the ensuing controversy led the Pentagon
to say the office was being disbanded.

But the government's attempts to manipulate public
opinion through propaganda operations did not end. In 2005,
the public learned the Bush administration had been paying
journalists, covertly, to promote its policy initiatives; in one
case, a syndicated columnist and TV analyst was paid a quarter of a million dollars for his clandestine public relations efforts on behalf of the administration. It also was disclosed
that government agencies had been producing and distributing videos of so-called news reports about administration
actions—often containing inaccurate information—which
were then used by TV stations across the nation. These
pseudo-news reports, produced at government expense, neither informed the public of the government's involvement

nor acknowledged that the reports lacked in independent assessments about their accuracy. In Congress, and in the General Accounting Office, these efforts were labeled "improper covert propaganda."

———

In drawing parallels between the ages of anxiety sparked by McCarthyism and terrorism, I am *not* suggesting the present period rivals McCarthyism in its most notorious excesses. While John Ashcroft's record, as well as those of Bush/Cheney operatives, uncomfortably recalls the days of McCarthyism, no demagogic Joe McCarthy has arisen to threaten our liberties. And while America's freedoms have been under assault, and in some cases abridged, basically they remain intact. Darkness has not descended on the land. But I am suggesting that the same kinds of dangers are present as in the McCarthy days, with the same kinds of battles being waged, and the same kinds of tactics being employed. And in some ways the present excesses have been worse.

Now as then, Congress and much of the press have been shamefully weak in checking executive branch abuses. However, now, as then, the courts have been the nation's indispensable protector of fundamental rights. In June 2004, for instance, the Supreme Court delivered a stinging rebuke to the president's post-9/11 claim of "inherent authority" to establish military commissions without congressional authorization. That claim had permitted the military to detain so-called enemy combatants without due process. After months of controversy and legal challenges, the Court held that those detainees had the right, previously denied by the administration, to use the U.S. federal courts system to fight their imprisonment.

Another signal court ruling, one of only a small number that has struck at the Bush administration's abuse of fundamental rights, came a week after the presidential election. A federal district court judge in Washington ordered the first military commission prosecution at Guantanamo halted on the grounds that it lacked basic elements of a fair trial and violated the Geneva Conventions.

Despite ideological pressure to impose conformity of thought and stifle dissent, Americans still display an independent cast of mind. To take one example, the Pentagon's uniformed military lawyers have been among the most outspoken critics, albeit internally, of the Pentagon's edicts on dealing with detainees. In another example, growing opposition to the Patriot Act has attracted prominent activists and organizations, from Amnesty International on the Left, to the American Conservative Union (ACU) on the Right. They have joined in strongly calling for major changes in, if not outright repeal of, the legislation.

These are positive signs; but negative ones abound. Nothing demonstrates this more than the disreputable tactics employed in the first post-9/11 presidential campaign. While we don't have a McCarthy, his methods—the Big Lie, fear, smear, and character assassination—live on.

TWENTY-FOUR

A House Divided

*Fear does work. You can make people
do anything if they're afraid.*

**—Jim McDermott, a congressman from the state
of Washington who is also a psychiatrist**

I t was a disgraceful campaign, marked from beginning to
end by smears—even doctored photos*—that evoked the
darkest memories of the McCarthy era.

In 1952, McCarthy accused the Democratic presidential
nominee, Adlai Stevenson, of being "soft on Communism" and
allied with traitors. In daily campaign appearances across the
nation, McCarthy called Democratic Party candidates handmaidens of the Communist conspiracy and the left-leaning

---

*A Bush TV commercial, aired in the closing days of the election, con-
tained digitally reproduced images repeating the same faces of U.S. soldiers, adding to the impression of military support for the president.

media. In the first post-9/11 presidential election, the Democratic nominee, John Kerry, was charged with "aiding and abetting the enemy," called "Commie Kerry," and accused of, if not being "soft on terrorism," then being too weak to combat it, and of being supported by the biased, liberal media.

The McCarthyistic tactics of 2004 were more disturbing than those of half a century ago, for this time they were employed by the president of the United States. Viciously destructive as the 1952 campaign was, the Republican nominee, Dwight Eisenhower, never stooped to character assassination, to leveling charges of un-Americanism, or to suggesting his opponent was unpatriotic. "This kind of rhetoric would never have come into a presidential campaign during the '50s or '60s," American historian Alan Brinkley has said. "It would come from people widely dismissed as extremists—people on the margin of the party who were tolerated or perhaps quietly encouraged—but never from anyone identified as the party. Now it has migrated to the very center of the campaign."

In 2004, President George W. Bush personally attacked Kerry as being weak on defense, a "cut-and-run" politician who lacked the character and the stamina to protect America from terrorists. He charged that Kerry was "blind" to terrorist dangers threatening the nation, and warned that terrorists might be planning an attack before the election. Vice President Dick Cheney, in perhaps the lowest blow of all, implied that a vote for Kerry was a vote for terrorists. Kerry, Cheney said, was incapable of understanding, much less acting upon, the terrorist threat; Cheney raised the specter of terrorists infiltrating American cities with nuclear bombs "to threaten the lives of hundreds of thousands of Americans." If Kerry had been president instead of Bush, Cheney suggested, the

Soviet Union might still be standing, a nuclear-armed Saddam Hussein would still be in power and solidly in control of the Persian Gulf, and the United States would have ceded its national defense to the United Nations. Attorney General Ashcroft suggested that God had spared America from another 9/11-type terrorist attack because President Bush's administration was assisting "the hand of Providence."

Other Republican allies made similar attacks. The Republican Speaker of the House, Dennis Hastert, told a campaign rally that terrorists "would like to influence this election" just as they had influenced the Spanish national election by bombing trains in Madrid. When a reporter asked Hastert if this statement meant he thought terrorists would operate with more comfort if Kerry were elected, he replied: "That's my opinion, yes." Right-wing talk radio ideologues such as Rush Limbaugh also kept sounding the theme that terrorists supported Kerry and the Democrats. At one point, Limbaugh told his audience of some twenty million listeners: "If you want the terrorists running the show, then you will elect John Kerry."

The character attacks were relentless. The Bush camp and its cable TV allies hammered Kerry daily with charges of irresolution and deceitful conduct during his Vietnam service thirty years before. In the closing weeks of the campaign, a conservative advocacy group aired an attack ad featuring photos of Osama bin Laden, Saddam Hussein, and 9/11 hijacker Mohammad Atta, along with a grainy image of Kerry. "These people want to kill us," the commercial's narrator said. "They killed hundreds of innocent children in Russia, two hundred innocent commuters in Spain, and three thousand innocent Americans. Would you trust Kerry against the fanatic killers?" The advocacy group, the Progress for America Voter Fund, was headed by Tony Feather, the political director of George

W. Bush's 2000 presidential campaign and a former student of Karl Rove, the White House's chief political strategist and architect of the 2004 campaign.

Other fearsome pictures marched across TV screens: wolves in the woods, smoking wreckage of the twin towers. They were interspersed with images of staged rallies at which, in the president's case, only people pledged to the candidate (either in writing or by campaign contributions) were permitted to attend. Dissenters were forcibly removed by security guards. Viewers were left with the impression that the cheering crowd represented a true cross section of the electorate. Further adding to the Orwellian attempt to manipulate opinion, candidates habitually spoke against a backdrop of slogans crafted by image merchants to play upon current anxieties: STRENGTH. SECURITY. A SAFER AMERICA.

In the end, as Jim McDermott said, fear worked.

Writing in the *New York Times* the day Bush's victory was decided, Maureen Dowd drew the lesson of the election well: "The president got reelected by dividing the country along fault lines of fear, intolerance, ignorance, and religious rule."*

For the hapless Democratic Party, the 2004 campaign fell into a familiar pattern also seen in the McCarthy era: an inability to fashion a strong, coherent reason for voters to elect its candidates, and a reluctance—indeed, a fear—to confront its rivals forcefully.

Immediately after the Democratic Convention in Boston, Kerry became the target of a shameful right-wing national TV

---

*Bush didn't create the divisive national fault lines; he exploited fault lines that already exist, thus creating even greater ideological fissures.

ad campaign. He was called a traitor—"Commie Kerry"—accused of being a coward, and termed unfit to become the nation's commander-in-chief. In yet another example of McCarthyistic character assassination, the combat medals he had won for valor as the commander of a Swift boat in Vietnam— the Silver Star, the Bronze Star, and three Purple Hearts— were alleged, falsely, to have been improperly awarded through deceitful claims made by Kerry and his shipmates.*

These TV attack ads were sponsored by the Swift Boat Veterans for Truth, a group of Vietnam-era naval veterans who had served on the same kinds of patrol boats as Kerry. The group was funded by Texas Republicans and others with close Republican ties. Its ads became the most successful—and dishonorable—negative commercials of the modern media age, with an impact on the electorate that eclipsed even that of the Willie Horton ads run repeatedly against Michael Dukakis, the Democratic nominee in 1988. Night after night during the 1988 campaign, America's TV screens depicted a stream of prisoners entering and leaving jail through a rapidly revolving door, the camera finally focusing on Willie Horton, a black murder convict who had raped and stabbed a white woman while released from jail under a Massachusetts weekend prison furlough program when Dukakis was governor. Words superimposed over the image informed viewers that hundreds

---

*An even more disgraceful McCarthyistic smear earlier involved Max Cleland, a Democrat, who lost three limbs in combat in Vietnam, became head of the Veterans Administration, and then a U.S. senator from Georgia. He was defeated in 2002 when his conservative opponent, Saxby Chambliss, accused him of being weak on national security. More disreputably, Chambliss, who had gained a deferment from service in Vietnam, ran negative ads linking Cleland with Osama bin Laden.

of such prisoners had escaped, and "Many are still at large." The message was frightening, and was meant to be: dangerous men were on the loose and headed straight for you, all because the liberal Dukakis was soft on crime.

Like the Willie Horton ad, the Swift boat attacks were shot in ominous black-and-white tones. The first wave of ads in early August accused Kerry of deceiving the military to receive his medals. A second batch, aired later that month, used Kerry's anti-Vietnam War testimony to Congress in 1971 to accuse him of betraying his military mates.

The "Swifties," as they came to be called, planned to air their attacks mainly in small and midsize media markets. But by repeatedly airing the commercials on their ideological shoutfests, the cable TV channels' newscasts enabled the attacks to reach a majority of Americans—far more than Joe McCarthy ever reached. Constant repetition over cable outlets had an echo chamber effect that greatly magnified the ads' false charges. In effect, the newscasts gave the commercials free air time, and powerfully affected public attitudes of Kerry and his campaign. Before the first attack ads aired, Kerry and Bush were locked in a statistical dead heat in the polls; three weeks later, a CBS poll showed Bush leading Kerry by eighteen points. In September, three-fourths of respondents nationally said they knew about the Swift boat ads. More than sixty percent thought Kerry was either "hiding something" or "mostly lying" about his Vietnam record.

Compounding the public perception of Kerry as untrustworthy to lead America in a moment of wartime peril was a relentless Republican attack campaign that brilliantly, if disingenuously, persuaded voters he was a "flip-flopper" lacking conviction and principle, a politician who shifted his position on issues with the winds.

Attacks calling Kerry a flip-flopper were repeated so frequently that the charge became an inseparable aspect of Kerry's public image. For example, a LexisNexis computer search of headlines and lead paragraphs printed in major papers over the final six months of the campaign yielded four hundred forty-six articles on the "Swift Boat Veterans for Truth" ads, but a similar search for "flip-flopper" prompted the user to refine his or her query. "Flip-flopper" yielded more than the database's per-search maximum of one thousand documents.

The flip-flopper charges stuck, though they were unfair. Every politician compromises on almost every bill under consideration; the give-and-take necessary to reach an agreement is a central part of the legislative process in a democracy.°

°The "flip-flop" charge is a traditional staple of American political campaigns. In 1952, Adlai Stevenson in a TV ad accused Ike of flip-flopping on whether or not he was fully committed to fighting the Iron Curtain; Nixon used it against McGovern in 1972 after McGovern dropped his running mate; Carter against Reagan on contradictory statements on nuclear proliferation; Bush Sr. and Dole against Clinton in both 1992 and 1996. It was even leveled against Kerry by his then-opponent, Howard Dean, in 2003 when the Dean camp deposited a pair of flip-flops on Kerry's doorstep, and Dean's press spokesmen explained that "Sen. Kerry has been flip-flopping on issues throughout his career and campaign, and we thought we could make things a little more comfortable for him." The real problem for Kerry was the almost total failure of the press to put this charge into political context, explaining, for instance, that when Kerry made his famous remark, "I actually did vote for the $87 billion before I voted against it," he meant he had voted for the bill when it included a provision to reduce tax cuts for the wealthy to pay for it, but voted against it without that amendment. Of course, it was Kerry's failure as a candidate to clarify his remark—or to make it in the first place.

This was not made clear to voters, either by the press and certainly not by the Kerry camp. Neither was the president's own record of changed positions. To cite only a few: Bush opposed, then supported, creation of the Homeland Security Department; opposed, then supported, creation of the 9/11 Commission; opposed, then supported, his national security adviser Condeleeza Rice testifying before the congressional investigation into how repeated warnings and evidence of coming terrorist attacks were ignored before 9/11; opposed, then supported, a constitutional amendment banning gay marriage; opposed, then supported, using the military for nation-building attempts as in Iraq. He also changed positions on, among other things, regulation of air pollution and tariffs for steel manufacturers.

Finally, far too late, Kerry began responding to these attacks and launched ones of his own. He attempted to portray himself as tougher, smarter, and more capable of winning the war on terrorism; he would be more aggressive, he claimed, in seeking out and killing more terrorists. He "had a plan," though in substance it differed little from the course being followed by the Bush administration. Kerry also employed fear as a tactic. He warned, without proof, that the president was secretly planning to reinstate the military draft and order a call-up of U.S. reservists. He even warned that a Bush victory could precipitate a nuclear attack on U.S. soil.

In the end, the Bush campaign's appeal to fear—and its portrayal of Bush as a stronger, more resolute leader in a time of fear—prevailed. But the campaigning ineptitude that cost Kerry the election owed as much to the Democratic Party's response to the Bush administration's use of fear as to that Republican use of fear itself.

In the spring of 2004, Kerry and his campaign strategists consciously refrained from responding to coordinated attacks on his patriotism after he wrapped up the nomination by winning the Iowa primary. Immediately afterward, Republican members of Congress who had also served in Vietnam took to the floor of the House to attack Kerry as "Hanoi John," as a politician whose "true colors" were not "red, white, and blue," and as having engaged in "nothing short of aiding and abetting the enemy." Kerry also refrained from responding to accusations of flip-flopping. Even more disastrous, for weeks in the late summer he ignored the Swift boat TV commercials airing daily throughout the country. When placed alongside the flip-flop allegations, the commercials—greatly magnified by the megaphone cable TV news programs—defined, and demonized, him. He never recovered.

This was not Kerry's fault alone. Democrats, in yet another echo from the McCarthy era, had cowered before the president's post-9/11 appeal. They refused to challenge Bush and his policies—and not only in the 2004 presidential election, but also two years earlier in the first congressional elections after 9/11. So fearful were Democratic leaders in 2002 of seeming unpatriotic by not supporting a president in a time of war—that course would be "political suicide," they privately argued—that they endorsed a congressional resolution granting Bush authority to launch a unilateral strike against Iraq. Uniting behind the president were then-Senate majority leader, Democrat Tom Daschle of South Dakota, and the Democratic House leader, Richard Gephardt of Missouri.

Daschle set the tone for his party. He pointedly refrained

from voicing criticism, but merely asked the president for better consultation and the sharing of information with Congress. When Daschle mildly called on the president to clarify his goals in expanding the war and also to define his terms for success in Iraq, he was accused of undermining the war effort. "How dare Senator Daschle criticize President Bush while we are fighting the war on terrorism, especially when we have troops in the field," stormed Trent Lott, then the Senate's Republican leader. In the House, the powerful Tom DeLay of Texas, attacked Daschle's comments as "disgusting."

Most Democrats fell in line behind their leaders. Fear of being labeled unpatriotic, and of triggering a backlash from voters in their home districts, kept them from debating the war. As a result, while Democrats campaigned on domestic issues in 2002, Republicans ran against terrorism. Republicans portrayed themselves as the bulwark of national security, and won across the board, regaining control of the Senate and picking up eight more seats in the House. This gave left them a 229-to-204 advantage over the Democrats.

Two years later, in the presidential and congressional elections of 2004, history repeated itself. Not only did Bush win; voters gave him a stronger hand in Congress, with Republicans gaining four more Senate seats and adding another four in the House. It was the first time in eighty years that the reelection of a Republican president also brought GOP gains in the House and Senate. Among the losers: Senate Democratic leader Tom Daschle.

———

The way Daschle lost spoke volumes about the fearful currents being stirred by the threat of terrorism, and the ability of the Bush campaign to exploit those fears. So conflicted was Daschle over the war, and so determined not to offend voters, that he ran a campaign TV commercial featuring the president in which the announcer lauded Daschle for having helped the president "forge a consensus to rebuild our military." Yet the South Dakota GOP chairman described Daschle as "an embarrassment" to voters there, saying Daschle had "given aid and comfort to America's enemies." On a special pre-election NBC *Meet the Press* broadcast, moderator Tim Russert pressed Daschle's opponent, former representative John Thune, for his reaction to this kind of McCarthyistic smear. Thune not only defended, but reinforced, the charge. He accused Daschle of using words that "embolden the enemy" and undermine "the morale of our troops."

Tom Daschle became the first leader of the Senate to be defeated since 1952. That was the year Barry Goldwater, with campaign help in Arizona from Joe McCarthy, defeated the Democratic Majority Leader Ernest McFarland, who had strongly opposed McCarthy in the Senate.

The press's failure to make the comparison between the tactics of the McCarthy era and of the election of 2004 was striking. As far as I can tell, the historical analogy was seldom drawn for the public by the army of journalists covering the campaign. A notable exception came not in the mainstream print or TV media, but in a Salon.com online article by Eric Boehlert, entitled "Joe McCarthy Lives." "For the first time in decades," Boehlert wrote, "journalists find themselves reporting on a kind of public character assassination that's reminiscent of McCarthyism." He then quoted a number of respected journalists who had covered the McCarthy era, as well as distinguished historians who remembered its lessons, as bemoaning the fact that the media, as in McCarthy's day, was allowing itself to be used as a conveyer belt for reckless, unsubstantiated charges. "The press can't simply report flat-footed a smearing accusation against somebody's loyalty," said Murray Marder, who did some of the sharpest reporting on McCarthy in the *Washington Post*. "I think the press certainly can recognize quicker than anyone else when a loaded accusation, questioning somebody's loyalty, is coming out. The press should ask the accuser, 'What do you mean? What justification do you have?' That's real work, and it's called journalism."

This kind of accountability reporting was lacking in 2004. Instead, at a time of momentous issues that will define the course of the nation for years, the campaign degenerated into charges that recalled Cold War-era Red-baiting. Despite intense, and heartening, public interest in the election, and a welcome reversal of declining voter participation, too many of the issues were either ignored or insufficiently addressed by the press and our political leaders. Even if the issues were raised, daily personal attacks and relentless negative commercials drowned them out.

The three nationally televised presidential debates, for instance, were serious and substantive. But even in these encounters, not a single question was asked about a number of important topics: Not about the Abu Ghraib horrors or those in Guantanamo Bay and Afghanistan—how they happened, who was responsible, what steps were being taken to prevent their reoccurrence, whether the United States still supported the Geneva Conventions protocols about humane treatment of prisoners.* Not about the makeup of a Supreme Court facing the prospect of historic turnover that will affect the nation's course for decades to come, an issue that drew one reference in the debates. Not about the Bush administration's assaults on civil rights. Not about a real examination of how the nation's leaders had stumbled into the morass of Iraq; how the administration had so miscalculated the support the Iraqi people would give to an American invasion; how U.S. policymakers had failed to produce a realistic assessment of the manpower, materiel, and money required to occupy a land riven by ancient tribal and religious rivalries; how those leading the war on terror planned to respond to other threats with a military stretched to the breaking point. Not about how to pay for the immense needs of an aging America, an America facing historic national and personal debt amid presidential promises to enact more tax cuts that will make the fiscal task of addressing long-term problems like Social Security benefits exponentially more difficult.

As Thomas L. Friedman commented in a *New York Times* analysis of the election:

> At one level this election was about nothing. None of the real problems facing the nation were really discussed. But at another level, without warning, it actually became about

---

*The President's White House counsel, Alberto Gonzales, in a Jan. 25, 2002, legal memo to the president had described the Geneva Conventions strictures on humane treatment of prisoners as "obsolete" and "quaint," opening the door to torture of prisoners held by Americans in Iraq, Afghanistan, and Cuba. A week after his reelection, Bush nominated Gonzales to replace John Ashcroft as Attorney General.

everything. Partly that happened because so many Supreme Court seats are at stake, and partly because Mr. Bush's base is pushing so hard to legislate social issues and extend the boundaries of religion that it felt as if we were rewriting the Constitution, not electing a president . . . Despite an utterly incompetent war performance in Iraq and a stagnant economy, Mr. Bush held onto the same basic core of states that he won four years ago—as if nothing had happened. It seemed as if people were not voting on his performance. It seemed as if they were voting on which team they were on. This was not an election. This was a station identification. I'd bet anything that if the election ballots hadn't had the names Bush and Kerry on them but simply asked instead, 'Do you watch Fox TV or read the *New York Times*?' the Electoral College would have broken exactly the same way."

The Bush campaign had convinced many Americans that being pro-war and antiterrorism meant being on the president's team.

———

Despite claims that voters had given him a "mandate," Bush was reelected with the smallest margin for a presidential incumbent since Woodrow Wilson in 1916. Wilson's 49.2 percent of the popular vote and 277 Electoral College ballots remain the closest for a president winning a second term in U.S. history. Most reelected presidents receive landslide proportions the second time around. For example: In 1936, FDR won 60.8 percent of the popular and 523 of the electoral votes. In 1956, Eisenhower won 57.4 percent of the popular and 457 of the electoral votes. In 1964, LBJ won 61.1 percent of the popular and 486 of the electoral votes.* In 1972, Nixon won 60.7 percent of the popular and 520 of the electoral votes. In 1984, Reagan won 58.8 percent of the popular and 525 of the electoral.

Bush won with only 50.8 percent of the one hundred twenty-two million popular votes—a margin of 2.5 percent over Kerry's popular total—and by 286 to 252 of the electoral ballots. Narrow as his victory was, no amount of rationalization could obscure the cold reality for Democrats: they had sustained a crushing defeat, and one that threatened them with becoming a permanent minority party lacking the strength to affect the American future. This, at a time when the nation appeared moving even more toward the Right, with conservatives empowered—and determined—to fundamentally reshape the nation's social and economic fabric as much as FDR was able to do during the New Deal. The newly installed conservative congressional Republican majority, backed by President Bush, immediately initiated a bold, if not radical, attempt to transform their electoral gains into basic changes in the role and makeup of America's government. They set about achieving this goal by seeking to privatize Social Security, further deregulating longstanding government rules affecting business, and opening public lands to private development. Most dramatic of all, in concert with the strong backing of the religious Right which exploited an emotional right-to-life case involving a brain-dead Florida woman named Terry Schiavo kept alive in a vegetative state for fifteen years on artificial life support, they launched an aggres-

---

*I count this as a second-term election, following the term Johnson fulfilled after the Kennedy assassination.

sive campaign to transform the nation's judiciary by installing rigidly ideological nominees to the courts and curbing the historic checks-and-balances independent role of the Supreme Court. They would do this by applying a litmus test that would ban or remove justices who did not meet their agenda of having religiously acceptable judges whose rulings conformed to the ideological views of the majority in the legislative branch of government. Whether the Democrats can summon the will, and the unity, to counter these moves will determine the shape of Bush's second term, and, perhaps, the American social and political future.

No sooner had the presidential votes been counted than the mythmaking began. Aside from that of Bush's "mandate," the central myth was that Bush won because voters shared his, and the Republicans' "moral values" over those of Kerry and the Democrats. This, at least, was the message pulled from a misleading media consortium exit poll conducted on election day.

The inclusion of a single question on a survey of seven thousand voters leaving their polling places quickly led to this accepted—and wrong—interpretation of the election outcome. Voters were asked: "Which one issue mattered most in deciding how you voted for president?" Of the seven options given, "moral values" was chosen by the most respondents; 22 percent picked it. Of respondents who voted for Bush, 80 percent cited "moral values" as their determining reason. Following "moral values" in importance in the poll results were "economy/jobs," picked by 20 percent; "terrorism," at 19 percent; Iraq, 15 percent; and health care, taxes, and education in a cluster of single digits.

Thus was born the great "moral values" explanation for

the post-9/11 American political mood. Moral values had sup-posedly trumped Iraq, terrorism, the economy, and health care in importance to the American people.

Such a broadly generalized question is near to worthless in determining voter attitudes, however. Which morals, which values? Yours or mine? The morality taught by Jesus, Moses, Mohammed, Buddha, Confucius, or agnostics and atheists? The morality of sanctioning torture, of imprisoning innocents, of lying about the reasons for launching a preemptive war, of trampling on civil rights and liberties, of helping the power-ful at the expense of the powerless?

Leading pollsters attempted to set the record straight. Gary Langer, the polling director for ABC News, had been among the group that designed the exit poll issue options list and from the beginning had objected to including the all-encompassing "moral values" category. As he explained in a *New York Times* op-ed column immediately after the elec-tion, "this hot-button catch phrase had no place alongside de-fined political issues on the list of most important concerns in the 2004 vote. Its presence there created a deep distortion— one that threatens to misinform the political discourse for years to come."

The same exit poll had been proven disastrously wrong election night after its false projections created the impres-sion of a clear-cut victory for Kerry. Still, the "moral values" explanation continued to be widely expressed, and believed. Bush operatives and cultural conservatives assiduously peddled this theory to "prove" that a hidden political force, driven by previously undetected Christian "values voters," had turned out in great numbers for Bush. As Tucker Carlson articulated this new "truth" on his CNN *Crossfire* program: "Three days after the presidential election, it is clear that it was not the war on terror, but the issue of what we're calling moral values that drove President Bush and other Republicans to victory this week."

Giving this theory credence was the fact that citizens in eleven so-called red—or Republican—states had voted for ballot initiatives banning gay marriage. The emotional public reaction to the gay marriage issue—and to abortion and stem-cell research—unquestionably aided Bush and contributed to the sharp polarization over so-called social issues that the election outcome revealed. But the actual election statistics punctured the myth that Bush won because of a massive turnout of church-going, social conservative, religious Right voters. In 2004, the percentage of voters who attended church weekly—forty-two—was exactly the same as in 2000. Of those church goers, Bush received 58 percent of their votes in 2004, an increase of only a single percentage point from 2000. Instead, Bush won more votes from those who never went to church: he received 4 percent more of their votes in 2004 than in 2000.

Bush *was* aided by the intense voter mobilization effort of evangelical Christians, which was central to Karl Rove's strategic plan. Therein lay another myth punctured by the election of 2004: that a significant increase in voter turnout would unquestionably benefit Democrats. Democrats *did* significantly increase their voter turnout, attracting nearly seven million new voters, or 16 percent more than four years earlier. But the Republicans turned out more than ten million new voters, up 23 percent from the last presidential election. This fact spawned yet another myth: that the press had missed this supposed determinative factor of the 2004 election. As

CNN's Candy Crowley said in a speech, "All of us missed this moral values thing."

This was also untrue. Coverage of Rove's plan to mobilize Christian conservatives was visible and continuous in 2004, although much more so in the mainstream print media than in TV reportage. It was prominently reported that Rove had set a goal of attracting four million more evangelicals in 2004 than in 2000; that he and other White House operatives had been meeting with Christian conservatives and urging them to turn over their church directories and identify friendly organizations in key swing states; that an intensive effort was being made to accomplish these ends. Numerous stories highlighted the fact that values could be a central campaign theme.*

---

*Two examples: in the *Los Angeles Times,* July 12, under the headline "Initiatives to Ban Gay Marriages Could Help Ballot Measures in Key States; Strategists Hope Ballot Measures in Electoral Battlegrounds Will Boost Conservative Turnout," Janet Hook reported: "Same sex marriage remains a potent political issue because the segment of the population that is concerned about it cares so intensely. GOP pollster Bill McInturff said . . . the issue may rouse potential Bush supporters who need an extra shove out the door on election day . . . as well as the 4 million Christian conservatives who did not vote in the 2000 elections, to the frustration of Bush political strategist Karl Rove." In the *Christian Science Monitor,* on July 16, under the heading, "Early Signs of a Values Campaign," Peter Grier and Liz Marlantes reported: "To the GOP, references to abortion, opposition to gay marriage, and other positions on hot-button social issues may be a way of keeping core conservative voters happy while attempting to woo some conservative Democrats." See also the front-page stories in the *New York Times* and *Los Angeles Times* on Sept. 4 at the end of the GOP convention, "A Hidden Swing Vote: Evangelicals" (N.Y.) and "Christian Conservatives Leave Convention in Great Spirits" (L.A.), or the meticulously reported *Washington Post* analysis on Oct. 25, "Politics and Pulpit Combine to Sway Swing-State Voters."

None of this should have come as a surprise. The rise of the so-called religious Right—from the moral majority to televangelists—has been extensively reported and commented upon. For twenty-five years it has been a central aspect of American politics, and a critical factor in the gathering conservative ascendancy. Ronald Reagan courted and won these voters with his appeals to "flag, faith, and family." Long before Karl Rove, Republican strategists were skillfully targeting evangelicals and fundamentalists with the goal of mobilizing a group of Americans that traditionally had voted the least into a formidable, though by no means a majority, political force.

Then as now, the message crafted to win them was fueled by appeals to anxieties and prejudice and fears: fears of a "coarsening of the culture"; of courts "coddling criminals"; of expanded rights for gays, lesbians, African-Americans, Native Americans, and abortion advocates; of a "liberal elite" in New York, Washington, and Hollywood and a media out of touch with and contemptuous of "traditional values"; of an America besieged by alien forces and un-Christian beliefs. These concerns certainly played a role in the 2004 election, but they were neither new nor decisive.

The real story of the moral values factor in 2004 was not that Americans were suddenly shocked into political action by the questions of whether abortion or same-sex marriages should be legal. They were troubled by something more elusive, and powerful: fear of threats external and internal, real and imagined; threats from terrorists lurking in the shadows; threats from Americans practicing "immoral" acts around them; threats from Americans deemed unpatriotic and irreligious; threats to the accepted "American way of life" by "un-American" elements of society. In this fear-driven environment, the road to political office, Oval or otherwise, was through appeals to voters' visceral emotions and deep-seated anxieties.

Joe McCarthy understood this well, and played upon the same kinds of fears. With his witch hunts, his hounding of homosexuals, his sowing of suspicions of enemies within, his appeals to Christian conservatives by warning of godless Communism and atheistic beliefs, his targeting of the aliens among us, his attacks on those who didn't conform to the accepted view of what was "normal," he carved a divisive path that others could follow, and did.

In the end, the 2004 presidential election came down to three elements: Bush and the Republicans were far better at expressing what they stood for than the Democrats, who seemed to be for everything—and nothing. In the first post-9/11 election, the specter of terrorism and concern over national security overshadowed every other issue. And most crucial, employing fear as a factor in gaining, or holding, political power works as well—or better—in the new millennium as in the old.

Epilogue

THE AGE OF ANXIETY

Walking the Tightrope

T wo days after his reelection, in only his second news conference of the year, George Bush thanked his fellow citizens for giving him new political capital—which he intended to spend, he promised. How wisely and how well he does that will determine the course of the United States for years, if not decades, after his inauguration on January 20, 2005.

Four years before, after losing the popular vote but even more decidedly prevailing in the Supreme Court in the closest and most divisive election since 1876, the president had pledged to be "a uniter, not a divider." That promise was not fulfilled in his early months in office, but fate intervened in the form of the flames and wreckage of 9/11 to give him a historic new opportunity. Every American will forever remember the shock and the deep emotions stirred by the terrorist attacks of that day. In a millisecond, the United States was transformed from a divided society into the most united one since the attack on Pearl Harbor. Americans rallied behind their president; his approval ratings soared to the highest levels ever recorded in public opinion surveys.

The scenes I witnessed in New York only days after 9/11 remain indelible.

Prompted perhaps by my old reporter's instinct to witness events firsthand, after taking the train to New York from Washington (all planes were grounded), I immediately hailed a cab to drive me down the West Side Highway to the lower end of Manhattan. Dense clouds of smoke were still rising from the ground. All along the way, firefighters and rescue workers—many slumped in fatigue, covered with dust and grime, their heads in their hands—sat beside their vehicles flanking the Hudson River. As we drew closer to the vast wreckage that occupied the World Trade Center grounds, I saw unbroken lines of young people. They were wildly cheering the rescue workers, holding up signs that said, "our heroes" and "our angels," and passing out bottles of water. It was an incredibly powerful scene, one that inspired in me a fierce surge of pride in my fellow countrymen and women, and a belief that out of this tragedy a more unified, mature America was being forged.

In the days that followed, this belief was reinforced as Americans joined in displays of patriotism and emotional rallies supporting their leaders and their country. Yes, some of the flag waving was excessive, and some was motivated by a crass commercial desire to cash in on patriotic feelings. But I believed we were witnessing something more profound: a more tempered patriotism—hard-eyed, not jingoistic—born of an America that had suffered and survived the bloodiest day in its history, an America ready to unite, confront common problems, and put aside its obsession with frivolous around-the-clock news media scandal presentations, trivial "reality TV" mass entertainment, and get-rich-quick dreams of what I have called the "bubble years" of the 1990s.

These memories of 9/11 now belong to a vanished America. The hope that the shock of the terrorist attacks would propel the nation into a more realistic, tough but tolerant era has not been realized. The president squandered the historic opportunity—presented by the enormous national unity after 9/11, and the near-universal backing of the American people—to bring the nation together in common purpose to deal with immensely complex long-term problems. Instead of being a uniter, he was a divider. Bush's first term was not that of a consensus builder, nor of a "compassionate conservative." He never asked Americans to unite by sharing common sacrifice. He never issued a call for greater public service, a summons to the best in us, not the worst.* Other than pledging to kill the terrorists wherever they existed, and bellicosely taunting "them" to "bring it on," he never tried to prepare the country for what to expect in the years to come. He never articulated clearly defined goals for the future. He governed narrowly, stubbornly, ideologically, arrogantly.

---

*Five months into his second term, Bush did deliver a welcome, if belated, call to public service. During a Calvin College commencement address in Grand Rapids, Michigan, May 21, 2005, he cited as his theme Tocqueville's *Democracy in America* as providing an "agenda for our time." He urged the graduates and their generation "to serve a cause greater than yourself." In asking them to consider whether to "be a spectator or a citizen?", he counseled that "to make a difference in this world, you must be involved."

Now, the problems he and America confront are more difficult—and more dangerous—than they were four years ago. Only the most optimistic, or naïve, can believe that Americans are more secure now than then, or, despite Bush's cocky and vastly premature boast of "mission accomplished," that the "war on terrorism" is being won.

The hard evidence, played out daily before our eyes, is that our military actions in Iraq have engendered more hatred, more terrorism, more suicide bombers. Whether the U.S. invasion and occupation of Iraq ultimately leads to a welcome new era of democracy and freedom in the Middle East, as the president has hopefully expressed in the wake of free elections in Iraq early in 2005 and the stirring of reform movements in Lebanon, Egypt, Palestine, and Saudi Arabia, will not be known for years, and probably decades. However history's final judgment on these events, an interim assessment on the conception, rationale, and execution of the U.S.'s preemptive invasion already has been rendered. Collectively, it was a political, military, diplomatic blunder. At the least, it left the United States more isolated in the world than at any time in memory. If the end result emboldens terrorists to intensify their attacks abroad, for Americans at home this means more anxieties and more fears will affect their thoughts and actions.

———

In looking ahead, I see three areas to be examined: the political system, the media, and the legacy of the war on terror.

Despite the preoccupation with red vs. blue America, there is nothing new about a divided America. Regional, racial, religious, ethnic, economic, educational, and class divisions have always afflicted this most pluralistic and diverse society—and always will. The question is whether these social, cultural, and political divisions are more severe than in the past, and, if so, what to do about them.

One of the glories of American democracy is that citizens have the right to associate with whom they wish, and to live where they desire—so long, of course, as they do not deny their fellow citizens similar opportunities. What has developed in recent decades, however, is an America in which increasingly large groups of citizens have less contact with other elements of society—urban vs. exurban, rural vs. metropolis, inner city vs. gated community, college vs. high school, blue collar vs. white collar, military vs. civilian—and thus less understanding of the beliefs and, yes, values of their fellow countrymen and women. And this was the state of the nation before post-9/11 fears intensified the sense of a sorely divided America. America's new divisions are born of fears and anxieties that deepen our differences, make us mistrust each other more, sow suspicions that further drive us apart, and force us to draw inward.

No easy method for breaking down these barriers exists, but I have long (for at least twenty years) advocated compulsory national service as one possible remedy. As a price of the privilege of citizenship, every American upon reaching the age of eighteen would be obligated to serve for six months in some form of public service. This could mean working in a drug prevention program, a library, a hospital, an environmental cleanup effort, or serving in a branch of the armed forces. It's not a panacea, but at least millions of young Americans would be exposed to people they would not otherwise know. They might even develop a greater appreciation for shared public service and a commitment to the greater society. The alternative is to do nothing, to continue to sit back while others do the work and take the risks.

Beyond this, the political system appears broken. In a period of bitterly partisan divisions, heightened by fears and uncertainties, sternly ideological one-party dominance has emerged. The result is an inevitable arrogance of power and an absence of political accountability. Abominable continued redrawing of congressional districts to preclude genuine election contests only worsens this condition. The House of Representatives, by constitutional design the chamber closest to the people because its members are elected every two years, is approaching a state in which elections don't matter. Its incumbents are virtually unbeatable; in 2004, accelerating a long-term trend, only four of four hundred thirty-five House incumbents lost. In the words of my colleague, David S. Broder, the House now operates as a "House of Lords"—a power unto itself, impervious to opposition, functioning without the check of popular rebuke.

It was this arrogant cast of mind that led Republican House leaders to demonstrate their disdain for public opinion immediately after their 2004 election gains by seeking to eliminate decades-old House rules drawn to insure representatives' high ethical conduct. The GOP leaders urged members to change a basic rule that enabled colleagues to admonish fellow lawmakers for ethical infractions. Under their plan, members could keep their positions of power even if they were indicted for criminal offenses. Republican leaders also proposed redrawing conflict-of-interest guidelines that restricted lawmakers from accepting foreign and domestic trips from groups interested in legislation before the House.

These acts of blatant self-interest ultimately triggered a political reaction stemming from revelations concerning the close ties of House Majority Leader Tom DeLay of Texas to lobbyists, foreign trips he made that were funded by private groups dealing with the federal government, and huge salaries paid his wife and daughter from fundraising allies of the congressman. The growing controversy eventually forced Republican House leaders to remove changes in ethics rules governing its members they had earlier imposed. DeLay had further engendered intense controversy by his strong attacks on the federal judiciary in the wake of the Terry Schiavo incident. The *New Yorker*'s Hendrick Hertzberg drew the political lesson of the situation by linking DeLay's attack on the courts to the larger conservative agenda: "So there you have it," he wrote, "the DeLay agenda: no separation of church and state, no judicial review, no right to privacy. Next to this the President's effort to repeal the New Deal social contract by phasing out Social Security is the mewing of a kitten. DeLay may stay or DeLay may go. But the real danger is not DeLay himself. It's DeLay's agenda. It's his vision. It's his 'values.'"

Witnessing these kinds of dismal examples of lowered political standards makes me yearn for candidates who express a militant but wise and tempered Americanism, such as Theodore Roosevelt's "Speak softly and carry a big stick"; or who issue bold calls for social and economic justice while battling for the people, as did the La Follettes and their Progressive followers; or for an Eisenhower who would really attempt to rally Americans to reject extremism by forming a new political coalition composed, as he said in private rage at McCarthy's demagoguery, of all the sensible, independent-minded people in the great middle of American life.

I yearn, too, for an American politics that presents fierce debates of issues without descending into the hateful, and destructive, invective that so often characterizes the electoral process. As we've seen, demagogues such as McCarthy and his successors have so deprecated the term "liberal" that most politicians shun it as a kiss of death. That the United States is a liberal democracy, born of the liberal ideas of the western Enlightenment—tolerance, independence, the rejection of rigid religious or political orthodoxy, respect for facts and knowledge—is seldom expressed. Similarly, those on the left too often employ the same venom in characterizing all conservatives as ignorant, zealous hatemongers, deserving of scorn for their lifestyles and religious values. America's present ideological and cultural divide is often presented as though all Americans in the great heartland possess dramatically different attitudes than those along the coasts and the industrial north. This is simply not true; I say this after having spent a great deal of some forty years of my professional time talking to Americans in their homes and offices in all areas of the nation, attempting to fathom these elusive common denominators of thought that bind, as well as divide, us.

In railing against "the artillery of the press" leveled against his administration, Thomas Jefferson, the greatest exponent of a free press, complained that America could not then be governed with the press—or without it. Jefferson's remark about the promises and problems of the press appears as pertinent today as it was two hundred years ago.

At a time with so much at stake, the quality, and reliability, of public information becomes ever more important. Instead, we have a mass media that too often offers a daily menu of ignorance and fear, especially on twenty-four-hour cable TV news. By failing to provide essential information, the media exacerbates national divisions and endangers the democracy it is supposed to serve. The years since 9/11 have produced some of the best reporting in my lifetime—and some of the worst, notably on ideological cable outlets such as Fox News.

The trouble stems from both the new media and the old. The new encompasses the rise of the twenty-four-hour cable TV channels, the expanding reach of the Internet, and the army of bloggers who fill the electronic ether with reports and commentary at times incisive and valuable, at other times wildly inaccurate. In the midst of the rapid reshaping of broadcast and print operations, with accelerating corporate consolidations and bottom-line management favoring entertainment over news, an undeniable erosion of standards for fairness and accountability has occurred.* As daily newspapers shrink in numbers and readership, and the audience of the traditional TV networks declines, a vacuum has been created. Filling it are the ideological cablecasts offering cheap sensations and false accusations that further divide us. They have a right to be wrong, of course, but as more and more Americans get their news from these outlets, damage is being done to the essential role of a free press: to provide

---

*An ominous development in the 2004 campaign, illustrating the danger of ideological media monopoly control, came when the Sinclair Broadcast Group, owner of the largest number of TV stations in the nation, ordered all 62 of them to air a patently biased program attacking John Kerry's Vietnam record in the closing days of the campaign. It was a clear case of political propaganda intended to influence the election by employing the publicly-owned airwaves. This took place at the same time that the government was aggressively embarked on a multi-million-dollar "covert propaganda" effort of its own to manipulate print and broadcast presentation of "news" reports, analyses, and commentary with false accounts produced at government expense and provided to, and used by, legitimate news outlets nationwide.

reliable, substantive information so citizens can make informed decisions.

For years, the idea that the national TV networks could supply the basic news of the world in a mere twenty minutes of nightly broadcasts was hopelessly inadequate; it is even more so now as ever-more complicated issues arise that demand fuller exploration. The media is not meeting this challenge. As a result, the American public is receiving either inadequate, inaccurate, or biased—and government manipulated—information in the news presented to it.

An example of old media problems created by the pressures of declining viewership and intense battles for ratings came shortly before the election in the CBS-Dan Rather story about the National Guard record of George W. Bush, just out of Yale during the height of the Vietnam War. CBS claimed it had obtained official documents that depicted Bush as avoiding Vietnam service by landing a spot in the Texas Air National Guard through political influence. He then failed to meet his military service duty obligations to such an extent that a commanding officer ordered him to "be suspended not just for failing to take a [required] physical . . . but for failing to perform to U.S. Air Force/Texas Air National Guard standards." Furthermore, as CBS alleged in the Rather broadcast, Bush was permitted to transfer to a military base in Alabama, but failed to report for duty and instead spent his time there campaigning for a Republican candidate. Driven by the desire to break a major story, CBS—the network that set the news standards from the days of Edward R. Murrow on—therein violated all its rules for determining the accuracy of highly controversial material before presenting it to the public. When CBS's report was exposed as having been based on documents that were easily determined to be fabricated, the network suffered the greatest blow to its reputation in its history. Rather, the veteran anchor and successor to the respected Walter Cronkite, was forced to step down. The entire news media was dealt one more blow to its credibility with the public.

Preparing Americans to understand the complexities and challenges of the long "twilight struggle"—to borrow a Cold War term—of the war on terrorism requires not only a far more aggressive and responsible press, but also tough-minded, realistic, independent leaders willing to break the ideological confines that now keep our politics in a perpetual state of division through daily charge and countercharge.

None of this litany of difficulties means that George W. Bush, or America, is doomed to failure; it means that he, and we, now have another opportunity to start afresh.

In the weeks following his second inaugural, Bush began evoking the spirit—and the example—of such presidents as Lincoln, Wilson, FDR, and Reagan. It was America's mission, Bush told his fellow citizens, to bring democracy and freedom to the world. He was determined to pursue those goals however long it took and however great the cost. Whether the president's crusading, indeed messianic-sounding message ultimately produces success in the war against terror—or engenders greater resentment, hatred, and acts of violence against the United States—remains a critical but unresolved question. At the time Bush sounded this call, however, it came against a backdrop of accelerating murderous acts by insurgents in Iraq and amid evidence that the threat of terrorism was increasing, not diminishing.

Finally, some observations about the part fear plays in our lives.

Though fear has been exploited as a political tool, today's threat of terrorism is real. It might even pose greater dangers than the nuclear threat of the early Cold War era. During the Cold War, containment policies kept the two superpowers, the U.S. and the USSR, from launching their weapons out of the knowledge that neither side could "win" such an exchange. The only result would be mutual, assured destruction. Today's terrorists are motivated by one purpose, the destruction of their enemies, and are not hampered by the existence of their own nation-state against which retaliation can easily be aimed. There can be no doubt that terrorism's suicidal footsoldiers will employ without hesitation the full range of biochemical and radiological weapons they might obtain as the availability of such weapons continues to spread—and employ them not only against the armed forces of their enemies, but against civilians, from infants to the aged. These are the terrible realities of the new Age of Anxiety.

During the McCarthy era, as we have seen, the domestic Communist menace was exaggerated, largely for political purposes, as the Soviet Union itself was growing steadily weaker, not stronger, in its military, economic, and political competition with the United States. Still, forces of international Communism seeking worldwide dominion did pose a genuine threat. Then as now, nuclear weapons—and the biochemical weapons that existed then as they do now—did raise the terrifying prospect, as Einstein warned so long ago, of extinguishing "any life on earth." They still do, and still inspire legitimate feelings of fear.

Our challenge is twofold:

First, not to be so overcome by fear that we overreact. We have already progressed down this road in the years since 9/11, which have been symbolized by the Patriot Act. Enacting repressive security measures, imposing security edicts for which no one is publicly accountable, and creating a climate of obsessive secrecy creates abuses against liberty rather than greater safety. These actions change the nature, and the promise, of our democracy. In allowing them, we risk becoming more like the enemies we combat.

Second, not to let fear blind us to a greater task necessary for providing national security: employing our best talents and energies toward eradicating the sources of the hatred that threaten us. True security requires not merely the ability to amass weapons and launch successful combat operations. It requires working to ameliorate the conditions that breed terrorism: poverty, ignorance, isolation, intolerance. It means changing the ways we educate and inform ourselves, mandating that foreign languages be taught, insisting on required study not only of the Islamic world and its cultural and religious values, but also of *our own* history and traditions. I have been dismayed as a college professor to discover how many bright students, even ones in graduate school, are ill-prepared to understand the complexities of the American constitutional system. An appalling ignorance exists, suggesting a breakdown in the basic teaching of civics, government, and history.

In view of America's current deep ideological divisions, this ignorance also suggests a lack of appreciation for *real* American values: values that celebrate personal tolerance for all faiths but shun the intolerant religious demagogues and merchants of hate who seek to impose their views on their fellow citizens; that teach respect for those among us with whom we might strongly disagree; that cherish opposition to excessive government secrecy and abuses of power; that prompt people to emulate the example, and the message, of Martin Luther King, Jr., who better than anyone in my lifetime successfully appealed to the conscience of the country, scaling barriers of prejudice and hatred and elevating the American standard of moral principles and actions in the eyes of the world. By upholding these quintessential American values, we can establish more solid grounds for lasting security than all the powers of military arms can ever achieve.

Only by being true to our principles, forged by the hardships of over two centuries, can the United States mobilize its great resources and strengths to meet what I fear are much greater challenges than those we have faced in the past. The United States can blunder ahead, leaving itself more isolated and resented, draining its blood and treasure while risking the fate of other great powers—Greek, Roman, Persian, Spaniard, French, British—that saw their strength and influence ebb and decline. Or it can summon its multiple talents and set out on a different course. By unifying and working more aggressively to strengthen our own society, we can make America a brighter beacon for the world to follow.

America's best instincts, those of the good neighbor seeking to work with others to alleviate human suffering, were demonstrated in the country's response to victims of the tsunami that brought incalculable death and destruction to Southeast Asia. Such humanitarian impulses will not lessen, and certainly not eliminate, the dangers of terrorism, but they exemplify true American values. The Age of Anxiety has not ended, nor is it likely to end soon, as the terror attacks on

London in the summer of 2005 demonstrated so shockingly. The American challenge, one that could last for decades, is not to let fears paralyze and further divide us.

This is not a new test for Americans; we've been through it before. As Rebecca West wrote when the darkest Cold War fears of nuclear incineration were setting the stage for McCarthyism, "Our task is equivalent to walking a tightrope over an abyss." It still is.

Afterword

*A wiretap requires a court order . . . When we're talking
about chasing down terrorists, we're talking about getting
a court order before we do so.*

**—George W. Bush, at a campaign rally in Buffalo,
April 20, 2004, six months before his presidential reelection**

A s with all his election-year appearances, the president's
stage at flag-draped Kleinhans Music Hall was carefully
set to dramatize his political message. Surrounding him were
hundreds of uniformed first responders from New York police and fire departments; members of local, state, and federal law-enforcement agencies; and relatives of National
Guard forces then serving in Iraq—soldiers in "the army of
compassion," as the president put it. Behind him, a huge sign
proclaimed:

PROTECTING THE HOMELAND

Underneath, other words reinforced his theme:

PROTECTION PREVENTION
ENFORCEMENT SECURITY

Once again, Bush evoked fearsome memories of 9/11, that "horrible day for our nation," and once again he exploited the fear factor to make political points. He boasted how his decision to invade first Afghanistan and then Iraq had made America more secure from terrorism abroad. "The world is more peaceful because the Taliban is gone," he said. The same was true with Iraq. "We're defeating the enemy there so we won't have to defeat them here," he told the wildly cheering, invitation-only crowd of loyal supporters.

He pledged to continue finding "killers before they kill us," and summoned Congress to renew and expand the Patriot Act, portions of which were due to expire at the end of that year. "I'm starting a campaign," he said, "to make it clear to members of Congress it shouldn't expire. It shouldn't expire for the security of our country." Already, he claimed, the Patriot Act was speeding up "the process whereby people can gain information to go after terrorists" by permitting such things as "roving wiretaps" and "delayed notification warrants."

To critics worried about erosion of American rights, the president was reassuring. "Now, by the way," he said, "any time you hear the United States government talking about wiretaps, it requires—a wiretap requires a court order. Nothing has changed, by the way. When we're talking about chasing down terrorists, we're talking about getting a court order before we do so."

Further addressing concerns of civil libertarians, he said: "It's important for our fellow citizens to understand . . . constitutional guarantees are in place when it comes to doing what is necessary to protect our homeland, because we value the Constitution."

As for protecting the homeland, he said his Homeland Security Department had been empowered with new law-enforcement tools to make America not only more secure from "evil-doers" but also from natural calamities.

"We do the same thing, by the way, for federal emergency response," the president explained. "We've done a better job of coordinating FEMA, for example, which is—means Federal Emergency Management Association [*sic*]. But it's now part of the Homeland Security Department." Thanks to Homeland Security's new policies, "the bureaucratic mindsets that prevented the sharing of information" have been eliminated. "We better coordinate with state and local authorities. So not only are we doing—coordinating activities when it comes to fighting terrorists, but we're doing so when it comes to responding to emergencies, as well."

An America more secure from terrorism abroad and from disasters at home; an America that carefully balances the need for military action to maintain national security in times of peril with safeguarding constitutional protections to ensure liberty: This was the president's election-year message. Politically, it was a winner. He was reelected and given more political capital to expend in a second term.

———

Fast forward, two years later, April 2006:

Virtually all of Bush's statements that day in Buffalo have turned out to be false:

Afghanistan is not a stable society; the Taliban is not "gone"; Osama bin Laden remains at large; Al Qaeda still uses Afghanistan as a base for terrorism and launching attacks against American forces. As for Iraq, exactly three years after the invasion even the war's most ardent supporters won't claim America is "winning," or that America and the world are more secure because of the U.S. intervention.

As the Iraq war began, I said it would be years, if not decades, before we had history's judgment on that military engagement. I was wrong. There now exists definitive evidence of how great a historical debacle the Iraq intervention has been.

What emerges from sworn testimony, newly revealed classified documents, memoirs of leading military and civilian participants, and public calls for Defense Secretary Donald Rumsfeld's removal made by half a dozen retired generals who led U.S. forces in Iraq is a record of the Bush administration's reliance on, or cynical misuse of, falsified intelligence about the existence of weapons of mass destruction; catastrophic strategic miscalculations from within the top levels of the Pentagon and the White House; near-criminal negligence in failing to provide sufficient troop levels on the ground and proper protective equipment for U.S. personnel; ignorance of Iraq's divisive historical past and culture and the bitter enmity between its rival religious factions; astonishing hubris in assuming the Iraqi operation would be a "cakewalk"; and a tragic lack of postinvasion planning for what would be required militarily, economically, and tactically to provide security, stability, and an improved standard of living for the "liberated" Iraqi people.

The great majority of the American people now see Iraq as a U.S. failure. Nearly two-thirds of those polled say the invasion was a mistake—a stunning reversal from the 27 percent who thought so when the invasion began. Along with this reversal in opinion, the president's personal approval ratings have plummeted to as low as 29 percent. Even more startling has been the defection of Bush's bedrock supporters. Among influential conservatives who have broken with Bush on Iraq are such notables as William F. Buckley, George F. Will, and Francis Fukuyama. As a result, by the spring of 2006 a majority of the public no longer believes the president to be truthful or thinks his policies are leading America in the right direction.

The president's other national-security claim made that day in Buffalo—that the Homeland Security Department stands ready to respond swiftly and effectively to emergencies at home—has also turned out to be disastrously wrong. A portrait of governmental ineptitude, bureaucratic bungling, cronyism, cover-up, and incompetence was presented for all to see after a long-predicted hurricane named Katrina devastated the Gulf Coast over Labor Day 2005, inundated the city of New Orleans, and left death and destruction in its wake. Exposed were massive failures of the Homeland Security Department and the state and local emergency agencies with whom it was supposed to coordinate emergency relief actions.

Beginning with the landfall of Katrina and continuing day after day, week after week, month after month, citizens witnessed heartbreaking scenes of America's worst natural disaster. When placed alongside daily pictures of death and destruction in Iraq, Katrina taught Americans a bitter lesson: Nearly five years after 9/11, despite all the government's assurances about an improved state of national security, the United States seems incapable of protecting itself from terrorists abroad or from forces of nature at home. That this inability stems largely from top-to-bottom governmental incompetence only makes the lesson more difficult to accept.

But of all the president's misstatements in Buffalo, most troubling was his assertion that constitutional protections against such civil-liberties violations as lawless wiretaps were being followed. "A wiretap requires a court order," he said then. "Nothing has changed, by the way. When we're talking about chasing down terrorists, we're talking about getting a court order before we do so."

What the president *didn't* say was that nearly two-and-a-half years earlier, in the days immediately after 9/11, he had secretly ordered a massive electronic wiretapping operation that authorized the National Security Agency—without obtaining a court warrant, as specifically required by law—to eavesdrop on American citizens suspected of being in contact with international terrorists. This action was undertaken despite objections about its legality expressed privately by senior government attorneys; without the knowledge of nearly all members of the secret U.S. court specifically charged with granting authority for such warrants in national security cases; and without adequate notification of the Congress that wrote the law mandating court approval of such warrants—a Congress that, constitutionally, is supposed to exercise oversight of the executive branch of government headed by the president.

When the *New York Times* exposed this secret warrantless wiretap operation more than a year and a half later at the end of 2005, Bush strongly defended his surveillance program and pledged to find and prosecute the "leakers" who had, in his view, endangered national security. He claimed he was acting under inherent powers granted him as commander in chief in a time of national peril. Top officials, including the attorney general, vigorously backed his claim and asserted an expansive, highly controversial theory of a "unitary executive" possessing near unlimited powers. To critics who questioned the legality of the president's actions—among them members of his own party—the president's aides cited a congressional resolution authorizing use of American force after 9/11 as granting Bush such power. Leading congressional members of both parties denied that that had been the intent of the earlier resolution.

Not since Richard Nixon had such sweeping assertions of unchecked presidential power been made. And not since Nixon had the nation seen the emergence of such an arrogance of power in the White House, accompanied by a contempt for constitutional protections and procedures; a deeply held belief in governmental secrecy; and a determination to withhold information from the public and the two other constitutionally coequal branches of government, the courts and the Congress.

In the aftermath of these disclosures, talk of impeaching the president began in Congress. A Wisconsin senator, Russ Feingold, who had been the only member of Congress to vote against passage of the original Patriot Act in 2001, called for a congressional resolution censuring the president.

These and other developments triggered an intense debate over presidential powers Bush claimed and exercised, raising again old questions about the inherent conflict between national security and liberty.

KATRINA: THE PERFECT STORM

I don't think anyone anticipated the breach of the levees.

—President Bush, in a TV interview September 1, 2005, two days after the levees were breached

Thirteen months before Katrina howled ashore, federal emergency planners conducted what they called a "doomsday" exercise to assess what calamities might occur if Louisiana, and New Orleans, experienced the full force of a Category 3 hurricane. The results of that July 2004 exercise were, to say the least, deeply disturbing.

Such a storm, the emergency planners predicted, might force a million people to relocate. Investigators also concluded that federal and state officials were aware that, at best, evacuation planning for the New Orleans area was dangerously inadequate.

One year later, as Katrina began sweeping across the Gulf of Mexico, Max Mayfield, the nation's leading hurricane expert as head of the National Hurricane Center in Miami, was sending out urgent warning after warning in daily videoconference briefings to federal officials in Washington, about the monster storm his agency was nervously tracking. By then Katrina had been elevated to a Category 5 storm, the most intense on the hurricane scale, and was heading directly toward landfall near New Orleans. The prospect of the New Orleans area taking such a blow was especially ominous, since 70 percent of the city was below sea level, protected by a series of levees long known to be incapable of withstanding anything more than a Category 3 storm. Now, Mayfield and his forecasters were predicting a storm surge there that could reach twenty-eight feet. The highest levees around New Orleans were eighteen feet.

On Sunday, August 28, Mayfield repeated his great concerns during a videoconference call to the president, then on a month-long vacation at his Crawford, Texas, ranch, and to Homeland Security and Federal Emergency Management Agency (FEMA) officials in Washington. So alarmed was Mayfield that he expressed a "very, very grave concern" about failure of the levees, and displayed a warning on the screen in capital letters:

SOME LEVEES IN THE GREATER NEW ORLEANS AREA COULD BE TOPPED

During this period similar urgent warnings were being made to officials by the National Weather Service. Its forecasters were calling Katrina "a most powerful hurricane with unprecedented strength," and saying that a Category 4 storm, to say nothing of a Category 5, could wreak massive havoc, destroy buildings, hurl small cars into the air, and cause the levees to fail.

During the videoconference with the president in Texas, the hurricane center in Miami, and U.S. emergency officials in Washington, even the FEMA director, Michael D. Brown— later to become the object of national scorn for his inept handling of the emergency—warned that the approaching storm was, "to put it mildly, the big one," that medical and mortuary teams might not be prepared for such a crisis, and that he was worried about the government's "ability to respond to a catastrophe within a catastrophe." He noted that the Louisiana Superdome, designated as a shelter of last resort for displaced people in New Orleans, was twelve feet below sea level and might lose its roof in the storm.

When six months later the taped videoconference that Sunday was "leaked" to the public to the vast embarrassment of the president and his emergency team, viewers saw that Bush appeared curiously unengaged. He asked no follow-up questions, though after he left the room other officials did. In the immediate hours before Katrina's landfall, more dire warnings were relayed to Washington and to the president, still on vacation in Texas. At 1:47 A.M., August 29, for instance, hours before Katrina struck, the White House received an official report bluntly stating: "Any storm rated Category 4 or greater will likely lead to severe flooding and/or levee breaching."

The fury of the storm more than lived up to the fearful

warnings. As predicted in that emergency disaster exercise the summer before, more than a million people suddenly found themselves forced to flee. In New Orleans alone, 100,000 residents were left isolated, with no place to go except for the city's Convention Center and the Superdome, both of which were below sea level and, as foretold, were quickly transformed into hellholes of despair. As feared, large portions of the Superdome roof were blown away, exposing the huddled throngs inside to the elements.

The entire Gulf Coast sustained extraordinary damage. Touring some of the disaster scenes immediately after Katrina moved inland, Mississippi's governor Haley Barbour said, "It looks like Hiroshima is what it looks like."

Two days later, after a flyby of New Orleans and the Gulf Coast on the way back from his Texas ranch, the president returned to Washington. There, on September 1, he told ABC-TV's Diane Sawyer: "I don't think anyone anticipated the breach of the levees." The next day he flew to New Orleans and was shown live on TV, standing next to FEMA director Brown, already the object of intense criticism. There, he made the remark that will outlive Bush's time in office: "Brownie, you're doing a heckuva job."

As all America, indeed all the world, understood by then, the emergency relief-and-rescue effort being made was anything but "a heckuva job." It was an unmitigated disaster that further eroded the impression of a can-do United States capable of dealing with emergencies and creating security for its citizens.

THIRD WORLD AMERICA

declared a headline in London's *Daily Mail*. "Law and order is gone," the paper commented, "gunmen roam at will, raping

and looting, and as people die of heat and thirst, bodies lie
rotting in the street. Until now, such a hellish vista could only
be imagined in a Third World disaster zone. But this was
America yesterday."

Recriminations began immediately; they have not abated
in all the months since. When juxtaposed against the continuing disasters in Iraq, the failures of the government's emergency planning for Katrina marked the unraveling of the Bush
presidency.

Just as Joe McCarthy refused to reveal documents that
damaged his credibility, so the Bush White House refused to
produce internal White House documents on actions taken
before and after Katrina struck, or to allow key officials to testify under oath before investigating congressional panels. The
administration imperiously rejected attempts by congressional committees—controlled by Republicans—to gain access to White House files, documents, e-mails, and reports on
the executive branch's response to Katrina. For more than two
months, a special House committee chaired by a conservative
Republican, Thomas M. Davis III of Virginia, was repeatedly
rebuffed. Finally, a deputy counsel to the president rejected
yet another congressional request for information about communications to and from three key presidential advisers, their
deputies, and senior staff members. Were the president to
agree to such a request, William K. Kelley informed the investigators, it "would impinge on the separation of powers of
the legislative and executive branches."

Senate investigators seeking to learn lessons from the mishandling of Katrina were thus unable to compile a complete
record in the public interest. This kind of stonewalling, to employ a term from another embattled presidency locked in a

collision course with Congress, led, inevitably, to the leaking of the damaging prestorm videoconference between the president in Texas and emergency officials in Washington.

After the video was seen, criticism of the White House was as severe from Republicans as it was from Democrats.

Five months after Katrina, a scathing report by the government's investigating arm, the General Accounting Office, placed blame across all levels of government, but particularly at the top of the White House. After reading the GAO report, Chairman Davis of the special investigating committee said: "The director . . . of the National Hurricane Center said this was the big one," but "when this happened . . . Bush is in Texas, [White House chief of staff Andrew] Card is in Maine, the vice president is fly-fishing. I mean, who's in charge here?"

Similar harsh criticism came from a Senate investigating panel, and from 9/11 Commission members who strongly rebuked both the Bush administration and Congress for "minimal progress" in enacting many of their panel's year-old recommendations meant to bolster domestic security agencies' abilities to respond to terrorist attacks and natural disasters like Katrina. One Republican commission member, John F. Lehman, a former Navy secretary under Ronald Reagan, said he feared the "unconscionable" failures of the Katrina rescue effort would embolden terrorist groups to attack again on American soil.

Katrina revealed more than governmental incompetence. By highlighting the suffering of trapped poor and black citizens of New Orleans, Katrina exposed the ever-present but too-little-noted world of the underclass that still exists in America. The president's mother, Barbara Bush, showed how great the societal gulf between the haves and have-nots remains, when she carelessly demonstrated a Marie-Antoinette-meets-Lady-Bountiful let-them-eat-cake attitude toward the plight of the evacuees.

Days after Katrina's landfall, she toured a Houston relocation site housing displaced victims from the storm. "What I'm hearing, which is sort of scary," she told a radio interviewer immediately afterward, "is they all want to stay in Texas, and so many of the people in the arena here, you know, were underprivileged anyway, so this is working very well for them."

OF WIRETAPS, SECRECY, AND LIBERTY

I did not and could not address . . . any other
classified intelligence activities.

—Attorney General Alberto Gonzales, replying to a Senate
Judiciary Committee request that he clarify his testimony
implying that secret operations other than warrantless
wiretapping might be occurring

In response to the senators, the attorney general carefully noted that in his previous testimony about the president's authorization of the secret wiretapping program, "I was confining my remarks to the Terrorist Surveillance Program as described by the President, the legality of which was the subject" of Gonzales's Senate appearance several weeks earlier in February 2006. The attorney general therefore was suggesting that the government might be engaged in other—unspecified—spying operations in which American citizens were secret targets.

His response added to the controversy about both the legality and the extent of post-9/11 clandestine surveillance activity approved by the president without the knowledge of the courts, Congress, or the public. Nor was the criticism only from civil libertarians. Noted conservative constitutional scholars like Bruce Fein, who held top posts in the Nixon, Carter, and Reagan administrations, among them associate deputy attorney general, also sharply challenged the constitutionality of the warrantless surveillance program.

After testifying before the same Senate Judiciary Committee that had questioned the attorney general, and then learning of Gonzales's equivocal response concerning other possible domestic spying operations, Fein told the *New York Times*: "It seems to me he is conceding that there are other NSA [National Security Agency] surveillance programs ongoing that the president hasn't told anyone about." (Months later, Fein reacted strongly after learning that President Bush personally had blocked a Justice Department investigation of NSA's warrantless surveillance operation by refusing to give security clearances to lawyers who were attempting to conduct the investigation. Gonzales's revelation of that unprecedented presidential intervention came after stern questioning before a Senate panel on July 18, 2006. Fein compared Gonzales's role in passively acceding to the president's action to that of Elliot Richardson, the attorney general who resigned on principle rather than obey President Nixon's order to fire the special prosecutor, Archibald Cox, during his investigation of the Watergate scandals, an action that ultimately led to the Nixon impeachment proceedings. "If he was like Elliot Richardson, he'd say, 'Mr. President, I quit,'" said Fein, referring to Gonzalez, in comments to the *Washington Post*.)

As of this writing, that issue hasn't been resolved.* Congressional attempts at oversight have been stymied by White House refusals to cooperate with investigators, or even to allow them to question the legal experts on whom the president relied for his authorization of these—and possibly other—secret operations. But in one important sense, the record is becoming clearer about the controversial roles played, and the advice rendered, after 9/11 by some of the most staunchly ideological conservatives inside the Bush administration.

Prominent among them is a young lawyer named John Yoo, now on the faculty of the University of California, Berkeley's School of Law, but previously a Justice Department attorney. Yoo's opinions shaped many of the administration's most controversial post-9/11 policies: the warrantless surveillance operation; the redefinition of what constitutes torture of prisoners to reject both the Geneva Conventions and federal antitorture laws that ensure humane treatment of

---

*On May 11, 2006, three months after Gonzales's testimony, *USA Today* published a blockbuster revelation under the banner headline: NSA HAS MASSIVE DATABASE OF AMERICANS' PHONE CALLS. 3 TELECOMS HELP GOVERNMENT COLLECT BILLIONS OF DOMESTIC RECORDS. The story reported that the NSA "has been secretly collecting phone call records of tens of milions of Americans using data provided by AT&T, Verizon, and BellSouth . . . The NSA program reaches into homes and businesses across the country by amassing information about the calls of ordinary Americans—most of whom aren't suspected of any crimes." President Bush immediately rejected the idea that this was another illegal surveillance operation, saying: "We're not mining or trolling through the personal lives of millions of innocent Americans. Our efforts are focused on links to Al Qaeda and their known affiliates." Administration aides insisted this new revelation "is lawful and very carefully done," and that disclosure of the classifed program had harmed national security.

prisoners; and the expanded claim for sweeping executive powers.

John Yoo deserves more than a passing note in these pages, for he symbolizes how the anticommunist fears of the Cold War that created McCarthyism form a continuous connection to abuses spawned by fears of terrorism in our own time. In a *Washington Post* profile published at the end of 2005, Yoo told reporter Peter Slevin how his coming of age in a strongly anticommunist household—his parents had emigrated to the United States from Korea in 1967, when he was three months old—made him associate the opposition to communism with the Republican Party. From that background, and through associating with others of similar political views, Yoo became one of many dedicated young conservatives who thrived during the Reagan years.

With the help of contacts in such conservative organizations as the Federalist Society and the American Enterprise Institute, he became a clerk with U.S. Appeals judge Lawrence H. Silberman, was hired at Berkeley, then clerked for Supreme Court Justice Clarence Thomas and served under Senator Orrin Hatch on the Senate Judiciary Committee when Hatch was seeking "bright, conservative up-and-comers." Then, in July 2001, he became a member of the Justice Department's influential Office of Legal Counsel. That's where his ideological convictions came powerfully into play in the legal advice he offered Attorney General John Ashcroft and the White House after the 9/11 attacks.

Despite his age, he had great impact. As Slevin explained: "Yoo required a particular convergence for his views to become as influential as they did. He needed a well-placed position, a national crisis and a receptive audience. He quickly got all three."

Two weeks after 9/11, Yoo argued in a memo to the White House that the Constitution confers "plenary"—or absolute—authority for the president to use force abroad, "especially in response to grave national emergencies created by sudden, unforeseen attacks on the people and territory of the United States." He expanded his argument for unprecedented presidential power in wartime by also contending that when Congress passed a joint resolution three days after 9/11 authorizing the president to use force if required against Al Qaeda, that gave the president license to undertake other unilateral actions.

Bush later argued that this, plus his inherent plenary power as commander in chief, gave him the right to order his warrantless wiretapping operation. This claim was in direct conflict with the clear language of the twenty-eight-year-old Foreign Intelligence Surveillance Act (FISA), which requires the government to obtain warrants from a newly created, secret FISA court before being legally authorized to wiretap U.S. citizens and residents in terrorism and espionage cases.

Yoo's assertion of unlimited presidential power was breathtaking: "The President's broad constitutional power to use military force to defend the Nation, recognized by the Joint Resolution itself, would allow the President to take whatever actions he deems appropriate to pre-empt or respond to terrorist threats from new quarters."

Subsequently, Yoo's advice on torture became critical in what happened next in the "war on terror."

On August 1, 2002, he was the principal author of what became known among civil libertarians as the infamous "torture memo." In his opinion, the administration was not bound by federal antitorture laws. To be considered torture, he wrote, techniques must produce lasting psychological damage or cause suffering "equivalent in intensity to the pain accompanying serious physical injury, such as organ failure, impairment of bodily function, or even death."

Thus the legal rationale—and the green light—for the ensuing tortures at Abu Ghraib, Guantanamo, and other prisons, which have stained the good name of the United States and brought dishonor to those civilian officials and members of its armed forces who permitted such abuses to occur. As a black mark on America's standing in the world, these prison scandals were worse than anything that occurred during the McCarthy era.

Subsequent charges that some American troops had murdered Iraqi civilians, plus the revelation that innocent Iraqis were slaughtered by U.S. troops on patrol in the Sunni village of Haditha in November 2005, only further blackened the good name of America. The so-called Haditha massacre—and attempts to cover it up—came after a homemade bomb detonated under a Humvee, killing Marine Lance Cpl. Miguel Terraza of El Paso, Texas. In an ensuing act of murderous rage and revenge, Marines stormed into four homes, breaking down doors, hurling grenades, firing indiscriminately, and killing men, women, and children. At least twenty-four Iraqis were slain, including an eighty-nine-year-old amputee, his wife, three sons, a daughter-in-law, and a five-year-old grandson. In another of the house assaults, an Iraqi father and seven others inside, including five children, were killed.

Since leaving the administration, Yoo has continued to stir controversy through his public speeches and writings.

Ultimately more important for the role he played in further-
ing the new Age of Anxiety, Yoo has yet to receive definitive
public or political judgment on the acceptability of his legal
opinions.

One memorable warning about the dangers of an imperial president in this democracy bears noting, however. It
came when Supreme Court justice Sandra Day O'Connor
eloquently rebuked the Bush administration's claim that the
president is answerable to no one. In a June 2004 majority
court opinion involving the wartime power of a president to
detain U.S. citizens as enemy combatants without access to
courts or attorneys, Justice O'Connor expressed, in the best
American tradition, the fear of unlimited presidential authority when she said: "A state of war is not a blank check for the
President when it comes to the rights of the Nation's citizens."
In directly addressing controversies over the president's claim
of expanded wartime powers, she also said that "even the war
power [of a president] does not remove constitutional limitations safeguarding essential liberties."

Two years later, on June 29, 2006, in what legal scholars
called a "stunning rebuke to the Bush presidency," the Supreme Court ruled by five to three that the military tribunals
Bush sought to try foreign terror suspects were illegal under
both U.S. military law and the Geneva Conventions. By
strongly upholding the rule of law, the court dealt a blow to
one of the key powers the administration claimed to possess
in fighting the war on terror. In writing the majority opinion, Justice John Paul Stevens rejected the administration's
claims for Bush's inherent—or absolute—powers as commander in chief and also denied that the congressional resolution authorizing the use of force after the 9/11 attacks

had conferred unilateral power for the president to act. There is nothing in the resolution's legislative history "even hinting" that such an expansion of the president's powers was considered, Stevens wrote. The Navy lawyer assigned to defend one of the terror suspects hailed the decision, calling it "a return to our fundamental values." Standing before the Supreme Court immediately after the ruling, Lt. Commander Charles Swift said, "That return marks a high-water mark. It shows that we can't be scared out of who we are, and that's a victory, folks."

O'Connor's surprising retirement two months before the death of Chief Justice William Rehnquist on September 4, 2005, set off an intense ideological battle to reshape the U.S. Supreme Court. With the quick Senate confirmations of Bush's two conservative appointees, John G. Roberts as chief justice and Samuel Alito as associate justice, and the absence of the highly influential O'Connor, questions were immediately raised about the direction the court would take in years to come. O'Connor, a conservative Republican appointed by Ronald Reagan in 1981 and the court's first female justice, had played a critical role as the court's centrist swing vote. She was also a staunch defender of the judiciary's critically independent role in the face of onslaughts from right-wing politicians and religious fundamentalists such as that which marked the bitter Terry Schiavo right-to-life case, in which the lives of conservative judges were threatened by zealots seeking to impose their views on the courts, and thus on the people.

The inherent conflict represented by the views of O'Connor and Yoo—and even of President Bush himself—lie at the heart of the great issues now presenting themselves for judgment by the American people: Are a president's powers unlimited in times of crisis, or must they be subject to checks and balances to prevent abuses? What kind of country do Americans believe in? What values do they celebrate most highly? What steps do they want their officials to take to ensure their security and protect their freedom? What lessons have they drawn from experiencing, as in the McCarthy days, the politics of fear employed as a political device to gain power? What is the proper role of secrecy and classification of vital intelligence information in a nuclear age of terrorism and suicide bombers? When is secrecy legitimate and necessary, and when is it employed as a means to cover up abuses, discredit critics, and maintain control and power?

To take the last question first, far more than in any administration in my experience dating back to the Eisenhower presidency, the Bush administration has set an all-time record for secrecy. Examples are almost too numerous to count, but some of the latest to surface since I finished the original manuscript for this book include:

- During Katrina, FEMA officials ordered the news media not to take pictures of those killed during the storm and its aftermath, much like the administration's earlier ban on showing photos of flag-draped coffins bearing U.S. dead returning from Iraq. Though the administration claimed its motivation was to preserve the dignity of victims and protect their families, it was a clear case of censorship to prevent the public from seeing images documenting unwelcome bad news that might embarrass the administration.

- A vivid example of the administration's manipulation of the news came in the April 2006 disclosure that the claim of supposed mobile WMD labs "discovered" in Iraq, which the government repeatedly cited as evidence of Saddam's secret cache of weapons of mass destruction, was known by the Pentagon three years earlier to actually be, as *Newsweek* reported, "harmless weather balloons." The White House subsequently blamed the false claims on "bad intel."

- Also in April 2006, it was revealed that the National Archives had cooperated with the Air Force, CIA, and other federal agencies to withdraw 55,000 pages of decades-old historical documents from public access, even though those records had long been declassified. Beginning in 2002, archives officials secretly began removing documents for possible reclassification, concealing the identities of anyone involved in the project. All of these documents had "already been available publicly from the open shelves for extended periods of time," an internal archives memo read. After this story appeared, Thomas S. Blanton, executive director of the respected, private National Security Archive, told the *Washington Post* that the memo "shows that the National Archives basically aided and abetted a covert operation that whited out the nation's history by reclassifying previously released documents." After this secret archival operation was made public, an audit by the National Archives revealed that the reclassification efforts were far more extensive than previously disclosed: The CIA and other agencies had wrongfully kept secret about a third of the records removed from public shelves, the audit concluded.

- This development came after the revelation that in November 2001 George W. Bush had signed Executive Order 13223, which virtually negated the Presidential Records

Act. This act mandated that all presidential papers are the
property of the U.S. government and, with certain exceptions for national security, must be released for public examination within twelve years of the end of a presidential
term. Under the Bush executive order, any U.S. president,
whether still in office or not—and even the immediate
family of a deceased president—has carte blanche to withhold documents that might be incriminating or embarrassing. There is no appeal process to limit that so-called family
veto provision. This last provision was added as thousands
of presidential documents relating to the Iran-Contra
scandal, when the United States secretly sold arms to Iran
in exchange for release of American hostages, were due
to be released. Some of these documents reportedly involved actions of the first President Bush, then Ronald
Reagan's vice president. Subsequently the right-wing watchdog group Judicial Watch, which had already filed more
than 350 Freedom of Information requests with the George
W. Bush administration, commented conspiratorially in
March 2006: "Truth be told, the president was likely trying to keep secret possibly incriminating information involving his father."

So much for learning the lessons of history, or for understanding abuses of power that might have occurred during a previous presidential term.

• Added to this was the disclosure that the FBI sought an ac-
cumulation of fifty years of personal files from the late columnist Jack Anderson in a search for any classified documents
they might find. This action, also in April 2006, signaled a
widening of the Bush administration's crackdown on leaks
of "sensitive" information, no matter how old or relevant
the material might be. The dragnet of the files of Anderson, who had died just four months earlier, was part of a

campaign, the *Washington Post* noted, that "already includes several FBI inquiries, a polygraph investigation inside the CIA and a Justice Department warning that it might seek to criminalize conversations about classified subjects by non-government officials such as journalists, researchers and think-tank analysts." Anderson's family branded the FBI request for the files as outrageous and a "dangerous departure" from First Amendment protections, a view shared by many academic and legal experts. This development came as the administration announced its intent to criminalize the leaking of information: Through the widespread use of polygraph tests, government employees now face intimidation, ruined careers, and criminal charges should they disclose critical information they believe to be in the public interest.

• Meanwhile, the White House repeatedly refused to release internal documents or photos involving contacts between Jack Abramoff and executive department officials, including the president. Abramoff, a disgraced and now criminally indicted former lobbyist, stands at the center of a spreading congressional corruption scandal that promises to rival that of the Gilded Age of criminality and bribery after the Civil War. The Abramoff affair already has caused the indictments of a White House official, a Republican congressman, and top former aides to former House Majority Leader Tom DeLay, with more indictments expected. The greatest political casualty to date of the Abramoff scandal has been DeLay, by far the most powerful Republican congressional legislator in recent history. The fall of DeLay, after his own indictment and his announcement that he would not seek reelection in 2006, provided fresh evidence of the corrupt and dysfunctional U.S. political system.

But the most notable example of secrecy and government manipulation—and the most disturbing example of McCarthyism at work—involves the revelation that President Bush authorized the leaking of highly classified intelligence information to selected reporters to discredit critics of the Iraq war.

This revelation grew out of the controversy that resulted when the name of Valerie Plame, a classified CIA operative working on uncovering weapons of mass destruction, was made public. Plame's husband, former ambassador Joseph C. Wilson IV, had been sent by the CIA in 2002 to the African nation of Niger to investigate reports that Iraq was secretly seeking to obtain a nuclear material called yellowcake, a processed form of uranium ore essential in creating nuclear fission. Wilson found no such evidence.* After the Bush administration began citing the yellowcake story as a rationale for removing Saddam Hussein in the months leading up to war, Wilson debunked the administration's claims of Iraqi weapons of mass destruction in an op-ed article in the *New York Times*. The Bush administration retaliated in a concerted, albeit secret, attempt to discredit Wilson, claiming his

---

*The claim that Iraq was seeking to obtain yellowcake now stands as the most egregious example of manipulating intelligence about Saddam Hussein's supposed weapons of mass destruction. It was cited repeatedly by the Bush administration as a key rationale for the war in Iraq, including most famously Bush's nationally televised State of the Union address in 2003 in which the president declared: "The British government has learned that Saddam Hussein recently sought significant amounts of uranium from Africa." Bush made that statement based on information purporting to prove that Italian intelligence had uncovered classified documents detailing Saddam's attempt to purchase yellowcake uranium. Later investigation showed those documents to have been a crude forgery.

trip to Niger was a "boondoggle" arranged by his wife, Valerie Plame, whose identity as a covert CIA operative they then disclosed. Vice President Cheney's chief of staff and national security assistant, I. Lewis (Scooter) Libby Jr., also an assistant to the president and one of the most powerful men in the administration, was instructed by Cheney to leak sections of a highly classified National Intelligence Estimate supposedly documenting the administration's case that Saddam was acquiring nuclear materials from Niger.

After Plame was identified in a column by Robert D. Novak, one of the recipients of the government leak, the CIA asked the Justice Department to find out who had violated the law by making public the name of a classified operative. Disclosure of classified information about an individual's CIA employment, according to the Intelligence Identities Protection Act, "has the potential to damage the national security in ways that range from preventing the individual's future use in a covert capacity, to compromising intelligence-gathering methods and operations, and endangering the safety of CIA employees and those who deal with them." FBI agents began extensive interviewing, a grand jury was formed, and a special counsel was named to oversee the criminal investigation. The president, who has repeatedly attacked leaks of secret information as threats to national security, stated he was determined to cooperate with the special counsel's inquiry; if a member of his administration was guilty of leaking Plame's name, he said, that person would be removed and punished.

Three years since this controversy first surfaced in July 2003, Libby has been indicted for perjury, obstruction of justice, and making false statements in his grand jury testimony about the Plame/Wilson case. His criminal trial is scheduled for January 2007. Then, on April 6, 2006, Special Counsel Patrick J. Fitzgerald dropped a bombshell. In a court filing, Fitzgerald disclosed that Libby had told the grand jury that President Bush, through Vice President Cheney, had authorized him to disclose secret prewar intelligence about Iraq to reporters. Immediately, critics derisively, but accurately, proclaimed Bush "the leaker in chief."

In recounting Libby's secret testimony to the grand jury, Fitzgerald described "a concerted action" by "multiple people in the White House" to use the classified information to "discredit, punish, or seek revenge against Mr. Wilson." Vice President Cheney, Fitzgerald said, was at the center of the campaign to use classified information to mislead the public. A less circumspect way of describing what had happened was that this was a case of character assassination. "The evidence will show," Fitzgerald said, "that the July 6, 2003, op-ed by Mr. Wilson was viewed by the Office of the Vice President as a direct attack on the credibility of the vice president (and the president) on a matter of signal importance: the rationale for the war in Iraq."

Cheney "specifically directed" Libby to leak classified CIA documents, including the highly sensitive, closely guarded National Intelligence Estimate, and an account summarizing Wilson's trip to Niger. This attempt to manipulate opinion and discredit critics came even though Cheney and top officials were well aware that the central claim they sought to make—that a "key judgment" in the intelligence assessment showed a consensus existed among most senior U.S. officials that Hussein was "vigorously" seeking to obtain nuclear material from Niger—was fraudulent. In fact, no such consensus existed; the actual CIA document stated no such key judgment. Instead, the assessment about the risk of Iraq acquiring nuclear materials was relegated to a section far back in the Intelligence Estimate, which was not shown to reporters at the time the estimate was leaked. And at that time strong doubts had already been raised about the yellowcake story by top intelligence officials at both the CIA and the State Department, whose Bureau of Intelligence and Research called the claim "highly dubious"—to say nothing of knowledge about the "crude forgery" of yellowcake intelligence documents.

That didn't stop the White House from pressing the supposed Iraqi nuclear threat on the public through speeches and leaks. As Barton Gellman and Dafna Linzer reported in the *Washington Post* after Fitzgerald had made public limited portions of Libby's grand jury testimony, a White House Iraq Group had been formed in the summer of 2002 to foster "public education"—a polite term for propaganda—about Iraq's "grave and gathering danger" to the United States, and it "repeatedly pitched the [false] uranium story" to the media, which then delivered that message to the public.

THE LONG WAR AND THE AMERICAN FUTURE

. . . that will be decided by future presidents . . .

**—President Bush responding March 20, 2006,
to a news-conference question about when American
troops will be out of Iraq**

As the Iraq war enters its fourth year, President Bush has signaled that his successors, not he, will have to grapple with the difficult decisions about how to prosecute, or withdraw, from that war, with all the consequences those decisions will entail.

Whether the president's statement was a way of prolonging the war without specifically saying so cannot be known, but at the least it indicated a rare concession of error by Bush. Three years after he stood on the deck of the aircraft carrier USS *Abraham Lincoln* before a huge MISSION ACCOMPLISHED banner and declared that "major combat operations in Iraq have ended . . . the United States and our allies have prevailed," Bush was acknowledging that conflict would likely extend long into the future. But even extricating the United States from Iraq will not end the larger conflict growing out of the 9/11 attacks. That greater "war on terror," of which Iraq is only a part, is already being likened to historical episodes like the Cold War, which lasted for decades— the Long War, as some historians and military specialists are now dubbing it. By itself, the Iraq war now stands as one of the longest in the American experience dating back to the beginning of the nation with the seven years of the American Revolution. It exceeds the length of the War of 1812 (two years), the Spanish-American War (four months), World War I (nineteen months), and the Korean War (three years), and rapidly approaches the four years each of the Civil War and World War II. Only the eight years of Vietnam eclipse it in duration.

While the outcome of Iraq may not be known for years, the challenge of global terrorism could not be more immediate, as the outbreak of war between Israel and the terrorist organizations Hamas in Palestine and Hezbollah in Lebanon tragically demonstrated in the summer of 2006.

Instead of helping forge an international coalition to combat terrorism, the invasion of Iraq has isolated the United States from the world. Instead of diminishing the threat of terrorism, it has united more fanatics in their hatred of America and diverted America's attention and resources from other threats in the Middle East and elsewhere. As yet another example of how Islamist hatred of the United States has spread beyond Iraq since the invasion, new developments in North Korea and the Middle East have raised fears about further destabilization and violence. The Palestinian election of the terrorist organization Hamas, sworn to the destruction of Israel, makes a mockery of the Bush administration's hopes for installing democratic regimes in that region and fuels new violence between Hamas terrorists, Israelis, and—in a second terrorist front—Hezbollah in Lebanon, igniting renewed open warfare that threatens to spread throughout the entire Middle East. At the same time, Iran's defiant announcement that it rejects a U.N. demand to cease an enriched uranium program that could lead to its possession of nuclear weapons comes amid reports that the United States is studying military options about launching a preemptive strike against Iran that would include use of its own nuclear weapons. These developments increase the dangers confronting the United States; they make America more, not less, of a target for terrorists. As Congressman John Murtha said in his call for a phased withdrawal of U.S. forces, "Our troops have become the primary target of the insurgency. They are united against U.S. forces and we have become a catalyst for violence." Murtha also put it well when he said, "The threat posed by terrorism is real, but we have other threats that cannot be ignored." Therein lies America's central challenge: not to let fears and hubris drive us further into a destructive abyss, but instead to fashion realistic policies that address *all* of America's long-term problems at home and abroad.

In my original text, I enumerated a number of parallels between the politics of fear in the McCarthy era and the present. Many more parallels can now be cited. In McCarthy's time, there were many accusations of disloyalty, but few convictions and even fewer Communists exposed. In our time, setting off orange, yellow, and red alerts and posting spy tips on billboards have set the nation's nerve ends jangling, but have not yet led to uncovering major terrorist networks. In his time, McCarthy's attacks on the military led to the Army-McCarthy hearings that eventually destroyed him. In ours, a revolt of generals has seriously damaged the president's public standing and that of civilian Pentagon leaders. In McCarthy's time, reputations were ruined and careers destroyed. In ours, similar character assaults have been launched against noted military figures such as General Anthony Zinni, who commanded American troops in the Middle East and questioned the administration's strategy for Iraq, and General Eric K. Shinseki, the Army chief of staff. Shinseki's congressional testimony stating that the occupation of Iraq would require "several hundred thousand troops" led to bitter denunciations of him by civilian Pentagon leaders and ultimately to his retirement. Valerie Plame lost her CIA job after she was "outed," and then jointly with her husband filed suit against Cheney, Libby, and presidential advisor Karl Rove after what she called the "media storm that destroyed my family's privacy, significantly heightened concerns for our security, and challenged Joe and me in a myriad of ways we could not have imagined when this episode began." She added:

After years of service to my country, I felt compelled to resign from the CIA . . . because I could no longer effectively
perform the job that I was trained and honored to do. The
right wing has sought to destroy Joe's reputation, despite
his twenty-three years of service to his country, and
mounted a searing and relentless smear campaign against
him. It has been a disheartening and discouraging time for
those who care about the rights of citizens to hold their
government accountable for their words and actions.

And also the veteran CIA analyst Mary McCarthy was fired
after she was accused—falsely, she maintains—of leaking
classified information about secret torture prisons abroad or
of merely having contact with reporters. And these are not
the only casualties of the Bush *et al* "reign of terror" in our
time. Sowing of fears and suspicions has also damaged many
anonymous U.S. Muslims. In my list of parallels, what now
appears most analogous to McCarthy's destruction is not the
ruined careers of "leakers" and civil servants falsely accused
of disloyalty. It is the self-destruction of the present-day
fearmongers-in-chief, since absolute power does corrupt absolutely, as it did with Joe McCarthy. As I write, we are beginning to see the unraveling of the unitary presidency, and with
it a hopeful sign that the public once again—if belatedly, as
in the McCarthy era—could be ready to reject appeals to the
politics of fear and smear. A source of optimism that the political system is reasserting itself to check abuses of power
came after the Supreme Court rejected the administration's
claims for unlimited presidential authority, and the White
House was forced to acknowledge that the secret FISA court
could review the legality of the covert intelligence operation
that had been conducting warrantless wiretaps.

During the McCarthy years, out of varying motives described earlier, both political parties were essentially quiescent, even cowardly, in combating McCarthyism. To a large extent, the same was true, with notable exceptions, for the press. That combination of a climate of fear, indifference, and cynicism permitted McCarthy to flourish unchecked for nearly five years, leaving a legacy that has affected our politics negatively to this day. Eventually the political system, the press, and the public combined to render a decisive verdict on McCarthy. In our period, until very recently, similar timidity—cheerleading, even—has marked the reaction of politicians of both parties and important segments of the press, who have failed to examine the administration's many false premises for preemptive war.

Differences also exist. Chief among them is that in the McCarthy witch-hunting days, the Eisenhower administration was aligned against his abuses. Though Ike failed for too long to employ the powers of his presidency to summon the will of the people in checking the Wisconsin demagogue, Ike's belief that McCarthy ultimately would self-destruct was proved correct. In our time of terrorism, it's not only the presidential circle itself but many members of Congress as well that have been responsible for many of the abuses that have occurred.

In these concluding pages, I have described a number of tests before the public. Many are self-evident and spring from the daily drumbeat of news: creating stability, if possible, in Iraq to permit the withdrawal of U.S. forces; working to repair damage done to the U.S. reputation abroad by forging greater international cooperative efforts, not out of messianic desire to spread democracy but out of mutual self-interest in dealing with the spread of nuclear weapons in the hands of terrorists; containing such nuclear-armed rogue states as Iran and North Korea; addressing the looming perils of global warming and forecasts of an avian flu pandemic.

Difficult to resolve as these issues are, even more daunting is the challenge of finding a way to deal with America's internal problems: from immigration, to energy costs, to courts, to religion, to health care, to public education, to poverty, to inner-city pathologies, to the national debt, to the powers of the respective branches of government, to the competence of government itself.

These issues have become so polarized, so subject to bitter ideological attacks, that necessary consensus on what course to take has been virtually destroyed. In our post-9/11 years, the politics of personal destruction, cynical manipulation of public opinion, lies, leveling of false charges, and divide-and-conquer exploitation of fears have prevailed.

At the least, these issues will not be resolved—or even seriously addressed—until public and political leadership emerges to demand a unified national approach. That will require a different brand of leadership—leadership that embraces a politics of inclusion, not exclusion; leadership that appeals to a truly united America, not panders to ideological blocs cynically labeled by political manipulators as red or blue; leadership that summons the public to coalesce for the common good, sacrificing if necessary; leadership of candor, so absent from the Bush presidency's cheerleading proclamations and public falsehoods; leadership that demands accountability—oversight, not cover-up; leadership that levels with the people, that, as with great leaders like FDR and Churchill, relates the bad news as well as the good to prepare the nation for greater long-term challenges ahead. Ultimately, it requires leadership that moves the nation out of an

Age of Anxiety into, if not an Age of Reform, then an Age of Realism.

Two major lessons emerge from the Iraqi experience. The first involves the transparent, but paramount, need to get America's fiscal house in order. The United States has been fighting its "war on terror" by recklessly accumulating historic levels of national debt fueled by tax cuts and deficit spending that risk the nation's future.

As I write in April 2006, the cost of maintaining an American presence in Iraq has spiraled to well beyond the $300 billion mark, with no end in sight. Some estimates put the ultimate cost of the war at one trillion dollars. Congress has just raised the national debt by $781 billion, to its highest level ever of $9 trillion. This cripples America's ability to attend to pressing national needs.

In fact, the great long-term debt problem confronting the United States is even worse than those figures show. In yet another example of pernicious secrecy and cover-up, that bad news has been deliberately kept from the public. That revelation came in the hardly known but critical Financial Report of the United States, produced by the Treasury Department. The inherent secrecy of this report, which the government did not even call to the public's attention through a news release, led my journalistic colleague David S. Broder to comment: "You might think that the subject matter is as sensitive as the National Intelligence Report that President Bush declassified to discredit Joe Wilson. And it is. The cover letter in the report from Treasury Secretary John Snow contains the bad news. Whereas the budget deficit for 2005 was officially given as $319 billion, the government accrual-based net operating cost was $760 billion in 2005." Broder adds: "That $760 billion is the real difference between the money the government received and the obligations it added in the past year—in other words, the unfunded costs being passed on to our children and grandchildren."

The second lesson involves the government itself. Here again we find another parallel with the McCarthy era. Decades-old damage, dating from those witch-hunting McCarthy days that saw reputations blackened and careers destroyed, has resulted from ideological attacks not only on public service and public servants but on journalists, members of Congress, and just plain people as well—bequeathing yet another destructive legacy to the present. The nation has paid dearly for the long-term climate of distrust that has enveloped fellow citizens and public institutions. Our post-Iraq, post-Katrina period of political cronyism, corruption, and mismanagement has heightened cynicism about public servants and the functioning of the political system. As a consequence, from the McCarthy days to now the proper role of government has been demonized and diminished: that is, of government neither big nor small, liberal nor conservative; rather, government that works, government that strikes a proper relationship between the public and private sectors, government capable of dealing with national emergencies and formulating effective long-term plans for the nation's well-being.

Bad as the McCarthy era was, even then there were notable examples of bipartisan approaches to national problems. The select Senate committee that censured McCarthy, led by the sternly conservative Republican Arthur Watkins of Utah, and formed by the liberal Democratic leader Lyndon B. Johnson of Texas in cooperation with the conservative Republican leader William Knowland of California, stands as a superb

example of how Democrats and Republicans can put aside
ideological and regional differences to work together in the
national interest.

This kind of bipartisanship has all but disappeared in recent
years—as has the essential oversight responsibility of Congress to investigate and hold officials accountable for abuses.
"Where is the outrage?" a frustrated Senator Arlen Specter,
the Republican chairman of the Judiciary Committee, complained about the lack of congressional reaction to months of
stonewalling by the administration when asked to provide information about the warrantless surveillance program.

How these questions will be resolved or addressed is
presently unanswerable, but the next election cycles should
offer clues about the public and political responses to these
tests. It's a cliché to say the American system now stands at a
crucial crossroads, but that is where we are. Compelling evidence exists about the need for a fundamental change in direction—or a new political party, if necessary, to force desired
action. But as I write now, the prospect looms of more politics of division and fear in the forthcoming elections.

For instance: On the January 20, 2006, anniversary of
George Bush's second inaugural, Karl Rove, the president's
chief political adviser and architect of Bush's winning elections,
spelled out the latest Republican strategy for the midterm
congressional elections and the presidency two years later.

Once again, Rove employed the fear factor. America faces
a "ruthless enemy," he told members of the Republican National Committee. Its citizens "need a commander in chief,
and a Congress, who understand the nature of the threat and
the gravity of the moment America finds itself in. President
Bush and the Republican Party do. Unfortunately, the same

cannot be said for many Democrats." Rove added: "Republicans have a post-9/11 world view, and many Democrats have a pre-9/11 world view. That doesn't make them unpatriotic—not at all. But it does make them wrong—deeply and profoundly and consistently wrong."

Though he carefully refrained from labeling Democrats unpatriotic, that was his clear intent, and his attack was typically unsparing—"lacerating," in the view of one political analyst. He attacked Democrats for their weakness on terrorism and national security, their "cut-and-run" stand on Iraq, their challenging of the administration's secret surveillance operation, and their opposition to Bush's efforts to reshape the federal judiciary along right-wing lines. And, once more, Rove described national security as preeminently the major issue before the nation.

Six months later, Rove cited that campaign tactic as the key to Republican victory. Moments after learning he would not be indicted by the special counsel in the Valerie Plame leak case, Rove told Republican supporters in the key presidential primary state of New Hampshire that such Democratic critics of Iraq as John Murtha and John Kerry—both decorated combat veterans—"give the green light to go to war, but when it gets tough, they fall back on that party's old platform of cutting and running. They may be with you for the first few bullets but they won't be there for the last tough battles." Rove also took that occasion to capitalize on the news that the brutal terrorist Abu Musab al-Zarqawi had been killed days before by an American attack in Iraq. If Democrats had had their way, he said, Zarqawi would not have been killed. Republicans in Congress immediately picked up the same "cut-and-run" phrases in attacking Democrats. President

Bush employed the same language against Democratic critics of his Iraqi policies after he completed a quick photo-op trip to Iraq. This became the central theme of the Republican's congressional elections campaign for the fall. After the terrorist plot to blow up trans-Atlantic airliners was exposed by British security forces, the GOP began employing this slogan to link Democratic "weakness" on terrorism and "cutting-and-running" in Iraq: "Weak and Wrong: Meet the Defeat-o-crats."

Those kinds of remarks close the circle on the exploitation of fear from the Cold War days of Joe McCarthy to the present era of terrorism. When I read Rove's remarks, I recalled Edward R. Murrow's words in his *See It Now* broadcast of March 9, 1954, challenging Senator McCarthy—words even more pertinent today than they were then: "We will not walk in fear, one of another. We will not be driven by fear into an age of unreason if we dig deep in our history and remember we are not descended from fearful men . . . who feared . . . to defend causes which were unpopular."

About Sources

As Samuel Johnson famously admitted long ago, I too have ransacked
a library to make this one book. In that process, I have accumulated
an immense debt to all the authors, especially the historians and biographers, who cumulatively have created a great body of work dealing with
the era of Joseph R. McCarthy and McCarthyism. My own effort draws
on those works and with the vast and growing storehouse of sources covering the period of the Cold War and beyond into our new Age of Anxiety and terrorism. In my bibliographical notes, I'll cite and assess those
works I found most useful. Among other critical sources are recently declassified government documents from the McCarthy era; oral histories of
the leading players and archival material housed in a number of libraries,
but primarily at the Wisconsin State Historical Society in Madison, at
Marquette University in Milwaukee, and at the invaluable and often over-
looked oral history collection of the U.S. Senate Historical Office in Washington; transcripts of testimony and reports from presidential commissions
and congressional committees examining the 9/11 terror attacks on the
United States; my own interviews and personal connections to and observations of some of the events described in these pages.

A further word about sources: Despite the voluminous amount of available material, unfortunately much of the record of Joe McCarthy's life and times continues to be deliberately hidden. After McCarthy's death, his widow Jean, a determined keeper of his flame even after her remarriage, donated the "McCarthy Papers" to Marquette University. The papers consist of twenty-five segments, of which the first thirteen are routine: texts of speeches, sound recordings, film and video recordings, lists of speaking engagements declined, congressional bills introduced, published hearings, Senate committee reports, and press clippings. She specified that the remaining segments be closed to the public during her lifetime and that of the daughter she and McCarthy adopted shortly before his death in 1957.

Jean Kerr McCarthy Minetti, who had been a key young aide to McCarthy before their marriage in 1953, died at the age of fifty-five in 1979, twenty-two years after McCarthy. A quarter century after her death, and almost half a century after his, the papers remain closed. The surviving daughter, five weeks old when she was adopted and now in her late forties, rejects inquiries about the papers. At Marquette, here's how those remaining segments of the McCarthy Papers are described: Senate subject files, and files from the years 1933, 1937, 1943, 1946–57: *Sealed*. Desk calendars: *Sealed*. Telephone logs and visitor's logs: *Sealed*. Marine Corps records: *Sealed*. Photographs (Private): *Sealed*. Financial and legal records: *Sealed*. Personal subject files: *Sealed*. Manuscripts: *Sealed*. Senate files: *Sealed*. Campaign records: *Sealed*. The last segment, which may also contain valuable information, are the Jean Kerr Minetti Papers: *Sealed*.

For these reasons, and many others, my effort here cannot possibly be considered definitive. But then no work can ever truly claim to offer the final word, for time and new evidence continually alter perceptions and judgments. Thus, I offer only a fragment of the backdrop of a much greater story about the links between the McCarthy era and America's new period of fear and anxiety.

H. J.

Source Notes

Quotes before Preface

Page

    x. "Must a government . . .": from Abraham Lincoln, *Speeches and Writings, 1859–1865.* New York: The Library of America, FN:p. 641. Cf., Wahlke, John C., Editor. *Loyalty in a Democratic State: Problems in American Civilization. Readings Selected by the Department of American Studies, Amherst University.* Boston: D.C. Heath and Company, 1952, p. xi.

    x. "We should be eternally . . .": from dissenting opinion of Justice Oliver Wendell Holmes, in *Abrams et al v. United States,* 250 U.S. 616.

Preface to the Paperback Edition

Page

    xii. "I'm the decider . . .": Bush, in remarks defending Defense Secretary Donald Rumsfeld against generals calling for Rumsfeld's removal, news conference, April 18, 2006. See CNN.com transcript.

xii. "Brownie, you're doing . . .": Bush, during a Hurricane Katrina briefing at Mobile, Ala., airport, Sept. 2, 2006, from transcript of the Office of the Press Secretary.

xiii. "surrender to the terrorists . . .": Charles Babington, "Hawkish Democrat Joins Call for Pullout," *Washington Post,* Nov. 18, 2005, p. A1.

xiii. "cynical and pernicious . . .": "Cheney Calls War Critics 'opportunists,'" MSNBC.com, Nov. 17, 2005.

xiii. "The Democratic Party . . .": Cf., Howard Kurtz and Shailagh Murray, "Web Site Attacks Critic of War," *Washington Post,* Jan. 14, 2006, p. A5.

Prologue: A NEW KIND OF WAR

Page

2. "You've probably wondered . . .": full page ad, *New York Times,* March 28, 2003, p. W8.

4. "The arrogance of power . . .": Fulbright used the phrase in the first of three Christian A. Herter lectures at Johns Hopkins University, April 21, 1966. Later, it became the title of his book *The Arrogance of Power,* New York: Random House, 1966.

4. "It is excellent . . .": Cited, in Fulbright speech, "The Price of Empire," Aug. 8, 1967, before the American Bar Association in Honolulu.

PART ONE: McCarthyism

1. The List

Page

9. "Good afternoon, Senator . . .": William Manchester, *The Glory and the Dream: A Narrative History of America, 1932–1972.* Boston: Little, Brown and Company, 1973–1974. p. 521.

10. "in violation of . . .": Robert Griffith, *The Politics of Fear: Joseph R. McCarthy and the Senate* (2d ed.) Amherst: The University of Massachusetts Press, 1987, p. 28.

11. "fictitious amendment . . .": David M. Oshinsky, *A Conspiracy So Immense: The World of Joe McCarthy*. New York: The Free Press, 1983, p. 66.

13. "weedy, with a . . .": Rebecca West, *The New Meaning of Treason*, first published 1947 as *The Meaning of Treason*, republished, under revised title, New York: The Viking Press, 1964, p. 177.

13. "I do not intend . . .": James Chace, *Acheson: The Secretary of State Who Created the American World*. New York: Simon & Schuster, 1992, p. 227.

13. "radioactive poisoning . . .": Einstein's warning came on Jan. 31, 1950: Manchester, *op. cit.*, p. 512.

14. "How much more . . .": *Chicago Tribune*, Feb. 8, 1950. Cf. Manchester, *op. cit.*, p. 512.

14. "The Republican Party . . .": *The Wheeling Intelligencer*, Feb. 7, 1950, p. 1.

15. "thus a willing . . .": *Chicago Tribune*, Feb. 2, 1950.

15. "The great lesson . . .": Manchester, *op. cit.*, p. 521. Nixon's speech to the House was Jan. 26, 1950.

19. "As Lewis began . . .": Edwin R. Bayley, *Joe McCarthy and the Press*. Madison: The University of Wisconsin Press, 1981, p. 18.

20. "realized that he . . .": Manchester, *op. cit.*, p. 522.

20. "others deplored treachery . . .": *Ibid.*

22. "What about it . . .": Bayley, *op. cit.*, p. 20. The *Denver Post* ran a photo of McCarthy peering into his briefcase for his non-existent list on Feb. 11, 1950.

23. "Last night I . . .": *Ibid.*, pp. 20–21.

24. "McCarthy Charges 57 . . .": *Ibid.*, p. 21.

25. "We opened the . . .": *Ibid.*, pp. 26–27.

29. "McCarthyism . . .": Herblock's *Washington Post* cartoon appeared March 29, 1950.

2. Tail Gunner Joe

Page

30. "When I was . . .": Richard Rovere, *Final Reports: Personal Reflections on Politics and History in Our Time.* New York: Doubleday & Company, 1978, p. 17. Hereafter cited as Rovere *Reports.*

31. "lightning quick . . .": This quote and others in this chapter from McCarthy's early associates and friends, are drawn from the Joseph R. McCarthy Papers at Marquette University and the archives of the Wisconsin Historical Society. Hereafter cited as McCarthy Papers and Wisc. Hist. Soc. Files.

32. "the source of . . .": *Ibid.*

33. "the family's shy . . .": from the invaluable Thomas C. Reeves Papers in the Wisconsin Historical Society archives, containing correspondence, interview notes, documents, and transcripts. Hereafter cited as Reeves Papers.

39. "you could watch . . .": Thomas C. Reeves, *The Life and Times of Joe McCarthy,* Madison Books, 1997, originally published by Stein and Day in 1982, p. 37.

39. "Joe worked like . . .": Michael O'Brien, "Young Joe McCarthy, 1908–1944," *Wisconsin Magazine of History,* Vol. 63. No. 3, spring, 1980, p. 181. This 49-page seminal article is the best on his formative years and remains indispensable for an understanding of his character.

39. "I remember . . .": O'Brien, *op. cit.*

40. "be the first . . .": Reeves Papers, *op. cit.*

40. "I never saw anybody . . .": From O'Brien, *op. cit.,* as are the other quotes cited here.

41. "lying in the dirt . . .": *Ibid.*

41. "start kicking . . .": John G. Adams, *Without Precedent: The Story of the Death of McCarthyism.* New York: W.W. Norton, 1983, p. 149.

44. "He not only drove . . .": Reeves, *op. cit.,* p. 31.

45. "Joe and I . . .": *Ibid.*, tells this story briefly on p. 17, but a fuller account is in the Reeves Papers, which includes his extensive interview notes with Curran and many others.

46. "enlisted as a buck . . .": *Ibid.*, p. 43. See also official McCarthy documents falsely stating this as fact in McCarthy Papers.

47. "honest acting men . . .": *Green Bay Press Gazette*, McCarthy Papers. Cf., O'Brien, *op. cit.*, p. 219.

47. "obsessive preoccupation with . . .": O'Brien, *op. cit.*, p. 224.

48. "hare-brained, illogical . . .": *Ibid.* Cf., Reeves, *op. cit.*, p. 23. Cf., Oshinsky, *op. cit.*, p. 18.

48. "Of all the brainless . . .": O'Brien, *op. cit.*

48. "hard-hitting, personal . . .": O'Brien, *op. cit.*, p. 201.

52. "expose the guy . . .": Letter from Capt. Jack Canaan to Editor William Evjue of the *Madison Capital Times*, Evjue Papers, Wisconsin Historical Society. Cf., Oshinsky, *op. cit.*, p. 31.

52. "Sometimes, to ease . . .": Oshinsky, *op. cit.*, pp. 31–32.

54. "I was within . . .": Reeves Papers.

3. Progressivism to McCarthyism

Page

56. "'Ideal Commonwealth' . . .": Lincoln Steffens, quoted in Karl E. Meyer, "The Politics of Loyalty: From La Follette to McCarthy in Wisconsin, 1918–1952." Meyer's brilliant 1956 Ph.D. Princeton dissertation is the best I've read on the La Follettes and Wisconsin.

57. "a creed as . . .": *Ibid.*

57. "No other living . . .": *Ibid.*

58. "Who shall rule . . .": Meyer, *op. cit.*

58. "If we don't stop . . .": *Ibid.*

58. "an outgrowth . . .": *Ibid.*

58. "more wages, more education . . .": *Ibid.*

59. "If Franklin had . . .": Rexford G. Tugwell, *The Democratic Roosevelt: A Biography of Franklin D. Roosevelt.* Garden City, NY: Doubleday and Company, 1959, p. 298.

59. "that the rich . . .": "Young Bob La Follette . . .": Patrick J. Maney, *Young Bob: A Biography of Robert M. La Follette, Jr.* Madison: Wisconsin Historical Society Press, 2003, p. xi.

61. "smooth, suave, impeccably . . .": *Ibid.*, p. 70.

61. "Tom, you're a . . .": *Ibid.*

61. "I have been doing . . .": McCarthy Papers.

62. "raided by outsiders": McCarthy Papers.

62. "a system for . . .": McCarthy Papers.

62. "shaking hands, swapping . . . :" Reeves, *op. cit.*, p. 26. Cf., Maney, *op. cit.*, p. 290.

63. "darting in and . . .": Reeves, *op cit.*, p. 27.

63. "like having the . . .": *Ibid.*, p. 27.

64. "He cut a . . .": Oshinsky, *op. cit.*, p. 45.

66. "had once owned . . .": Roger T. Johnson, *Robert M. La Follette, Jr., and the Decline of the Progressive Party in Wisconsin.* Madison: State Historical Society of Wisconsin, 1964, p. 132.

66. "Mr. La Follette, the gentleman . . .": *Ibid.*, p. 13.

67. "How Did La Follette . . .": Maney, *op. cit.*, p. 291.

67. the man "who is . . .": Johnson, *op. cit.*, p. 133.

67. "playing into the . . .": *Ibid.*, p. 131.

68. "expressed more concern . . .": Six months after his defeat by McCarthy, La Follette wrote a widely publicized *Colliers* article, "Turn the Light on Communism" (Feb. 8, 1947) that began: "In my opinion, Communist and fellow-traveler activities in America have be-

come a serious menace to our democracy." But he also warned that in fighting communism, Americans must not resort to totalitarian methods. America's challenge, he added, was "to take intelligent action to combat the menace without at the same time impairing civil liberties." Maney, *op. cit.*, pp. 307–308.

68. "denunciation of our . . .": Johnson, *op. cit.*, p. 140.

68. "actually charges that . . .": *Ibid.*, p. 141.

68. "The Communists definitely . . .": *Ibid.*, p. 138.

69. "So they cranked out . . .": Jack Anderson and Ronald May, *McCarthy: The Man, the Senator, the Ism.* New York: Crown Forum, 1952, p. 104.

69. "running on my . . .": Johnson, *op. cit.*, p. 151.

70. "Senator Robert M. . . .": James Reston, *New York Times*, Aug. 13, 1946, p. 18.

70. "I am proud . . .": Johnson, *op. cit.*, p. 157.

70. "one of the most . . .": *Milwaukee Journal*, Aug. 14, 1946.

71. "In our day only . . .": *New York Times*, Aug. 15, 1946, p. 24.

71. "I didn't go . . .": *Time*, March 9, 1953.

71. "a little megaphone . . .": *Milwaukee Journal*, Oct. 17, 1946.

71. "Red-baiting became . . .": Reeves, *op. cit.*, p. 104.

71. "make every effort . . .": *Ibid.*, p. 105.

72. "Pro-McCarthy newspapers . . .": *Ibid.*, p. 105.

73. "Communism and Republicanism . . .": David Caute, *The Great Fear: The Anti-Communist Purge Under Truman and Eisenhower.* New York: Simon and Schuster, 1978, p. 26.

73. "The people will vote . . .": *Ibid.*

73. "The Moscow-PAC . . .": *Ibid.*, p. 27.

4. The Remarkable Upstart

Page

76. "Mr. McCarthy, what . . .": Oshinsky, *op. cit.*, p. 59. Cf., Richard H. Rovere, *Senator Joe McCarthy*. New York: Harcourt, Brace and Company, 1959, p. 105. Hereafter cited, Rovere *Senator.*

77. "When you want me . . .": *Ibid.*, Oshinsky, p. 59. Cf., Rovere *Senator, op. cit.*, p. 105.

77. "hustling, whirlwind": *Ibid.*, p. 55.

77. "The Senate's Remarkable . . .": *Saturday Evening Post,* Aug. 9, 1947.

78. "painfully clear before . . .": From a transcript of the then-popular weekly radio program, *America's Town Hall Meeting of the Air,* forerunner of *Meet the Press*-type shows, April 3, 1947. McCarthy Papers.

79. FN. Reagan fable, described, Haynes Johnson, *Sleepwalking Through History: America in the Reagan Years.* New York: Norton, originally published 1994, 2003 edition, p. 60.

80. "He looked at me . . .": Christine S. McCreary, oral history interview, Senate Historical Office, Washington, D.C., May 19, 1998.

5. The Way to Wheeling

Page

82. "Has the Communist . . .": Bayley, *op. cit.*, Nov. 9, 1949, p. 128.

82. "an active and . . .": *Ibid.*

82. "I'm not going . . .": McCarthy's Madison speech was May 7, 1950. Quoted, Bayley, *op. cit.*, p. 129.

83. "It was a disgusting . . .": Oshinsky, *op. cit.*, p. 69.

84. "embarrassingly small . . .": *Ibid.*, p. 70.

84. "squandering $37 million . . .": *Ibid.*, p. 70.

84. "turned up another . . .": *Ibid.*, p. 71.

85. "assign the book . . .": *Ibid.*, p. 71.

85. "One pleasant day . . .": Rovere *Reports, op. cit.*, p. 100.

87. "watch out for . . .": Oshinsky, *op. cit.*, p. 76.

87. "somehow convinced himself . . .": Arthur Herman, *Joseph Mc-Carthy: Reexamining the Life and Legacy of America's Most Hated Senator.* New York: The Free Press, 2003, p. 54.

88. "worse than anything . . .": *Ibid.*, p. 75.

88. "had strutted around . . .": *Ibid.*, p. 75.

89. "By every objective . . .": Herman, *op. cit.*

89. "charges of a . . .": *Malmédy Massacre Investigations. Hearings.* 81st Congress. U.S. Senate Committee on Armed Services, 1st Sess., 1949.

91. "criminally responsible": Rovere *Senator, op. cit.*, p. 112; Cf., Griffith, *op. cit.*, p. 25.

91. "We, his colleagues . . .": Malmédy Hearings Report. Cf., Griffith, *op. cit.*, p. 25, Oshinsky, *op. cit.*, p. 80, Reeves, *op. cit.*, p. 179.

PART TWO: The Past as Prologue

6. In the Beginning

Page
96. The first act . . . : All the acts are reprinted verbatim in Henry Steele Commager, Editor, *Documents of American History, Volume Five,* Section 101, "The Alien and Sedition Acts," New York: Appleton-Century-Crofts, 1949, pp. 175–78.

96. "demonical societies" and "nurseries of sedition": Carey McWilliams, "The Modern American Witch Hunt," from Walke, *op. cit., Loyalty in a Democratic State*, p. 8.

98. "Mobs broke into . . .": Carey McWilliams, *Witch Hunt: The Revival of Heresy.* Boston: Little, Brown and Company, 1950.

100. "Communism does not . . .": John Earl Haynes and Harvey Klehr,

Venona: Decoding Soviet Espionage in America. New Haven: Yale University Press, 2000, p. 57.

100. "an infernal machine . . .": Frederick Lewis Allen, *Only Yesterday: An Informal History of the Nineteen-Twenties*. New York: Harper & Brothers, Publishers, 1931, p. 49.

104. "made the Sedition Act . . .": Henry Steele Commager, editor, *Documents of American History*, 5th edition, New York: Appleton-Century-Crofts, Inc., 1949, p. 325.

106. "My motto for . . .": *Ibid.*, p. 58.

107. "to tear out . . .": A. Mitchell Palmer, "The Case Against the Reds," *Forum*, 1920, 63: 173–185.

108. "kept there for . . .": *Ibid.*, p. 57.

110. "It was an American . . .": *Ibid.*, pp. 69–70.

111. "the censorious eye . . .": Howard K. Beale, *Are American Teachers Free?* New York: Charles Scribners Sons, 1936.

111. "There is no danger . . .": Cited, "America Responds to Terrorism. The Palmer Red Raids." Constitutional Rights Foundation, www.crf-usa.org/terror/PalmerRedRaids.htm. Cf., Geoffrey R. Stone, *Perilous Times: Free Speech in Wartime*. New York: W. W. Norton, 2004. Cf., W. Dennis Dugan, "Palmer Do Not Let This Country See Red," Constitutional Rights Foundation, *op. cit.*

112. "I have seen . . .": Justin Kaplan, *Lincoln Steffens: A Biography*. New York: Simon & Schuster, 1974, pp. 239–245. Cf., *The Autobiography of Lincoln Steffens*. New York: Harcourt, Brace and Company, 1931.

112. "the bright young . . .": Haynes and Klehr, *op. cit.*, p. 333.

114. The 1938 congressional . . . : For HUAC citations I have relied on William Gellermann's *Martin Dies*, New York: Da Capo Press Reprint Edition, 1972, of the original John Day Company edition, plus congressional testimony. I also drew from Frank J. Donner's, *The Un-Americans*. New York: Ballentine Books, 1961.

115. "Before you testify . . .": *Ibid.*

7. Cold Warriors

Page

117.　"extremely critical situation . . .": Commager, *op. cit.*, reprints full text, Section 577, "The Truman Doctrine," pp. 719–22.

121.　"America's answer to . . .": Harry S. Truman, *Memoirs: Years of Trial and Hope. 1946–1952. Volume Two.* New York: Doubleday & Company, 1956, p. 105.

122.　FN. "the most baleful . . .": Daniel Patrick Moynihan, *Secrecy: The American Experience.* New Haven: Yale University Press, 1998, p. 2.

122.　"knew that . . .": Derek Leebaert, *The Fifty-Year Wound: How America's Cold War Victory Shapes Our World.* Boston: Back Bay Books, 2002, p. 108.

123.　"adroitly stolen": Griffith, *op. cit.*, p. xiii. Cf., Caute, *op. cit.*, pp. 32–33, effectively documents this state of mind. He cites Clifford proposing in a memo to Truman that Henry Wallace be "red-baited" in the 1948 presidential campaign. Caute also quotes the well-informed commentator, Alistair Cooke, as noting then that "the Democrats and the Republicans are now racing each other for the anti-Communist stakes." Cf., Ellen Schrecker, *Many Are the Crimes: McCarthyism in America.* Princeton, N.J.: Princeton University Press, 1998, p. 287, hereafter cited as Schrecker *Crimes.* Schrecker quotes Clifford saying Truman and his advisers were not worried about disloyal federal workers: "We did not believe there was a real problem. A problem was being manufactured."

124.　"potentially disloyal . . . they entertain today . . .": L. A. Nikoloric, "The Government Loyalty Program," *American Scholar*, XIX (Summer, 1950).

124.　"that one cannot . . .": L. A. Nikoloric, "The Government Loyalty Program," *American Scholar*, XIX (Summer, 1950). Hereafter cited as *American Scholar*.

127.　being on the "wrong . . .": Cf., Ellen Schrecker, *The Age of McCarthyism: A Brief History With Documents.* 2d Edition. Boston: Bedford/St. Martins, 2002. A superb guide to the era.

128. "The Truman administration . . .": Griffith, *op. cit.*, p. xii.

128. "Those who do not . . .": Caute, *op. cit.*, p. 15.

128. "It was the liberals . . .": *Ibid.*, p. 22.

129. "Wherever Stalinism conquered . . .": Irving Howe, "Ideas in Conflict," *A Margin of Hope.* San Diego: Harcourt Brace Jovanovich, 1982, p. 206.

130. Nelson Polsby says . . . : Prof. Polsby's two important essays on McCarthy and McCarthyism are: "Toward an Explanation of McCarthyism," *Political Studies,* Oct. 1960, and "Down Memory Lane with Joe McCarthy," *Commentary,* Feb. 1983.

130. "The atmosphere in . . .": *American Scholar, op. cit.*

131. "By 1953, the . . .": Leebaert, *op. cit.*, p. 111.

132. "an enormously expanded . . .": cited, Stephen E. Ambrose, *Rise to Globalism: American Foreign Policy Since 1938.* Fourth Revised Edition. New York: Viking Penguin, 1985.

132. "Chickens had come home . . .": *Ibid.*

PART THREE: Dealing with a Demagogue

8. The Press

Page

137. "Many of the . . .": Bayley, *op. cit.*, pp. 7–8.

138. "If the press . . .": *Ibid.*, pp. 16–17.

140. "Joe loved to play . . .": George Tames, Oral History Interviews, Jan. 13 to May 16, 1988, Senate Historical Office, Washington.

142. "That's great, great . . .": Bayley, *op. cit.*, p. 29, and 26–27.

143. "Everything was by inference . . .": Bayley, *op. cit.,* p. 29.

144. "Reporters covered politics . . .": *Ibid.*, p. 30.

146. "Joe tried to . . .": *Ibid.*, p. 35.

148. "just a political speech . . .": *Ibid.*, p. 36.

9. The Politicians

Page

149. "Let me have him . . .": Adams, *op. cit.*, p. 25.

150. "a subject which concerns . . .": For debate quotes see *Congressional Record*, 81st Congress, 2nd Session, Feb. 20, 1950.

151. The Lee list . . . : Manchester, *op. cit.*, p. 521, contains the best background on the Lee list. For excellent summation, see Griffith, *op. cit.*, pp. 40–41, 54–57.

152. "the most sinister . . .": Griffith, *op. cit.*, p. 56.

156. "With his funny waddling . . .": Richard Fried, *Men Against McCarthy.* New York: Columbia University Press, 1976, p. 54.

157. "a perfectly reckless . . .": Manchester, *op. cit.*, p. 524. Cf., Oshinsky, *op. cit.*, p. 114.

158. "If one case doesn't . . .": Manchester, *op. cit.*, p. 527. Cf., Rovere *Reports, op. cit.*, p. 124. Rovere describes how McCarthy called him and a few reporters to his office a month after Wheeling and said Taft urged him "to keep on talking" about charges of Communist traitors saying, "to keep going ahead, and if one case doesn't work out, proceed with another." Typically, McCarthy later denied making that comment to the reporters, but Rovere said they all had the exact same quotes in their notes.

158. "curiously unprepared . . .": Oshinsky, *op. cit.*, pp. 113–114.

159. "photographs of records": Reeves, *op. cit.*, p. 239.

160. "I have more . . .": *Ibid.*, p. 243.

161. "Similar—perhaps identical . . .": *Ibid.*, p. 243.

161. "Let me have . . .": Oshinsky, *op. cit.*, p. 119.

10. The Network

Page

163. "I tell you . . .": Reeves Papers.

163. FN. The fascinating Surine file is in Reeves Papers.

165. "'Oh,' said Wherry . . .": Oshinsky, *op. cit.*, p. 147. Cf., Reeves, *op. cit.*, p. 248.

165. "Joe never had . . .": Oshinsky, *op. cit.*, p. 117.

165. Source for Chambers is Nellor, Reeves Papers.

166. "On the day when . . .": Reeves, *op. cit.*, p. 237.

166. "the top Russian . . .": Rovere, *Senator, op. cit.*, p. 151. Cf., Manchester, *op. cit.*, p. 527. Cf., Oshinsky, *op. cit.*, p. 136.

167. "unworthy of a Senator . . .": Reeves, *op. cit.*, p. 273. Cf., Schrecker, *op. cit.*, for an excellent exposition on the Lattimore episode, pp. 247–253.

169. "Well, to my . . .": Reeves, *op. cit.*, p. 277. Cf., Oshinsky, *op. cit.*, p. 150.

170. "Quickly people associated . . ." Oshinsky, *op. cit.*, p. 141.

170. "Do you think . . . ?": "The President's Press & Radio Press Conference," March 30, 1950, Truman Presidential Library, Independence, Mo. Cf., Oshinsky, *op. cit.*, p. 143.

171. "I think that the greatest asset . . .": Reeves, *op. cit.*, p. 270.

171. "bitter and prejudiced . . .": Reeves, *op. cit.*, pp. 269–270.

171. "They pointed out . . .": Oshinsky, *op. cit.*, pp. 144–145.

172. "egg-sucking phony liberals . . ." Manchester, *op. cit.*, p. 526. Cf., Griffith, *op. cit.*, p. 89. Oshinsky, *op. cit.*, p. 157. Reeves, *op. cit.*, p. 278.

172. "Some write columns . . .": Reeves, *op. cit.*, p. 278.

172. "completely incompetent . . .": Griffith, *op. cit.*, p. 217.

173. "I'll never let that go . . .": Oshinsky, *op. cit.*, p. 161.

174. "This is a land . . .": *Ibid.*, pp. 159–160.

175. "The issue is . . .": Reston column, *New York Times,* May 19, 1950,p. 12.

175. "a hit-and-run . . .": Reeves, *op. cit.*, p. 296.

175. "Nearly all the . . .": Allan Nevins, *Herbert H. Lehman.* New York: Scribner's Sons, 1963, pp. 334–35.

176. "phony . . . raped . . .": McCarthy's Midwest Council of Republicans speech was May 6, 1950, La Salle Hotel, Chicago.

11. The Opposition

Page
178. FN. "I am reminded . . .": George J. Mitchell, "The Not-So-Secret History of Filibusters," op-ed article, *New York Times,* May 10, 2005, p. A21.

179. "on to something . . .": Further reading on this subject can be found at the Margaret Chase Smith Library, Northwood University, Skowhegan, Maine; and at the Senate Historical Office and Web site. Senator Smith's memoir, Margaret Chase Smith, *Declaration of Conscience,* New York: Doubleday, 1972, reprints the full text of her famous "Declaration," pp. 12–18. Hereafter cited, Smith *Conscience.*

179. "Joe began to get . . .": Oshinsky, *op. cit.*, p. 164.

183. "The man who . . .": Griffith, *op. cit.*, p. 72. Cf., Reeves, *op. cit.*, p. 262.

183. "behind-the-iron-curtain . . .": Reeves, *op. cit.*, p. 617.

183. "Snow White and . . .": *Ibid.*, p. 298. Cf., Oshinsky, *op. cit.*, p. 215.

183. "Joe had the Senate . . .": Smith *Conscience, op. cit.* Cf., Reeves, *op. cit.*, p. 298.

184. "a fraud and . . .": For the official Tydings Committee report see: U.S. Congress, Senate, Committee on Foreign Relations, *State Department Loyalty Investigations: Hearings of S. Res. 231.* 81st Cong., 2d Sess., Feb. 22, 1950 et seq., S. Rept. 2108, 281 pp., and 34 pp. of minority views. Hereafter cited as Tydings. Cf., Schrecker, *op. cit.*, p. 249. Cf., Oshinsky, *op. cit.*, p. 169. Cf., Reeves, *op. cit.*, p. 304.

185. "Not before in . . .": Reeves, *op. cit.*, p. 304.

186. "taken punishment . . .": *Ibid.*, pp. 309–310.

186. "whitewash": Griffith, *op. cit.*, p. 100.

187. "How can we . . .": Oshinsky, *op. cit.*, p. 169.

187. "You know, I have been . . .": *Ibid.*, p. 171.

187. "You will find out . . .": *Ibid.*, p. 171.

187. "'farce' and a 'whitewash'": Griffith, *op. cit.*, p. 100.

187. "conducting the most . . .": Reeves, *op. cit.*, p. 311.

187. "was such a brave . . .": *Ibid.*, p. 312.

188. "a green light . . .": *Ibid.*, p. 307.

188. "Acheson spilled blood . . .": McCarthy's speech before the Military Order of the Purple Heart in Worcester, Mass. was covered by the *Washington Times-Herald*, Aug. 27, 1950, p. 2. Similarly, the *Times-Herald* reported on his Charleston, S.C., speech, "McCarthy Puts Acheson in Molotov Class," Sept. 2, 1950, p. 4.

188. "a great American . . .": Oshinsky, *op. cit.*, p. 161.

190. "despicable 'back street' . . .": Griffith, *op. cit.*, p. 127. For official record of the Maryland investigation of Tydings's defeat, see: U.S. Congress, Senate, Committee on Rules and Administration, Subcommittee on Privileges and Elections, *Maryland Senatorial Election of 1950: Hearings on S. Res. 250*, 82d Cong., 1st Sess., Feb 20, 1951, et seq., 1222 pp. and Report 647.

190. "sponsored Owen Lattimore . . .": Reeves, *op. cit.*, p. 339.

191. "In every contest . . .": *Ibid.*, p. 343.

12. The Demagogue

Page
193. "I will have to . . .": Oshinsky, *op. cit.*, p. 207.

194. "the paranoid style . . .": Richard Hofstadter, *The Paranoid Style in*

American Politics and Other Essays. New York: Alfred A. Knopf, 1965.

194. "McCarthy's blunderbuss . . .": Oshinsky, *op. cit.*, p. 206.

195. "There are those . . .": *Ibid.*, p. 207.

198. "Someday I'm . . .": *Drew Pearson Diaries 1949–1959*. Edited by Tyler Abell. New York: Holt, Rinehart and, Winston, 1974. Diary entry for May 13, 1950, p. 128.

198. "whether to kill . . .": *Ibid.*, diary entry for April 21, 1950, p. 124.

198. For Pearson-McCarthy libel suit see the official transcript, "Drew Pearson, Plaintiff, v. Joseph R. McCarthy, et al., Defendants." *Deposition of Drew Pearson*. In the United States District Court for The District of Columbia. Civil Action No. 897-51, Washington, D.C., Sept. 25, 1951. McCarthy Papers.

203. "I won't turn . . .": *Ibid.*

203. "in the nuts . . .": Reeves, *op. cit.*, p. 349.

203. "I have an exclusive . . .": *Ibid.*

204. "about as effective . . .": Oshinsky, *op. cit.*, p. 180.

205. "Such foolishness . . .": *Ibid.*, pp. 180–181.

205. "Joe I've heard . . .": *Ibid.*, p. 181.

205. "For combat duty . . .": Reeves, *op. cit.*, p. 349.

205. "McCarthy, don't do . . .": Oshinsky, *op. cit.*, p. 181.

PART FOUR: Prelude to Power

13. Twenty Years of Treason

Page

211. "The son of a bitch . . .": *Milwaukee Journal*, April 12, 1951.

212. "old Yalta crowd . . .": Quotes here from text of McCarthy remarks, McCarthy Papers.

213. "I am reminded . . .": All of McCarthy's Marshall speech quotes here and following pages are from *Congressional Record* of June 14, 1951, and republished in his *America's Retreat From Victory: The Story of George Catlett Marshall.*

216. "Berserk eruption . . .": McCarthy himself proudly quoted this press criticism of him in his *America's Retreat from Victory: The Story of George Catlett Marshall.* New York: The Devin-Adair Co., 1952, pp. 174–180.

217. "What I said . . .": Oshinsky, *op. cit.*, p. 201.

217. "With a seeming . . .": William S. White, *New York Times,* Jan. 7, 1951.

218. "a general expression . . .": *Ibid.*

218. "to pin him . . .": Oshinsky, *op. cit.*, p. 199.

218. "For whom . . .": *Ibid.*

219. "He made the . . .": Haynes Johnson and Bernard M. Gwertzman, *Fulbright: The Dissenter.* New York: Doubleday & Company, 1968, p. 163. Hereafter cited, Johnson & Gwertzman.

220. "No help from . . .": Robert A. Caro, *Master of the Senate: The Years of Lyndon Johnson.* Volume Three. New York: Alfred A. Knopf, 2003, p. 543.

220. "destroying civil liberties . . .": *Ibid.*, p. 547.

220. "Something, somebody . . .": Caro, *op. cit.,* p. 543.

221. "only by the . . .": Griffith, *op. cit.*, p. 151.

222. "hit-and-run . . .": Reeves, *op. cit.*, p. 404.

223. "six Communist fronts . . .": Griffith, *op. cit.*, p. 148.

223. FN. Reeves, *op. cit.*, p. 387.

223. "affirmed their . . .": Griffith, *op. cit.*, p. 150.

223. "a controversial figure . . .": *Ibid.*, p. 150.

224. "filed and forgotten . . .": *Ibid.*, p. 157. For the official record, with transcripts of testimony, see: U.S. Congress, Senate, Committee on

Rules and Administration, Sub-Committee on Privileges and Elections. *Investigation of Senator Joseph R. McCarthy: A Resolution to Determine Whether Expulsion Proceedings Should Be Instituted: Hearings on S. Res. 187.* 82d Cong., 1st Sess., Sept. 28, 1951, and May 12-16, 1952. Unnumbered report (The Hennings Report) December 31, 1952, 400 pp. Cf., U.S. Congress, Senate, Committee on Rules and Administration. Sub-Committee on Privileges and Elections. *Investigation of Senators Joseph R. McCarthy and William Benton: Hearings On Sen. Res. 304.* 82d Cong., 2d Sess., July, 1952. Unnumbered report (The Hennings Report) December 31, 1952, 400 pp.

224. "should initiate . . .": *Ibid.*, p. 157.

224. "Connecticut's odd mental . . .": Oshinsky, *op. cit.*, p. 203. Cf., Reeves, *op. cit.*, p. 382, in separate quotes has McCarthy saying at one point, "odd little mental midget."

224. "Benton did what . . .": Reeves, *op. cit.*, p. 375.

224. "seems to thrive . . .": Oshinsky, *op. cit.*, p. 219.

225. "motley, Red-tinted . . .": Griffith, *op. cit.*, p. 175.

225. "shouting and screaming . . .": Reeves, *op. cit.*, p. 398.

226. "a means of . . .": *Ibid.*, p. 399.

226. "sweat . . .": *Ibid.*

226. "Instead of pursuing . . .": Griffith, *op. cit.*, p. 176.

226. "lies and slander . . .": Reeves, *op. cit.*, p. 379.

227. "If Truman wants . . .": *Ibid.*, p. 380.

227. "almost completely morally . . .": *Ibid.*, p. 397.

227. "The Democratic label . . .": Manchester, *op. cit.*, p. 526, Cf., Caute, *op. cit.*, p. 45.

228. "editorialized against . . .": *New York Times,* Sept. 19, 1951.

228. "what is pure and noble . . ." Reeves, *op. cit.*, p. 382.

229. "People wouldn't talk . . .": Taken from Oral Histories, Interviews, U.S. Senate Historical Office.

230. "He never really . . .": Darrell St. Claire, Oral History Interview, Senate Historical Office, Dec. 1976 to April 1978.

231. "Misguided zealots . . .": Jazzes H. Halsey, "Higher Education's Appalling Responsibilities: Correcting the Cultural Lag," delivered at the opening convocation of the University of Bridgeport's college year Sept. 25, 1951, published, *Vital Speeches,* Nov. 1, 1951, pp. 61–64.

238. "Ladies and gentlemen . . .": Reeves, *op. cit.*, p. 424.

239. "My good friends . . .": *Ibid.*, p. 425. Cf., for full McCarthy text, McCarthy Papers.

14. Taking More Scalps

Page
241. "He exposed all . . .": Bayley, *op. cit.*, p. 63.

242. "This is not only . . .": "The Man They Nominated," editorial, *Milwaukee Journal,* Sept. 10, 1952. Cf., Bayley, *op. cit,* p. 99.

243. "I'm not going to . . .": Author's Goodpaster interview, Sept. 11, 2003.

244. "I never heard . . .": William Bragg Ewald, Jr., *Who Killed Joe McCarthy?* New York: Simon & Schuster, 1984, p. 33.

244. "We had a very . . .": *Ibid.*

245. "Let me be . . .": *Ibid.*

245. "Deliberately, intentionally . . .": *Ibid.*

247. "mouse-trapped . . .": Goodpaster interview, *op. cit.*

247. "the theme of every . . .": Griffith, *op. cit.*, p. 199.

248. "the chameleon from . . .": *Ibid.*, p. 175. McCarthy made these and other charges at a congressional hearing on July 4th, 1952.

248. "Well, we got . . .": Oshinsky, *op. cit.*, p. 239.

248. "With that . . .": *Ibid.*, p. 239.

248. "Alger—I mean . . .": McCarthy's speech was Oct. 27, 1952. Text, McCarthy Papers.

249. "When I heard . . .": Oshinsky, *op. cit.*, p. 243.

249. "character assassin . . .": Reeves, *op. cit.*, p. 379.

250. "Hell, half my voters . . .": Arthur M. Schlesinger, Jr., *A Thousand Days: John F. Kennedy in the White House.* New York: Boston: Houghton Mifflin Company, 1965, p. 13.

251. "an old, blind . . .": Caro, *op. cit.*, p. 548.

251. "a disdain and contempt . . .": Griffith, *op. cit.*, p. 182, and Hennings Report. Cf., *New York Times*, Jan. 2, 1953.

252. "a new low . . .": Griffith, *Ibid.*

15. Junketeering Gumshoes

Page
253. "My God, I'm glad . . .": Roy Cohn, *McCarthy,* New York: Lancer Books, 1968, p. 46.

255. "I was brash . . .": *Ibid.*, p. 181.

258. "old and dusty . . .": Griffith, *op. cit.*, p. 218.

261. "There was no . . .": Oshinsky, *op. cit.*, p. 291.

262. "Communists, Fellow Travelers . . .": Reeves, *op. cit.*, pp. 480–481. Cf., Schrecker, *op. cit.*, p. 257, for even more telling details about the infamous Dulles directive on banning books from the overseas libraries: at one point, the directive on the "subversive" books policy ordered the banning of books "by any controversial persons, Communists, fellow travelers, et cetera . . ." Subsequently, the "any controversial persons" phrase was dropped, but the directive still included the all-embracing "et cetera" language, in effect, to cover all potential "subversive authors and artists." Cf., Caute, *op. cit.*, p. 322, on this policy.

263. "an obsessive and . . .": Maney, *op. cit.*, p. 313.

263. "ate away at . . .": *Ibid.*, p. 314.

264. "told how he . . .": Drew Pearson column, " 'Young Bob' Felt He'd Failed Dad," *Washington Post*, March 4, 1953.

265. "tear McCarthy . . .": Ewald, *op. cit.* Also other citations Ike diaries.

265. FN. "loathed McCarthy as . . .": Ewald, *op. cit.*, p. 67.

266. "Senator McCarthy is . . .": *Ibid.*, p. 66. The diary entry is for April 1, 1953. All subsequent diary citations for Eisenhower, Hagerty, C.D. Jackson, and others on the then-White House staff are from Ewald, who also was on the White House staff and later had access to all these and more documents while helping Eisenhower write his memoirs at Gettysburg.

266. "Don't join the book burners . . .": Ewald, *Ibid.*, p. 67.

267. "In all that . . .": *Ibid.*, p. 151.

268. "My brother . . .": *Ibid.*, p. 147.

269. "the build and . . .": Rovere, *Senator, op. cit.*, p. 193.

269. "sallow, sleekly coiffed . . .": *Ibid.*

270. "stood as Exhibit A . . .": Ewald, *op. cit.*, p. 51.

270. "ready-made plot . . .": Rovere, *Senator, op. cit.*, p. 199.

270. "was marked from . . .": *Ibid.*

271. "By the time . . .": *Ibid.*, p. 201.

271. "junketeering gumshoes": *Ibid.*, p. 204.

272. "Mr. Cohn and Mr. Schine . . .": Hans N. Tuch recalls the episode after Cohn's death in a letter to the editor, "Roy Cohn's Descent on the Libraries of Europe," *New York Times*, Aug. 17, 1986, Sect. 4, p. 22.

272. FN. Bayley, *op. cit.*, p. 168 notes that *"Time* magazine, almost always on McCarthy's 'left-wing' list, had been skeptical about his charges from the start."

272. "swear word . . . when I said . . .": *Ibid.*

273. "these two brash . . .": Griffith, *op. cit.*, p. 214. Cf., Reeves, *op. cit.*, pp. 488–89.

273. "a colossal mistake": Cohn, *op. cit.*, p. 81.

274. "Specifically, what was . . .": *Meet the Press*, transcript, May 3, 1953, courtesy NBC.

277. "Reds and Our . . .": J. B. Matthews, *American Mercury*, July 1953.

277. "headed for disaster . . .": Robert F. Kennedy, *The Enemy Within*. New York: Popular Library, 1960, p. 170.

279. "the spies popped up . . .": LeCarré quoted, *New York Times*, May 4, 1993.

280. "car body shelter": Patricia Leigh Brown, "Ideas and Trends: Armageddon Again: Fear in the 50's and Now," *New York Times*, Aug. 10, 2002. Other sources from which I've drawn include: "The Red Scare: A Filmography," The All Powers Project, an excellent summary, from http://www.lib.Washington.edu./exhibits/AllPowers/film; the equally valuable "Movies of the 1950's," Media Resources Center, UCB, http://www.lib.berkeley.edu/MRC/movies1950; the superb rendering, "American Cultural History, 1950–1959," Kingwood College Library's Web and library guide, http://kdlibrary .nhmccd.edu/decade50. In addition, see "1950s Bestsellers," 1950 through 1959, provided by Cader Books, http://www.caderbooks .com/best50, and the telling collection of *Life* magazine covers for 1950, especially the *Life* cover of Feb. 27, 1950, shortly after McCarthy's Wheeling speech, that shows a rising mushroom cloud from an atomic bomb explosion in the Pacific and headline: "The Danger of War and Our Ability to Face It," http://www.life.com/Life/covers/1950.

PART FIVE: Witch Hunts

16. Inquisitions

Page
285. "Are you a witch? . . .": "Salem Witchcraft Hysteria," Nationalgeographic

.com., 1997. Cf., Douglas Linder, "An Account of Events In Salem," Salem Trials Web site.

288. "judge, jury, prosecutor . . .": Erwin Griswold, *The Fifth Amendment Today.* Cambridge: Harvard University Press, 1955.

288. "It didn't really . . .": John G. Adams, *Without Precedent: The Story of the Death of McCarthyism.* New York: Norton, 1983, p. 53.

289. "a new and . . .": Reeves, *op. cit.*, pp. 524–525. Cf., See the remarkable transcripts of the McCarthy closed-door sessions, stamped secret and deposited in the National Archives until they were declassified and made public after 50 years, in January 2003: *Executive Sessions of the Senate Permanent Subcommittee on Investigations of the Committee on Government Operations.* 83d Congress, 1st Sess., 1953. Volumes 1 through 5. Printed for the use of the Committee on Governmental Affairs. Washington: U.S. Government Printing Office, 2003. All quotes in my narrative describing these hearings are from these volumes. Hereafter cited as Closed Hearings.

289. "No real research . . .": Kennedy, *op. cit.*, p. 291.

289. "McCarthy ignored . . .": Adams, *op. cit.*, p. 67.

291. "Seeking any sign . . .": Closed Hearings, *op. cit.*, commentary from Donald A. Ritchie. U.S. Senate Historical Office.

292. "give it a more . . .": *Ibid.*

292. "Do not just . . .": Closed Hearings, *op. cit.*

298. "It seemed like . . .": Oral History Project, American Music, Yale University. Cited, Aaron Copland and Vivian Perlis, *Copland: Since 1943.* New York: St. Martin's Press, pp. 398 and 181. In his biography, Copland writes about his McCarthyism experience. Hereafter cited as Copland.

299. "The master of . . .": Copland, *op. cit.*, p. 185.

299. "The Republican Party . . .": *Ibid.*

299. "I have no . . .": *Ibid.*

299. "I am an American . . .": *Ibid.*, p. 187.

300. "because we didn't . . .": *The Nation,* Jan. 31, 1953.

302. "He seems to enjoy . . .": Copland, *op. cit.*, p. 195.

303. "sense of being pursued . . .": *Ibid.*, p. 198.

303. "passports to individuals . . .": *Ibid.*

303. "Aaron Copland . . .": *Ibid.*

303. "avowedly anti-Communist . . .": *Ibid.*

303. "I regret to . . .": *Ibid.*, p. 200.

304. "After I talked . . .": Arnold Rampersad, *The Life of Langston Hughes. Volume II: 1941–1967: I Dream a World.* Second Edition. Oxford University Press, 1988, p. 209.

305. "YOU ARE DIRECTED . . .": Rampersad, *op. cit.*, p. 210.

305. "radical . . . great Red flag . . .": Closed Hearings.

308. "Hughes had given in to brutish . . .": *Ibid.*, p. 219.

309. "Politics can be . . .": *Ibid.*

309. In a poem . . . : "Un-American Investigators," published in Langston Hughes, *The Panther and the Lash: Poems of Our Times.* New York: Alfred A. Knopf, 1967, p. 67.

311. "I knew that . . .": Theodore Kaghan, "The McCarthyization of Theodore Kaghan," *The Reporter,* July 21, 1953.

329. "Eric Kohler . . .": Lynn Sweet, "Hunt for Homosexuals at Roosevelt University," *Chicago Sun-Times,* May 6, 2003.

330. "completely incompetent . . .": Closed Hearings, *op. cit.*

17. The Case of Private Schine

Page
333. "our young friend . . .": All quotes cited from verbatim telephonic conversations between Stevens, his aides, Army and defense officials, and others cited between pp. 413–449 are drawn from the transcriptions made over Stevens' office phone detailed in Ewald,

op. cit., from papers deposited in the Eisenhower presidential library, Abilene, Kansas. Also published, in part, Army Hearings.

336. "gold mine . . .": Ewald, *op. cit.,* p. 81.

336. "a rolling . . .": *Ibid.*

339. "Don't give me that, General . . .": Closed Hearings, *op. cit.*

348. "A few days ago . . .": Text, McCarthy Papers.

352. "I would love . . .": Closed Hearings, *op. cit,* as are the others cited in this section.

360. "a disgraceful performance . . .": Reeves, *op. cit.,* p. 545.

360. "avenging angel . . .": *Chicago Tribune,* Feb. 25, 1954.

361. "no intention of . . .": Ewald, *op. cit.* Again, Ewald cites the verbatim phone conversations that I quote here and elsewhere from papers eventually deposited in the Eisenhower presidential library, Abilene, Kansas. Also published, in part, Army Hearings.

361. "Mr. Secretary . . .": Ewald, *op. cit.*

367. "Bob, you've been had . . .": *Ibid.,* p. 213.

368. "Senator McCarthy this afternoon . . .": *London Times,* Feb. 26, 1954.

369. "He couldn't have . . .": *New York Times,* Feb. 26, 1954, p. 1. Cf., Ewald, *op cit.,* p. 218.

369. "He had gone into . . .": Ewald, *Ibid.,* p. 217.

370. "I heard about . . .": Ewald, *op. cit,* p. 220.

371. "I shall never . . .": *Ibid.,* p. 222.

372. "totalitarianism . . . his cold, calculated . . .": Walter Lippmann, op-ed column, *Washington Post,* March 25, 1954.

372. "If the President permits . . .": Alsop op-ed column, *Washington Post,* March 25, 1954.

373. FN. "McCarthy is grabbing . . .": *Ibid.,* p. 288.

373. "Such a statement . . .": Ewald, *op. cit.,* p. 238.

373. "Why, the yellow . . .": Bayley, *op. cit.*, p. 189. The quote is from an interview by Bayley with Willard Edwards of the *Chicago Tribune* on June 27, 1977. Edwards told Bayley he and Alsop were sitting together at the news conference, expecting, as did all observers, that "Eisenhower was going to tear McCarthy's head off. . . . I sat next to Alsop and we listened with bated breath. Ike started reading his statement, and it became obvious that he was going to be very mild. Joe Alsop stood up and said in a loud voice, 'The yellow sonofabitch!'"

373. "only under tyranny . . .": *Ibid.*, p. 238.

374. "If a stupid . . .": *Ibid.*, p. 188.

375. "A group of . . .": Ewald, *op. cit.*, p. 246.

376. "The networks will . . .": Reeves, *op. cit.*, p. 562.

376. "Some people think . . .": Ewald, *op. cit.*, p. 270.

376. "that prick . . .": Reeves, *op. cit.*, p. 562. The quote is from Van Susteren. Cf., Bayley, *op. cit.*, quoting Van Susteren as telling him in 1976 that McCarthy disliked Nixon, "you could almost say he hated him," p. 137. Cf., Rovere *Senator, op. cit.*, quoting George Sokolsky as telling him McCarthy "particularly felt betrayed by Vice President Nixon . . . ," p. 246.

377. "dead set [on] . . .": Ewald, *op. cit.*, p. 247.

378. "loose the dogs . . .": *Ibid.*, p. 250.

378. "dons his war . . .": Flanders' Senate speech was March 9, 1954. Cf., Reeves, *op. cit.*, p. 563.

378. "America needs to hear . . .": Eisenhower to Flanders, March 9, 1954, Eisenhower papers, presidential library.

18. Point of Order!

Page
381. "He complained bitterly . . .": Cohn, *op. cit.*, p. 208.

381. "on an extremely . . .": Ewald, *op. cit.*, p. 298.

383. "'Boys,' Welch . . .": Oshinsky, *op. cit.*, p. 457.

383. "an unerring instinct . . .": Cohn, *op. cit,* p. 132.

384. "should return . . .": Oshinsky, *op. cit,* p. 458.

384. "several bottles of . . .": *Ibid.*, p. 458.

385. "a different story . . .": Ewald, *op. cit.*, p. 302. Cf., Oshinsky, *op. cit.*, p. 458.

386. "drove the snakes . . .": Oshinsky, *op. cit.*, p. 410.

388. "the television camera . . .": David T. Bazelon, his introduction, Emile De Antonio and Daniel Talbot, *Point of Order! A Documentary of the Army-McCarthy Hearings.* New York: W.W. Norton & Company, 1964, p. 5. Hereafter cited as *Documentary.* For all public Army-McCarthy Hearings quotes from testimony, see the official record: U.S. Congress, Senate, Committee on Government Operations, *Charges and Counter-Charges Involving Secretary of the Army Robert T. Stevens, John G. Adams, H. Struve Hensel, and Senator Joe McCarthy, Roy M. Cohn, and Francis P. Carr: Hearing on S. Res. 189,* 83d Cong., 2d Sess., Apr. 22–June 17, 1954, 2,980 pp., and S. Rept. 2507, 130 pp. Hereafter cited as Army Hearings. For TV statistics, see Bayley, *op. cit.*, p. 176.

389. during the hearings' . . . : Oshinsky, *op. cit.*, p. 416. Cf., *Newsweek,* reported a surge of TV sales. Cf., *Washington Times-Herald,* headline: "MCCARTHY-ARMY TELECASTS DISRUPT HOUSEWORK ROUTINE," cited Adams, *op. cit.*, p. 167.

390. "our national obsession . . .": Lippmann, op-ed column, *Washington Post,* March 25, 1954.

390. "Van . . . do you . . .": Among many accounts of McCarthy's drinking, see: Reeves, *op. cit.*, pp. 669–670, and Oshinsky, *op. cit.*, pp. 231–232, 504. Both biographers quote Van Susteren on McCarthy's "kiss my ass" comment.

390. "The walls have . . .": Oshinsky, *op. cit.*, p. 412.

392. "preferential treatment . . .": *Documentary, op. cit.*

393. "He complained bitterly . . .": Cohn, *op. cit.*, p. 208.

394. "Does that mean . . .": *Documentary, op. cit,* as are the hearings quotes that follow here.

402. "This is nothing but . . .": Ewald, *op. cit.*, p. 365.

403. "The executive branch . . .": *Ibid.*

406. "Don't threaten me . . .": Cohn, *op. cit,* p. 71.

410. "would not consent . . .": Army Hearings, *op. cit.*

19. "Have You No Shame, Senator?"

Page

413. "Until this moment . . .": Army Hearings, *op. cit.*

413. "There's a little matter . . .": Cohn, *op. cit.*, p. 200.

415. "That night . . .": *Ibid.*, p. 202.

419. "Roy Cohn grimaced . . .": *Ibid.*, p. 203.

419. "This is the subject . . .": *Ibid.*

426. "I got physically ill . . .": Nellor and Van Susteren quotes, Reeves Papers.

427. "What did I do? . . .": Adams, *op. cit.*, p. 229.

PART SIX: Judgment

20. Belling the Cat

Page

431. "I think they . . .": McCarthy made this remark to reporters after the hearings that day. After his quote made the front pages the next day (*New York Times*, June 11, 1954), he typically denied saying it.

434. "Just a minute . . .": *New York Times*, Sept. 1, 1954.

434. "The senator is . . .": *Ibid.*

434. "the gavel crack . . .": Griffith, *op. cit.*, p. 299.

434. "I think it's . . .": *New York Times,* Sept. 1, 1954.

434. "improper influence . . . inexcusable actions . . .": U.S. Congress, Senate, 83d Congress, 2d sess., Committee on Government Operations, Permanent Subcommittee on Investigations, *Charges and Counter-Charges . . .*, Senate Report 2507, Washington, D.C., 1954.

435. "We realize the . . .": *New York Times,* Sept. 1, 1954, p. 1.

435. "He has posed . . .": For the full charges, see the 68-page, Report of the Select Committee to Study Censure Charges, United States Senate, 83d Congress, 2d Session, Pursuant to S. Res. 301 and Amendments. *A Resolution to Censure the Senator from Wisconsin, Mr. McCarthy.* Printed for the Use of the Select Committee to Study Censure Charges. Washington: United States Government Printing Office, 1954. For the record of the Watkins Committee investigation, see: U.S. Congress, Senate, Select Committee to Study Censure Charges. *Hearings on S. Res. 301,* 2d Sess., Aug. 28–Sept. 16, 1954, 399 pp., and Report No. 22508, Nov. 8, 1954, 68 pp.

436. "The committee denied . . .": Griffith, *op. cit.*, p. 297.

437. "Red skunk . . .": Oshinsky, *op. cit.*, p. 487. From August to November, as the censure fight drew to a conclusion, Fulbright received literally thousands of hate letters, vile, profane, and many illiterate. In a Senate speech Nov. 30th, the day before the censure vote, he read excerpts from many of the letters, citing them as examples of McCarthyism: "By his reckless charges [McCarthy] has so preyed upon the fears and hatred of uninformed and credulous people that he has started a prairie fire, which neither he nor anyone else may be able to control. If there are ten million people in this country similar to the authors of these letters, I believe it is something about which all of us ought to be deeply concerned." Among comments he read were: "a fine dirty red rat are you." Censuring McCarthy, he hoped, would put a stop to "the reckless incitement of the hatreds and fears of people who are suffering from a lack of in-

formation or a lack of understanding." Cf., Johnson & Gwertzman, *op. cit.*, p. 140.

438. "symbol of resistance . . .": Oshinsky, *op. cit.*, p. 483.

438. "lynch-bee . . .": Rovere, *Senator, op. cit.*, p. 230. McCarthy repeatedly described the Senate censure debate as a "lynch-bee" in a national TV-radio address Nov. 7, 1954. In that speech he also attacked the Watkins Committee as being "involuntary agents" and "attorneys in fact" of the Communist Party, and accused its members of being "handmaidens" of the Communist conspiracy.

438. "The strategy of . . .": Oshinsky, *op. cit.*, p. 484.

439. "given the gas . . .": Robert G. Spivack, then Washington correspondent of the at-the-time liberal *New York Post,* interviewed Texas oil man G. G. Gurley by phone and wrote about his letter to Fulbright under the headline "Mr. Gurley Elaborates," *New York Post,* Dec. 1, 1954, p. 5. Gurley's letter was among those Fulbright had read to the Senate the day before, Nov. 30.

439. "Ten Million . . .": "Petitions Go to Capital, Shy by 9 Million Names," *Ibid.*, p. 5.

440. "Each of us . . .": Spivack, "Senate Begins Vote Today, Hears Bush Denounce," *Ibid., New York Post.*

440. "If I ever saw . . .": Spivack, *op. cit.*

21. Oblivion

Page

443. "There he was . . .": Dorothye G. Scott, Oral History Interview, June 3 to June 24, 1992.

444. "very splendid job": Ewald, *op. cit.*, p. 381.

444. "During the Eisenhower . . .": Oshinsky, *op. cit.*, p. 493.

445. "dispirited and bewildered . . .": Cohn, *op. cit.*, p. 243.

447. "What other explanation . . .": Oshinsky, *op. cit.*, p. 497.

447. "Had the censure vote . . .": *Ibid.*, p. 498.

448. "dry him out . . .": Reeves, *op. cit.*, p. 691.

449. "He had a much . . .": Pat M. Holt, Oral History Interview, Sept. 9, 1980, to Dec. 12, 1980.

449. "Who the hell . . .": Reeves Papers, *op. cit.*

450. "It was fascinating . . .": Francis R. Valeo, Oral History Interview, July 3, 1985, to March 11, 1986.

451. "I'm Joe McCarthy . . .": Johnson & Gwertzman, *op. cit.*, p. 140.

452. "Of the dead . . .": "Hundreds View McCarthy Bier," *Washington Post and Times Herald,* May 3, 1957, p. B-3.

452. "In some respects . . .": Pearson, *op. cit.* Diary entry for May 2, 1957, p. 379.

453. "People were a little . . .": "Hundreds View McCarthy Bier," *Washington Evening Star,* May 4, 1957, p. A-2.

454. "a role which . . .": Mary McGrory, "Cathedral Rites Laud McCarthy," *Evening Star,* May 6, 1957, p. A-1.

454. "There was his casket . . ." Dorothye G. Scott, Oral History Interview, June 3 to June 24, 1992.

PART SEVEN: Legacy

22. The Politics of Fear

Page

459. "Between 1950 and 1954 . . .": Griffith, *op. cit.*, p. 320.

463. "that stinking hypocrite . . .": Manchester, *op. cit.*, p. 505. Cf., Rovere *Senator, op. cit.*, p. 250.

463. "McCarthy was murdered . . .": Reeves, *op. cit.*, p. 672, found Loeb's *Union Leader* editorial, undated, in Box 13 of the Flanders Papers, Wisc. Hist. Soc. Files.

464. FN. "What the country needed . . .": Ann Coulter, *Treason: Liberal Treachery From the Cold War to the War on Terrorism.* New York: Crown Forum, 2003, p. 69.

23. Parallels

Page

466. "We've cleared whole . . .": "After Terror, a Secret Rewriting of Military Law," *New York Times,* Oct. 24, 2004.

468. "Unannounced, the FBI . . .": "Sanctioned Bias: Racial Profiling Since 9/11," ACLU, Feb. 2004, p. 5.

468. "In a massive . . .": *Ibid.*, p. 6.

469. "The human costs . . .": *Ibid.*, p. 11.

470. "What's the record there . . .": Ray Suarez interview, *The NewsHour With Jim Lehrer,* transcript, Nov. 11, 2004.

470. "This is an . . .": *Ibid.*

471. "tantamount to torture": Neil A. Lewis, *New York Times,* Nov. 30, 2004.

472. "so sensitive that . . .": Tim Golden, "Tough Justice: New Code, New Power," first of two articles, "After Terror, A Secret Rewriting of Military Law," *New York Times,* Oct. 24, 2004, p. A-1.

473. "communications blackout . . .": From Justice Department's IG Report.

474. "that the detainees . . .": *Ibid.*, as are all other quotes cited on following pages of this section.

474. "It soon became . . .": IG Report, *op. cit.*

478. "a nightmare of . . .": Joseph S. Nye, op-ed column, *New York Times,* Nov. 29, 2004.

479. On September 22 . . . : "Detained Cat Stevens Heading Home," CNN.com, Sept. 22, 2004.

24. A House Divided

Page

494. "Fear does work . . .": McDermott's quote is from a transcript of the Michael Moore film documentary, *Fahrenheit 911*. McDermott responded to an off-camera question, "And how do you make them afraid?" by saying, "You make them afraid by creating an aura of endless threat . . . It's like training a dog. You tell him to sit down or you tell him to roll over at the time. Dog doesn't know what to do. Well, the American people were being treated like that. It was really very . . . ugly what they did."

495. "This kind of . . .": Eric Boehlert, "Joe McCarthy Lives," Salon.com, Sept. 30, 2004.

496. "to threaten the . . .": "Scare Tactics," *International Herald Tribune*, Oct. 22, 2004. Cf., Jim VandeHei and Howard Kurtz, "The Politics of Fear," *Washington Post*, Sept. 29, 2004.

496. "the hand of . . .": *Ibid., International Herald Tribune*, Oct. 22, 2004.

496. "That's my opinion . . .": Boehlert, *op. cit.*

496. "If you want . . .": *Ibid.* Limbaugh's broadcast was March 18, 2004.

496. "These people want . . .": *Ibid.* The commercial began airing the last week in Sept 2004.

497. "The president got reelected . . .": Maureen Dowd, "The Red Zone," op-ed column, *New York Times*, Nov. 4, 2004.

502. "Hanoi John . . .": E. J. Dionne Jr., "Stooping Low to Smear Kerry," op-ed column, *Washington Post*, April 27, 2004.

503. "How dare Senator . . .": Gail Russell Chaddock, "Soft Debate Surfaces on Terror War," *Christian Science Monitor*, March 4, 2002.

503. "disgusting . . .": *Ibid.*

504. "an embarrassment . . .": *Meet the Press*, transcript, Sept. 19, 2004, courtesy NBC News.

504. "Joe McCarthy Lives . . .": Boehlert, *op. cit.*

505. "The press can't . . .": *Ibid.*

505. This kind of . . . : *Ibid.*

506. "At one level . . .": Thomas Friedman, "Two Nations Under God," op-ed column, *New York Times,* Nov. 4, 2004.

510. "this hot-button . . .": *New York Times,* Nov. 6, 2004.

510. "Three days after . . .": CNN *Crossfire,* transcript, Nov. 5, 2004, 4:30pm, EST.

512. "All of us missed . . .": Scripps Howard News Service, November 17, 2004.

Epilogue: THE AGE OF ANXIETY

Page
520. "House of Lords": David S. Broder, op-ed column, "No Vote Necessary," *Washington Post,* Nov. 11, 2004.

521. "So there you . . .": Hendrik Hertzberg, "Without DeLay," *The New Yorker,* April 25, 2005, pp. 33–34.

522. "the artillery of the press": Cited in Haynes Johnson, "The American Press and the Crisis of Change," Goldstein Program in Public Affairs, in *Contemporary Views of American Journalism,* Chestertown, Md.: Literary House Press at Washington College, 1997, p. 18.

529. "Our task is . . .": Rebecca West, *The New Meaning of Treason,* first published 1947 as *The Meaning of Treason,* republished, under revised title, New York: The Viking Press, 1964, p. 370.

Afterword

Page
530. "A wiretap requires . . .": White House transcript, "Remarks by the President in a Conversation on the USA Patriot Act, Kleinshans Music Hall, Buffalo, New York," 9:49 a.m. EDT, April 20, 2004.

536. "I don't think . . .": Bush interview with Diane Sawyer, ABC-TV, Sept. 1, 2005.

536. they called a "doomsday" . . . : See the extensive account of the "doomsday" planning in Joel K. Bourne, Jr., "Gone With the Water. The Louisiana bayou, hardest working marsh in America, is in big trouble, with dire consequences for residents, [and] the nearby city of New Orleans . . . ," *National Geographic Magazine*, Oct. 2004.

537. SOME LEVEES . . . : John Fain, "Hurricane Katrina Forecast Was Remarkably Accurate," USA Today.com, Sept. 16, 2005.

538. "Any storm rated . . .": Eric Lipton, "White House Was Told Hurricane Posed Danger," *New York Times*, Jan. 24, 2006, p. A14. Cf., Spencer S. Hsu and Linton Weeks, "Video Shows Bush Being Warned on Katrina," *Washington Post*, March 2, 2006, p. A1.

539. "It looks like Hiroshima . . .": Joseph B. Treaster and N. R. Kleinfeld, "New Orleans Is Inundated as 2 Levees Fail; Much of Gulf Coast Is Crippled; Toll Rises," *New York Times*, Aug. 31, 2005, p. A1.

539. "I don't think . . .": Bush, Diane Sawyer interview, *op. cit.*

539. "Brownie, you're doing . . .": *op. cit.*

539. THIRD WORLD AMERICA . . . : London *Daily Mail*, Sept. 3, 2005.

540. "would impinge on . . .": David E. Rosenbaum, "Fight in House for White House Files on Katrina," *New York Times*, Dec. 8, 2005, p. A33.

541. "The director . . . of . . .": Spencer S. Hsu and Amy Goldstein, "Administration Faulted on Katrina; GAO Report Blames Bungled Response on Failures That Started at the Top," *Washington Post*, Feb. 2, 2006, p. A5.

541. feared the "unconscionable" . . . : Philip Shenon, "Commission Criticizes Storm Response," *New York Times*, Sept. 15, 2005, p. A23.

542. "What I'm hearing . . .": Barbara Bush's interview was with the radio program "Marketplace," Sept. 5, 2006, after she toured the Houston Astrodome complex housing Katrina evacuees with her husband, former President George H. W. Bush.

542. "I did not . . .": Charles Babington and Dan Eggen, "Gonzales Seeks to Clarify Testimony on Spying; Extent of Eavesdropping May Go Beyond NSA Work," *Washington Post,* March 1, 2006, p. A8.

543. "It seems to me . . .": *Ibid.*

545. a *Washington Post* profile . . . : Peter Slevin, "Scholar Stands by Post-9/11 Writings on Torture, Domestic Eavesdropping," *Washington Post,* Dec. 26, 2005, p. A3.

545. "bright, conservative up-and-comers . . .": *Ibid.*

545. "Yoo required a . . .": *Ibid.*

546. "The President's broad . . .": *Ibid.*

547. "equivalent in intensity . . .": *Ibid.*

548. "A state of war . . .": Justice O'Connor's ruling was on June 30, 2004, in *Hamdi v. Rumsfeld.*

551. "harmless weather balloons . . .": Jory Warrick, "Lacking Biolabs, Trailers Carried Case for War," *Washington Post,* April 12, 2006, p. A1.

551. "already been available . . .": Christopher Lee, "Archives Kept a Secrecy Secret," *Washington Post,* April 12, 2006, p. A6.

551. "shows that the National Archives . . .": *Ibid.*

552. "Truth be told . . .": Peter S. Canellos, "Questions Raised on President's Role," *Boston Globe,* April 7, 2006.

553. "already includes several . . .": Spencer S. Hsu, "FBI Rebuffed on Reporter's Files," *Washington Post,* April 18, 2006. Cf., Scott Shane, "F.B.I. Seeking Access to Dead Columnist's Papers," *New York Times,* April 18, 2006, p. A1.

553. "dangerous departure . . .": *Ibid.*

554. Wilson debunked . . . : Wilson's op-ed *New York Times* article was published July 6, 2003.

555. "has the potential . . .": Office of Special Counsel, "White House Official I. Lewis Libby Indicted . . .": Oct. 28, 2005.

556. "a concerted action" by "multiple people in the White House": *Ibid.*

557. White House Iraq Group . . . : Barton Gellman and Dafna Linzer, "A 'Concerted' Effort to Discredit Bush Critic. Prosecutor Describes Cheney, Libby as Key Voices Pitching Iraq-Niger Story," *Washington Post,* April 9, 2006, p. A1.

557. "that will be decided . . .": Bennett Roth, "Exit from Iraq is up to 'future presidents,'" *Houston Chronicle,* March 22, 2006, p. A1.

558. "major combat operations . . .": For Bush transcript, see "Bush makes historic speech aboard warship," CNN.com, May 1, 2003.

559. "Our troops have become . . .": For full text of Murtha's remarks see his congressional office news release, "War in Iraq," Nov. 17, 2005.

560. "several hundred thousand . . .": Eric Schmitt, "Pentagon Contradicts General on Iraq Occupation Force's Size," *New York Times,* Feb. 28, 2003, p. A1.

564. "You might think . . .": David S. Broder, "Red Ink Run Amok," op-ed column, *Washington Post,* April 13, 2006.

566. "Where is the outrage . . .": Cited, Walter Pincus and Charles Babington, "Specter Wants More Debate on Spying," *Washington Post,* April 28, 2006, p. A4.

566. "ruthless enemy . . .": E. J. Dionne Jr., "Rove's Early Warning," op-ed column, *Washington Post,* Jan. 24, 2006.

568. "We will not walk . . .": Text of Murrow's broadcast, reprinted, *In Search of Light: The Broadcasts of Edward R. Murrow 1938–1961,* Edward Bliss Jr., editor, New York: Knopf, 1967, pp. 247–8.

Bibliographical Notes

A s I noted in my manuscript, the first serious book on McCarthy, Richard Rovere's *Senator Joe McCarthy,* remains incomparably the best-written and most provocative portrait both of the man and the times forty-six years after it was published—a remarkable achievement considering it came only two years after McCarthy's death when so many critical sources were unavailable. Since Rovere, three major McCarthy works have become indispensable. The first, Robert Griffith's *The Politics of Fear: Joseph R. McCarthy and the Senate,* published in 1970, is an admirable work of scholarship and analysis, and especially good for its grasp of McCarthy and the Senate and the interplay of politics, personalities, and issues. It provides a solid framework for all others that have followed. A second edition, published in 1987, contains a superb new introduction by Griffith that updates the story to then and includes an excellent overview of published works on McCarthy, McCarthyism, and anticommunism, which complements and strengthens his own excellent bibliographical essay of 1970. After Griffiths, came two full-length biographies that draw from the extensive and growing McCarthy archival information—those still not closed to public scrutiny, I should say—official and secondary works, and source interviews. Thomas C. Reeves's, *The Life and Times of Joe*

McCarthy: A Biography, the product of six years of prodigious and painstaking research, published in 1982, is required reading for any serious student of McCarthy and his era. Scholars in particular will forever be in his debt for the voluminous collection of his interview notes and other material now housed in the Historical Society of Wisconsin. Important as the Reeves biography is, it is marred by a chip-on-the-shoulder defensiveness about McCarthy and its tendency to explain away McCarthy's actions as just "Irish blarney" or as behavior misunderstood by biased critics, especially "liberals" in Washington and New York. Reeves, as a young Wisconsin scholar, frankly set out to debunk Rovere and other McCarthy critics. In a preface to his paperback edition, published fifteen years later in 1997, he displayed the same dogged, if not ideological, determination to correct what he maintains is still "a crude caricature" of McCarthy portrayed in works about him, a portrait of the real McCarthy "virtually ignored by journalists and historians." That is a sweeping, and absurd, conclusion. These caveats of mine aside, the Reeves biography is a fine resource. The other major biography, David M. Oshinsky's *A Conspiracy So Immense: The World of Joe McCarthy,* published a year after the Reeves work in 1983, is better written and offers a deeper portrait of the clash of politics of the time, both in Washington and the nation. All three of these works, Griffith, Reeves, and Oshinsky, remain essential reading for anyone interested in the McCarthy story. In 2000, Arthur Herman produced another worthy full-length biography, *Joseph McCarthy: Reexamining the Life and Legacy of America's Most Hated Senator.* Written from a frankly conservative viewpoint, Herman's is a serious work that sheds light on how McCarthy is seen by conservatives all these years later. In the fall of 2004, Ted Morgan published a massive, exhaustively researched study, *Reds: McCarthyism in Twentieth-Century America,* that seeks to link, as do I, the McCarthy era to past times of repression. Since I was in the midst of my own effort, I consciously did not read Morgan until my work was finished. Morgan offers another important telling of the subject, yet to my mind one that is often heavy and discursive. Among other works that I found especially useful, Ellen Schrecker's writings are essential. Her *No Ivory Tower,* a study of the impact of McCarthyism on American colleges and universities, is splendid, and so is her most valuable collection of documents on the McCarthy era and anticommunism, *The Age of McCarthyism. A Brief History with Documents* (2nd edition), published in 2002. Her 1998 *Many Are the*

Crimes: McCarthyism in America, is another serious offering, but somewhat dry and bloodless. In the growing literature on Communist activity in America, including spies, essential is John Earl Haynes and Harvey Klehr's *Venona: Decoding Soviet Espionage in America,* published in 2000; and Derek Leebaert's most impressive major history of 2002, *The Fifty-Year Wound: How America's Cold War Victory Shapes Our World.* Sam Tanenhaus's 1997 definitive biography of Whittaker Chambers (*Whittaker Chambers: A Biography*) is essential for understanding that crucial, complex figure, and helps fill in much of the questions arising out of Chambers's own remarkable account of his undercover Communist years, *Witness.* For an overview of the McCarthy hysteria, David Caute's 1978 *The Great Fear: The Anti-Communist Purge Under Truman and Eisenhower* is the best, but it must be read from the perspective of the New Left historical revisionism of the Vietnam/Watergate era. William Manchester's masterly history, *The Glory and the Dream: A Narrative History of America, 1932–1972, 1973–74,* becomes even more impressive the more you examine it a generation after its publication. Two other works, among the many I cite in the formal bibliographical listing following these notes, deserve special praise. Edwin R. Bayley's 1981 *Joe McCarthy and the Press* is far and away the best, and most sophisticated, on the subject—and a subject that cries out for a similar treatment on today's press-government relations in the Bush era. William Bragg Ewald, Jr.'s *Who Killed Joe McCarthy?* is indispensable for its behind-the-scenes account of the Eisenhower administration's maneuverings on McCarthy. For the La Follette story, the two excellent biographies on which I have relied are Roger T. Johnson's *Robert M. La Follette, Jr.,* in 1970, and Patrick J. Maney's *Young Bob.* I will not attempt here to assess the outpouring of excellent works on our current post 9/11 anxieties, which are listed below, except to say that two accounts on the 9/11 investigations are obviously crucial: the official rendering, *The 9/11 Commission Report: Final Report of the National Commission on Terrorist Attacks Upon the United States* (Norton, 2004); and a complementary offering, *The 9/11 Investigations,* providing staff reports of the 9/11 Commission, excerpts from the House-Senate Joint Inquiry Report, and testimony from fourteen key witnesses, including Richard Clarke, George Tenet, and Condoleeza Rice (Public Affairs Press, 2004).

Critical to my own effort are the following research files from which I drew essential material:

From Marquette University Libraries, Department of Special Collections and University Archives: Joseph R. McCarthy Papers: Series 1, General Correspondence, 1939–1946; Series 21, Court Records, 1946, 1951–1956; Series 3, Speeches (Released Texts), 1942–1957; Series 9, Memorabilia; Series 12, Press Clippings, 1939——; FBI (Federal Bureau of Investigation) Records, J. Edgar Hoover Official and Confidential File, 1925–1977; Series 16, Box 17, Folder 105, Senator Joseph R. McCarthy, March 18–July 14, 1953; Biographical Information Files, Record A-4, 5, Series 9, Drawer 16, McCarthy, Joseph R. (Alumnus——Law, 1935; U.S. Senator from Wisconsin).

From the Wisconsin Historical Society: William Benton Papers, 1951–1961; Thomas E. Coleman Papers, 1914–1964; William Theodore Evjue Papers, ca. 1880–1969; Miles J. McMillin Papers, 1951–1979; Karl Ernest Meyer Papers, 1951–1979; Ivan Nestingen Papers, 1942–1961; James A. Pike Sermons, 1954; Thomas C. Reeves Papers; William A. Roberts Papers, 1942–1956; Leonard F. Schmitt Papers; Bradley R. Taylor Papers, 1917–1963; Urban P. Van Susteren Interview, 1965; Urban P. Van Susteren Papers concerning Senator Joseph McCarthy, 1930–1978; Burton K. Wheeler, 1882–1975, Interviewee; Oral History Interview with Douglas Anderson, 1963; Oral History Interview with Laurie E. Carlson, 1979; Bill Grede Papers; James P. Held, Photographs of the funeral of Joseph McCarthy, 1957, May; Benjamin G. Leighton Papers, 1951–1955; Albert J. O'Melia Papers, 1911–1962; Wisconsin State Journal, Joseph McCarthy files, 1946–1957.

From the U.S. Senate Historical Office, Washington, D.C., the following Oral History Interview files: Darrell St. Claire, Dec. 1976 to April 1978; Pat M. Holt, Sept. 9 to Dec. 12, 1980; Warren Featherstone Reid, July 1 to July 23, 1981; Leonard H. Ballard, Aug. 18, 1983 to Jan. 10, 1984; Francis R. Valeo, July 3, 1985 to March 11, 1986; George Tames, Jan. 3 to Aug. 16, 1988; Roy L. Elson, April 27 to Aug. 21, 1990; Dorothye G. Scott, June 3 to June 24, 1992; Christine S. McCreary, May 19, 1998; F. Nordy Hoffman, June 28 to Aug. 30, 1988.

Cited in my foregoing page-by-page Source Notes are the renderings, with full titles, from official congressional records, and particularly from the critical extensive hearings and investigations affecting McCarthy: the Malmédy investigation of 1949; the Benton Expulsion Resolution and debates of 1951 and 1952; the Army-McCarthy Hearings of 1954; and the Censure Hearings of 1954.

Herewith, the formal bibliographical listings:

BIBLIOGRAPHY

1. McCarthyism

Adams, John G. *Without Precedent: The Story of the Death of McCarthyism.* New York: Norton, 1983.

Allen, Frederick Lewis. *Only Yesterday: An Informal History of the Nineteen-Twenties.* New York: Harper & Brothers, Publishers, 1931.

Ambrose, Stephen E. *Rise to Globalism: American Foreign Policy Since 1938. Fourth Revised Edition.* New York: Viking Penguin, 1985.

Anderson, Jack and Ronald May. *McCarthy: The Man, the Senator, the Ism.* Boston: Beacon Press, 1952.

Barth, Alan. *The Rights of Free Men: An Essential Guide to Civil Liberties.* Edited by James Clayton. New York: Alfred A. Knopf, 1984.

Bayley, Edwin R. *Joe McCarthy and the Press.* Madison: The University of Wisconsin Press, 1981.

Bell, Daniel. *The New American Right.* New York: Criterion, 1955.

Bohlen, Charles E. *Witness to History.* New York: Norton, 1973.

Block, Herbert. *Herblock's Special for Today.* New York: Simon and Schuster, 1958.

————. *Herblock: A Cartoonist's Life: Self-Portrait and Views of Washington from Roosevelt to Clinton.* New York: Macmillan Publishing Company, 1993.

Buckley, William F., Jr. and L. Brent Bozell. *McCarthy and His Enemies: The Record and Its Meaning.* Chicago: Henry Regnery Company, 1954.

————, Editor. *The Committee and Its Critics: A Calm Review of the House Committee on Un-American Activities.* Chicago: Henry Regnery Company, 1963.

Caro, Robert A. *Master of the Senate: The Years of Lyndon Johnson.* Volume Three. New York: Alfred A. Knopf, 2002.

Caute, David. *The Great Fear: The Anti-Communist Purge Under Truman and Eisenhower.* New York: Simon and Schuster, 1978.

Chambers, Whittaker. *Witness.* New York: Random House, 1952.

Chase, James. *Acheson: The Secretary of State Who Created the American World.* New York: Simon & Schuster, 1998.

Cohn, Roy. *McCarthy.* New York: Lancer Books, 1968.

Congressional Record. *Major Speeches and Debates of Senator Joe McCarthy.* New York: Gordon Press, 1975.

Commager, Henry Steele. *Documents of American History.* Fifth Edition. New York: Appleton-Century-Crofts, Inc., 1949.

Cook, Fred. *The Nightmare Decade.* New York: Random House, 1971.

Coulter, Ann. *Treason: Liberal Treachery From the Cold War to the War on Terrorism.* New York: Crown Forum, 2003.

Crosby, Donald F., S.J. *God, Church and Flag: Senator Joseph R. McCarthy and the Catholic Church, 1950–1957.* Chapel Hill: The University of North Carolina Press, 1978.

De Antonio, Emile and Daniel Talbot. *Point of Order! A Documentary of the Army-McCarthy Hearings.* New York: W.W. Norton & Company, 1964.

Donner, Frank J. *The Un-Americans.* New York: Ballantine Books, 1961.

Donovan, Robert J. *Eisenhower: The Inside Story.* New York: Harper's, 1956.

———. *Tumultuous Years: The Presidency of Harry S. Truman, 1949–1953.* New York: Norton, 1982.

Douglas, Helen Gahagan. *A Full Life.* New York: Doubleday & Company, 1982.

Ewald, William Bragg, Jr. *Who Killed Joe McCarthy?* New York: Simon and Schuster, 1984.

Fulbright, J. William. *The Arrogance of Power.* New York: Random House, 1966.

———. *Old Myths and New Realities*. New York: Random House, 1964.

Gellermann, William. *Martin Dies*. New York: Da Capo Press Reprint, 1972.

Griffith, Robert. *The Politics of Fear: Joseph R. McCarthy and the Senate*. Second Edition. Amherst: The University of Massachusetts Press, 1987.

Goodman, Walter. *The Committee: The Extraordinary Career of the House Committee on Un-American Activities*. New York: Farrar, Straus and Giroux, 1968.

Griswold, Erwin. *The Fifth Amendment Today*. Cambridge: Harvard University Press, 1955.

Haynes, John Earl and Harvey Klehr. *Venona: Decoding Soviet Espionage in America*. New Haven: Yale University Press, 2000.

Halberstam, David. *The Best and the Brightest*. Greenwich: A Fawcett Crest Book, 1973.

Herman, Arthur. *Joseph McCarthy: Reexamining the Life and Legacy of America's Most Hated Senator*. New York: Free Press, 2000.

Hoffer, Eric. *The True Believer: Thoughts on the Nature of Mass Movements*. New York: Harper & Brothers, 1951.

Hofstadter, Richard, *The Paranoid Style in American Politics and Other Essays*. New York: Alfred A. Knopf, 1965.

Hughes, Emmet John. *The Ordeal of Power: A Political Memoir of the Eisenhower Years*. New York: Atheneum, 1963.

Johnson, Haynes and Bernard M. Gwertzman. *Fulbright: The Dissenter*. New York: Doubleday & Company, 1968.

Johnson, Roger T. *Robert M. La Follette, Jr. and the Decline of the Progressive Party in Wisconsin*. Madison: State Historical Society of Wisconsin, 1964.

Kaplan, Justin. *Lincoln Steffens: A Biography*. New York: Simon & Schuster, 1974.

Kennedy, Robert F. *The Enemy Within*. New York: Popular Library, 1960.

Lattimore, Owen. *Ordeal by Slander*. Westport, Conn.: Greenwood Press, 1950, revised, 1971.

Leebaert, Derek. *The Fifty-Year Wound: How America's Cold War Shapes Our World*. Boston: Back Bay Books, 2002.

Manchester, William. *The Glory and the Dream: A Narrative History of America, 1932–1972*. Boston: Little, Brown and Company, 1973–1974.

Maney, Patrick J. *Young Bob: A Biography of Robert M. La Follette, Jr.* Madison: Wisconsin Historical Society Press, 2003.

McCarthy, Joseph R. *America's Retreat From Victory: The Story of George Catlett Marshall*. New York: Devin Adair Company, 1952.

———. *The Fight for America*. Random Lake, WI: Times Printing Co., 1985.

McWilliams, Carey. *Witch Hunt: The Revival of Heresy*. New York: Little, Brown and Company, 1950.

Morgan, Ted. *Reds: McCarthyism in Twentieth Century America*. New York: Random House, 2004.

Moynihan, Daniel Patrick. *Secrecy: The American Experience*. New Haven: Yale University Press, 1998.

Navasky, Victor. *Naming Names*. New York: Viking, 1980.

Nevins, Allan. *Herbert H. Lehman and His Era*. New York: Charles Scribner's Sons, 1963.

Oshinsky, David M. *A Conspiracy So Immense: The World of Joe McCarthy*. New York: The Free Press, 1983.

Reeves, Thomas C. *The Life and Times of Joe McCarthy*. New York: Stein and Day, 1982, Lanham, MD: Madison Books, 1997.

———, Editor. *McCarthyism*. Third Edition. Malabar, FL: Krieger Publishing Company, 1989.

Rovere, Richard. *Final Reports: Personal Reflections on Politics and History in Our Time.* New York: Doubleday & Company, 1984.

———. *Senator Joe McCarthy.* New York: Harcourt Brace, 1959.

Schrecker, Ellen. *The Age of McCarthyism: A Brief History with Documents.* Second Edition. Boston: Bedford/St. Martins, 2002.

———. *Many Are the Crimes: McCarthyism in America.* Princeton: Princeton University Press, 1998.

———. *No Ivory Tower: McCarthyism and the Universities.* New York, Oxford University Press, 1986.

Schlesinger, Arthur M., Jr. *A Thousand Days: John F. Kennedy in the White House.* Boston: Houghton Mifflin Company, 1965.

Sherrow, Victoria. *Joseph McCarthy and the Cold War.* Woodbridge, CT: Blackbirch Press, 1999.

Smith, Margaret Chase. *Declaration of Conscience.* New York: Doubleday & Company, Inc., 1972.

Stacks, John F. *Scotty. James B. Reston and the Rise and Fall of American Journalism.* Boston: Little, Brown and Company, 2003.

Tanenhaus, Sam. *Whittaker Chambers: A Biography.* New York: Random House, 1997.

Truman, Harry S. *Memoirs: Years of Trial and Hope. Volume Two. 1946–1952.* New York: Doubleday & Company, 1956.

U.S. Senate. *Executive Sessions of the Senate Permanent Subcommittee on Investigations of the Committee on Government Operations. Eighty-Third Congress, First and Second Sessions. 1953–1954. Five Volumes.* Made Public January, 2003. Washington: U.S. Government Printing Office, 2003.

Weinstein, Allen. *Perjury: The Hiss-Chambers Case.* New York: Alfred A. Knopf, 1978.

West, Rebecca. *The Meaning of Treason.* New York: 1947, reissued as *The New Meaning of Treason.* New York: The Viking Press, 1964.

White, William S. *The Professional: Lyndon B. Johnson.* Boston: Houghton Mifflin, 1964.

Zinert, Karen. *McCarthy and the Fear of Communism in American History.* Berkley Heights, NJ: Enslow Publishers, 1998.

Zion, Sidney. *The Autobiography of Roy Cohn.* Secaucus, NJ: Lyle Stuart, 1988.

2. Terrorism

"Anonymous" (Michael Scheuer). *Imperial Hubris: Why the West Is Losing the War on Terror.* New York: Brassey's, 2004.

Brown, Cynthia, Editor. *Lost Liberties: Ashcroft and the Assault on Personal Freedom.* New York: The New Press, 2003.

Chang, Nancy. *Silencing Political Dissent.* New York: Seven Stories Press, 2002.

Clarke, Richard A. *Against All Enemies: Inside America's War on Terror.* New York: Free Press, 2004.

Cole, David. *Enemy Aliens: Double Standards and Constitutional Freedoms in the War on Terrorism.* New York: The New Press, 2003.

Cole, David and James X. Dempsey. *Terrorism and the Constitution: Sacrificing Civil Liberties in the Name of National Security.* New York: The New Press, 2002.

Coll, Steve. *Ghost Wars: The Secret History of the CIA, Afghanistan, and Bin Laden, from the Soviet Invasion to September 10, 2001.* New York: The Penguin Press, 2004.

Danner, Mark. *Torture and Truth: America, Abu Ghraib, and the War on Terror.* New York: The New York Review of Books, 2004.

Dean, John W. *Worse Than Watergate: The Secret Presidency of George W. Bush.* New York: Little, Brown, 2004.

Ferguson, Niall. *Colossus: The Price of American Empire.* The Penguin Press, 2004.

Frum, David. *The Right Man: The Surprise Presidency of George W. Bush.* New York: Random House, 2003.

Hentoff, Nat. *The War on the Bill of Rights and the Gathering Resistance.* New York: Seven Stories Press, 2003.

Hersh, Seymour M. *Chain of Command: The Road from 9/11 to Abu Ghraib.* New York: HarperCollins Publishers, 2004.

Krugman, Paul. *The Great Unraveling: Losing Our Way in the New Century.* New York: Norton, 2003.

Leone, Richard C. and Greg Anrig, Jr., Editors. *The War on Our Freedoms: Civil Liberties in an Age of Terrorism.* New York: A Century Foundation Book. Public Affairs Reports, 2003.

Lyon, David. *Surveillance after September 11.* Cambridge, UK: Polity Press, 2003.

Parenti, Christian. *The Soft Cage: Surveillance in America.* New York: Basic Books, 2003.

Phillips, Kevin P. *American Dynasty: Aristocracy, Fortune, and the Politics of Deceit in the House of Bush.* New York: Viking Press, 2004.

Red Cross, International Committee of. *Report of the International Committee of the Red Cross and Other Protected Persons by the Geneva Conventions in Iraq During Arrest, Internment and Interrogation by Delegates of the International Committee.* February 2004.

Schlesinger, Arthur M., Jr. *War and The American Presidency.* New York: W. W. Norton & Company, 2004.

Schulhofer, Stephen J. *The Enemy Within: Intelligence Gathering, Law Enforcement, and Civil Liberties in the Wake of September 11.* New York: The Century Foundation Press, 2004.

Sifry, Micah L. and Christopher Cerf, Editors. *The Iraq War Reader: History, Documents, Opinions.* New York: Touchstone, 2003.

Suskind, Ron. *The Price of Loyalty: George W. Bush, the White House, and the Education of Paul O'Neill.* New York: Simon & Schuster, 2004.

Taguba, Major General Antonio M. *Article 15-6 Investigation of the 800th Military Police Brigade (The Taguba Report).*

Wilson, Joseph. *The Politics of Truth: Inside the Lies That Led to War and Betrayed My Wife's CIA Identity.* New York: Carroll & Graff, 2004.

Woodward, Bob. *Plan of Attack.* New York: Simon & Schuster, 2004.

———. *Bush at War.* New York: Simon & Schuster, 2003.

Acknowledgments

Once again, I regret being unable to acknowledge all those friends, colleagues, and professional sources to whom I am deeply indebted for help in this long book project. To these few then, out of so many, my special appreciation: To Jim Silberman, of James H. Silberman Books, my editor, and Philippa Brophy, of Sterling Lord Literistic, my agent, who have been the best of professional counselors and most steadfast of friends. To André Bernard, vice president and publisher of Harcourt, and Dan Farley, its president and CEO, who from the beginning could not have been more supportive and encouraging. At Harcourt, I'm also indebted to David Hough, its managing editor, to Stacia J.N. Decker, its associate editor, to Sara Branch, its assistant managing editor, and to copy editor Margaret Jones, for their great skill and care in processing the manuscript. In Wisconsin, to Kimberly Louagie, Curator of Exhibits, Outagamie County Historical Society, who went out of her way to provide access to and background information on the wonderful McCarthy exhibit in Appleton. To Phil Runkel, Archivist, Department of Special Collections and University Archives, Marquette University Libraries in Milwaukee, and to Harry Miller, Reference Archivist, Wisconsin Historical Society in Madison, for their many courtesies in meeting my requests and guiding me to the resources of their collections on McCarthy, the McCarthy Era, and Wisconsin. In Washington, to Donald A. Ritchie, Associate Historian, the Senate Historical Office, U.S. Senate, who was unfailingly patient and generous with his time in suggesting new areas of worthwhile material in that office's superb collection; to Laura W. Murphy, Director, ACLU's Washington National Office, and her colleagues, who provided valuable documentary material; to Doris Meissner, former Commissioner of the U.S. Immigration and Naturalization Service, who took time from a busy schedule to offer important insights and background information; to General Andrew J. Goodpaster, USA (Ret.), Senior Fellow and Chairman Emeritus, the Eisenhower Institute, for his compelling recollections of Eisenhower and McCarthy (General Goodpaster died at the age of ninety, just as this book was in final phase before publication. He was an exemplar, the best in public service.); and to Susan Eisenhower, the President's granddaughter, a Senior Fellow at the Institute, who earned my gratitude for urging me to read William Bragg Ewald, Jr.'s *Who Killed Joe McCarthy?* for the inner workings on the Machiavellian struggle between the Eisenhower Administration and McCarthy. I also am indebted to Paul Mihailidis and Svetlana Markova, my Ph.D.-candidate graduate assistants, and to my graduate and undergraduate students who over the last two years produced worthy papers from which I drew material on the Bush administration and terrorism.

Finally, and more personally, to Mike Goelzer, my stepson, whose support and interest were more important than I'm sure he realizes, especially for his insights on the McCarthy era as seen from the vantage of a generation born long after that period. And, once again, I owe an incalculable debt to two people: to Lisa Larragoite, my indispensable assistant, without whom this project literally could not have been accomplished; and to Kathryn Oberly, my wife, best critic, confidante, and counselor.

Index

impact of, 118–20
origins of, 117–18
support for Greece and Turkey in,
118, 119
Tuch, Hans N., 272
Turkey, Truman Doctrine support for,
118, 119
Turner, Anne, 487
Tydings, Millard
attacks on, 186–92
end of political career, 191, 218
McCarthy's vow to destroy, 189–91
reelection campaign of 1950,
189–92, 218, 224
Senate censure of McCarthy and, 91
Tydings subcommittee final report
and, 184–92
Tydings subcommittee investigation
of McCarthy and, 160–61,
166–76, 222–23

Unconstitutional (film), 488
unitary executive, 535
United Electrical Workers (UE)
union, 314–16
U.S. Department of Defense, 132
Senate Permanent Subcommittee
on Investigations and, 309–11,
330–31, 334–35, 340, 351–52
see also Army-McCarthy hearings
U.S. Department of Homeland
Security, 2–3, 97, 480–82, 501,
532, 534, 537
U.S. Department of Justice, 435,
467–71, 543
Office of the Inspector General
(OIG), 471–72, 476–77
Palmer raids and, 107–12, 129n,
470–71

USA Patriot Act and, 97, 467–71,
478, 484–89
see also Federal Bureau of
Investigation (FBI)
U.S. Information Agency, 300–302
U.S. Marine Corps, and McCarthy,
36–37, 45–47
exploitation of military record,
45–47, 49–54, 64–65, 67,
78–79
fraudulent medals, 52–53
joins as commissioned officer, 46
resignation, 46, 49–54
speaking tour of 1950 and, 21
"tail gunner Joe" myth and, 49–54,
65, 78–79
U.S. Senate campaign of 1944 and,
46–47
USS *Abraham Lincoln* and "Mission
Accomplished," 558
U.S. National Hurricane Center, 537
U.S. Senate
campaign of 1944, 46–47, 49–51
campaign of 1946, 47, 57, 60–74,
80, 248, 249, 263–64
campaign of 1950, 9–29
campaign of 1952, 241–45,
247–51
censure and condemnation of
McCarthy, 90–92, 224–26,
228, 230, 251–52, 411, 411n,
431–42, 445–48, 453,
459–60
death of McCarthy and, 35–37,
453–54
intimidation of, by McCarthy,
156–57, 183, 218–26, 228–31,
278
Malmédy massacre hearings and,
85–92